COUNTERFEIT WORLDS
PHILIP K. DICK ON FILM

Counterfeit Worlds
Philip K. Dick on Film
1 84023 968 9
ISBN-13: 9781840239683

Published by
Titan Books
A division of
Titan Publishing Group Ltd
144 Southwark St
London
SE1 0UP

First edition July 2006
2 4 6 8 10 9 7 5 3 1

Front cover painting by Aaronu. Used with permission.
For more information about Aaronu's art, including paintings for sale, visit his online gallery:
www.aaronu.tk
Or contact: **aaronuart@gmail.com**

Grateful acknowledgment is made to the following for the use of their visual material, used solely for the advertising, promotion, publicity and review of the specific motion pictures, television programmes and publications they illustrate. Academy Entertainment, Ace, Agave, Alliance, Berkley, Born Pockets, Carolco Pictures, Columbia Tristar Home Entertainment, Corgi, Daw, DeNoel, Doubleday, DreamWorks LLC, Editrice Nord, FAN, First Run Features, Fox Lorber Home Video/Orion Home Video, Granada Books, Kentaur, The Ladd Company/The Blade Runner Partnership, McFadden Books, Miramax Film Corp, Nemira, Panther, Paramount Pictures, Penguin, Prism Leisure Corp. PLC, QM Productions, Robert Laffont, Team Entertainment Group, Triumph Enterprises, Inc., 20th Century Fox, Warner Independent Pictures, Universal. Special thanks to The Tony Hillman Collection, and to James Van Hise. Any omissions will be corrected in future editions.

Visit our website:
www.titanbooks.com

Did you enjoy this book? We love to hear from our readers. Please e-mail us at: **readerfeedback@titanemail.com** or write to Reader Feedback at the above address. To subscribe to our regular newsletter for up-to-the-minute news, great offers and competitions, email:
titan-news@titanemail.com

A CIP catalogue record for this title is available from the British Library.

Printed and bound in Great Britain by MPG, Bodmin, Cornwall

COUNTERFEIT WORLDS
PHILIP K. DICK ON FILM

BRIAN J. ROBB

TITAN BOOKS

"I've seen things you people wouldn't believe…
Attack ships on fire off the shoulder of Orion.
I watched c-beams glitter in the dark near Tanhauser Gate.
All those moments will be lost in time, like tears… in rain.
Time… to die."

ACKNOWLEDGEMENTS

Many thanks to Philip K. Dick's daughters Isa Dick-Hackett and Laura Leslie, and Russell Galen of Scovil Chichak Galen Literary Agency, Inc., for their invaluable input and advice.

The world of Philip K. Dick scholarship and *Blade Runner* fandom would be all the poorer without Paul M. Sammon, so a huge tip-of-the-hat to Paul for his work in *Cinefantastique* and the definitive *Future Noir*, as well as for kindly taking the time to offer his views on Dick for this current volume.

Thanks are due to Gary Goldman and Richard Linklater, two of Philip K. Dick's greatest champions in Hollywood, who took time out of their busy schedules to contribute to this book. Thanks also to Peter Weller for sharing his thoughts, and to Sandy Stone for conducting the interview with him.

Due thanks to everyone who has contributed to the growing field of Philip K. Dick studies, whether academic or fan. Your varied thoughts and theories have been an inspiration.

Thanks to my editor Adam Newell, for setting me on this course and providing vital direction just when it was needed. Also thanks to all at Titan Books and Titan Magazines, without whom…

Most of all, thank you to Philip K. Dick. After all, it's his world. We only live in it.

CONTENTS

THE WORLD DICK MADE

He's been dead for over twenty years, but the counterfeit worlds of Philip K. Dick continue to fascinate readers and cinema audiences...

"I, in my stories and novels, often write about counterfeit worlds, semi-real worlds, as well as deranged private worlds inhabited, often, by just one person, while the other characters either remain in their own worlds throughout or are somehow drawn into one of the peculiar ones..." — Philip K. Dick, 'If You Find This World Bad, You Should See Some of the Others', 1977 speech delivered at the Metz Festival, France.

One of the most successful writers in Hollywood today has been dead for over twenty years. Philip K. Dick created the future in which we now live; at the very least, he was writing about it long before it ever took shape. That foresight makes this acclaimed writer of the American pulp SF era of the 1950s and 1960s a kind of 'pre-cog' — a precognitive who, like the characters in the film *Minority Report* (based on a Dick short story), can somehow discern the future... Now, movies and TV shows based on ideas from his short stories and novels feed our heads, as the world around us becomes ever more like the counterfeit worlds in his fiction.

Art Spiegelman, acclaimed writer/illustrator of the holocaust graphic novel *Maus*, said of Dick: "What Franz Kafka was to the first half of the twentieth century, Philip K. Dick is to the second half." Fellow American SF author Ursula K. LeGuin saw Dick as "our own homegrown Borges", while 1960s counter-culture guru Timothy Leary called him "a major twenty-first century writer, an influential 'fictional philosopher' of the quantum age." Dick's work appealed across a broad spectrum of readers worldwide, from philosophers and other writers and thinkers, to SF fans, scientists and, of course, filmmakers.

If science fiction can be defined as the literature of ideas, then the work of Philip K. Dick is science fiction par excellence, as it contains more off-the-wall ideas per page than most. Dick returned obsessively to a set of key themes, with the nature of reality and what it means to be human being his two main philosophical concerns. He wrapped these often deep and meaningful cognitions in all-out, action-packed pulp science fiction storylines.

It is this fertile feeding ground for high concept notions that has made Dick's considerable volume of work the prime source for many of the biggest grossing science fiction movies of the past twenty years. Direct adaptations of his work include the blockbusters *Total Recall* and *Minority Report*, as well as the critically acclaimed *Blade Runner*, but other successful films like *The Truman Show* and *The Matrix* trilogy would likely not have existed as they do (or have been so readily accepted by the movie-going public) if the ideas and concepts put forward in his work had not entered the popular consciousness, along with their very own adjective: 'phildickian'.

***Opposite:** Philip K. Dick, pulp fiction practitioner and pop philosopher, pictured in September 1981. Photo © James Van Hise.*

Dick began to ply his trade in the early 1950s for US science fiction short story

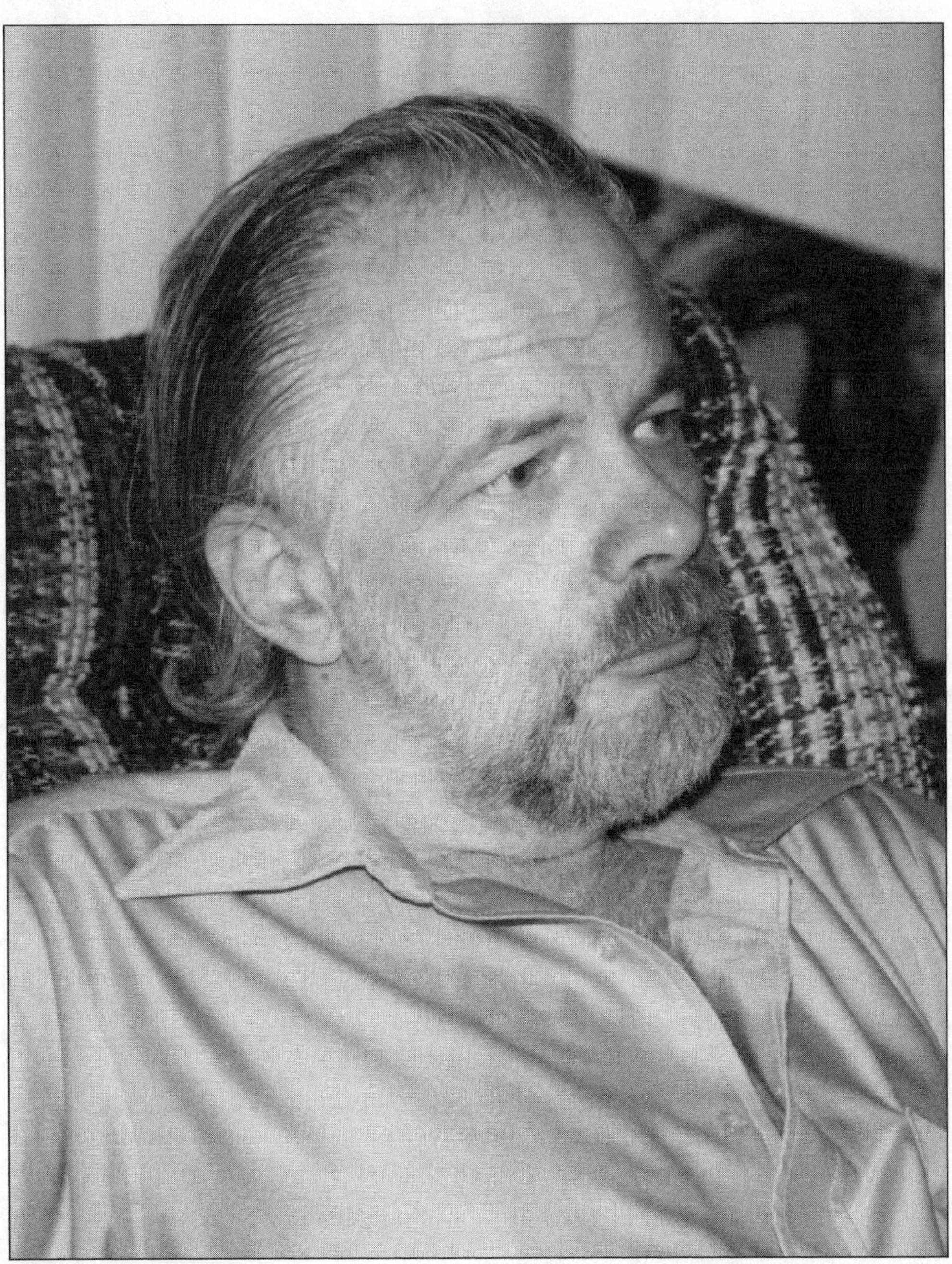

magazines like *If*, *Astounding* and *Galaxy*. He worked fast, churning out hundreds of stories, often selling them for little more than $100 each. Eventually, Dick moved onto the growing field of science fiction novels where he could earn up to $1000 as an advance. While Dick gained a growing and loyal fan following during the 1960s, the wider fame and critical acclaim he sought eluded him. He also lived much of his life struggling to make ends meet, as his writing failed to provide anywhere near an adequate income for him or his family. His agent, Russell Galen, admitted as much in *Wired* magazine: "Phil's work came out of an atmosphere of want and struggle. He was as prolific as he was because he needed money." Ironically, movie rights to his short stories have recently been sold to Hollywood studios for sums that hugely exceed Dick's entire lifetime earnings. A case in point: 'Paycheck'. The original short story sold to *Imagination* magazine in 1954 for the princely sum of $195. The film rights reportedly cost Paramount around $2 million, over 10,000 times the amount Dick was paid for originating the ideas in the first place. "I think he would have fallen over backwards to see what Steven Spielberg paid for the rights to the short story 'The Minority Report'," noted fellow author and Dick acolyte James Blaylock in *The San Francisco Chronicle*. "Philip was the archetypal writer who lived on nothing but his meager royalties… and then he died."

Dick's frequent attempts at writing mainstream fiction, reflecting suburban life in 1950s and 1960s California, remained largely unpublished until after his death. The popular perception of Dick in the science fiction community was of a drug-addled (he admitted to using copious amounts of speed to fuel his writing), would-be messiah who'd gone off the rails after claiming to have seen God in 1974. Apart from some early radio and television dramatisations, his work remained un-adapted for other media until Ridley Scott's *Blade Runner* in 1982. By then, Philip K. Dick had died of a heart attack at the tragically early age of fifty-three.

It was only after his death and the failure of *Blade Runner* at the box office that the cult of Philip K. Dick really took off. "Clearly Dick was ahead of his time," wrote Russell Galen in *Writer's Digest*. "The very elements that once branded him not fit for mainstream audiences now seem enlightened and fresh, raising disturbing questions that force us to think about the implications of modern life." Throughout the 1980s Dick's science fiction came back into print, and many of his mainstream novels were finally published, providing a more rounded picture of the author and his work. Biographies began to appear, while the visuals and atmosphere of *Blade Runner* (a film which enjoyed growing critical stature and a huge audience on home video) exerted an influence on advertising and SF filmmaking that has yet to diminish. Dick's questioning of the nature of reality and the nature of humanity started to become common currency in the media as the millennium approached. Suddenly, the exploration of counterfeit worlds was cool.

Creative people in Hollywood had not given up on Philip K. Dick, despite the initial failure of *Blade Runner*. The release of *Total Recall* in 1990 — which proved to be the theatrical blockbuster that *Blade Runner* was not — was the result of many years of endeavour to get another Philip K. Dick project into cinemas. Then the floodgates opened: *Screamers*; a *Total Recall* TV series that seemed stylistically closer to *Blade Runner* than the original feature; *Impostor*; Steven Spielberg's *Minority Report*; John Woo's *Paycheck*; Richard Linklater's *A Scanner Darkly* and Lee Tamahori's *Next*. The long-dead Philip K. Dick had become the hottest 'ideas man' in Hollywood.

Dick himself would have appreciated the films made from his work, especially perhaps the French character drama *Confessions d'un Barjo* (a faithful — though transposed to France — version of his realist novel *Confessions of a Crap Artist*), and Richard Linklater's pseudo-animated take on his confessional drug culture novel *A Scanner Darkly*. Dick did see some footage from *Blade Runner* before his untimely death and despite initially fighting the project, he was won over by the dense visual world director Ridley Scott was creating. "I thought, these guys have figured out what life is going to be like forty years from now," Dick told interviewer Gregg Rickman in 1982. "I'm completely convinced."

Dick was a confirmed movie fan, though he preferred to watch them on cable TV later in his life than at cinemas, as he suffered from anxiety in crowds. According to Lawrence Sutin's definitive Dick biography, *Divine Invasions*, his father Edgar wrote an unpublished family memoir called *As I Remember Them*. That source indicates that in telling Dick about his experiences in the First World War, where he'd served on the front lines, Edgar had taken his son to see his first movie: 1931's *All Quiet on the Western Front*. Early in his pulp writing career, it seems Dick was a more regular attendee at the cinema. Kleo Apostolides, Dick's second wife, recalled their 1950s movie-going habits: "Movies were a little difficult. The Roxy Theatre was an artsy theatre that showed strange, foreign films we wanted to see, but we didn't always have the money. We'd sneak in. Every so often our timing was off and Phil would be acutely embarrassed and make a big show of saying goodbye to me, buying my ticket and going home…"

"It's important to note how much impact films did have on Dick's life, his work and his emotions," claimed biographer Daryl Mason. "He was pushing from the mid-1950s onwards to get films and TV shows made from his stories. Obviously the fees paid were influential, but from his first exposure to the cinema at three years old, and the reality-defining World War Two-era newsreels he watched as a teenager, he never lost his love for movies and consciously wrote some stories that he hoped would interest producers."

By the time *Blade Runner* was in production, Dick was being invited into Hollywood elite circles to see the results of his work being transferred to the big screen. If he'd lived beyond 1982, it's likely that he would have become directly involved in many of the film productions made from his novels and short stories, despite his initial reluctance to play the Hollywood game. He may also have pursued his wish to write directly for the screen (he adapted his own novel *Ubik* as a screenplay in the early 1970s).

By 2005, Dick's star had risen so far — both as a literary figure and as a source for some of cinema's most mind-bending movies — that he was inducted into the Science Fiction Hall of Fame. With *Minority Report* director Steven Spielberg, stop-motion pioneer Ray Harryhausen and SF artist Chesley Bonestell, Dick took his place alongside thirty-six other such science fiction literary luminaries as Mary Shelley, H.G. Wells, Jules Verne, Sir Arthur C. Clarke, Edgar Rice Burroughs, Ursula K. LeGuin and Isaac Asimov.

Philip K. Dick created visions of a media-manipulated world in which global corporations ride roughshod over ordinary folks, where memory cannot be trusted and moods can be controlled and altered through drugs and technology, where the very 'human-ness' of the person next to you cannot be taken for granted. Was he simply a writer ahead of his time? Perhaps the truth is stranger… perhaps our counterfeit world has been a Philip K. Dick novel all along… ■

THE VARIABLE MAN

The shifting realities of Philip K. Dick, from his troubled childhood to his pulp fiction days to his late-life triumphs and early death...

"People have told me that everything about me, every facet of my life, psyche, experiences, dreams and fears are laid out explicitly in my writing, that from the corpus of my work I can be absolutely and precisely inferred. This is true."
— Philip K. Dick, from the Introduction to *The Golden Man*, 1981.

Born in Chicago on 16 December 1928, Philip Kindred Dick was accompanied into the world by his twin sister Jane Charlotte. The twins were six weeks premature and in a strange numerical twist Jane died exactly six weeks later... Although he could not possibly remember the actual event, the death of his sister was to haunt Philip K. Dick's writing and his personal life through to his own death, a mere fifty-three years later.

Dick's mother, Dorothy Kindred, was a tall, gaunt-looking woman who had no idea that in that winter of 1928 she was due to deliver not one but two children. His father, Joseph Edgar Dick (known as Ted or Edgar), worked for the US Department of Agriculture, which had recently relocated the couple from Washington to Chicago.

Dick had been born first, at noon, twenty minutes ahead of his ill-fated sister. He weighed in at a frail four-and-a-quarter pounds. Despite his tiny size, he was able to make an astonishing amount of noise. Jane, dark-haired and a mere three-and-a-half pounds, followed her brother into that unforgiving 1928 Chicago winter.

Undernourished and cared for by a mother who was not prepared for the task and a father who was often absent at work or at his men's club, the newly born twins struggled for survival. Strangely, by the mid-1930s Dorothy would be employed by the Federal Children's Bureau as the author of publicly-available childcare pamphlets, suggesting she must have been an authority on raising children. Dorothy's own mother, Edna, joined the family to help out as 1929 dawned, but even she — an experienced mother — could do little to help the fading twins. At least Edna realised the seriousness of the situation and arranged for the suffering children to be taken to hospital, but on 26 January 1929, Jane Charlotte Dick died en route. Her brother spent weeks on a ventilator until, reaching the weight of five pounds, he was allowed home, along with a supply of a special formula food. Jane was buried in the Fort Morgan cemetery in Colorado, near the town where Edgar and Dorothy had met.

***Opposite:** Philip K. Dick with a copy of* Flow My Tears, the Policeman Said. *Photo courtesy of Isa Dick-Hackett.*

This was all related to Dick in some detail in a letter from his mother dated 2 August 1975. Dorothy had repeatedly told young Phil the nightmarish story of his and Jane's birth

FLOW MY
TEARS,

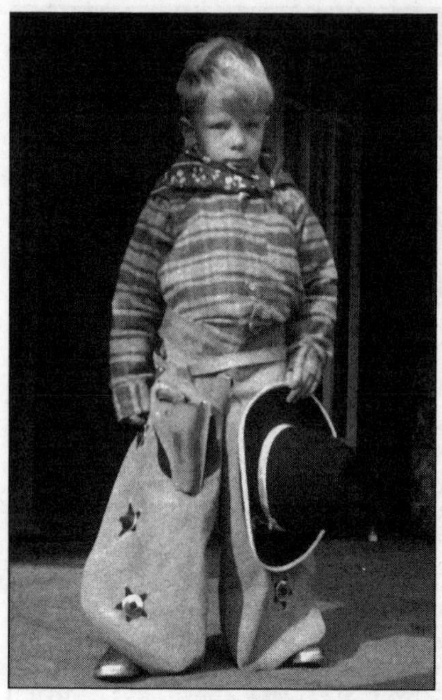

Above: *Philip K. Dick in 1935, in his cowboy costume. Photo courtesy of Isa Dick-Hackett.*

throughout his childhood. His missing sister came to life in his imagination, taking firm hold, so much so that her absence would later come to dominate his creative life. Repeatedly told the story of those traumatic first few weeks by Dorothy, as if in some form of guilty mea culpa, Dick later realised that this knowledge had not served him in a positive way. "I heard about Jane a lot, and it wasn't good for me," he told his third wife Anne, according to her memoir *In Search of Philip K. Dick*.

The death of his sister didn't just have a profound effect on Dick's psyche and psychological make-up, it made an immediate difference to his family situation. The previously strong relationship between his mother and father broke down in the wake of their daughter's death, and by 1933 Edgar had departed from the family, leaving Dick with the mother he would grow to blame for the death of his sister.

The impact of the loss of Jane on Dick's fictional universe cannot be over-estimated. Several of his stories and novels rely on notions of twinning, such as the real/unreal or human/android dichotomies that dominate much of his best work. In particular, *Dr Bloodmoney* (1965), *Flow My Tears, The Policeman Said* (1974), *A Scanner Darkly* (1977), *Valis* (1981) and *The Divine Invasion* (1981) feature twins or twinned characters, such as Edie and Bill in *Dr Bloodmoney*, Fred/Bob Arctor in *A Scanner Darkly* and Horselover Fat/Phil Dick in *Valis*. Edie and Bill most vividly capture the concept Dick sometimes expressed that his dead twin somehow lived on within him. Little girl Edie has within her an unborn twin in the form of Bill, located in her left side near the appendix. In the post-apocalyptic 1981 setting of *Dr Bloodmoney*, many characters have suffered mutations. The spin here is that Edie can hear Bill talking to her, expressing his desire to one day be 'born' like everyone else. In the *Exegesis* — a kind of religious and philosophical diary Dick wrote daily in his later years — he vividly expressed the idea that Jane lived on within him: "My sister is everything to me. I am damned always to be separated from her and with her, in an oscillation. I have her in me and often outside me, but I have lost her. Two realities at once: yin/yang."

This notion of two realities co-existing is at the centre of so much of Dick's writing. However, his loss also found expression in his childhood days through the creation of imaginary friends. One was a girl named Teddy (according to his fifth wife Tessa), while another was dubbed Becky (according to third wife Anne). His mother's repeated recounting of the story of his birth and Jane's death seems to have caused Dick to conjure up his missing sister as an invisible playmate. Dick's last wife Tessa even recalled that sometimes his imaginary 'other half' (the yin to his yang) was simply called Jane: "[Imaginary] Jane was small, with dark eyes and long hair. She was also very gutsy, always daring Phil to do things he was afraid of, helping him to get into trouble."

In an in-depth interview with Paul Williams in 1974, which formed the basis of an influential *Rolling Stone* profile and for Williams' book on Dick, *Only Apparently Real*, the author spoke of his sister's death: "I feel that my mother let her die. I resent the fact that my sister could have lived very readily had she been given normal treatment as a premature baby. I was a very lonely child and I would have loved to have had my sister with me all these years..."

To date, the twin theme in Dick's work has been expressed most significantly in the cinema adaptations of 'We Can Remember It For You Wholesale' (filmed as *Total Recall*) and *A Scanner Darkly*. The visualisation of *Total Recall*'s rebel leader Quato (Kuato in the movie), known as The Oracle, is a malformed congenital twin who has a secondary head and arms growing out of his body — a symbiotic mutated twin within the body of another. This is a characteristic Dick concept first brought to life body-horror style by David Cronenberg's script for an aborted version of the film. The concept survived through to the completed feature, though in diluted form. The Fred/Bob Arctor split in *A Scanner Darkly* is at the centre of Richard Linklater's movie version of the story (which stars Keanu Reeves, and uses groundbreaking animation and rotoscoping techniques to bring Dick's unique perspective to life).

Dick would search throughout his life for the dark-haired girl of his dreams, the figure who embodied the imaginary attributes he'd given to his lost sister. The heroines who featured in his novels, alternately brave and evil, were manifestations of Jane, as were the women with whom he involved himself in real life — especially his five wives — almost all slight, dark-haired and strong-willed.

During Dick's earliest years the family relocated several times. Following Jane's death and Phil's recovery to health, they moved in 1930 from Chicago via a brief stay (for Dorothy and Phil, at least) in Colorado, to Sausalito and Alameda, before finally settling in Berkeley, California in 1931. Edgar took up a new position with the Department of Agriculture's San Francisco office and two-year-old Philip was enrolled in the experimental Bruce Tatlock School, a progressive nursery. Dick was to remain in California for the rest of his life, specifically in the San Francisco area and then Orange County for his final decade.

Given the fate of his sister and his father's reported phobia of germs, combined with his mother's belief in then-prevalent 'tough love' theories of child-rearing, it's not surprising that Dick developed a series of physical and mental ailments from early childhood. In the mid-1940s he received intensive psychiatric treatment for agoraphobia and other ailments. In 1946 he was also diagnosed as suffering from tachycardia, a rapid heartbeat, an unusual condition in an eighteen-year-old. This condition, however, would contribute directly to his early death.

While at school, in seventh grade, Dick had suffered from severe vertigo: this recurred throughout his life, especially during his brief time as a university undergraduate. His late teens saw a diagnosis of schizophrenia, a condition that terrified him. How much of this was psychosomatic reactions to his troubled childhood and upbringing, including hearing his mother's tales of what had happened to Jane, is hard to tell. Whatever the causes, for Dick the effects of his illnesses and medical conditions were very real.

Dick biographer/interviewer Gregg Rickman, who was in contact with the author shortly before his death, suggested in his partial biography *To The High Castle* that Dick had

***Above:** The young Dick was excited to discover the "magic" of* Stirring Science Stories *and other pulp magazines.*

even been a victim of sexual abuse. Despite a lack of any real evidence, and drawing heavily on Dick's psychological ailments to form a diagnosis, Rickman even went so far as to select Dick's maternal grandfather Earl Grant Kindred as the perpetrator. Rickman's maverick, unsubstantiated claims caused a great deal of consternation in Philip K. Dick circles, resulting in one-time administrator of the Dick estate and custodian of the Philip K. Dick Society Paul Williams to speak out against "the Rickmanisation of Philip K. Dick." Rickman's theories remain little more than an interesting sideline in Dickian biography, with no clear proof to suggest they should be dwelt upon.

Dick's interest in science fiction and fantasy developed during his childhood and early teens. In a 1968 'Self Portrait', later published in the Philip K. Dick Society Newsletter#2 (December 1983, and republished in Lawrence Sutin's *The Shifting Realities of Philip K. Dick*), Dick wrote: "I was twelve [in 1940] when I read my first SF magazine… It was called *Stirring Science Stories*. I came across the magazine quite by accident; I was actually looking for *Popular Science*. I was most amazed. Stories about science? At once I recognised the magic I had found, in earlier times, in the [Wizard of] Oz books…"

The pulp science fiction magazines, to which Dick would contribute in earnest, had begun in 1926 with Hugo Gernsback's *Amazing Stories*. Printed on cheap paper manufactured from chemically-treated wood pulp (hence the term 'pulp magazines') and boasting garish, colourful and increasingly fanciful covers which aimed to capture the fickle reader's attention (if not to always accurately reflect the contents!), the pulps' lurid success reached a peak in the 1930s and 1940s. Typically paying struggling authors a cent per word (or even a half cent in some cases), the pulps were cheap to make and cheap to buy. The economic depression of the late 1920s and early 1930s fed the American population's desire for escape, often to the fantastic worlds and freaky situations of the SF pulps. Whereas individuals could seemingly make little difference to frightening global events in the real world of the 1930s, in the magical worlds of pulp fiction it was heroic, often put-upon individuals who saved the world, and sometimes other worlds too. The pulps emphasised action and romance, heroism and fantasy adventure, more often than not with a triumphal, or at least a happy, ending. While some of pulp's practitioners did work too often and too fast, churning out crude formulaic tales, others rose above the limitations of style and formula to become the key science fiction writers of the following decades. The pulps would directly feed into the post-World War Two SF paperback boom. The work of various writers in the post-war years solidified the concept of science fiction as a bona fide genre within which story-tellers could legitimately work.

In his lifetime, Dick would write hundreds of short stories and around forty novels, most of them categorised in the critically despised, but commercially successful, genre of science fiction. By the age of fourteen, at least according to Dick himself, he'd written his first novel, entitled *Return to Lilliput*. The manuscript has since been lost, perhaps justly depriving later readers of Dick's first juvenile attempts at novel writing.

It wasn't only pulp science fiction which interested Dick. He read far and wide, as recounted in his 1968 'Self Portrait': "I gorged myself on classics of literature: Proust and Pound, Kafka and Dos Passos, Pascal… I gained a working knowledge of literature from *The Anabasis* to *Ulysses*. I was not educated on SF, but on well-recognised serious writing by authors all over the world." Although he continued to write, hoping one day to be published in the prestigious literary publication *The New Yorker*, Dick's later teenage years saw him drift away from his vague ambitions as real life intervened and he was forced to get a job.

From the age of about fifteen into his early twenties, Dick was employed in two Berkeley music stores, University Radio and Art Music, both owned by Herb Hollis. Developing a passion for music to rival that he already had for writing, Dick found a mentor in Hollis. The small businessman father-figure character would recur in Dick's fiction, notably as Leo Bulero in *The Three Stigmata of Palmer Eldritch*. Many of Dick's other 'little guy' characters, the TV repairmen and appliance salesmen, were drawn from his time working in the music stores where he would sell not only records, but radios and the new-fangled television sets.

Working for Hollis was the only formal job that Dick ever held, other than being a writer. The stores were landmarks in liberal Berkeley, and Hollis cultivated a clientele among the students of the area who found a wide range of classical and obscure jazz and folk records in stock. Dick celebrated the end of World War Two in 1945 in the company of a gang from Hollis' stores. Hollis supplied records to and ran commercials (scripted by Dick) on local FM station KSMO in San Mateo in the late 1940s. Dick captured the milieu of a small town radio station in his posthumously published mainstream novel *The Broken Bubble*, written in 1956 and published in 1988. So accurate and atmospheric is the novel that Dick's unsubstantiated claims to have hosted a classical music show on KSMO in the 1940s may have some basis in fact. Dick's biggest ambition at the time was to own and manage a record store, just like his mentor Herb Hollis.

Dick's initial serious attempts at writing came in the late 1940s and were not science fiction at all. Both the lost novel *The Earthshakers* and the posthumously published *Gather Yourselves Together* were 'realist' novels which drew on the author's own coming of age experiences, including a short-lived marriage which ended in divorce in 1948.

Living in a shared loft house at 2208 McKinley Street with several arty types, some of whom were gay, Dick had taken to questioning his own sexuality. These doubts resulted in Dick recklessly committing to marrying Jeanette Marlin, a regular customer at the Hollis stores and several years Dick's senior, being in her late twenties. At only nineteen Dick was actually below the 'age of majority' in California and so his mother, Dorothy, had to sign the paperwork to make the marriage legal.

While Dick had initially wooed Marlin over shared musical interests, resulting in him losing his virginity with her in the basement of Herb Hollis' University Radio store, it was his continual late-night playing of records that was cited as the cause of the end of the relationship in their divorce several months later. According to his fifth wife Tessa, only two months into the marriage Dick had been shocked to discover that Marlin felt it was her right to see other men. This resulted in their separation, but the official reason for divorce (branded as "silly grounds" by the judge) was a threat from Marlin that she'd get her brother to come round to smash Dick's precious and extensive record collection.

Whether in response to his failed marriage or through peer-pressure as a result of living in an academic community, Dick spent the last months of 1949 trying one last time to adapt to college life, something he'd previously avoided after his less than stellar success at school. In September he enrolled in the University of California at Berkeley, studying philosophy, history and zoology. In addition, he had to attend military training, something he was deeply opposed to. Continuing to suffer from recurring bouts of vertigo and agoraphobia, Dick dropped out of college in November 1949 and was given an official honourable dismissal from military training in January 1950. That didn't stop him claiming to have been expelled due to his opposition to the mandated military training, giving his academic failure a more heroic and anti-establishment sheen. Ironically, dropping out of college made Dick eligible for the draft — compulsory service in the American armed forces. Much to his relief, he was rejected due to his high blood pressure and general ill health.

All through this turmoil Dick was writing and gaining in confidence. At this time his work continued to strive to be realist and mainstream, and though his period of loft-living with the arty crowd had broadened his literary tastes, he still cultivated a strong interest in science fiction, continuing to build up an impressive collection of pulp magazines. "I was living in Berkeley, and all the milieu-reinforcement there was for the literary stuff," Dick said in a *Twilight Zone Magazine* interview in 1982. "I knew all kinds of people who were doing literary type novels. I knew some of the very fine avant-garde poets in the Bay Area — Robert Duncan, Jack Spicer, Philip Lamantia, that whole crowd. They all encouraged me to write, but there was no encouragement to write science fiction and no encouragement to sell anything. I wanted to sell, and I also wanted to do science fiction. My ultimate dream was to do both literary stuff and science fiction."

Dick was certainly among literary company, and he is mentioned in Ekbert Fass' biography of Duncan: "With such young poet celebrities as Jack Spicer, Philip K. Dick and George Haimsohn living at 2208 McKinley Street, the rooming house had become a focus of literary activity… Philip K. Dick, from [the room] next door, who worked at a phonograph store, had an appliance for making records, a device they were quick to explore for its poetic potential… They would do charades, screaming and laughing till deep into the night… There was constant noise and laughter, as if they were celebrating a never-ending party."

Post-marriage, Dick's sexual horizons had been broadened too. In the company of buddy and fellow Hollis employee Vincent Lusby, he was on the lookout for the kind of girl who'd be impressed with his musical knowledge and access to rare records. One such was an Italian named Mary, who worked in a drug store and was trapped in an unhappy marriage. Dick's brief affair with her was to inform and inspire several of the love triangles that feature in his earliest attempts at writing social realist novels in the 1950s, most of which were not published until after his death. Dick was writing mainstream short stories too, and the occasional fantasy-tinged SF tale, all of which were regularly rejected by the editors of literary journals and pulp magazines alike. In the first half of the 1950s, in both romance and writing, the twentysomething Philip K. Dick was floundering.

Dick had learned much about life under the patient tutelage of Herb Hollis. It was however, another father figure who would help Dick to become a published author. Anthony Boucher was a Berkeley resident and renowned science fiction editor. Boucher's writing career had begun in 1941 for *Unknown*, and he became a regular contributor to that title and *Astounding*, turning out science fiction with an often humorous bent. By 1949 he was one of the founding editors of *The Magazine of Fantasy and Science Fiction*. A perceptive editor, Boucher was credited with raising the literary standards of much science fiction through the 1950s, especially via his criticism which appeared regularly in *The New York Times* and *The New York Herald Tribune*.

Despite having his free time to write restricted by his job at Hollis' stores, Dick continued to persevere with his mainstream writing, collecting a steadily mounting pile of demoralising rejection slips. Dick would write late into the night. So began a habit which he would maintain for the rest of his life: playing classical music records while writing. His rejection slips were defiantly and proudly taped to the walls. Even the return of seventeen manuscripts, all rejected in one single day, failed to knock the confidence of the would-be author.

Like so many of the people he met during the 1950s, Dick first met Anthony Boucher in the Art Music store. Boucher was also a record collector and hosted his own show, *Golden Voices of the Opera*, on KPFA in Berkeley. In his 1968 'Self Portrait', Dick recalled: "I listened to the program [and] I got to meet him. He came to the record store in which I worked and we had a long talk." Boucher was something of a revelation to the conflicted Dick. "I discovered that a person could be not only mature [Boucher was in his early forties], but mature and educated, and still enjoy SF! Tony Boucher had entered my life, and by doing so, had determined its whole basic direction."

Boucher held writing classes at his home on Thursday evenings. For a nominal one dollar fee, aspiring writers could submit their manuscripts to Boucher for analysis, discussion and critical feedback. Among the eight to ten students who regularly attended were Ron Goulart (in 1951), later a successful SF writer, and Philip and Dorothy Dick (often, when he was overcome with fear or literary stage fright, Dorothy would attend in Dick's stead as well as in her own right). "Tony dutifully read my painful first efforts," wrote Dick in his 'Self Portrait'. "The literary ones he did not respond to, but to my surprise he seemed quite taken with a short fantasy..."

Boucher's advice was both literary and economic: he liked the short story, entitled 'Roog', but perhaps more importantly he believed that Dick could actually sell it to one of the pulps. Boucher made Dick revise 'Roog', until he finally bought it himself for *The Magazine of Fantasy and Science Fiction*. Dick was a proper, albeit pulp, writer at last. In

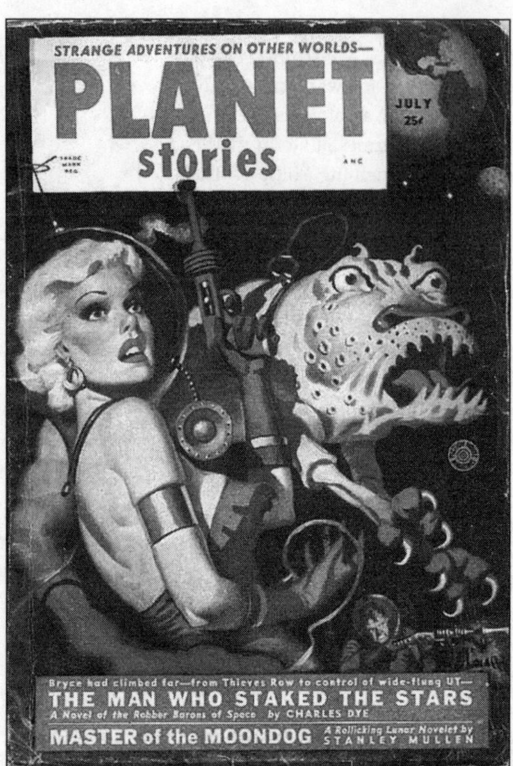

Above: *The July 1952 issue of* Planet Stories, *containing Dick's first published work: 'Beyond Lies the Wub'.*

October 1951, at the age of twenty-two, Philip K. Dick had made his first professional sale for the sum of $75. Although 'Roog' was his first sale, the first story to actually appear in print was 'Beyond Lies the Wub', which appeared in the July 1952 edition of *Planet Stories*. "This caused me to begin to write more and more fantasy stories, then SF," he wrote. Apart from occasional periods of writer's block, Dick would not stop writing until his death.

It seemed Dick's life was on a roll. Just prior to meeting his mentor Anthony Boucher, he'd met his second wife, eighteen-year-old Kleo Apostolides, also in the Art Music store. The Greek, dark-haired Kleo and Dick had bonded over their shared love of opera and she'd soon moved into his shared attic apartment, displacing his roommates and lodgers. Kleo was a student attending the University of California at Berkeley who was also holding down a variety of part-time jobs. In May 1950 the pair moved to a new house at 1126 Francisco Street in West Berkeley, which Phil had been making down payments on, and by June 1950 they were married. Kleo strongly supported Dick's writing ambitions and — like his mother — was even roped into attending Boucher's classes on his behalf to take notes. When Dick was fired by Herb Hollis for supporting another fired member of staff in an argument, Kleo was convinced that the timing — just after he'd begun selling stories to magazines — was a sign that it was time he moved on with his professional life.

Following 'Roog' and 'Beyond Lies the Wub', Dick began submitting stories to the pulps regularly. "I began to mail off stories to other magazines, and lo-and-behold, *Planet Stories* bought a short story of mine," wrote Dick in his 'Self Portrait'. "I forgot my [retail] career in seconds and began to write all the time. Within the month after quitting my job, I made a sale to *Astounding* and *Galaxy*. They paid very well, and I knew then that I would never give up trying to build my life around a science fiction career."

By May 1952 Dick had sold four more stories, all through his own efforts. On the advice of Boucher, though, he decided it was time he had an agent who could more effectively represent him to the twenty-five or so pulp magazines that were around in the early 1950s. Dick followed many other pulp writers to the door of Scott Meredith, who'd just set up his own agency specialising in material for the pulp magazines. Dick initially tried to get Meredith to represent only his mainstream work, still believing he could sell it, but Meredith wisely insisted on the SF material too.

Dick was ideally placed to take advantage of the explosion in pulp fiction. Meredith was also ideally placed to supply material of decent quality to the New York pulp editors who, by 1953, were filling twenty-seven regular magazines. It was a hungry market, one which appreciated authors like Philip K. Dick who could quickly turn out imaginative stories, to length and to deadline. In 1952 Dick published four short stories. By 1953 his annual total had leapt to thirty, including seven published in June 1953 alone. In 1954, twenty-eight stories saw print. By 1955, fifteen of his stories were grouped together for hardback book publication in the UK by Rogers and Cowan under the title *A Handful of Darkness*. Such hardback publication was almost unheard of for US pulp writers. Issued in the US in 1957 by Ace Books, *The Variable Man* was a second collection of short stories in book form. Philip K. Dick was writing and selling stories at the rate of one a week: he was now what he'd always yearned to be, a published writer with a solid income and a secure future.

October 1956 saw the first media adaptation of a Philip K. Dick short story. Science fiction radio anthology show *X Minus One* aired a version of 'Colony', a story published in the June 1953 edition of *Galaxy*, edited by Horace Gold. Gold was an eccentric agoraphobic Canadian-born writer and editor who'd been toiling in the SF sphere since the 1930s. Dick bonded with Gold over their mutual medical problems, but he eventually stopped selling stories to the editor as he was repeatedly upset by Gold's habit of altering writers' work. A handful of other radio adaptations of his stories followed, including 'The Defenders' for *X Minus One* and others for *Exploring Tomorrow* on New York station WOR in 1958.

Below: *Philip K. Dick as a young professional. Photo Courtesy of Isa Dick-Hackett.*

The only story which Dick ever sold to John W. Campbell's *Astounding*, the prime title among the SF pulps, also appeared in June 1953. 'Impostor' contains much that Dick would later expand upon in his novels and was the first significant outing for themes and situations which would recur in his fiction and, as a result of the film *Blade Runner*, come to dominate the popular perception of what Dick's work was about. It's no surprise, then, that 'Impostor' was also to form the basis for a TV adaptation and a movie.

Spence Olham, a defence researcher in Earth's war with the 'Outspacers', is suspected of being a humanoid robot. He is accused of having killed and replaced the real Olham in an attempt by the aliens to infiltrate Earth's defence establishment. Implanted memories convince Olham that he's not the replacement, but the real thing, and he goes on the run. Adding to the danger is the 'U-bomb' carried within

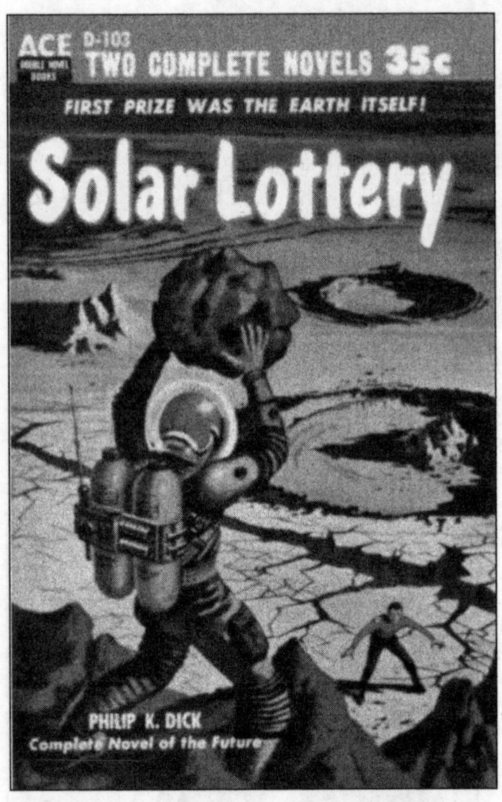

Above: *Like the pulp magazines, SF paperback covers in the 1950s often had little to do with the story inside.*

the android which will explode in response to a key phrase. It's the pursuers, determined to kill Olham at all costs, who appear to be inhuman. The robot replacement they are pursuing engages the reader's sympathy. It's all here in this one story: androids replacing humans, the intriguing question of 'What is real?' and 'What is human?' and totally convincing implanted, fake memories — all the major elements of the 'phildickian' universe were in place by 1953 with 'Impostor'.

America in the 1950s was in the grip of widespread political paranoia, with the rise of the 'red menace' feared by those in power. Post-war political expression was regarded as suspicious by the authorities and the FBI was tasked with the job of compiling dossiers on potential political subversives. Dick's wife Kleo had attended several political meetings as a student and had been photographed by FBI agents. In the mid-1950s, two black-suited FBI agents visited Kleo and Dick at home, intent on questioning her about others pictured in the photos. Agents Smith and Scruggs got more than they bargained for at the Dick household and found themselves drawn into in-depth discussions of the local Berkeley political scene. Scruggs, in particular, became friendly with the couple, according to Kleo. The FBI man even provided driving lessons for Dick, after he was given the gift of a 1952 Studebaker by a writer ex-neighbour who was relocating to New York. Later, the FBI men offered Dick and Kleo an all-expenses opportunity to study at the University of Mexico, if they would provide regular reports on student activities there. The pair politely declined the opportunity to spy for Uncle Sam and the visits by the FBI men slowly decreased.

For Dick, the feeling of being under surveillance by the authorities was to have a lasting impact. Although Smith and Scruggs appeared to have been on little more than a fishing expedition, looking for information, Dick was left with an uneasy feeling that he was being targeted by those in power. It was a feeling that would both inform much of his fiction and cause him much anguish in years to come.

In his 1968 'Self Portrait' Philip K. Dick was critical of his often hastily-written short story output. "With only a few exceptions, my magazine-length stories were second rate," he admitted. "Standards were low in the early 1950s. I did not know many technical skills in writing which are essential… the viewpoint problem, for example. Yet, I was selling; I was making a good living, and at the 1954 Science Fiction World Convention [WorldCon, an annual event since 1939, where Dick met fan and soon-to-be author Harlan Ellison], I was very readily recognised and singled out..."

Dick realised that if he were to move his work away from the pulp magazines and into a form that might be more accepted critically and have a chance of lasting longer, he should be writing novels. He prepared for months before embarking on his first SF novel aimed directly at publication. "I assembled characters and plots, several plots all woven together, and then wrote everything into the book that I could think up. It was bought by Donald Wollheim at Ace Books and titled *Solar Lottery*." Dick's mentor Anthony Boucher reviewed the book favourably in *The New York Herald-Tribune*, which was followed by other positive reviews in *Astounding* and *Infinity*. "It seemed to me that magazine-length writing was going downhill — and not paying very much. You might get $20 for a story and $4000 for a novel. So I decided to bet everything on the novel; I wrote *The World That Jones Made*, and later, *The Man Who Japed*." Dick considered his next novel, *Eye in the Sky*, to be his genuine breakthrough. "Tony [Boucher] gave it the Best Novel of the Year rating. [It turned out] I was a better novel writer than a short story writer. Money had nothing to do with it; I like writing novels and they went over well..."

Above: *Although he wrote over 80 short stories in the 1950s alone, Dick knew his future lay in novels like* The World Jones Made.

Dick was an industrious writer. Between 1951 and 1958, he wrote over eighty short stories and fourteen novels. Eight of these novels were mainstream, contemporary realist fiction which failed to sell, even though that was where his true literary ambitions lay. Six of his novels were science fiction and all sold.

In the 1950s Donald A. Wollheim's Ace Books was the major market for science fiction, publishing two novels every month in a single volume, known as an 'Ace Double'. The other major player was Ballantine, but their output was nowhere near as numerous or frequent. Although Ballantine paid better, it was to Wollheim's Ace Doubles (later DAW Books) that Dick would sell the majority of his work through to the middle of the 1960s.

Dick knew that his novels had to take a different approach from his many short stories. The short stories had been full of action and character, with ingenious twists (later to make them ideal source material for high concept Hollywood movies). The novels, however, were more character based and concerned with building a coherent future world. There were plots and action, but in nowhere near as concentrated a form as in the short stories.

The Ace Doubles were 22,000 word novellas, packaged back-to-back, giving each novel its own garish cover. Ace paid an advance of between $500 to $750 for an Ace

Something had upset the natural laws of the universe
EYE IN THE SKY
15¢

Double, with a royalty rate of between three and five per cent. The royalties may or may not have ever been earned or paid, so writers like Philip K. Dick relied almost exclusively on the advance. That's one of the reasons Dick was so prolific: he could write decent short novels very quickly, producing five or six each year, and he needed the money Wollheim and Ace could provide. By the time Dick finished *Eye in the Sky* in 1957, Ace were willing to offer him the ultimate accolade: publication of his latest story as a solo 'double'. For that, the advance was between $1,200 and $1,500. Dick had written *Eye in the Sky* over a compressed two-week period in 1955, fuelled — as was much of his writing — by an amphetamine rush brought on by pills obtained via Kleo's pharmacist father. It's the first of his novels to substantially tackle the notion of the failure of reality, which would provide the thematic and philosophical backdrop for so much of his work, and become central to the film versions of his stories and novels. Influenced by his readings of philosophy and by his first-hand experience of surveillance by the FBI, *Eye in the Sky* successfully fused Dick's obsession with the nature of reality with the paranoia that was slowly growing in him.

Above: *Deconstructing reality and exploring paranoia, Dick's 1957 novel* Eye in the Sky *was the first to explore his thematic obsessions in any depth.*

Philip K. Dick felt he'd stumbled into science fiction success too easily and so had a certain amount of contempt for his rapidly produced work. Most science fiction novels were published as paperback originals and so were not taken seriously by critics, especially those whose approbation Dick craved. Science fiction paperbacks were perceived as ephemeral and disposable, barely one step above the pulp magazines. However, as far as Phil and Kleo were concerned, critically approved of or not, the science fiction novels were paying the bills. Despite that, his mainstream ambitions would not go away.

For a year, between 1956 and 1957, Dick bravely abandoned science fiction altogether and concentrated on his realist work. His wife of the time, Kleo, noted: "Publishing a mainstream novel would have been his dearest dream. Not mainstream, necessarily, but just not science fiction."

From 1952 until around 1958, Dick produced eight mainstream novels alongside his science fiction. It was to be the major frustration of his life that none of these saw publication. Most were finally published (a few remain as titles only, as the manuscripts have been lost) during the 1980s, throwing a new and more complex light on the then-popular caricature of Dick as a paranoid, delusional science fiction hack. Dick's agents at the Meredith Agency tried hard to sell his non-science fiction work, and they came close to securing a sale on more than one occasion. Dick completed a major rewrite on *Mary and the Giant* in response to critical comments from one interested publisher, but it wasn't enough to actually get the book into print. In pursuit of his dream of mainstream publication and critical acceptance, Dick decided he would forego science fiction altogether and concentrate solely on his realist fiction.

It was a gamble: Dick knew he could reliably sell his science fiction and provide an income for him and Kleo, but the ambition to see his mainstream work published was so strong that he was willing to take the risk. His relationship with Kleo was on the slide around the same time.

The switch to mainstream writing failed to pay off. None of the mainstream works sold, and Dick found himself rapidly returning to science fiction. The one benefit of his continued attempts to write and sell realist stories was that he improved as a writer. By the time of *Time Out of Joint* in 1958, Dick was bringing the sensibilities of his mainstream work — the real-world contemporary settings, the confused and conflicted characters and the exploration of real human relationships — to bear on his previous pulp adventures.

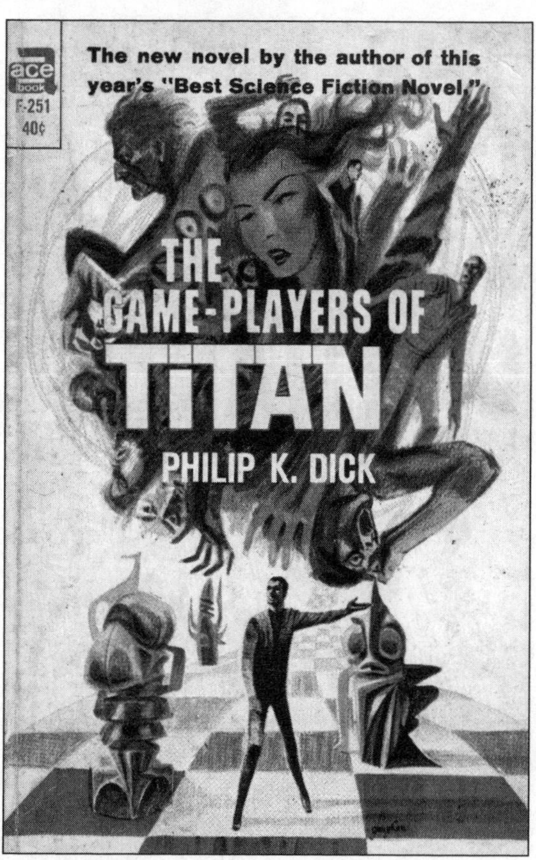

ace book
F-251
40¢
The new novel by the author of this year's "Best Science Fiction Novel,"
THE GAME-PLAYERS OF TITAN
PHILIP K. DICK

***Above:** When he failed to publish his 'mainstream' work, Dick fell back on SF, which he knew would sell.*

Time Out of Joint follows the reactions of Ragle Gumm, whose version of 1958 California is slowly crumbling: a soft drink stand dissolves before his eyes, to be replaced by a piece of paper simply stating 'soft drink stand'. Gumm discovers he's actually living within a simulation of 1958. It is in fact 1998 and Gumm's actions are being used to direct the conduct of a major war. The observed and monitored fake reality setting of *Time Out of Joint* would later become a staple of such Hollywood films as *The Truman Show* and *The Matrix*.

By the end of the 1950s, as success as an author was starting to become a reality, Philip K. Dick relocated to Point Reyes Station, a small dairy town in Marin County, Northern California.

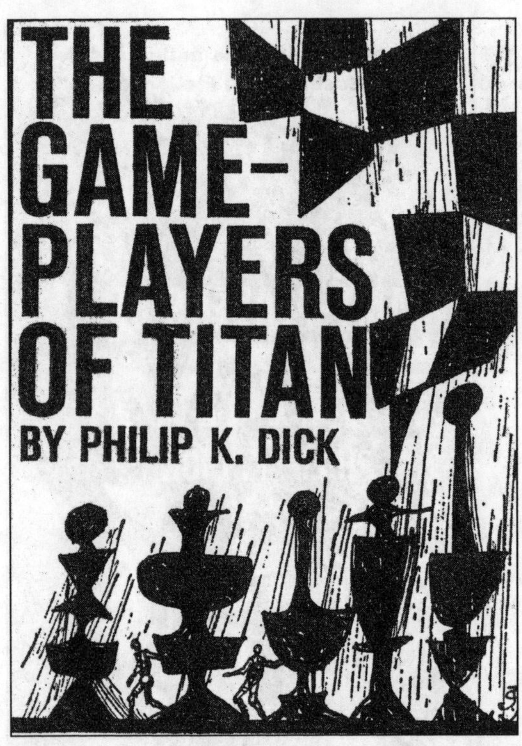

For the always-nervous Dick, small town life was an attractive proposition. Being a successful author — of whatever genre — was enough to make him stand out in the local community. It was also enough to attract the attention of thirty-one-year-old widow Anne Rubenstein. Her poet husband Richard Rubenstein had recently died of a severe allergic reaction to tranquillizers, leaving her to raise three daughters. Dick, then just twenty-nine and aware that his relationship with Kleo was crumbling, welcomed the attention.

While Dick was playing up his mainstream literary credentials, Anne was introducing him to a standard of living he had been previously unaccustomed to. Her house and surroundings (fairly accurately described in *Confessions of a Crap Artist*, which was also inspired by Dick's relationship at this time but not published until 1975), were unlike anything Dick had experienced before. Hitting it off from their first meeting, Dick and Anne had embarked upon a relationship within two weeks and as a result became the centre of a minor scandal in the usually sleepy Point Reyes Station.

Above: *Frontispiece of the first edition.*

The relationship with Anne led to Dick and Kleo getting divorced. Kleo left Point Reyes Station taking the couple's 1955 Chevy. Dick drew directly on his experience of the divorce court proceedings to describe the experience of Nathan Anteil in *Confessions of a Crap Artist*. Before long, Dick had acquired a ready-made family, moving in with Anne and her three daughters. Happy to play the role of instant father and husband, Dick married Anne Rubenstein on April Fools Day 1959 during a trip to Ensenada, Mexico. Upon returning to the US, he grew what would later become his trademark beard.

With Anne, Dick had found an intellectual equal with whom he could explore ideas of philosophy and notions about the nature of reality, much of which would later turn up in his novels. Still desperate to escape the SF ghetto in which he was fearful of being trapped, Dick agreed with Anne that he would once again devote some time to trying to develop as a mainstream literary novelist, claiming in conversation that success might not come for twenty or thirty years… Anne persuaded Dick to change his writing habits, switching from being nocturnal to adopting a more normal nine-to-five writing routine. This decision meant living on a tight budget, something Dick was very used to, Anne less so. Between Anne's income from her deceased husband's estate, Dick's funds from the sale of his previous house in Point Reyes Station and his annual income from his SF writing (in the region of $2,000), he reckoned they could manage for a while. By 1960 Dick was dealing with editors at respected mainstream publisher Harcourt Brace. Although they had turned down *Confessions of a Crap Artist*, they had liked his work enough to offer an advance and a contract for a new novel. Dick sensed success just around the corner.

On 25 February 1960, Laura Archer Dick was born. At the time of the birth of his first daughter (his wife's fourth), Dick's health problems had been recurring. Nervous about the new addition to the family and about his struggles to make it as a 'proper' writer, Dick was overdosing on vitamins and scrubbing the house and car clean of germs. According to Dick biographer Lawrence Sutin, the new father saw the birth of his first daughter as making up in some way for the traumatic death of his sister, Jane. After one visit from his mother and father, now grandparents, Dick resolved to severely limit their access to his child. He still blamed his mother for the traumatic death of Jane. Weeks after Laura was born, Dick was hospitalised with chest pains, warned off coffee by his doctors and sent home.

Following the rejection of *Confessions of a Crap Artist*, Dick submitted two other novels to Harcourt: *The Man Whose Teeth Were All Exactly Alike* (written in 1960, published posthumously in 1984) and *Humpty Dumpty in Oakland* (a 1960 redraft of *A Time for George Stavros*, written in 1956, published posthumously in 1987). Dick knew he had to keep the money flowing in, and produced two novels in 1960 as halves of the still-popular Ace Doubles paperback range. *Dr Futurity* and *Vulcan's Hammer* were both retreads of his 1950s short pulp magazine SF, and are rightly regarded as minor works.

While struggling with his attempts to achieve literary success, Dick was overjoyed to discover he was to be a father for a second time. However, after telling him she was pregnant again in the autumn of 1960, Anne also explained that she felt the family could not cope with a fifth child and she intended to have an abortion. This decision came as a shock to Dick, who maintained something of an ill-thought-out anti-abortion stance thereafter. His feelings and experience of this time informed the novel he later wrote in 1962, *We Can Build You*, a work which successfully mixed his mainstream ambitions and his science fiction skills.

After Anne's abortion, Dick buried himself in the I-Ching as the household returned to what passed for normality. He became fascinated by the ancient Chinese oracle and began studying it. Beginning to guide his life decisions based on his daily consultation with the I-Ching, Dick was surprised to find himself being 'misled' by his newfound oracle. In a bid to explain this phenomenon, Dick turned to fiction and through 1961 drafted *The Man in the High Castle*, one of his most accomplished works.

Below: Dr Futurity, *originally published by Ace, is an example of a 'new' novel expanded from an old short story.*

Hugo Award winning author
PHILIP K. DICK
DR FUTURITY

ACE
DOUBLE NOVEL BOOKS 35c
D-457
Battle of the Brain Machines
VULCAN'S HAMMER
PHILIP K. DICK
First Book Publication

The Man in the High Castle came about when Dick was on the verge of quitting. He'd been writing for close to ten years and had little to show for it, certainly financially. Anne had recently taken up a small home-based jewellery business, which was rapidly developing into a success. Dick had involved himself in the hand-making of jewellery as an alternative to writing, with which he was struggling. This so infuriated Anne that she suggested he find another place to work on his writing, away from the house. That way, they could both individually pursue their vocations without encroaching on each other's territory. Dick responded by renting a nearby hut, which he and Anne termed 'the hovel', into which he moved his typewriter, record player and precious collection of vinyl discs. It was in his 'hovel', in the company of the I-Ching and in an effort to show Anne that his writing was as worthwhile as her jewellery business, that Dick wrote *The Man in the High Castle*.

High Castle is one of Dick's more complex and profound novels. It takes the well-worn notion of a world in which the Axis powers prevailed during World War Two and uses it as a background against which he allows his characters to play out various permutations of what it means to be human. Dick's vision of a USA divided between a Fascist Nazi authority and Japanese hegemony contains within it a suppressed book, *The Grasshopper Lies Heavy*. That book, banned but widely read, implies there is an alternate world where the Allies triumphed. Driven by the I-Ching (as was Dick in his plotting), his characters confront the truth of this revelation at the climax of the book, but find they are still unable to escape the world in which they find themselves, despite the knowledge they now have. Dick continued to consult the I-Ching for the remainder of his life, though he remained suspicious of its pronouncements, believing it had let him down when it came to devising the climax of *High Castle*.

Above: Vulcan's Hammer *was Dick's last Ace Double; a final outing for his 1950s pulp fiction-style storytelling.*

Isolated in his writing hovel, in eighteen months across 1961 and 1962, Dick followed *High Castle* with another novel that would later be recognised as one of his masterpieces: *Martian Time Slip*. A superior example of Dick tackling his other prime concern beside 'What is human?', the book explores Dick's obsession with 'What is real?' Set among the struggling Earth colonies on Mars, Dick's avatar in the book is Jack Bohlen, a man who has had a tough time during his school years and suffers regular visions of reality collapsing around him. "With *High Castle* and *Martian Time Slip*, I thought I had bridged the gap between the experimental mainstream novel and science fiction," claimed Dick in 1974.

"I'd found a way to do everything I wanted to do as a writer. I had in mind a whole series of books, a vision of a new kind of science fiction progressing from those two novels."

It wasn't to be: *The Man in the High Castle* was initially published (and widely reviewed positively) as a political thriller, while *Martian Time Slip* was initially rejected, then published firmly in the SF category which Dick had been working hard to transcend. The author must have decided that the universe was trying to send him a message when, late in 1962, *High Castle* won a new lease of life published as a Science Fiction Book Club edition which won him, in September 1963, the highest SF literary honour: a Hugo award (named after pulp pioneer Hugo Gernsback).

"The Hugo was there to tell me that what I wanted to write was what a good number of readers wanted to read, amazing as it seems," noted Dick in his 1968 'Self Portrait'. Between 1963 and 1964 he proceeded to write a total of eleven full-length SF novels, including *Dr Bloodmoney, The Simulacra, Clans of the Alphane Moon* and a classic that stands comparison with *High Castle* and *Martian Time Slip*: *The Three Stigmata of Palmer Eldritch*. As life with his wife Anne descended into chaos and his drug intake increased ("I'm not sure I could have done it without the amphetamines, to turn out that volume of writing," Dick admitted), his productivity soared. In having failed to make the mainstream breakthrough he so craved, and in winning the Hugo award for *The Man in the High Castle*, and the recognition that came with it, Philip K. Dick found a new purpose in life. He redirected himself wholeheartedly to making the most of his new opportunities as a widely recognised, award-winning science fiction author.

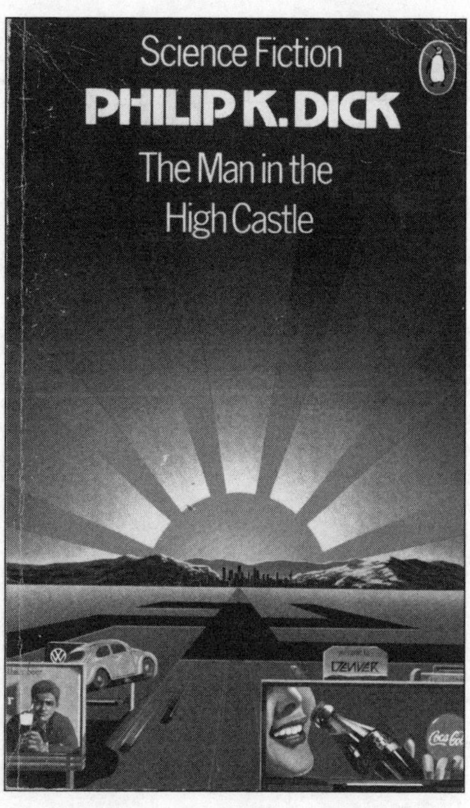

Above: The Man in the High Castle *marked the beginning of Dick's superior work of the 1960s.*

While welcoming his success (and the short-lived financial boost that came with it) in the SF ghetto, Dick's personal life was again in crisis. He and Anne were fighting worse than ever, to the stage where Dick became convinced (possibly as a result of his long working hours and increasing drug intake) that his wife was trying to kill him. After all, he reasoned, she'd 'killed' her first husband, Richard Rubenstein, and Dick was clearly just a temporary replacement… Retreating from his chaotic home life, Dick would visit his mother Dorothy, but whether this was for sympathy and support or simply to plunder the contents of her medicine cabinet is unclear. So convinced was Dick of Anne's ill-intentions towards him that he persuaded the local sheriff to serve her with non-voluntary committal papers, which resulted in a two week stay for Anne in a hospital ward for patients with mental

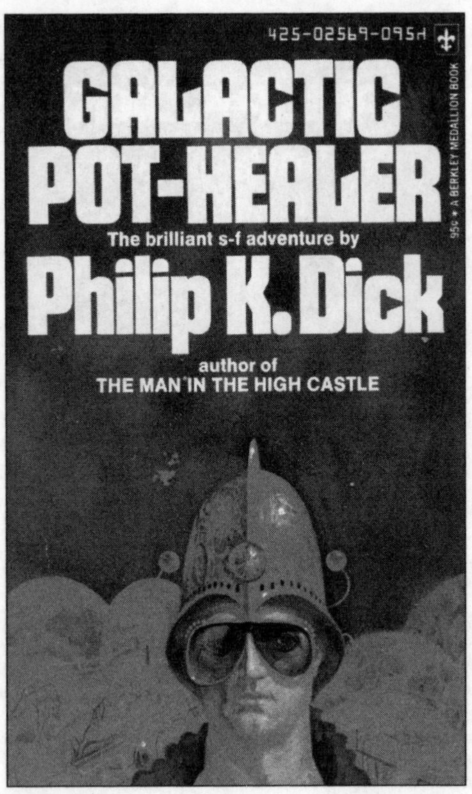

Above: *The early 1960s saw Dick enter a highly productive phase which disguised the writer's block which would torment him mid-decade.*

problems. After the deed, Dick reportedly claimed to his family and hospital staff that, in fact, *he* was the one who was ill and should be hospitalised. Seemingly still angry about Anne's 1960 abortion, Dick seems to have decided that he'd end the marriage in the most spectacular way he knew how. Much of these dramatic events would turn up in his later novels, lightly disguised but easily discernible. By 1964 the marriage was over and Dick had moved back to Berkeley, where he rapidly became a personality in the Bay Area SF scene.

During the mid-1960s, living in East Oakland, Dick found himself the centre of a group of SF writers who would meet regularly to brainstorm ideas and socialise. Among those attending were Ron Goulart, Avram Davidson (whose ex-wife Grania was involved with Dick for a while), Poul and Karen Anderson, Marion Zimmer Bradley, Ray Nelson and others. Ironically, Dick simultaneously found himself suffering from writer's block. His highly productive period of the early 1960s was now behind him. Knocked out of action by a car crash which saw him spending two months in a restrictive body cast to recover, and enjoying the benefits of a whole new panoply of drugs, Dick's writing all but ground to a halt. Luckily, there was a stock of already written novels to feed publishers now keen to regularly publish his SF work.

The 1964 SF WorldCon, the annual event held in a different city across the world every year, came to Berkeley. Dick attended, riding high on his celebrity, but it was from his behaviour at this event that many of the great myths of Dick's life took hold. Tales of him writing while high on LSD originated here (Dick took LSD fewer than half a dozen times in his life, though amphetamines were a different matter). Dick's reputation as a mad, drug-fuelled SF prophet emerged almost fully formed from the 1964 WorldCon, and persisted beyond his death.

By late 1964, the thirty-seven-year-old Philip K. Dick was living with twenty-one-year-old student Nancy Hackett, who was attending Oakland Art College and had moved into Dick's East Oakland house. Dick resumed his writing, but simultaneously withdrew from the Bay Area SF scene, partly as he was avoiding driving after his accident the previous year and partly due to the return of those social phobias from his youth. He was, it seems, content to stay home with Nancy and write. In 1965 the couple moved to San Rafael and Nancy took up a low-paid job in the post office. Dick was surprised to discover that her menial job actually paid better than his writing work. Through Nancy's relatives Dick struck up a friendship with the Episcopal Bishop of California, James A. Pike. Pike became something of a philosophical sparring partner for

Dick, always willing to debate outrageous ideas about the nature of reality, faith, life and death — even life after death, as Pike was something of a spiritualist, desperate to contact his son, who had committed suicide. Dick and Nancy would transcribe their notes of séance sessions Pike conducted.

Dick married Nancy in July 1966, with Bishop Pike officiating. Pike's presence in Dick's life would influence several of his books, notably *A Maze of Death* and, most directly and autobiographically, his last (and arguably greatest) book, *The Transmigration of Timothy Archer*.

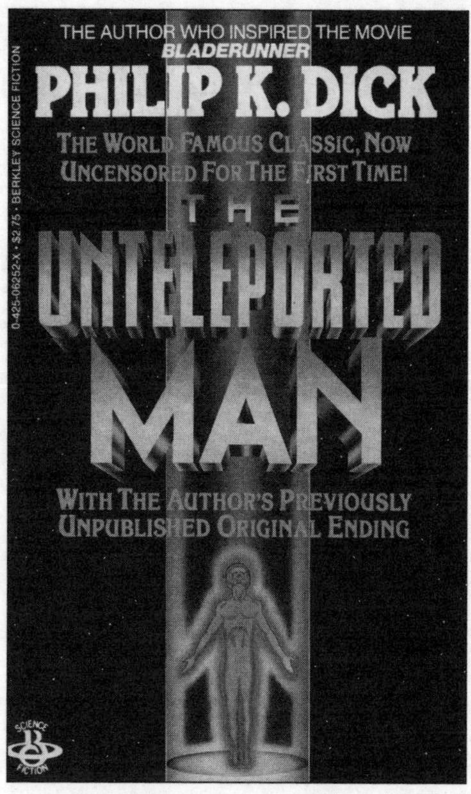

***Above:** Originally cut by 30,000 words for publication by Ace in 1966, the full version of* The Unteleported Man *appeared in 1983.*

The year 1966 saw Philip K. Dick write two of his best and most widely acclaimed novels: *Ubik* and *Do Androids Dream of Electric Sheep?*. *Ubik* follows the exploits of Joe Chip, who tests 'inertials' for Glen Runciter, his boss. Runciter Associates is engaged in a battle for supremacy with the villainous Ray Hollis (ironically named after Dick's one-time boss, Herb Hollis), who uses telepaths and precognitives to achieve his business goals. Inertials dampen telepathic ability and so can be used to even the psychic playing field. Chip comes across the intense and beautiful Pat Conley, an inertial whose talents extend even further: she can change the past, thereby throwing Hollis' precogs off the scent. Hollis lures Runciter, Chip and the team from Runciter Associates into a trap on the moon, where an explosion intended to kill them all seemingly propels Chip into an alternate reality, where messages from Conley and Runciter come to him about the mysterious Ubik, a product of apparently endless application. The novel *Ubik* draws on several of Dick's previous works (such a *Solar Lottery* and *Eye in the Sky*), and echoes others in its presentation of a crumbling reality, but it also displays Dick's search for answers. *Ubik* is often acclaimed by its critics for the open-ended nature of the narrative, but Dick's inability to end the story, to provide the answers to the questions he was posing about the nature of reality, simply reflected a wider need for some definite 'revelation' of the true nature of reality in his real life outside of his fiction.

Dick had married Nancy when she fell pregnant in 1966, and their daughter (Dick's second), Isolde Freya (known as Isa), was born on 15 March 1967. Around the same time, Dick bought a heavy-duty, fireproof safe to store his priceless collection of SF pulp magazines such as *Unknown Worlds* and *Astounding*, as well as other important papers and documents. Whether the prospect of a baby around the house or premonitions of darker forces brought about this purchase is unknown. Isa was, for a while, the focus of her father's attention. Concerned that his daughter be nourished properly, he took to bottle-feeding the new

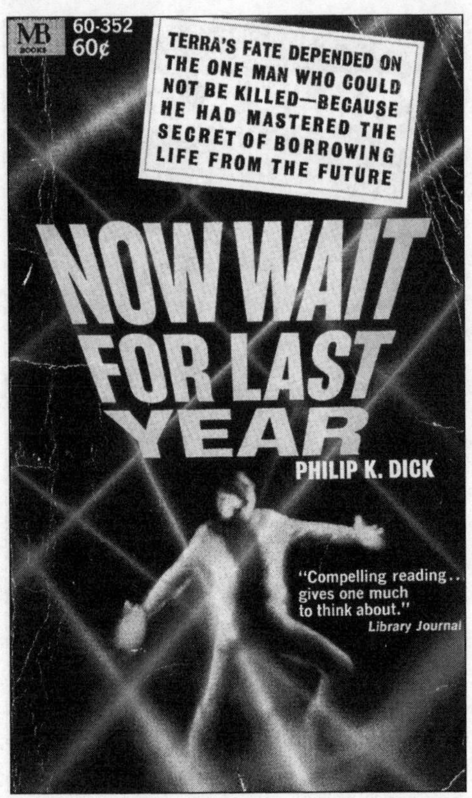

MB BOOKS
60-352
60¢
TERRA'S FATE DEPENDED ON THE ONE MAN WHO COULD NOT BE KILLED—BECAUSE HE HAD MASTERED THE SECRET OF BORROWING LIFE FROM THE FUTURE
NOW WAIT FOR LAST YEAR
PHILIP K. DICK
"Compelling reading.. gives one much to think about."
Library Journal

Above: *However lurid the covers, the off-the-wall SF ideas inside appealed to Dick's growing fan base.*

baby himself, as if he wanted to ensure that she didn't suffer the same fate as his twin sister, Jane.

During the years 1966 to 1968, Dick's dependence on drugs to write became ever stronger. Whenever money was needed, the author would throw himself headlong into another novel, turning out a manuscript on his typewriter at breakneck speed, completing a whole novel in three to four weeks. During the time he was writing, he'd immerse himself in the world he was imagining to such an extent that he'd identify strongly with the characters he was creating. Of the writing of *Do Androids Dream of Electric Sheep?* Nancy Hackett told Dick biographer Lawrence Sutin: "Phil was working all night, and when he came to bed he was talking like a different person. He'd had some kind of experience while writing and thought he was someone else or somewhere else…" Dick would regularly visit a rotating list of doctors in his attempts to obtain the prescription uppers and downers he was using to fuel his writing.

By 1968, the new Dick family had moved to a larger house in San Rafael, with a down payment made by his ever-worried mother, Dorothy. As the decade reached its end, so Philip K. Dick's precarious life began to spiral out of control. A series of deaths among friends and acquaintances set the writer on edge, while demands from the Internal Revenue Service (IRS) also tormented him, resulting in the seizure of his car in 1969 in lieu of back tax payments. He feared that his signature on a widely-published anti-Vietnam war protest document had resulted in the IRS having renewed interest in him.

Similarly, Dick was convinced that in his science fiction somewhere he had inadvertently revealed US Government scientific secrets and this would bring the secret services down upon him. The two works he felt were responsible were *The Penultimate Truth* (an extension of his short story 'The Mold of Yancy') and 'Faith of Our Fathers', a short story written for Harlan Ellison's groundbreaking 1967 collection *Dangerous Visions*.

No doubt Dick's paranoia was increased by his drug intake. Drugs were both a fuel for his creativity, in that they allowed him his white-heat bursts of writing, and a social lubricant. The process of obtaining and sharing drugs brought him into contact with many people whom he would otherwise not have met, and taking drugs removed a lot of the social anxieties that he'd always suffered, allowing him to enjoy being with new people. During this period, Dick churned out a recognised potboiler — *Our Friends From Frolix 8* — but he was also laying the groundwork for his masterpieces of the early 1970s: *Flow My Tears, The Policeman Said* and *A Scanner Darkly*.

Dick's new family was to collapse during 1970 under the strains introduced by his increased drug taking and Nancy's anxieties. At one point in early 1970, award-winning novelist Philip K. Dick was drawing welfare payments to make ends meet. As his relationship crumbled around him, Dick was writing *Flow My Tears, The Policeman Said*, a novel in which the answer to the question 'What is real?' is simple: love.

Jason Taverner is a big-name TV star, with all that implies: fame, fortune, good looks and his pick of the groupies. Thrust into an alternate world — the police state of General Felix Buckman — Taverner suffers the psychic shock of realising that not only does no one in this world know who he is, he doesn't exist at all... *Flow My Tears, The Policeman Said* is a bridge between the alternate realities and 'What is real?' questions of Dick's 1960s novels and the ever-present surveillance (whether by the state, omnipotent satellites or supreme beings) in his 1970s work, starting with *A Scanner Darkly*.

By September 1970, when Dick had completed *Flow My Tears, The Policeman Said*, Nancy and Isa had gone. For the forty-two-year-old writer it was the end of his fourth marriage and the loss of a second family.

In the early 1970s, Philip K. Dick was on his own, without his wife and daughters, but he couldn't stand to be alone. He opened his house to all-comers, with a succession of roommates (starting with Nancy's brother, Mike) and then extending to anyone from the neighbourhood who needed somewhere to crash. It was during this period that Dick's notorious paranoia really kicked in — really no surprise, considering the amounts of Dexedrine and Benzedrine he was consuming. Fearing he was being surveilled by 'them', Dick was on edge. Given the drug-consumers and drug-dealers he had regularly staying at his house, he probably had reason to be paranoid.

Below: *Dick's most widely-read masterpiece formed the basis for* Blade Runner.

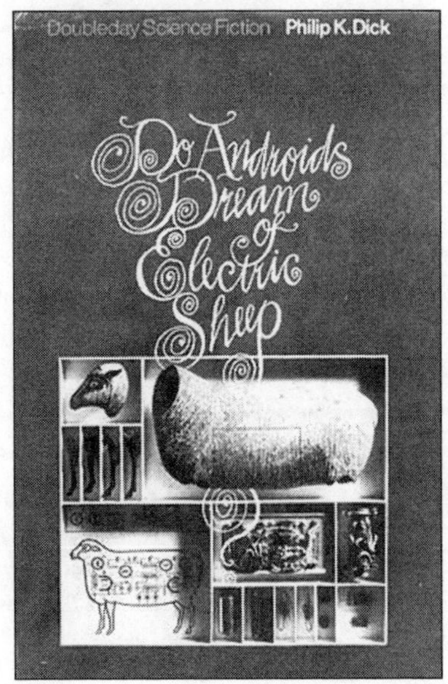

Dick was no fool: he was aware of the side effects of the drugs he was abusing and the long-term health implications. But he was also a writer, so this period of his life was to provide inspiration for one of his true literary masterpieces, *A Scanner Darkly* (written in 1973, revised in 1975, finally published in 1977 and released as a film in 2006).

Early in the decade, though, Dick was not in a fit state to write anything. Emotionally and economically, he was having a hard time. He borrowed freely from anyone he could, but especially his long-suffering mother. He lived life as inexpensively as possible, but the drugs cost money. Every royalty cheque that came in went straight out again on food and speed. The answer to generating more cash was to write, but that was the one thing Dick couldn't do. The house was too noisy, for a start, with all those people coming and going. Dick was staying awake (on speed) for days at a time, then sleeping for further days. The drugs may have helped him be productive in the 1960s, but that was within a stable family environment (in comparison to the early 1970s). Now, Dick was adrift, with no one and nothing to anchor him, least of all his work. A series of short and intense

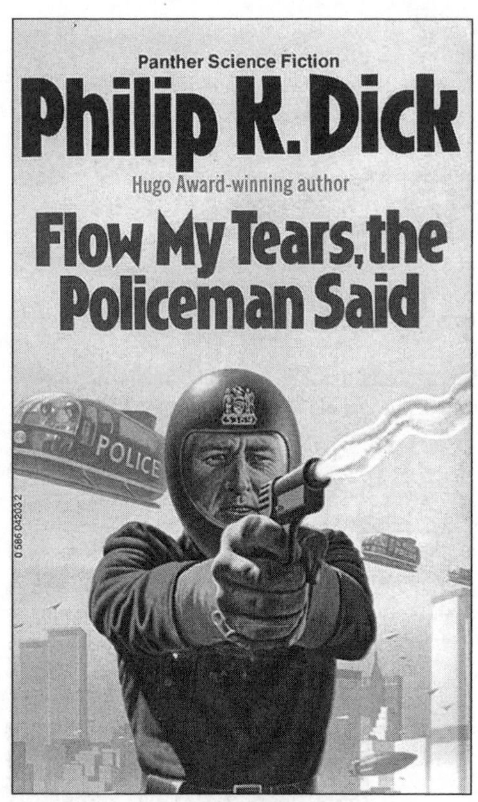

Above: *Written during a difficult period in Dick's life,* Flow My Tears *affirms the power of love.*

relationships (often with incredibly unsuitable women half his age whom he believed he could 'save') didn't help the author's creative or personal situation either. In many respects, it seemed Philip K. Dick had turned into a 'crisis junkie', needing one drama after another to affirm his existence. A few brief stays in hospital, usually for mental health reasons, followed.

While holding court to a younger generation — many of whom were unaware of Dick's status as an award-winning writer — and providing house space to drop-outs, addicts, young couples on the run and high schoolers, Dick was maintaining his friendships with a circle of science fiction authors from the old days. Terry Carr and his wife Carol, as well as Ray Nelson and his wife and others, regularly visited Dick. During these visits Dick went to great lengths to create some semblance of normality, even to the extent of keeping his writing space in immaculate condition: a sure sign that a writer is not actually writing. Despite his failure to put words on paper, Dick was absorbing details of all the people around him, and many of them have direct analogues in *A Scanner Darkly*.

Dick's paranoid fears were realised in November 1971, when he returned home to discover his house had been wrecked. The break-in he'd long feared had happened, but he had no idea who had done it or why. He formed countless theories, and outlined them to writer Paul Williams, who incorporated them into his *Rolling Stone* profile of Dick and his book *Only Apparently Real*. The break-in happened — clearly, it was a physical reality — but Dick's reaction, in spinning out theory after outlandish theory to explain it, was typical of the author of so many novels questioning the very nature of reality itself. Among those theories, Dick blamed the FBI, the CIA, right-wing fanatics, the local police (on a drugs bust), military intelligence agents, some of the criminal types who'd hung out at his house, religious fanatics and black militants. One theory even involved Dick — knowingly or otherwise — being responsible for the break-in himself (a theory actually pursued by the investigating police). That idea was filtered into *A Scanner Darkly* where Fred, the undercover narc, poses as Bob Arctor, a smalltime dealer, but becomes confused about who is who. As a result, he is unknowingly spying on himself. Dick went through the rest of his life without ever discovering who'd committed the break-in, or evolving an entirely convincing single theory that might explain it. The one positive, as far as Dick was concerned, to come out of these events was the confirmation that 'they' (whoever they were) really were out to get him. As he noted in his journals at the time: "The Nov. 17 hit didn't cause me to think someone was after me. It confirmed it. I thought when I saw it: 'At least I'm not paranoid!'"

Invited to be the Guest of Honour at the Vancouver Science Fiction Convention in February 1972, Dick saw a way to escape the life he felt trapped in, and an opportunity to get back to writing. He drafted a speech, 'The Android and the Human', to deliver at the con. It was the first sustained piece of writing he'd managed for a couple of years. He left his San Rafael house behind — following many missed payments it was being reclaimed by his loan financiers anyway. He also left his few remaining possessions to be claimed by anyone who wanted them. Canada, and a potential new start, beckoned.

Dick's appearance at the Vancouver con was a triumph and he decided, with nothing to return to in California, that he'd remain in Canada. For the first two weeks after the con he was put up by a young couple, SF fans who'd befriended Dick at the convention. He had soon rented his own apartment in Vancouver, but his paranoia, extreme loneliness and depression returned, resulting in a half-hearted suicide attempt in March 1972. As a result, Dick ended up in X-Kalay, a live-in drug rehabilitation facility, for a three-week stay. After nearly twenty years of dependence on speed, he emerged from X-Kalay ready to leave the drugs behind and begin a new life.

The final phase of Philip K. Dick's life and literary career began when a professor at Cal State Fullerton suggested the University as a suitable place to take possession of any of Dick's literary papers which had survived the break-in. Students of the professor offered to take Dick in until he got on his feet again, and one of those who met him at his arrival back in California was Tim Powers, then a wannabe science fiction writer and fan of Dick's work. Dick moved on again and was soon living in a shared apartment, but this time the strongest drug in evidence was the snuff which he'd taken up in place of speed. While recovering from recent incidents in his life, Dick was not writing, but ideas continued to brew in his head. He'd occasionally see other LA-based science fiction authors, including Harlan Ellison and Norman Spinrad.

By July 1972, Dick had met Tessa Busby, who was to become his fifth and final wife. Eighteen-year-old Tessa was a student with literary ambitions who soon became the anchor which Dick needed in his life to allow him to resume writing once more. The pair quickly moved in together, and Dick settled down to distilling his recent experiences into the manuscript of *A Scanner Darkly*.

Below: *Dick's real-life experiences with drugs were the inspiration for the literary triumph of* A Scanner Darkly.

The September 1972 WorldCon took place in Los Angeles, allowing Dick to bask in the acclaim of fans once again. Often up at 6am, but not going to bed until nearer 2am, Dick was writing during this period, but the paranoia and mood swings were never far away. In November 1972, during the first anniversary of the break-in at his old house, he stayed home all day, with every lock secured and fastened. Tessa learned to live with Dick's unusual lifestyle and selflessly provided the support he desperately needed, despite his mood swings.

Although he'd not sold a new novel since 1970, Dick's literary star was rising again in the early 1970s. His novels were in print and selling well in the UK, France and Germany. Critical works and surveys of science fiction history began to include him as a key figure in the genre. Heading towards fifty, it was perhaps easier for the poverty-stricken Dick to believe that his best work

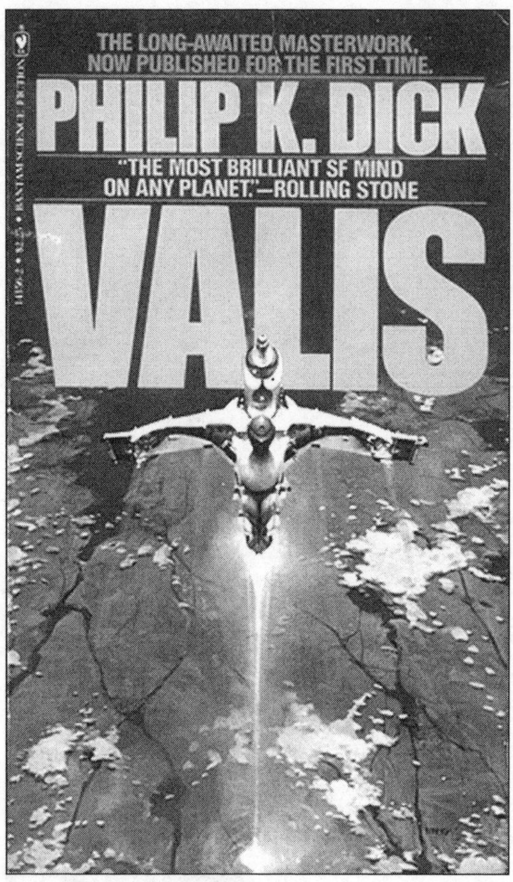

THE LONG-AWAITED MASTERWORK, NOW PUBLISHED FOR THE FIRST TIME.
PHILIP K. DICK
"THE MOST BRILLIANT SF MIND ON ANY PLANET."—ROLLING STONE
VALIS

Above: *Dick claimed to have 'met God' in 1974, an experience he revisited in his later novels, including* Valis.

and his earning days were behind him. *Ubik*, already acclaimed by the French, was published in Poland thanks to SF writer Stanislaw Lem. Dick corresponded briefly with Lem, before falling out spectacularly with him in a mysterious dispute over royalty payments.

Dick picked up and finished *Flow My Tears, The Policeman Said*, which had lain untouched since August 1970, followed by his first short story in almost five years. Recovering from a bout of pneumonia which almost killed him, Dick threw himself headlong into writing *A Scanner Darkly*. Between February and April 1973, Dick produced the first draft of what became the iconic anti-1960s drug culture novel. *A Scanner Darkly* concerned itself with the effects of 1960s drug abuse and the fall-out for those who, like the author himself, had participated. An accompanying author's note listed those (including Dick) killed or damaged by 1960s drug culture. Summer 1975 saw Dick revising *A Scanner Darkly* for publication, and pleading with his publisher Doubleday to treat the novel as a mainstream piece of work and not to bury it in the science fiction ghetto.

The final version of *Scanner* follows the decline of cop Fred, who infiltrates drug rings in the guise of dope-dealer Bob Arctor. His disguise is so convincing due to the use of a 'scramble suit', a computer-controlled disguise that totally alters the user's image as perceived by others. So fearful is Fred of infiltrators within his own police force, he is forced to keep his identity as Arctor secret from his colleagues. Tracking the source of Substance-D (nicknamed 'death'), the drug sweeping the youth of 1994, Fred himself becomes an addict. This results in an inevitable splitting of his personas, with Fred eventually investigating Bob Arctor, having lost track of the fact that he is both people…

Dick put much of himself and his experiences of real life junkiedom into *A Scanner Darkly*, making it one of his most personal and autobiographical novels, yet totally in keeping with his themes of deconstructing reality and personal identity. Dick's reputation was continuing to grow, with requests for interviews coming in (from the 'mainstream' media, as well as SF magazines), and fans and professionals making the pilgrimage to Fullerton to track him down. None of this acclaim and attention was bringing money in though, and Dick remained in a state of poverty and suffered recurring bouts of poor health while writing and revising *A Scanner Darkly*.

With Tessa pregnant, the pair were married in April 1973, with their son Christopher born on 25 July. Dick saw an opportunity to change, a chance to get things right with this third child. Christopher became the centre of his universe, sometimes to the exclusion of Tessa and his work. Conversely, he'd refuse to change nappies and insisted on quiet when he was writing, a state of affairs not easily obtained with a new baby in the house.

Dick's eternal cash crisis was eased briefly with the influx of an unexpected $2,000, when the film rights to *Do Androids Dream of Electric Sheep?* were picked up by United Artists, who continued to pay for extensions of the option over the next few years. As he would do over the later possibility of a film of *Ubik*, Dick got extremely excited about this potential movie, and set about devising ways he could ensure that his then-favourite actress, Victoria Principal, would feature in the film in the part of Rachael (eventually played by Sean Young in the 1982 movie).

In the early spring of 1974, a series of events took place which was to change Philip K. Dick's life and his work forever. What has become known in Philip K. Dick studies as the '2-3-74' events resulted in eight years of an in-depth combined diary and theological text which came to be known as Dick's *Exegesis* (in an attempt to explain the events) and the novels *Valis*, *Radio Free Albemuth* and *The Divine Invasion*. February 1974 had seen the publication of *Flow My Tears, The Policeman Said* and it proved to be Dick's most successful novel since *The Man in the High Castle*. *Flow* secured nominations for Nebula and Hugo awards and won the John W. Campbell Memorial Award for 1975. Paperback resales and foreign deals on his back catalogue had helped Dick's financial situation. The impending publication of one of his mainstream works, *Confessions of a Crap Artist*, the following year was to see a long-standing ambition fulfilled. The family — Dick, Tessa and young Christopher — were happily settled in Fullerton, where the nearby University was housing Dick's important papers. With the renewed stability and success, it seemed that nothing could possibly go wrong.

Instead, Dick finally found himself falling headlong into one of his own science fiction novels. An impacted wisdom tooth drove Dick to visit the dentist for the first time in many years, and following surgery a term of painkilling drugs was prescribed. On 20 February, his medication was delivered by a striking, dark-haired young woman. Dick was fascinated by her necklace as it was a symbol used by early Christian sects. The sight of this fish symbol seemed to trigger off in Dick a series of fantastical and outlandish visions, which he interpreted as past lives and 'DNA-memory' spilling over into the present and possessing him.

Whatever the cause, Dick sincerely believed that he suffered a series of vivid visions or hallucinations, in which it was revealed to him that First Century Rome in fact co-existed with the modern world, and that Dick himself was a Roman inhabitant named Thomas. It was as if elements of *Ubik* had forced their way into Dick's reality.

Through February and into March (hence '2-3-74', after the months and year) Dick continued to experience vivid dreams and daytime hallucinations of this other world. An information-based entity he called 'Firebright' was downloading material into Dick's head. Based on a magazine article he'd read, Dick came to believe that high doses of water-soluble vitamins (particularly vitamin C) improved neural-firing in schizophrenics. Somehow, he got it into his head that this could help him and took an overdose of vitamin C, which probably contributed to his visions rather than alleviating them…

Over several nights, Dick found himself blasted by information-rich pink beams of light and an endless parade of modern art, from Kandinsky to Klee. "I spent over eight hours enjoying one of the most beautiful, most exciting and most moving sights I have ever seen, conscious that it was a miracle," recorded Dick in his written accounts of the visions, which formed the basis of his 8,000 page *Exegesis*.

Were these blasts of art and information coming from an ESP lab in Russia, as part of an experiment which had made Dick their unwilling recipient? Or was the pink beam of light coming from an alien satellite in Earth orbit (which he dubbed 'Valis' for Vast Active Living Intelligence System)? Or was Dick finally in receipt of that which he craved all his life: actual messages from God? Or was he just imagining or dreaming it all? Perhaps it was the painkillers after his dental treatment, or flashbacks caused by his 1960s drug intake? It could even have been his twin sister, Jane, communicating from beyond the grave — an explanation which Dick explored for some time. More seriously, was Dick suffering from Temporal Lobe Epilepsy, as some commentators have speculated, or did he suffer a series of minor strokes, prefiguring the eventual cause of his death eight years later? Whichever, he was doomed to write about these experiences every night, in great detail and at great length, for the remainder of his life, exploring every possible explanation, however outlandish, for the next eight years.

It was as though Dick had finally fulfilled his own legend: the mad SF author who'd conjured such bizarre novels as *Ubik* and *A Scanner Darkly* had finally cracked, going mad himself and experiencing the plight of many of his characters. Perhaps the whole thing was a form of extreme research or role-playing for his next novel? One of his visions seemingly caused Dick to call the local Fullerton police to tell them: "I am a machine." He asked to be locked up for his own safety, but clearly having more pressing real-world concerns, the police did not respond. Dick cancelled his appearance as Guest of Honour at a July 1974 science fiction convention, preferring to stay at home and divine a meaning from what had happened to him.

There was a definite practical application of these visions, however, one which lends a tinge of the unexplained to Dick's whole experience. According to his own account, while listening to the Beatles' 'Strawberry Fields', Dick was zapped by the pink beam of light once more. This time it imparted to him the information that his son, Christopher, was suffering from a potentially fatal inguinal hernia. Taking their son to the doctor, Dick and Tessa were astounded when the diagnosis turned out to be correct. Surgery was performed in October 1974 and Christopher rapidly recovered.

This practical outcome of Dick's mystical experiences capped a weird year which ended with the approach of French filmmaker Jean-Pierre Gorin keen to make a movie of Dick's novel *Ubik* and of writer Paul Williams who wanted to profile Dick for *Rolling Stone* magazine. *Do Androids Dream of Electric Sheep?* also seemed to be progressing as a film project. While Dick was to wrestle with the meaning of his 1974 visions, he returned to the reality of everyday life as 1975 dawned and proceeded to do as he had with *A Scanner Darkly*: he incorporated these 'real-life' experiences into his fiction, in the form of three of his final novels, *Radio Free Albemuth*, *Valis* and *The Divine Invasion*.

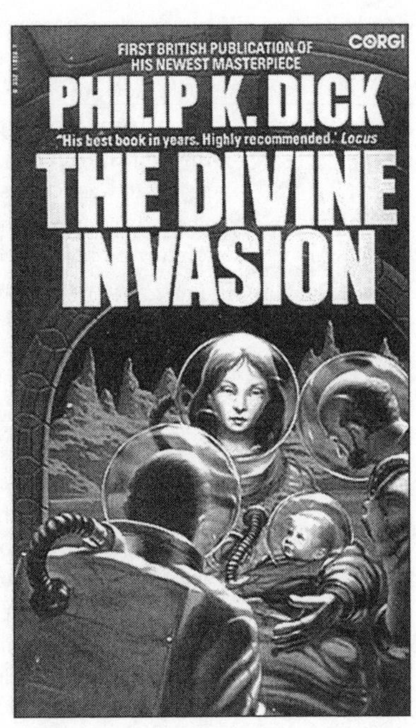

Above: Dick's sequel to Valis, again dealing with his 1974 experiences, was published just before his death.

There can be no doubt that in the final eight years of his life, Philip K. Dick was more troubled than ever before. Whether the cause was mental or physical, drugs or genuine messages from space satellites is impossible to say. Dick knew things had changed dramatically. In a 1978 entry in his hand-written *Exegesis*, his ongoing journal concerning the events of '2-3-74', he wrote: "My life is exactly like the plot of any one of ten of my novels or stories, even down to the false memories and identity. I am a protagonist from one of PKD's books, [a] mixture of 'Impostor', [*Time Out of*] *Joint*, [*A*] *Maze* [*of Death*], if not *Ubik* as well!"

Dick did not go public with his experiences, beyond a few close friends and colleagues. However, his focus on searching out an explanation for what had happened to him dramatically reduced his literary output. With every evening, into the small hours of the following morning, spent in a discussion with himself via his *Exegesis*, opportunities for actual writing for publication were few and far between. Having written a fictionalised account of his 'mystical' experiences as *Radio Free Albemuth*, the text was revised and published as *Valis* (the original, more truly autobiographical version only appeared posthumously). Before his death in 1982, Dick only published one other full-length novel, *The Transmigration of Timothy Archer*, based on his friendship with the late Bishop Pike. That final work, one of Dick's very best, capped the series of 'theological' novels which had followed '2-3-74.'

During 1976, Dick's final marriage had broken down. In an *Exegesis* entry, Dick had analyzed what he felt his role had been in many of his wives' lives: "It is as if I am a bridge [to adulthood] for fledgling girls, taking them to womanhood and motherhood, whereupon my value ends and I am discarded…"

Dick developed a strong friendship with a neighbour named Doris Sauter, and as that relationship deepened, his marriage crumbled, with Tessa and son Christopher leaving the family home, resulting in another suicide attempt. Dick tried to make sure he'd die this time by taking whatever pills he could find, slitting one wrist and sitting in his Fiat car in the garage with the engine running. The car stalled, the blood from the wrist wound coagulated and Dick vomited before the combination of pills he'd taken could have any real effect. It appeared Dick wasn't going to escape from his bizarre life that easily, and he turned the experience into a comic episode in chapter four of *Valis*.

Following a two-week hospital stay (some of that in the psychiatry ward), Dick returned to Fullerton to live with Doris Sauter, who was recovering from her own battle with cancer. The pair moved to Santa Ana, into the apartment complex that would be Dick's final home. Money was, finally, not a problem: Bantam republished three novels (*The Three Stigmata of Palmer Eldritch*, *Ubik* and *A Maze of Death*) for an advance of $20,000. Bantam also advanced the author a further $12,000 for the novel that would become *Valis* (published in 1981).

Despite the loss of his family, Dick's new-found financial security spurred him on to a new bout of creativity. He returned to writing, operating to a strict schedule starting at 10am, working through until 5pm when he'd eat, and then again overnight, often through to 6am the following day. He'd sleep, then be back at his typewriter at 10am again. It was a physically punishing schedule, but one that Dick believed he had to maintain, as when the ideas came he'd have to hurry to get them down on paper. It was a return to his pulp days when he'd knock out a novel in a matter of weeks.

This was too much for Sauter, who moved into the next-door apartment when it became available. As his divorce from Tessa was finalised in 1977, Dick was living alone again. He did enjoy a social circle, though, consisting of three fan friends who later became authors in their own right. Tim Powers, James Blalock and K. W. Jeter, among others, would meet regularly at Dick's home (and elsewhere) on Thursday evenings. The conversation would range from current projects to the state of the world, but would inevitably return repeatedly to Dick's latest theory for '2-3-74.'

Despite his failing health and periodic bouts of depression, Dick felt capable enough to take up an invitation to fly to Metz in France in 1977 to deliver a guest of honour speech at a science fiction convention. He wrote a piece entitled 'If You Think This World is Bad, You Should See Some of the Others'. His speech not only outlined a model of the universe consisting of constantly shifting parallel time tracks, it also tackled several themes and issues he'd been considering since his 1974 experiences. Shortly before he was due to deliver the speech, Dick was asked to shorten it by twenty minutes and proceeded to make on-the-run cuts. His translator, who was due to deliver a live translation to the largely French crowd, made different cuts. The resulting differing speeches managed to thoroughly confuse both French and English-speaking audiences, and to many confirmed Dick's status as science fiction literature's crown prince of the unreal. Dick capped the festival off by having a very public debate and falling out with fellow author and old friend Harlan Ellison.

As the 1970s drew to a close, Dick's financial fortunes continued to increase as foreign editions and more reprints of his earlier work multiplied. However, following the death of his mother Dorothy in August 1978 after a period of illness, Dick's thoughts were of a particularly morbid nature. Beyond initial grief, his mother's passing had little direct effect on Dick, such was his unrepentant anger with her over the demise of his infant twin sister, Jane. Always the hypochondriac, Dick even predicted his own death in a 1978 *Exegesis* entry: "After twenty-seven years of published writing, I now find myself signaled to die..." Delivering the manuscript of *Valis* to his agent at the end of 1978, Dick's covering note had a curious finality about it: "Here is *Valis* for Bantam. My work is done."

Bizarrely, Dick included himself as a character in his final novels. He was both 'Phil Dick' and 'Horselover Fat' in *Valis* ('Phil', in Greek, meaning 'a lover of horses' and 'Dick', in German, meaning 'fat'). *Valis* concerns Fat's search for God, while those around him (based on real people in Dick's life like his last wife Tessa, friends Powers and Jeter, Doris Sauter and others) doubt his sanity. It's a heavily fictionalised account of Dick's real life post-1974.

At one point in the book, Fat and two friends, believer David (based on Powers) and sceptic Kevin (based on Jeter) go to see a movie, which depicts events from the author's then unpublished novel *Radio Free Albemuth*, an earlier engagement with similar themes. The movie in the book, also called *Valis*, convinces Fat that there are others who know what he knows: that reality as he perceives it is not the whole story. The scene is based on a real trip to the movies, which Dick took with Powers and Jeter. The film was Nicolas Roeg's *The Man Who Fell to Earth*, starring David Bowie as a mysterious alien who arrives on Earth and is corrupted by human society. Dick became convinced that the movie revealed some hidden truth to him, though he was never quite sure exactly what. He spent many hours, often in the company of Jeter, listening to Bowie albums hoping to find some corroborating evidence...

Valis was greeted with some confusion by Bantam, who were expecting a more straightforward science fiction novel, rather than a deeply philosophical interrogation of the nature of reality. Bantam's concern about the novel meant that publication was delayed, and when it eventually came out it received a mixed reception from Dick's fans, who regarded it as the strangest book he'd ever produced (and that was saying something!). It was only much later, as Dick's posthumous reputation soared, that *Valis* could be reconsidered critically.

In a December 1980 letter, Philip K. Dick rather disparagingly summed up his own life: "He's crazy. Took drugs, saw God. Big fucking deal..." After *Valis*, there was another slump in Dick's writing, except for his nightly toils on the ongoing *Exegesis* project. In a 1979 letter to daughter Laura, Dick criticised this focus in the only way he knew how, through the use of his own literary themes: "I have become a machine which thinks and does nothing else," he wrote. "It scares me. How did this come about? Every day my world gets smaller. I work more, I live less..."

By 1980, Dick was writing fiction once more. Continuing to explore his religious obsessions and the speculations discussed at length in his *Exegesis*, Dick fashioned a sequel to *Valis* which he called *Valis Regained*. The novel was eventually published in 1981 as *The Divine Invasion*, less a science fiction novel than an attempt to encapsulate religious notions in the form of fiction.

The arrival of Dick's final year, 1981, saw a solid deal for a film based on one of his books, after years of on-and-off options. Producer Michael Deeley and The Ladd Company contracted to make a movie of *Do Androids Dream of Electric Sheep?*. It wasn't the first attempt to film that novel, but it was the one that came to fruition. Retitled *Blade Runner*, the film was directed by Ridley Scott and starred Harrison Ford as replicant hunter Rick Deckard. Something of a flop when initially released, with a very mixed critical reception, *Blade Runner* went on to be recognised as a science fiction movie classic which did much to bring the literary works of Philip K. Dick to the attention of a whole new generation. *Blade Runner* proved so influential that not only did its visual sense become incorporated into countless other productions (including films, commercials and music videos), but the film spawned the entire sub-genre of Philip K. Dick adaptations, which continue to this day.

Despite his delight over the project, Dick was distrustful of how the filmmakers would adapt his story, and he hated the first draft of Hampton Fancher's screenplay. So strong was his dislike of that version, he wrote a piece for *SelecTV Guide* which laid into the whole project and, particularly, the work of director Ridley Scott. Dick's ambivalence over

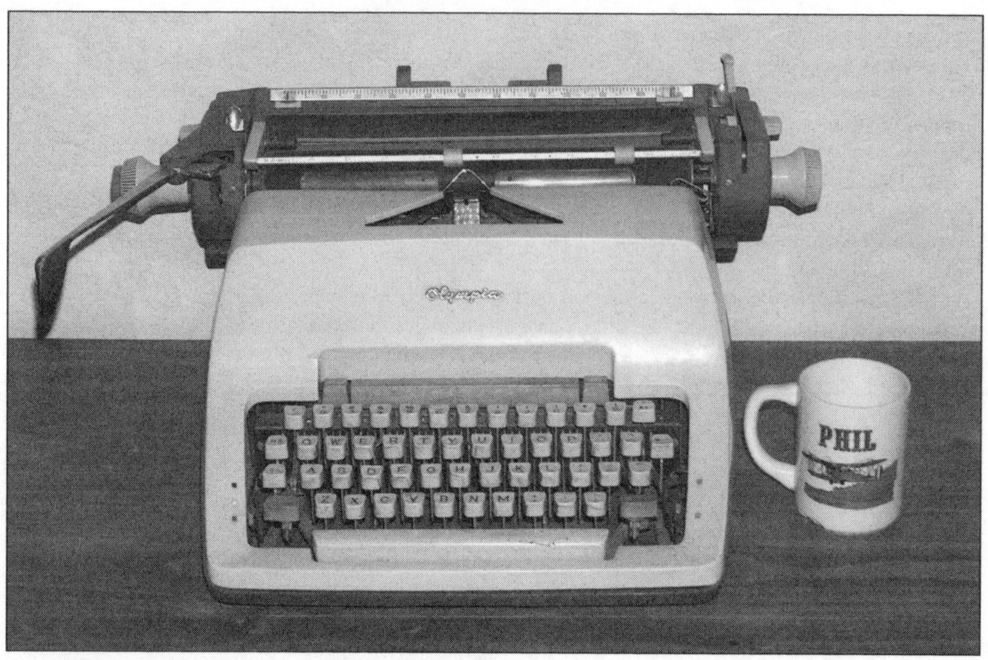

Above: *Philip K. Dick's typewriter and favourite mug. Photo courtesy of the Philip K. Dick Trust.*

Blade Runner swung the other way when he received David Peoples' rewrite of Fancher's work, which he then ridiculously over-praised. Very different from his original novel, the story of *Blade Runner* simplified some aspects and amplified others. Offered the opportunity to novelise the screenplay, Dick turned down a significant sum of money in favour of re-issuing the original novel in a movie tie-in edition.

Dick had engaged in a debate in the pages of *Science Fiction Review* with writer Ursula Le Guin over the religious themes of his recent work and his failure to write convincing female characters. Dick's response to her criticisms was the creation of Angel Archer, the warm, loving central character in his brilliant final novel *The Transmigration of Timothy Archer*, completed in May 1981. Writing his final book, Dick had a new drug of choice: copious amounts of Scotch whisky. The resulting novel is a much more accessible, readable and — above all — human recapitulation of those themes which had inspired *Radio Free Albemuth, Valis* and *The Divine Invasion*. Instead of recasting his metaphysical musings as a pulp science fiction plot and thrusting himself into the narrative as a character, Dick finally wrote his triumphant mainstream literary novel.

Dick had been contracted to write another science fiction novel, though he was once again yearning to dump his now-lucrative science fiction career to tackle mainstream projects like "the Archer book". His final work-in-progress was *The Owl in Daylight*. It featured a hack film composer working on a score for, in Dick's own words: "...this really rotten science fiction film about this detective who is tracking down these androids..." Aliens, who have no music but communicate through colour, discover the existence of the composer and embark on a sacred quest to track him down, treating him as their new God. Dick never finished the plot outline for the proposed novel.

In November 1981, Dick met with Ridley Scott when he was invited to view a reel of special effects footage from *Blade Runner*. Previously, Dick had caught a clip of the in-production movie on TV and had been fascinated by the future-noir look the director had brought to it. However, he didn't live to see the finished movie. Dick had even been rebuilding his relationship with Tessa, mother of his son, Christopher. Tessa claimed that in January 1982 the pair had decided to get remarried.

In his final week of consciousness, Dick was interviewed by Gwen Lee: "Although I think my writing is getting better all the time," he said, "my physical stamina is nothing like it used to be... I can still write well, but the cost... I can see the graph in my mind where the cost line is going to meet and then pass the use line. It's inevitable." Dick feared something was terribly wrong, beyond his usual hypocondria. He was aware he was contradicting himself in interviews, and he was having trouble with his eyesight.

Tim Powers had been due to host one of their regular Thursday evening gatherings (which Dick never missed) on 18 February 1982. When the author didn't show, concerned friends contacted Dick's neighbours who went next door and discovered him unconscious on his apartment floor. Powers was soon in attendance at Dick's condo, as an ambulance crew revived him and then took the semi-conscious author off to hospital. He had suffered a serious stroke.

Below: *Philip K. Dick at a bookstore signing. Photo courtesy of Isa Dick-Hackett.*

Powers recalled events, and the surprise of those who knew Dick, in the Philip K. Dick Society Newsletter in 1984: "[Dick] was writing some of his very best books, and was cheerfully aware of it. He was pleased with the increasing attention being given to his work by Hollywood. During his last few years he was in the enviable position of literally having more money than he knew what to do with..."

'Serious but recoverable' was the diagnosis presented to those who visited Dick in hospital to find him awake, but unable to speak. However, further strokes followed and Dick died of heart failure on 2 March 1982, aged just fifty-three. His father, Edgar, survived him and arranged for his son to be buried in Fort Morgan, Colorado, next to his sister Jane. There was no need for a new headstone. Back in the winter of 1929, his parents had been sure that their baby son would soon follow his twin into the earth. All his life, Philip K. Dick's name had been waiting for him on his grave. ■

PUTTERING ABOUT

Radio drama began the Philip K. Dick adaptations, but the author was more interested in breaking into television science fiction...

"When I started to write science fiction, the people in Berkeley would say, 'But are you doing anything serious?' That used to make me really mad. I'd say, 'My science fiction is very serious,' if I said anything at all. I usually just got so mad I couldn't talk." — Philip K. Dick, *Science Fiction Eye*, Vol. 1, No. 2.

Radio was a big part of Philip K. Dick's entertainment as a child. He listened to a show called *Betty and Bob*, which he dubbed "an ancient soap opera", also listened to by his character Virgil Ackerman in his recreation of his childhood (heavily based on Dick's own) in the novel *Now Wait for Last Year*. Dick was so taken with another radio programme that he sent away for a *Little Orphan Annie* decoder badge. The author later recalled listening avidly to radio adventure serial *Jack Armstrong, the All-American Boy*. As a child, he even wrote a report for his history class on 'Radio and History'. Dick's experience of World War Two came largely through radio coverage and the occasional cinema newsreel. Additionally, Dick's father Edgar, as part of his wartime job with the War Food Administration, hosted a radio show in Los Angeles called *This is Your Government*.

Music played an important role in Dick's life, and he claimed at one stage that he'd presented a classical music show while working for Herb Hollis at the Art Music store. Hollis sponsored a folk music programme on KSMO, a local radio station in San Mateo in the late 1940s. This sponsorship usually took the form of a steady supply of records for the show and on-air promotional material for his stores. Dick certainly seems to have written linking material for the DJs playing the records, essay-style introductions to particular composers or topical debates (such as the question of whether non-English language operas should be translated for performance in the English-speaking world) and the live commercials promoting Hollis' store. Dick was certainly a frequent visitor to the station on business for Hollis, and he captured the ambience of such a local station in his 1956 novel *The Broken Bubble* (published posthumously). Later in his life, Dick claimed to have hosted several classical music programmes on KSMO, particularly in a 1975 letter to Robert A. Heinlein. "I had a small AM radio programme each Saturday night in which I [played] classical music. I called [the programme] *Dr Jekyll and Mr Hayden*... [it was] on a commercial station so I had to do the ads as well. I kept a lot of humour going. I had a lot of fun, but what meant the most to me was playing opera." Also in 1975, Dick was quoted in the book *Contemporary Authors* claiming that he'd hosted a "classical music programme on KSMO radio, 1947." There's no evidence remaining of Dick's supposed radio show, and those

***Opposite:** The cast of* Mission: Impossible, *one of Dick's favourite TV shows, for which he drafted a typically 'Dickian' plot outline.*

interviewed for various biographies of the author cannot recall him presenting such a programme. It may have been a short-lived experience or it may have been a later exaggeration of his involvement in KSMO via his role at Art Music.

Dick's work wouldn't appear on radio again until the late 1950s, by which time he was rapidly establishing his profile in the pulp SF magazines. His then-wife Kleo Apostolides (whom he'd met in the Art Music store) recalled Dick adapting several of his own short stories for radio transmission, but the earliest radio versions of his short stories were adapted by others.

The growth of radio through the Depression years had established it alongside cinema as the prime entertainment medium for the American populace, unlike the 'elitist' pursuit of theatre. Fantasy dramas and tales of science fiction had always been attractive to radio producers, who could create new worlds, vast spaceships and alien species through a few words and judicious use of sound effects. It would take until the 1950s and the arrival of colourful SF B-movies to bring this level of invention to the big screen. The pulp SF magazines were a prime source of material for those radio stations with slots in their schedule dedicated to science fiction, fantasy, the weird, mysterious and bizarre.

The Mutual Broadcasting System had débuted the radio version of Alex Raymond's *Flash Gordon* newspaper comic strip in 1935. Orson Welles' infamous 1938 broadcast of H.G. Wells' *The War of the Worlds* did much to cement the power of radio as a medium of the fantastic. By the 1950s, radio science fiction had truly come of age. The Cold War stand off between the US and USSR — both with overwhelming nuclear weapons capabilities — created a new appetite for escapist fiction, as well as dire warnings of the possible futures mankind might face (or not, in the case of 'mutually assured destruction'.) Every major national radio broadcaster had a regular science fiction anthology show on air, with NBC airing *Dimension X* and CBS behind *Beyond Tomorrow*. Many of the scripts were written by the leading science fiction writers of the day, a pantheon which Dick was in the process of joining.

Both *Galaxy Magazine* and *Astounding Science Fiction*, at different times, were sponsors for the NBC series *X Minus One*, with John W. Campbell Jr's *Astounding* also involved with Mutual Broadcasting System's *Exploring Tomorrow* (which Campbell hosted during its short run between 1957 and 1958). It was on both *X Minus One* and *Exploring Tomorrow* that the earliest media adaptations of the work of Philip K. Dick were aired.

X Minus One premièred on 24 April 1955 on NBC and was a revival of *Dimension X*, the same channel's earlier science fiction anthology series. Like its predecessor, *X Minus One* featured full-cast dramatisations of stories by the biggest names in contemporary science fiction, including Ray Bradbury, Isaac Asimov, Robert A. Heinlein, Clifford D. Simak and Robert Bloch. NBC staff writers Ernest Kinoy and George Lefferts provided most of the adapted scripts, as they had several years earlier on *Dimension X*, which had aired from April 1950 to September 1951. The original authors were not involved in adapting their stories. According to Internet columnist Chuck Rees, "The first episodes of *X Minus One* re-used scripts from *Dimension X*, after which new stories were culled from the pages of *Galaxy Magazine* and adapted for radio. The series' producer Van Woodward and the staff at NBC went the adaptation route simply because that's where the best stories were. 'Bright ideas for science fiction tales don't come on order; they're usually the product of a moment's inspiration, by a writer who is steeped in the field,' pronounced Woodward." *X Minus One* ran until 9 January 1958 (and was re-run during the 1970s as part of NBC's *Omnibus* series).

Above: *George Lefferts adapted Dick's pulp tale 'The Defenders', first published in* Galaxy, *for radio anthology series* X Minus One.

All 124 episodic broadcasts were produced in New York. Fred Collins was heard every week as the announcer, intoning: "Countdown for blast-off. X Minus: Five, four, three, two, X Minus One! Fire! From the far horizons of the unknown come transcribed tales of new dimensions in time and space. These are stories of the future: adventures in which you'll live in a million could-be years, on a thousand maybe worlds. The National Broadcasting Company presents *X Minus One*." This verbal introduction was backed by a chorus of blast-off effects and voices.

Radio, in its hey-day, was often referred to as the 'theatre of the mind', making the medium ideal for the ideas-driven dramas of science fiction. Rather than relying on the special effects of SF and horror movies or those on early SF TV shows like *Space Patrol*, radio allowed the listening audience to create their own pictures, to imagine the action and settings more vividly than any on-screen portrayal of the same story. It was for this reason that shows like *X Minus One* were able to adapt some truly classic pulp fiction tales (and many more lesser stories) so successfully.

The two Philip K. Dick stories featured during the series ran in close proximity. They were 'The Defenders', broadcast on 22 May 1956, and 'Colony', following in the autumn of that same year on 10 October. 'The Defenders', with a script by George Lefferts, was described by NBC thus: "East and West make war above ground with robots while both sides live underground ... or do they?" The cast included Lydia Bruce, Warren Parker, Grant Richards, Mike Ingram and Stan Early. The drama was based upon Dick's short story which initially appeared in *Galaxy* in January 1953, and was later partially adapted by Dick for his novel *The Penultimate Truth*.

Similarly, Dick's short story 'Colony' had run in *Galaxy* in June 1953, before being adapted for *X Minus One*, this time scripted by Ernest Kinoy. The cast included Bill Quinn, Fredericka Chandler, John Larkin, James Stevens, Larry Robinson and Alan Bergman.

All 124 episodes of *X Minus One* are widely available (being out of copyright) and complete sets are available on CD from various 'old time radio' Internet sites: it's possible therefore to listen to Dick's *X Minus One* adaptations (unlike those later efforts for the Mutual Broadcasting System). Both plays are loose versions of their source stories, adapting the basic situations and twists, but picking up on little of the dialogue. Scenes are moved around, expanded, condensed and otherwise altered to create a different take on Dick's basic storyline, or to make the drama more suitable to the audio format (although a large amount of direct narration is still adopted, read by Norman Rose) and to the thirty-minute running time required. Both stories, of course, rely on surprise twist endings (which are intact) and that may be why these particular Dick stories were chosen to be adapted, as the twists are both very effective for the audio medium.

Above: *'Colony', from the June 1953* Galaxy, *was the second Dick story adapted for* X Minus One.

'The Defenders' was born of the Cold War era. Dick took the fear of imminent nuclear war and projected it into the future, a future in which humans live underground while robots continue endless warfare on the planet's surface. Of course, things are not exactly as they seem. It's now an anachronistic tale, with the Soviet Union apparently surviving far into the future. Don Taylor and his wife Mary are unquestioning denizens of the underground world where civilisation continues while the 'leadies', android war machines, fight humanity's wars. Deep underground, with artificial food and sunlight, mankind soldiers on. It's a life, and compared with the nuclear devastation on the surface of the planet, it's paradise. As Dick writes, "Nobody wanted to live this way, but it was necessary". For the past eight years, contact with the surface has been mediated by the leadies, the robot armies. As suspicions grow that recent robot visitors to the underground world of humanity have shown next to no radiation traces when surreptitiously scanned, a party — including Don Taylor — is convened to travel to the surface. Mankind must observe the progress of the war for himself. The trio of investigators are met by a group of leadies who try to obstruct their attempts to view a genuine sunrise. As the leadies escort the humans back to the Tube to take them below the surface, the team's back-up military squad arrive and the androids are defeated in a frantic battle. The trio discover that the surface world is perfectly healthy, populated by farms and animals. "As soon as you left, the war ceased. You're right, it was a hoax..." admits one of the androids. Believing the war unnecessary and mankind better off below the surface believing in the conflict, the androids have laboured for eight years to maintain the illusion of total war, in the belief that man would eventually grow out of his war-like ways. News, photos and artefacts have been manufactured, all to continue the 'reality' that man wanted to believe in. Instead of destroying the world, the leadies characterise themselves as the planet's caretakers, awaiting the eventual return of the true inhabitants.

Determined to turn this discovery to their advantage, the Americans propose returning to the underground world to raise an army to take over the Soviet hemisphere once and for all. The leadies have foreseen this, however, and sealed the Tube to the underworld. Introducing the American team to their Russian counterparts, the androids coerce the former enemies to work together with a view to creating a new time of prosperity for mankind, when the rest of the underground inhabitants can return to the surface. The key themes of Dick's oeuvre are here: the A-Class 'leady' is "almost human", while the fake reports of the war have created an alternate reality for humanity to believe in.

'Colony' was unusual for mid-1950s SF in that it featured a female hero, Commander Morrison, who is pushing for the colonization of a planet that seems to pass all tests. However, a series of attacks against her crew by inanimate objects soon leads to the realisation that the planet itself is resisting colonization, and is using the human's equipment against them. The climax sees the crew (naked, as they can't even rely on their clothing not to strangle them!) clamber aboard a rescue ship, only to be swallowed by one of the planet's malevolent life forms, which is merely mimicking the shape of a rescue ship. "The ultimate in paranoia is not when everyone is against you, but when every *thing* is against you," wrote Dick of 'Colony' in his introduction to the 1977 collection *The Best of Philip K. Dick*. "Objects sometimes seem to possess a will of their own anyhow... They don't do what they're supposed to, they get in the way, they show an unnatural resistance to change. The ending is the ultimate victory of a plotting object over innocent people..." Of course, Dick recycled elements of these ideas in both 'Impostor' and 'Second Variety' (both of which were adapted as movies).

These initial forays into the world of media adaptations of Philip K. Dick's work were necessarily limited because of their medium, but they were just the first in what would become a long line of audio, film and TV productions.

In 1957, Dick was apparently offered an assignment writing original scripts for the *Captain Video* radio show. The pay was (to the then-financially struggling twenty-eight-year-old) a massive $500 per week, but the problem was that the job meant moving to New York, something that Dick, hypochondriac that he was, simply wouldn't entertain. However, Kleo recalled this 'job offer' consisting of the opportunity to write one script, which Dick never followed up on.

Whether it was the same job or another one entirely, Dick did write at least one broadcast script in 1958, for a show called *Exploring Tomorrow* on the Mutual Broadcasting System. "It was kind of a kick, but it was just a one-shot," Kleo told Dick biographer Gregg Rickman. The script, an original not based on a published short story, was called 'Final Defence' and apparently aired on a New York station although there appears to be no surviving record. Other well-known SF authors whose stories inspired episodes of *Exploring Tomorrow*, or who themselves wrote scripts for the show, included Murray Leinster, Poul Anderson and Isaac Asimov.

Very few of the episodes of *Exploring Tomorrow* currently exist, Dick's 'Final Defence' being one of those generally believed lost (although it seems a reel-to-reel recording of this show, made by Dick himself, may be held by the Dick estate, as not all of the surviving material has yet been catalogued). His script dealt with the requisitioning of homes on Ganymede by Earth immigrants. One couple discover that the previous owner of their requisitioned new home is still around. He's charming enough, but his presence is a problem for the new arrivals. The couple then discover that many of their newly arrived Earth friends also have the same problem at their homes. Ganymedes (as Dick dubs the original inhabitants), declared unfit for space travel, continue to hang around the homes they once occupied, and are soon treated as pets by the new owners. When the Earth couple discover that their 'Gany' has a sick wife, the Earth couple voluntarily decide to move out, returning the home to the original owners, and find a place of their own. It seems that becoming a nuisance was the final defence of the Ganymedian people: annoy your occupiers until they finally get fed up and move away.

This surviving plot synopsis doesn't seem to offer much in the way of drama, though much of *Exploring Tomorrow*'s output was humorous in nature, so the script itself, which Dick wrote, may have been much more amusing than a plain plot outline reveals. Neither the script nor any recordings of the broadcast are currently available, so it remains to be

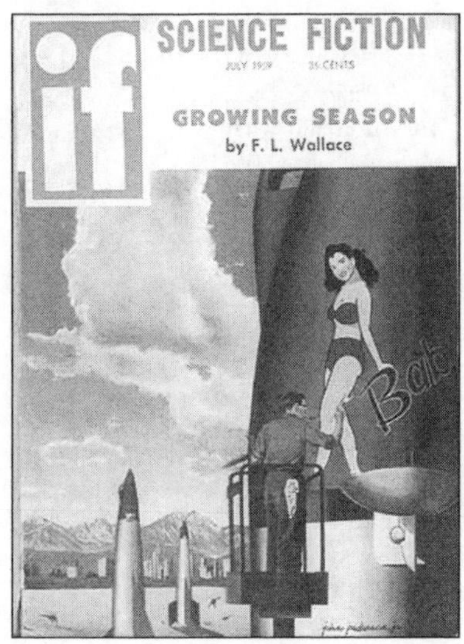

seen whether Philip K. Dick fans will ever discover if 'Final Defence' is a lost masterpiece or not.

Curiously, late in life Dick claimed (in a letter of 1978 and to interviewer John Boonstra in 1981) to have written multiple radio scripts for the Mutual Broadcasting System (all, presumably, for *Exploring Tomorrow*), although Kleo only recalls the one-off of 'Final Defence', and even that seems to have been written as something of an emergency replacement for another script which had fallen through.

The Scott Meredith Literary Agency records (dated 18 February 1958) reveal the existence of a radio script by Dick called 'New Economic Fact', seemingly intended for *Exploring Tomorrow*, but there is no synopsis available. Dick's 1959 short story 'War Game' seems to have originated from a script he'd drafted for *Exploring Tomorrow*, entitled 'Made in Avack'. Some sources indicate that 'Made in Avak' (note the spelling discrepancy) was broadcast as part of *Exploring Tomorrow* and that it concerned an interstellar trader's cargo of toys from the planet Avak, which arouse the suspicion of an Earth customs official. This was possibly a first draft of some of the ideas of the shape-shifting killer robots adopting the guise of teddy bears in 'Second Variety', the source for the movie *Screamers*. It may also have been the same script as the one entitled 'New Economic Fact'.

Above: *'Recall Mechanism' was published in* If *magazine in 1959, and may have been adapted for* Exploring Tomorrow.

Opposite and following page: *The front and back cover of British SF magazine* New Worlds *showcased the instalment of* Out of This World *based on 'Impostor'.*

It seems likely there was a third Philip K. Dick-scripted episode of *Exploring Tomorrow* from February 1958, entitled 'The Man Who Fell' and based on his 1955 story 'Recall Mechanism', published in *If* magazine in 1959. Most intriguing of all, the Philip K. Dick estate once held two reel-to-reel audio tapes labelled 'MBS SF scripts 2/58' and 'MBS Phobia' and 'Reverse Memory', suggesting possible alternative titles for 'The Man Who Fell' or perhaps even other Dick-penned scripts for *Exploring Tomorrow* which may not only have been produced but could still exist, recorded on those now-archaic tapes. The world of old time radio can sometimes seem as distant as prehistory…

While the 1950s was the decade in which Philip K. Dick made his mark as a pulp science fiction writer and had a handful of his stories adapted for radio, the swinging 1960s saw him become an acclaimed science fiction novelist, whose work was showcased by British television.

The thirteen-episode science fiction anthology drama series *Out of This World* was broadcast by Britain's ABC, part of the relatively young commercial television network, between June and September 1962. The series was Britain's first ever run of science fiction plays on television, and featured the first TV adaptation of Dick's work anywhere in the world.

Like the radio show *X Minus One* before it, *Out of This World* adapted a range of science fiction short stories by noted authors, among them John Wyndham (the opening tale 'Dumb Martian'), Isaac Asimov and Clifford Simak. The one-hour episodes were introduced by the seventy-five-year-old horror icon Boris Karloff. The series was created by ABC's chief

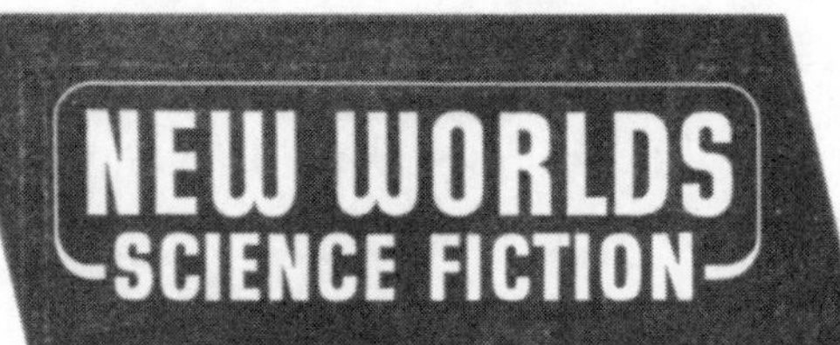

JULY 1962 2/6 Volume 40. No. 120

BORIS KARLOFF
hosts
ABC-TV's
new s-f
playhouse

Out Of This World

National Network
June 30 - September 22
See Article Inside

★

A Nova Publication

16th Year
of Publication

ABC TV's "Out Of This World" playhouse
IMPOSTER — July 21st

Fourth play in the science fiction drama and suspense series, written by Terry Nation from Philip K. Dick's short story and directed by PETER HAMMOND

BORIS KARLOFF hosts the "OUT OF THIS WORLD" series and introduces each play.

BORIS KARLOFF jokes with the cast of IMPOSTER
l. to r.
ANGELA BROWNE,
PATRICK ALLEN,
BORIS KARLOFF,
JOHN CARSON,
JUNE SHAW
and
GLYN OWEN

Photographs courtesy ABC Television Studios, Teddington.

story editor Irene Shubik (then best known for her ground-breaking work on *Armchair Theatre*) and produced by Leonard White (the initial producer on 1960s British fantasy adventure series *The Avengers*).

Aired at 10pm each Saturday night during the summer of 1962, the fifth episode in the run was a dramatisation of Philip K. Dick's June 1953 *Astounding* magazine short story 'Impostor', broadcast on 21 July and adapted by Terry Nation. Nation was then a scriptwriter for British comedian Tony Hancock, and just about a year away from creating the iconic villains the Daleks, as featured in the BBC's science fiction TV serial *Doctor Who*. It was *Out of This World* writer Clive Exton who introduced Nation to television science fiction when he suggested the comedy writer as a contributor to the short-lived series. As well as 'Impostor', Nation scripted his own story, 'Botany Bay', and adapted 'Immigrant' from a Clifford Simak story. In addition to his ongoing *Doctor Who* work (writing several Dalek adventures through to the late 1970s) and working on *The Avengers*, among many other 1960s shows, Nation would go on to create two further important British science fiction TV series: *Survivors* and the seminal *Blake's 7*.

Out of This World is often regarded as a forerunner to the BBC's more extensive *Out of the Unknown*, also script-edited and produced by Shubik for its first two seasons (although she did not return to Philip K. Dick's material as a source for these television stories).

The stories featured on *Out of This World* ranged from straight-ahead science fiction thrillers, like 'Impostor', to the wilder shores of satire. Show host Boris Karloff wrote an introduction to the series (more likely penned by Shubik, who also wrote his on-screen episode introductions), explaining his views on the offbeat tales the show would relate: "Science fiction is not only strange, it combines the aspects of terror and excitement with stories that set the spine tingling. Many other stories have all these qualities, but with science fiction there is an added dimension — the fact this *could* happen. What can be more terrifying? As we read our daily newspapers we find science fiction rapidly becoming fact. As little as ten years ago, science fiction writers had to rely mainly on their imagination. But now with projected journeys to other planets, satellites in space and astronauts circling the Earth, science fiction is in touch with reality and all the more frightening for it. That is why I think the stories in our series, which are admirably imaginative but not too far-fetched, will be so successful."

Director Peter Hammond and designer Robert Fuest brought Nation's low-budget version of Earth's war with the Outspacers to the small screen. Made in black and white, 'Imposter' (as the show was billed) featured Patrick Allen as security officer Major Peters, who suspects that an Outspacer robot bomb is masquerading as top scientist Roger Carter (changed from Spence Olham in the story, and played by John Carson). Carter is condemned to death, but tries desperately to prove his innocence. Additional members of the cast included Glyn Owen as Frank Nelson and Angela Browne as Jean Baron, Carter's secretary. Unfortunately, as with so much British television of the 1960s, Terry Nation's version of Philip K. Dick's 'Impostor' no longer exists for audiences to enjoy, having been wiped at some point during the purge of material that took place from the late-1960s through to the mid-1970s at both the BBC and the commercial broadcasters. The only episode of *Out of This World* that has survived is 'Little Lost Robot', an adaptation of an Isaac Asimov story.

Above: *Roy Thinnes, star of* The Invaders.

Throughout his life Philip K. Dick was keen for his work to be adapted to other media, whether radio in the 1950s, TV in the 1960s or film in the 1980s. More often than not, he would have preferred to have written these adaptations himself, despite having had next to no experience of script writing for any medium.

The success of the original *Star Trek* TV series, from 1966 to 1969, captured Dick's interest in either writing directly for television or in having some of his work adapted for the medium. The fact that some of his contemporaries, such as Harlan Ellison, Norman Spinrad and Theodore Sturgeon (on *Star Trek*) and Jerry Sohl (on *The Invaders*) were successfully writing for television may have spurred Dick on to have a go himself. It seems that during 1967, when Dick was writing little fiction (though he'd recently completed *Do Androids Dream of Electric Sheep?* and *Ubik*, as well as a children's novel, *Nick and the Glimmung*, which would not be published until after his death) he was determined to make a concerted effort to break into writing for television.

The first of his attempts was an unsolicited plot outline for the TV series *The Invaders*, registered with his literary agency Scott Meredith on 17 February 1967. *The Invaders* was created by prolific TV and film writer Larry Cohen (whose many credits from the past forty years range from *The Fugitive* TV series through cult B-movies like *It's Alive!* and *Q: The Winged Serpent* to big-budget twenty-first century movies like *Phone Booth* and *Cellular*).

The series had premièred in January 1967, so Dick was certainly quick off the mark in developing a storyline for a possible episode. That's no surprise, really, as the paranoid nightmare in which *The Invaders'* hero, architect David Vincent (Roy Thinnes) finds himself trapped could have come straight from a Philip K. Dick novel. Lost and tired on a lonely road late one evening, Vincent witnesses something amazing and terrifying in equal measure: the landing of an alien craft from outer space...! He discovers that aliens from a dying world are infiltrating Earth, disguised in human form, and are planning to make the planet their own. Somehow, it's up to this one man to convince a disbelieving world that the alien threat is real...

Produced by Quinn Martin Productions, Cohen had originally intended *The Invaders* to run as a three-nights-a-week serial (as the later 1980s alien invasion *V: The Mini Series* would). This was enough to interest broadcaster ABC, who commissioned twenty-two story outlines from Cohen. A change in format, to a once-a-week hourly series, mandated by

ABC, saw Cohen's proposed 'serial' ideas downplayed. ABC also brought in Quinn Martin Productions to produce the show, effectively sidelining the series' creator.

The Invaders débuted with a sixty-minute pilot episode entitled 'Beachhead' on 10 January 1967. Drawing on 1950s paranoia movies of alien invasion, such as *Invasion of the Body Snatchers*, *The Invaders* updated the premise to the 1960s, but dropped the political subtext, instead going for overt paranoia and subtle scares. As the series progressed, each episode settled into a standard format: Vincent would arrive at the scene of an alien sighting, investigate, defeat the aliens (who would in the process destroy all record of their existence) and be disbelieved by those in authority. This format fuelled the series through its first thirty episodes, into 1968, before Vincent attracted a group of followers (funded by a wealthy businessman) in an episode entitled 'The Believers'. For the final thirteen episodes of the show, the hero of *The Invaders* was no longer fighting his battle against the alien menace alone. The format change wasn't enough to bring the series a fresh lease of life, though, and it was cancelled, with the last of the forty-three episodes airing on 26 March 1968.

Dick was obviously impressed by the series' opening pilot show. In all, he may have seen the first five or so episodes of the show before submitting his own outline for an episode. These early episodes included 'The Experiment', which saw Vincent working with astrophysicist Curtis Lindstrom (played by Roddy McDowall) to expose the alien presence on Earth; 'The Mutation', in which Vincent investigates a reported saucer landing in Mexico only to fall into an alien trap; 'The Leeches', which sees Vincent investigating the mysterious disappearances of leading scientists and 'Genesis', in which Vincent discovers a sea lab where an alien project is creating a new form of life. These were all strong episodes, with solid science fiction ideas behind them, and were certainly enough to give Dick a clear idea of the scope and range of the series.

Dick's sixteen-page manuscript opens its first page with the description of the contents as being a "plot outline for [an] episode of [the] TV drama *The Invaders*." Entitled 'Warning! We Are Your Police', the episode would have opened in a junior high school, from which two students are playing truant. Decoding a time-and-place message from a billboard by using a special viewer (shades of the John Carpenter film *They Live!*), the students join a larger group meeting in a nondescript office building. It's clear this is a gathering

Below: *The aliens of* The Invaders *vanished in death, leaving no trace of their existence... ideal for fuelling paranoia.*

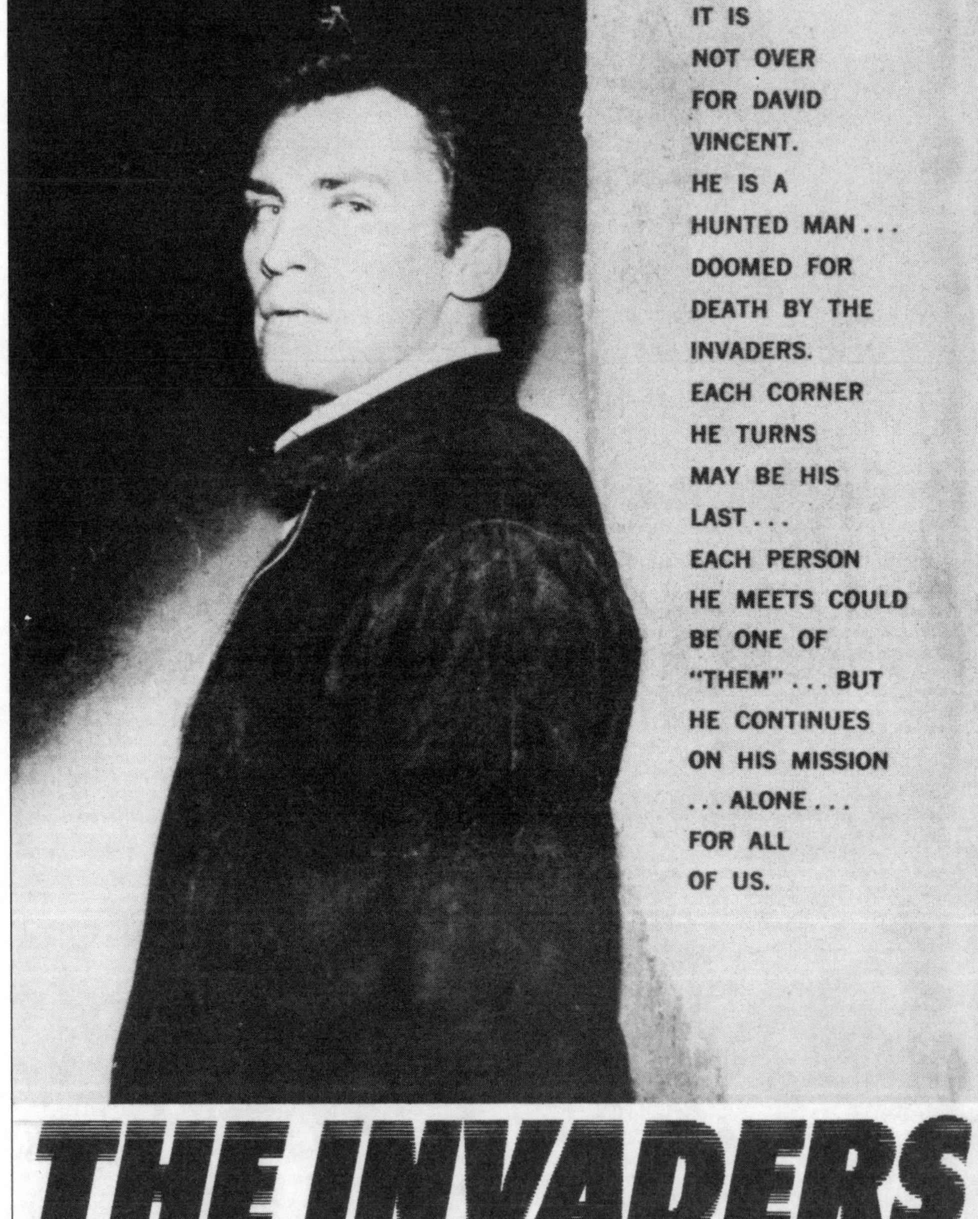
IT IS
NOT OVER
FOR DAVID
VINCENT.
HE IS A
HUNTED MAN . . .
DOOMED FOR
DEATH BY THE
INVADERS.
EACH CORNER
HE TURNS
MAY BE HIS
LAST . . .
EACH PERSON
HE MEETS COULD
BE ONE OF
"THEM" . . . BUT
HE CONTINUES
ON HIS MISSION
. . . ALONE . . .
FOR ALL
OF US.
THE INVADERS

of aliens preparing a new plan to subjugate humanity. The students (whom the viewer believes are also aliens) turn on the others, using futuristic ray gun weapons to destroy them. As Dick noted: "Their bodies shimmer and vanish, which as we all know is the way in which aliens die here on Earth." A latecomer to the meeting tries to fight back, killing one of the students, but the other — named Mumford — survives, having wiped out the last of the aliens at the gathering. Mumford discovers a file of papers and photos relating to David Vincent, which he takes with him. He leaves the office building, but the camera displays a final shot of his fallen schoolboy comrade, now revealed to have been a highly sophisticated robot body housing an organic brain.

Opposite: *Contemporary promotional material emphasised David Vincent's paranoia and fear of 'them', themes which appealed strongly to Dick.*

The next 'act' of the drama picks up with David Vincent at home (a location rarely seen in the series) marking a wall map of the US with the sites of UFO visitations. Along with a friend who believes his tales of alien invasion, Vincent is searching for a pattern in the landing locations. The phone rings and Vincent answers, while his friend picks up a second receiver and activates a tape recorder to record the call. The mysterious caller is aware he is being recorded and instructs Vincent to run his tape recorder at high speed before transmitting a high pitched, speeded up voice (which Dick describes as "bibble-bibble"). He then plays the message back at regular speed.

Vincent has been contacted by an "inter-galactic police agency", a different group of alien beings than those seen already in previous episodes of *The Invaders* (a plot development incorporated into the later 1990s series *The X-Files*, but not one pursued by *The Invaders* in the 1960s). These alien police are even less able to function on Earth than 'the invaders' themselves. They have discovered Vincent through the dossier their operative (Mumford) retrieved from the other aliens' files. It is their intention to gather all the information they can from Vincent about the invaders through the use of a brainscan process. He is to visit room 301 of the Benton Hotel, where their equipment is set up. And that's what Vincent fears this contact might be: a set up. However, he has no choice but to take the bait and visit the hotel.

En route to the hotel, Vincent's car knocks down what appears to be an ordinary schoolgirl. Getting out of the car to help her, Vincent is held at gunpoint by the uninjured girl, who says he's under arrest and will not be visiting the Benton Hotel. From the shadows emerge two uniformed aliens, flanking a man in a business suit: an exact duplicate of Vincent! The duplicate Vincent takes the car and continues the journey. Dick then writes: "Shot of the real Vincent, with a uniformed alien on either side of him, and the high schoolgirl still pointing her odd gun at him; Vincent is staring fixedly at his departing car. 'He'll keep your appointment for you,' one of the uniformed aliens says grimly. Fade out."

The start of the third act of the drama reveals that Vincent's captors are the benign 'inter-galactic police' who contacted him earlier. They are setting a trap for the invaders, who undoubtedly know of Vincent's trip to the Benton Hotel and will be lying in wait for him and the police aliens. They intend to turn the tables on the invaders, by allowing them to destroy the duplicate Vincent and their HQ, thus making them believe they have achieved a victory. Taking the real Vincent away with them in a TV rental van, the aliens explain this gambit will buy them time to establish whether Vincent is genuinely an enemy of the invaders. They fear the document they discovered may be an invader forgery: Vincent could be a collaborator out to trick them. He may even be an invader agent and not know

Above: *Vincent had the support of helpers in some episodes, but only gathered a group of 'believers' towards the end of the series.*

it (trademark Dickian paranoia, and shades of 'replicant' Deckard in *Blade Runner*). "False memories may have been grafted onto his brain," wrote Dick in his detailed plot outline. "The invaders have devices to accomplish this, and they've used them before in other takeovers. The fact that he [Vincent] remembers fighting them [the invaders] and running from them may mean nothing." All the inter-galactic police know for sure is that Vincent is somehow important to the invaders: he may be their key operative or their deadly enemy. Throughout this Dick maintains that Vincent remains calm (something he wasn't good at on the actual show!), showing no shock or anger at the alien police suggestions of his complicity in the invader's plans. Once they've established his true nature, the aliens say, he'll be given his instructions. "You'll be working under our direction from then on," Dick has one of the alien enforcers inform Vincent.

The aliens take Vincent to an ordinary suburban tract house: through the window he sees an apparently ordinary family watching TV. As they enter the building, however, it's clear that this is an illusion: this is the "nerve centre of the inter-galactic police on Earth." On a video monitor Vincent and the seemingly benign aliens watch the progress of his duplicate as he enters the Benton Hotel. As the duplicate Vincent reaches room 301, a thermal charge explodes, destroying him and the room. The aliens are still not sure of Vincent's bona fides however — the explosion either proves he's genuine or that the invaders were willing to sacrifice him. That trademark Dickian ambiguity continues…

For his part Vincent is suspicious of his new friends: they placed the call sending him to the Benton Hotel, then "saved" him from assassination. How would he know whether this was all an elaborate charade or not — and how would he know what faction of aliens is behind it, if indeed there are more than one type of aliens at all! "You say you're unsure of me," Dick has Vincent say to his alien hosts. "I'll tell you something; I'm darn unsure of you, all of you. How do I know that wasn't faked, that whole hotel sequence? How do I know this isn't all a show, staged to convince me? You're more of them, of the invaders. Maybe killing me is no longer enough — I have to be psychologically converted to a point where I actively co-operate with you? That's what you'll ask for next, won't you? My outright assistance?"

Vincent is correct. The inter-galactic police want to know everything Vincent does about the alien invaders. Before he'll co-operate, Vincent demands to see these new aliens in their true forms — he's seen the invaders and this will prove these aliens are of a different species. The alien leader obliges and reveals their true forms: "The busy room wavers, as if under water, and when it clears David Vincent and the viewer see not human forms, but organic brains lodged within artificial robot-like frames acting as bodies. After a pause, the humanoid forms reappear."

The aliens proceed to show Vincent a recording of the student's raid on the alien stronghold (which would have made up the episode's introductory teaser). At this point, the HQ comes under attack by invader aliens, on foot and from a saucer hovering above the building. The invaders have figured out the deception at the Benton Hotel and tracked Vincent to his current location. Vincent escapes, taking the schoolgirl alien with him, as the saucer grapples onto the building lifting it off its foundations. Vincent and the girl depart the scene in the TV repair van, as invaders fire after them. Escaping, Vincent swerves the van off the road and crashes to avoid a curiously old-fashioned vehicle heading straight for them. Vincent comes to and discovers sitting next to him in the wreckage of the crashed van is "not the girl, but an inert brain-and-machine creature. It is lifeless."

Setting things up for the later denouement of the episode, Dick notes: "An astute viewer might note that for an interval David Vincent was unconscious. The viewer would do well to file this observation away." Then, Dick's lengthy plot outline makes it very clear to less astute viewers that something odd is going on. Observing a glow in the sky which indicates that the battle between the invaders and alien police is still going on, Vincent is hit from behind and knocked unconscious (again). Standing over his prone body are two genuine invaders. "We can tell they are invaders because of the finger-bending propensity" — a reference to the giveaway stiff little fingers of the aliens featured in the series. One then asks the other if he thinks Vincent suspects, then orders the beginning of "stage four" before saying into a sleeve-mounted communicator: "We have him!"

As the invaders lift Vincent's unconscious body, their commander emerges from the shadows: it's the high school girl whom Vincent rescued, with a "cold and emotionless face. Fade out."

The next act switches location to an invader nerve centre, where Vincent is propped up unconscious in a chair. The aliens discuss how they will suffer casualties in the raid to come, yet it is necessary to convince Vincent. As the schoolgirl says, "He must see the pitched battle between ourselves and the inter-galactic police raiding unit." As Vincent begins to recover consciousness, the girl leaves and the aliens confirm it'll be five minutes until the staged raid begins. The aliens boast to Vincent of how they destroyed the base of the inter-galactic police, so he should not expect them to help him now. They try to impress upon Vincent how invulnerable they are — even the all-powerful inter-galactic police couldn't help Vincent repel their invasion of Earth. At this point, the 'police' raid begins and the invaders are wiped out, although there are clear casualties on both sides. The 'police' rescue Vincent, and continuing the theme of bluffs-within-bluffs attempt to persuade him they had the situation under control all along.

The alien 'police' leader explains to Vincent that they are now sure of his loyalties, but that it no longer matters as the invasion is at an end. The invaders have been vanquished and David Vincent can return to being a humble architect once more. "You can rest now," Vincent is told. "The long task is over. Our organisation will finish the job of mopping

Above: *Stephen Hill played IMF team leader Dan Briggs in* Mission: Impossible's *first season.*

them up." The alien police offer Vincent a way of contacting them if he should ever come across any future invader projects — after all, it's inevitable that some may escape their net.

Apparently convinced, Vincent leaves. He passes the wreck of the TV repair van and sees again the brain-and-machine construct, then catches a shape out of the corner of his eye. Pursuing the phantom figure into the woods, he discovers it's the supposedly dead schoolgirl. Vincent realises he has been the victim of an extremely elaborate hoax by the invaders, an attempt to convince him that he had no cause to fight on, that an all-powerful inter-galactic police force would relieve him of his burden of protecting humanity.

Attempting to escape Vincent, the girl runs from the woods back to the road and into the path of an incoming car. This is the real thing this time, no fake. Vincent's reaction displays a coldness towards another alien invader vanquished, but also a degree of pity for the creatures who feel it necessary to go to such extraordinary lengths to throw one man off their scent. Leaving the scene, Vincent leaves behind a confused driver who thought he'd hit someone, but now there's no body.

In the style of the show, Dick even provided the spoken narration for the end of the episode summing up the theme and indicating that Vincent's battle does go on: "A man who thought he could rest. A man told that others had come to take up the task, others better qualified and many of them — professionals who would win, who would spread their protective cloak around a defenceless Earth. For a little while — just a few hours, no more — David Vincent seemed not to be alone." Fade out.

Dick was obviously anxious that his first television submission should succeed. Writing in a letter to Cynthia Goldstone dated 27 February 1967, just ten days after submitting his outline to his agent, he notes: "I wrote a script [it wasn't, just an outline] for the TV show *The Invaders*. I wonder if they'll buy it (of course they will, it's superb!)" Writing to agent Scott Meredith on 24 April 1967, Dick was worried that his TV story proposal had gone astray as he'd heard nothing since submitting it: "Did you get my script for *The Invaders*? I never received an answer from you. Could it have gotten lost in the mail?" Dick needn't have worried. Meredith's agency had forwarded his outline to the producers of *The Invaders* immediately on 21 February 1967. With Larry Cohen's twenty-two story outlines and a roster of writers already lined up for the show, the potential episode openings for unsolicited story ideas on *The Invaders* were few and far between, so it's no surprise that

Dick's efforts were rejected and the manuscript returned to the author, via his agents, on 9 May 1967.

By then Dick had moved on to work on a story idea for another of his favourite TV shows — *Mission: Impossible*.

Mission: Impossible first aired in the US in September 1966 and ran, with a changing ensemble cast, for seven years until 1973. The series chronicled the adventures of the Impossible Mission Taskforce (IMF), a team of government spies and specialists who were assigned secret missions deemed impossible by the unseen 'Secretary', a government or secret service official. The main characters included the team leader (Dan Briggs in the first season, then Jim Phelps for the remaining six), a techno-savvy character (Barney Collier), the muscle (Willy Armitage), a master of disguise (first Rollin Hand, then The Amazing Paris), and various femme fatales (Cinnamon Carter, Casey, Dana Lambert, Mimi Davis). The stars of the series were Martin Landau (1966-69), Barbara Bain (1966-1969), Peter Lupus, Greg Morris, Peter Graves (1967-1973), *Star Trek*'s Leonard Nimoy (1969-1971), Sam Elliot (during the 1970-1971 season), Lesley Ann Warren, Lynda Day George and Barbara Anderson.

***Below:** A scene from 'The Legacy', one of the* Mission: Impossible *episodes Dick may have seen before writing his own multiple realities storyline.*

Mission: Impossible was best remembered for its opening sequence, setting out the terms of the week's mission via the gimmick of a self-destructing recorded message tape, voiced by uncredited actor Bob Johnson. Other notable elements of the episodic formula of the series were the team leader's selection of mission agents from a dossier, the opening briefing meeting, the intricate use of disguises and a typical unveiling scene near the end of most episodes, where a mask or disguise is removed. The show also boasted a set of cardboard characters, who showed no development and little change across the years…

Episodes Dick may have seen before submitting his own idea (during the show's second year on the air) include the pilot which saw the team assembled to recover stolen nuclear warheads; 'Operation Rogosh' which sees a mass murderer who is targeting LA tricked into believing he's in a prison cell three years after his capture (a play on the nature of subjective reality which may have caught Dick's attention); the use of a phoney psychic in 'Zubrovnik's Ghost'; the defeat of some junior Nazis in 'The Legacy' and the exposure of the use of faked propaganda footage of American soldiers committing atrocities in 'Action!'.

ELITE
JANUARY • ONE DOLLAR
MODEL OF
THE YEAR
CINNAMON
CARTER

***Above:** Cinnamon Carter (Barbara Bain) was used as bait to lure a dictator into a trap in Dick's* Mission: Impossible *outline.*

Some of the themes of the show may have intrigued Dick, especially the emphasis on disguise and the questions of identity and perceived reality. Each episode featured one or more members of the IMF team faultlessly disguising themselves as someone else in order to achieve the mission. This passing off one person as another perhaps had resonance with Dick as he'd just written *Do Androids Dream of Electric Sheep?*, one of several of his novels which deal with the issue of fake/android humans passing themselves off as the real thing, or being entirely unaware of their own true natures.

Dick's idea for an episode of *Mission: Impossible* is untitled, simply headed 'Plot Idea for *Mission: Impossible*'. It opens by outlining the details of the mission: it takes place in a Latin American country (Dick admits he's basing his fake country on 1960s Cuba), where the dictator was recently assassinated. His young, left-wing revolutionary replacement (simply called 'R' early in Dick's plot outline) has aligned his country with the Soviet empire. The US wants regime change, but won't go as far as assassination as that would simply make a martyr of the country's newest dictator. The mission is to arrange for the dictator to voluntarily return to Western patronage, an act which will simultaneously undermine him with his own people and remove him from power. Using Cinnamon as bait, the IMF team capture 'R' when he is indulging himself at one of the old dictator's out-of-the-way pleasure palaces. Taking his cue from the movie *The Great Man*, Dick proposes the team use 'word cuts', edits from 'R's previous speeches to fake a message from him explaining his absence.

Faking the interior of a mental asylum, the IMF team revive 'R' and introduce him to the chief 'psychiatrist', in reality IMF leader Jim Phelps. They attempt to convince 'R' that he has never ruled his country, but has instead suffered a "catatonic schizophrenic state" for over a year. He's been suffering from the delusion that the previous dictator (referred to in the synopsis only as 'D') was assassinated: in fact, he's very much alive and is still in power!

Using faked TV reports (perhaps referring directly to 'R's mental state) and faked newspapers, the IMF team have to convince 'R' of his new reality. 'R' is convinced that his henchmen and supporters are either dead or in the pay of 'D'. As Dick notes: "The appearance of 'D' on the TV screen is done by Rollin, using his handy rubber-face apparatus." Then, Dick promises "the most overwhelming fakery is yet to come..."

This can't be real — 'R' is not that easily fooled. He remembers delivering a rousing speech to the nation promising them a shining 'anti-capitalist' future. He is shown a recording of that speech, with 'R' in a medical gown addressing his fellow mental patients. However, 'R' spots a pile of magazines in this supposed year-old film which have also been used to convince him of his present condition and location: the IMF team have made a mistake! Without revealing that he knows of their trickery, 'R' must find a way to free himself from their clutches.

Dick's idea was to match the IMF team against someone as adept at deception as they are. As he writes: "I don't recall a *Mission: Impossible* episode in which the team faced someone expert in their own sort of electronic sleight-of-hand before." Cinnamon, posing as a fellow patient, inadvertently gives 'R' what he needs to affect his escape: her miniature walkie-talkie, which 'R' steals from her purse. Breaking into the basement to rewire the walkie-talkie, 'R' discovers Barney's electronic control centre, the heart of the IMF team's deception.

Attempting to contact the outside world, 'R' is confronted by Barney. The young dictator defeats the IMF operative and takes his gun — now he can simply shoot his way out. Escaping the building, he comes across Willy, whom he rapidly eliminates using Barney's gun. Dick points out that, as 'R' makes his way down a country road "the viewer will think that not only has 'R' gotten away and the mission failed, but also that Barney and Willy are dead."

Below: *Master of disguise Rollin Hand (Martin Landau) played a key role in Dick's proposed storyline.*

Presenting
Rollin Hand
MAN OF A MILLION FACES
WORLD'S GREATEST IMPERSONATOR - QUICK CHANGE - ILLUSION - FEATS OF DISGUISE

Eventually, 'R' comes across a cadre of his own men guarding a checkpoint. Here Dick finally gives this character a name: Ernesto Guardia. However, it seems his men don't recognise their leader and fire upon him. 'R' has no choice but to take out his own squad. Discovering contemporary newspapers and listening to a radio broadcast, 'R' discovers that he himself has been overthrown in his absence and two of his henchmen and their respective followers are battling each other for power: it's civil war! Additionally, he has been discredited through the release of papers showing how 'R' was working with the CIA... There is no way he can reclaim his power base. Killing a pilot and stealing his plane, 'R' voluntarily flies to the United States and political asylum.

Dick reveals his final trick: "This means that 'R' fell for a fraud within a fraud." The IMF team are all alive and the outside world through which 'R' travelled, apparently unhindered, was just another fake reality they had constructed to convince him to flee to the US. "The IMF did its job," wrote Dick. "It only appeared to have lost control of the situation for a time… when in actuality everything went exactly as planned."

Needless to say, this plot was similar to (if slightly less complicated) than the one Dick had devised for *The Invaders*. It plays out some of his key themes of identity and the nature of reality. The fact that the spy world and the plots of *Mission: Impossible* are all about deception made them a natural home for the sensibility of Philip K. Dick. It's a shame, then, that neither of his ideas for episodes of two of his favourite 1960s TV shows were ever developed.

As he was in so much of his writing, Dick's approach to television drama was perhaps ahead of its time. His take on the dubious nature of reality, and how easily it can be faked to political ends, may have found more resonance in the America of 1974 when President Nixon fell following Watergate (the year after the original IMF team retired from the small screen). Right through to the present day, episodes of serial TV shows have played with the faking of reality, with key recent examples including the wonderfully paranoid and 'phildickian' *Nowhere Man* starring Bruce Greenwood, and the high-spirited espionage hijinks of *Alias*, starring Jennifer Garner. Philip K. Dick's take on episodic television just wasn't ready for prime time. Or perhaps prime time wasn't ready for Philip K. Dick.

Despite these two setbacks, Dick did make a third attempt at breaking into 1960s television. If established producers wouldn't let him write for shows already on air, then he'd create his own series. In another 1967 document, simply headed 'TV Series Idea', Dick outlined his notions for an ongoing episodic TV show that would capture his approach to fiction on the small screen. He seems to have had little notion about to how transform his idea from some notations on paper to an actual proposal suitable for submission to TV producers. It seems unlikely that this proposal went any further than the offices of the Scott Meredith Literary Agency, and there's certainly no record of any correspondence in which any potential producers express an interest in Dick's TV series idea.

The setting for Dick's proposed untitled TV series is Heaven, a grey, foggy landscape peopled by guardian angels. This is the base of operations for 'We Are Watching You, Inc', (WAWY, Inc), a slightly sinister sounding name for one of the smaller firms of guardian angels watching out for humanity. This is a family style business, modelled — as are so many of the small businesses in his novels and short stories — after Dick's own experiences of Herb Hollis and the Art Music store.

The characters who staff this organisation are Anastasia Kelp, the company patriarch; Miss Theola Feather, the receptionist and secretary; Morris Nimbleman, director of research; Ludlow Orlawsky, the sales manager; Fred Engstrom, the repairman for the angel's equipment; and the series' lead protagonist, Herb DeWinter, head of field operations, who makes trips back and forward between Heaven and Earth on missions of mercy.

'We Are Watching You, Inc' is a tiny outfit when it comes to organisations of guardian angels, battling against the big boys of the business and forever in danger of losing its franchise due to its size, despite a nearly 100 per cent record of success. Our hero, DeWinter, is a typical Dickian 'little man', in a position of great responsibility, who somehow manages to muddle through and ensure everything comes out right in the end. His biggest antagonist is Mr Vane, a ghostly, booming voice, representing Heaven's supervising authorities.

Vane is always checking up on DeWinter, threatening an 'audit' and the ultimate closure of WAWY, Inc.

For his part, Kelp is aware he should throw in the towel as they can't compete with the more corporate outfits. Everything about WAWY, Inc is old fashioned. Dick describes a headquarters office location that is redolent of the early 20th Century: no chrome or gadgets, just old-fashioned telephones and wooden desks. "The locale is like an old-fashioned small store, with much personal relatedness [sic] between the employees, so that they form a bickering, loving small family, with Kelp, of course, as the father."

Dick makes an exception to this "old-fashionedness" for the magical gadgets required in the guardian angels' line of work. These are "advanced electronic super-science gimmicks. Each time the gimmicks differ according to the assignment. [They] are really quite spectacular, so that Herb becomes a parody of James Bond with his magic attaché case… This is the dominant mood of the drama: a sort of supernatural James Bond, except well intentioned, unsophisticated and a bit bungling."

Dick's idea was that each episode of the series would feature a different field trip for Herb DeWinter. A dead client (that is, a resident of Heaven and "a good many odd-balls") would come to WAWY, Inc for help with a problem being suffered by a friend or relative who is still alive on Earth. A guardian angel is needed to bail this relative out of whatever "wild and kookie mess [that is] ensnaring him…"

DeWinter's approach is to be as straightforward as possible. Dressed like an FBI Agent or an IBM salesman, in a "natty New York-style suit of the latest cut", DeWinter would approach the person he's to help and come straight out with the explanation that he's a guardian angel hired by their grandmother (or whomever) to solve their problem. Rather then milk the comedy of this situation or have the person to be assisted baulk at the idea, Dick proposed that "double takes are as brief as possible; then the two of them get down to brass tacks… The shortness of the double take can be explained by the urgent peril surrounding the beleaguered loved one; he can't afford to be sceptical, not at a time like this…" The characters in Dick's drama simply accept the existence of Heaven and guardian angels, and welcome their assistance. Dick may have found more dramatic success if he had his agents working in secret, like the later similarly themed TV shows *Touched By An Angel* or the SF time-hopping drama *Quantum Leap*.

DeWinter, of course, complicates the situation long before he solves it, thus providing a half-hour of drama and adventure each week. A further error Dick makes is in characterising the person to be helped as "often faster and brighter" than DeWinter. If that's so, why does he need DeWinter in the first place? It's fine to make the protagonist bumbling and inefficient, but to make him less smart than those he's out to help seems like a step too far in denigrating the central character.

Dick proposed that DeWinter should find himself regularly up against a 'Mr Big' character, "head of the mob." Mr Big also accepts Herb as a guardian angel, and in fact, "Mr Big compares his electronic gimmicks with the supernatural magic ones that Herb is equipped with, and often Mr Big's are more advanced…" Again, mere Earth technology is ahead of that in Heaven, partly explained by the WAWY, Inc's inherent old-fashioned nature. There is no suggestion that 'Mr Big' might be working for the 'other side' (ie. Hell), which would have been a nice twist in the drama and provided a cosmic motivation to this recurring antagonist.

Dick does suggest "a particular 'evil' human, who shows up in various guises from time-to-time. The sinister man's name changes, and so does the modus operandi of his activities, but he is always pitted against Herb…" From Sherlock Holmes and Professor Moriarty, every hero needs a strong, recurring antagonist. "This guy gives Herb's rescue activities the faint hint of being a perpetual crusade in the name of God and Good against Evil, as personified by the recurring evil figure who seems to haunt Earth. Of course, since this is an action-comedy series, philosophical undertones such as this will be played down, yet will be there for anyone who wants to pick them up."

The gadgets were supposed to be like those featured in spy shows of the period, like Dick's favourite *Mission: Impossible*, but there would always be some doubt about whether Herb's equipment would function at all. "The pendulum swings from miracle to complete bust of Herb's arsenal of wild supernatural gimmicks — the fact that any gimmick may work spectacularly or be a total dud would help keep audience interest."

Dick saw the owner of WAWY, Inc, Anastasia Kelp, as a frustrated field operative, stuck in his office but always willing to stick his nose into Herb's business, often not to his aid. They have a bickering and goading relationship, and Kelp often appears to berate DeWinter when he's least welcome. DeWinter also (at least once an episode, according to Dick's outline) calls on engineer Engstrom in Heaven, to effect repairs to his equipment or to whip up a gadget to solve a specific problem. Engstrom is the go-to gadget guy, described as "a nervous, twitchy electronics genius type", a character archetype familiar from countless movies and TV shows, from 'Q' in James Bond to Marshall J. Flinkman in the twenty-first century TV spy show *Alias*. Occasionally, Engstrom will get to make the trip to Earth in person to help out DeWinter with particularly fiendish gadgets.

This contact with Engstrom requires that DeWinter first go through the sexy and flirtatious secretary Miss Feather (in a kind of Bond and Miss Moneypenny relationship). DeWinter can also be put in touch with the client, who "old-ladywise" can comment on his progress (or lack of it) in solving the problem. The videophone used for these contacts is a brilliant conceit on Dick's behalf: "a mixture of science fiction and the supernatural: any object can be used as a Terrascreen, such as the mirror of the medicine cabinet in the bathroom…"

Another person who can call on DeWinter during his missions is Mr Vane, God's representative, who can study his progress and often feels the urge to similarly comment on events. All of this puts Herb DeWinter under great pressure: while Kelp, Vane, the client and the victim all require action from him, he can only really rely on Engstrom and Miss Feather to help him fulfil his weekly mission. And fulfil it he does, every week, but only just. At the last minute, DeWinter pulls victory from the jaws of defeat, so Mr Vane reluctantly gives WAWY, Inc a stay of execution, while Mr Kelp continues DeWinter's precarious employment. "The episode ends," Dick writes of the formula of the show, "with Herb back in Heaven in the front office of the firm, and an identifying coda note closes each [episode]: the entrance to the firm's office, with the shadow of a new client falling across it as the client prepares to enter."

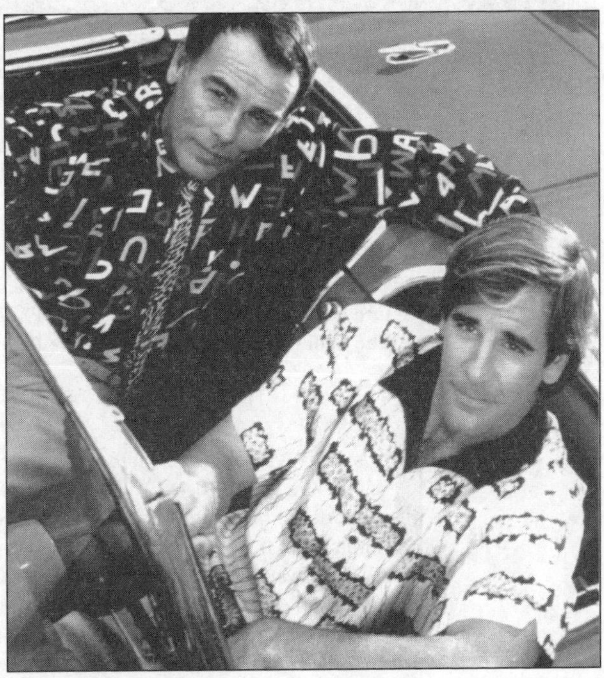

Above: *The 1990s show* Quantum Leap, *starring Dean Stockwell and Scott Bakula, had echoes of Dick's 1967 TV series idea.*

In his outline, Dick admits to several influences from the *Topper* novels of Thorne Smith to *The Man From U.N.C.L.E.* TV series, with a dash of James Bond and *The Twilight Zone* thrown in for good measure. Dick was keen to see the series adopt a globe-trotting perspective, noting that guardian angels can tackle problems in any country across the world, although this might have been something of a stretch for the show's budget, with many US series faking international locations in Los Angeles (where most 1960s US episodic TV was shot). Locations suggested include the Volpo in East Berlin (this was 1967, remember), Cambodia or Pocatello, Idaho, from the exotic to the mundane.

Overall, it's not a bad mid-1960s idea for an ongoing TV series. In fact, in the 1990s a slew of series seemed to show echoes of Dick's idea. There was *Quantum Leap*, with time-travelling scientist Dr Sam Beckett occupying the bodies of others throughout modern post-War history in a mission to "set right what once went wrong." Beckett even encountered a recurring, evil counterpart (dubbed the 'evil leaper') and seemed to meet 'God' in the series' metaphysical finale. Other shows like *Brimstone* and *Good Vs Evil* (aka *G Vs E*) put the battle between the forces of good and evil, or God and the Devil, at the forefront of their weekly episodes. *Dead Like Me* had 'reapers', well-intentioned dead folks, recovering the souls of the departed.

Dick's idea needed a lot of refinement and development if it was ever to stand a serious chance of success in the TV environment of the mid-1960s. It would have needed a star name actor and a brand name writer-producer, perhaps like Quinn Martin of *The Fugitive* and *The Invaders*, to pick it up and drive it forward. Dick fails to provide a batch of episodic plot outlines, usually required by producers to show that the proposed series has 'legs', and won't run out of story ideas.

Of course, none of this happened, so Philip K. Dick's untitled 1967 TV series idea remains an unproduced curiosity. Dick did not have the contacts, or perhaps the ambition, to pursue his half-formed ambitions to write for television. If he got stuck or frustrated, he'd always fall back on what he knew and was successful at: writing novels.

By early 1968, less than a year since his first attempt to write for TV, Dick had forgotten all about his ambitions to write a teleplay. He had a potentially much bigger dramatic project to deal with: a possible film of his recently published novel, *Do Androids Dream of Electric Sheep?*. ■

ANDROID DREAMS

The late 1960s saw Philip K. Dick get very excited about a possible film adaptation of his novel *Do Androids Dream of Electric Sheep?*

"I did not know that a work of mine or a set of ideas of mine could be escalated into such stunning dimension…" — Philip K. Dick in a letter to Jeff Walker of The Ladd Company regarding *Blade Runner*, October 1981.

It is perhaps no exaggeration to say that the film *Blade Runner* largely created the Philip K. Dick industry. There had always been fans of his work, from the 1950s onwards, but prior to the first movie based on one of his novels, Dick did not scale the heights of literary name recognition achieved by contemporaries like Isaac Asimov or Robert Heinlein. His work was an acquired taste and something of a well kept secret among SF aficionados. Ironically, it was only after Dick's death that his literary reputation was boosted and his 1950s mainstream novels finally saw publication. It's unlikely this would have happened to the same extent, or that Dick would be enjoying the high profile he does today, if it hadn't been for Ridley Scott's *Blade Runner*, the first successful attempt to bring the counterfeit worlds of Philip K. Dick to the big screen.

Interest in turning Dick's 1968 novel *Do Androids Dream of Electric Sheep?* into a film began almost with its original publication. The novel was written in 1966 — the same year as *Ubik* — when Dick was living in a tiny, rented house at 57 Meadow Drive in San Rafael, which backed onto a canal. Dick was thirty-eight and producing some of his finest work during this period, while his fourth wife Nancy Hackett was working at a nearby post office to bolster their income.

Set in 1992 (later editions changed the date to 2019 to reflect the date indicated in the movie *Blade Runner*), the novel features bounty hunter Rick Deckard as its protagonist. It's his job to hunt down and eliminate 'andys', rogue androids (the *Blade Runner* movie term 'replicant' is never used in the novel) who have escaped their roles as slave labourers in the Martian colonies and returned to a post-nuclear holocaust Earth (after World War Terminus), hoping to pass for human. Deckard in the novel is far from being the movie's hard-bitten cop who sees no problem in 'killing' artificial people. In fact, the novel's hero begins to sympathise with the artificial humans and comes to appreciate the genuine differences between true humans and the human-like machines. It's the purest exploration of Dick's favourite theme, 'What does it mean to be human?'

Roy and Irmgard Baty (with one 't' unlike in the *Blade Runner* movie, pre-figuring a later spelling change for the Rekal, or Rekall, Corporation in the film *Total Recall*) are the primary android antagonists (modelled by Dick after his friends, science fiction writer Ray

Above: *Dick's 1968 novel would eventually become* Blade Runner *in 1982, but interest in a movie of* Do Androids Dream of Electric Sheep? *began almost as soon as it was published.*

Nelson and his wife Kirsten, on whom Dick had a serious crush). The other androids featured include Pris Stratton, unreciprocating love interest for John Isidore. Isidore (named after Jack Isidore from Dick's at-that-point unpublished mainstream novel *Confessions of a Crap Artist*) is a 'chickenhead', one of the 'specials', a new grouping of low-IQ humans impaired due to the fall-out from the nuclear conflict. The nearest similar character in the film is android builder J. F. Sebastian, played by William Sanderson. Rachael Rosen is another android, with whom Deckard has an unfulfilling affair when things are not going well with his own wife Iran (patterned by the author after his own new wife, Nancy).

The Deckards find solace in their use of the Penfield 'mood organ', a piece of technology that replaced mood-altering drugs in Dick's vision of the future. Various settings are available to users, including the prescient #888: "The desire to watch TV, no matter what's on it." One setting Deckard makes full use of in relation to Iran is #594: "Pleased acknowledgement of husband's superior wisdom in all things..." The opening chapter alone sees Deckard faced with a gulf of choices from "Awareness of the manifold possibilities open to me in the future..." to "a six-hour self-accusatory depression." The 'mood organ' would prefigure the Sublimator, an alternate-reality/dream-manufacturing device featured in the *Blade Runner/Do Androids Dream of Electric Sheep?*-like TV series *Total Recall 2070* (see Chapter 10).

A further effect of the nuclear war is the rarity of any living animals, making them much sought after. A real status symbol in this version of 1992 is the ability (both

Above: *Dick's tiny rented home at 57 Meadow Drive, where he wrote* Do Androids Dream of Electric Sheep?. *Photo © Brian J. Robb.*

financially and through your contacts) to own a real, living owl or sheep. Most people have to make do — like Deckard — with a 'simulacra', an artificial replacement for the real thing. This aspect of the novel, echoing the main theme of the android 'humans' and raising the question of the perception of 'What is real?' (as the simulacra are virtually indistinguishable from the real thing), was omitted almost entirely from the eventual film.

Both Deckard and Isidore find themselves descending into Dick's 'tomb world' of depression, brought to life through alternate realities. They are revived from these states by evangelist Wilbur Mercer, whose 'religion' of Mercerism has swept the planet. The use of an 'empathy box' links users with each other and Mercer, giving humans a sense of collective consciousness and an awareness of each others' existence. The empathy box echoed a device in Dick's 1964 short story 'The Little Black Box' and the 'Ludens maze', another manifestation of empathy, in his potboiler novel *The Zap Gun* (published in novel form in 1967, but also written in 1964).

When Mercer is exposed by TV prankster Buster Friendly (a character akin to Norman Spinrad's TV phone-in host Jack Barron in *Bug Jack Barron*) as a two-bit actor named Al Jarry, the religion of Mercerism built around him is doomed. None of the Mercer elements of the novel were retained in the film.

"It is one of my favourite novels," said Dick to *Future Noir* author Paul M. Sammon of *Do Androids Dream of Electric Sheep?*. "Although it's essentially a dramatic novel, the moral and philosophical ambiguities it dealt with are really very profound. The book stemmed from my basic interest in the problem of differentiating the authentic human being from the reflexive machine, which I called an 'android'. In my mind, 'android' is a metaphor for people who are physiologically human, but who behave in a non-human way."

Dick's notion of people who look human but act in a non-human way seems to have been partly inspired by his relationships with the women in his life, from his various wives to his troubled relationship with his own mother. *Do Androids Dream of Electric Sheep?* "was written when things were really quite stable for me," Dick told Gregg Rickman in *Philip K. Dick: In His Own Words*. "Nancy and I had a house and a child [Isa] and a fair amount of money. Things were good. At that point, I was contrasting Nancy's warmth with the coldness of the people [wives] I'd known before. I was beginning to develop the idea of the human versus the android, the bipedal humanoid that is not essentially human. She [Nancy] had shown me for the first time what a real human could be like, tender and loving and vulnerable. I was beginning to contrast that to what I had been brought up with [his often-distant mother, Dorothy]."

Dick's analysis of the 'non-human' also brought in some ideas which had been lingering since his research for *The Man in the High Castle*. That Hugo Award-winning novel, written in 1961 and published the following year, featured a post-World War Two alternate reality in which the victorious Nazi and Japanese forces had divided the USA in much the same way that Germany was divided in the real world. Dick had researched his novel in the 1950s through access to original Gestapo documents held in the private collection of the University of California at Berkeley. Reading diaries (in the original German) by SS operatives stationed in Poland, Dick had come across a sentence that had a profound effect on him, and formed the basis for much of his concern with the question of 'What is human?' The sentence, attributed to a concentration camp guard, which so troubled Dick read: "We are kept awake at night by the cries of starving children..." Dick was given cause to wonder what kind of person could write such a sentence and not be moved to do something about the situation. "There was obviously something wrong with the man who wrote that," noted Dick, quoted in *Cinefantastique*'s coverage of the making of *Blade Runner*. "I later realised that, with the Nazis, what we were essentially dealing with was a defective group mind, a mind so emotionally defective that the word 'human' could not be applied to them..."

Extrapolating this idea, Dick saw the question of 'non-humanity' as one which stretched beyond the core idea of 'evil Nazis'. "I felt that this was not necessarily a solely German trait. This deficiency had been exported into the world after World War Two and could be picked up by people anywhere at any time. I wrote *Do Androids Dream of Electric Sheep?* during the Vietnam War. At the time, I was revolutionary and existential enough to believe that these android personalities were so lethal, so dangerous to human beings, that it ultimately might become necessary to fight them. The problem in killing them would then be: 'Would we not become like the androids in our very effort to wipe them out?'"

Because the novel formed the basis of the first film successfully completed from any of his work, Philip K. Dick's *Do Androids Dream of Electric Sheep?* has enjoyed more attention from literary critics and theorists than most of his work.

"[It] is one of Dick's most important novels," claimed Patricia S. Warrick, Professor of English at the University of Wisconsin, Fox Valley, in her book on Dick's work, *Mind in*

Above: *The Japanese attempt to link sheep and dreaming on their cover for* Do Androids Dream of Electric Sheep?.

Motion, published in 1987. "It explores a question of great importance to Dick: How do we tell the authentic human from that which only masquerades as human?" Warrick recognised that the novel was a partial reworking of some of the ideas presented by Dick in *We Can Build You* (written in 1962, but not published until after *Do Androids Dream of Electric Sheep?* in 1969).

Dick's obsession with recognising the human and the non-human was best outlined in his essay 'The Android and the Human' delivered to the 1972 Vancouver SF Convention. "What is it in our behaviour that we can call specifically human? That is special to us as a living species? And what is it that, at least up to now, we can consign as merely machine behaviour, or by extension, insect behaviour, or reflex behaviour? And I would include in this the kind of pseudo-human behaviour exhibited by what were once living men — creatures who have become instruments, means rather than ends, and hence, to me, the analogues of machines in the bad sense, in the sense that although biological life continues, metabolism goes on, the soul — for lack of a better term — is no longer there, or at least no longer active." Dick's worry about the 'non-human' extended not just to the mechanical or artificial person, but to those otherwise human (at least biologically) people who exhibit non-human traits, as in the example of the Nazi diary he cited in his research.

Dick's earliest short stories had featured robots or androids in key roles, such as 'Impostor',. 'Second Variety' and 'The Defenders'. It's interesting to note that once *Blade Runner* established Dick's cinematic name in connection with 'replicants', artificial humans, it was to these robot stories, like 'Impostor' and 'Second Variety', that other producers turned for their own Philip K. Dick movies.

Warrick perceives a change in Dick's fiction with *Do Androids Dream of Electric Sheep?*. "His interest now is in exploring inner rather than outer space, because he has become aware — as he tells us — that 'the greatest pain does not come down from a distant planet, but up from the depth of the human heart.'" The novel's predominant single point of view, that of Rick Deckard, stands in contrast to Dick's prior novels, many of which employed an unusual multiple-point-of-view technique to a greater extent.

Warrick also identified the problem with the novel that would initially throw off those attempting to adapt it into a screenplay. "At first reading, the novel appears to be a conventional cops and killers tale, with the future setting and the robot killers giving the required science fiction twist. It is tightly knit: the action occurs in a single day, in a single setting — the post-holocaust, nearly lifeless, wasteland of San Francisco. Rick Deckard wants to make money — make a killing — so he can buy a big, live animal." Deckard's job — to kill six rogue androids in one day — will provide him with the cash to buy the status symbol he craves, a live sheep. This reduction of the plot to a chase-and-kill scenario, often eliminating the artificial animal angle altogether (Deckard's original motivation, after all!) was how some scriptwriters would attempt to adapt the novel, much to Dick's chagrin.

Above: *This striking British paperback cover went for a literal approach.*

Douglas A. Mackey tackled Dick's *Do Androids Dream of Electric Sheep?* as part of the Twayne's United States Authors Series (which included volumes on Kafka, Orwell, Huxley, Poe and Tolkien, as well as science fiction authors Ray Bradbury, Robert Heinlein and Frank Herbert). "Perhaps in no other novel did Dick grapple as boldly with the question 'What does it mean to be human?'" Mackey wrote. "The reader is continually challenged to evaluate how human the androids are and how mechanical the humans are. The androids are not mere machines like most of the simulacra in Dick's other novels: they are artificial people made from organic materials; they have free will and emotions like fear and love. Physically and behaviourally they are indistinguishable from real people. Although these androids can believe themselves to be human (due to the implanted 'memory tapes'), they do lack one thing: empathy — the ability to identify with the suffering or joy of others..."

For novelist Kim Stanley Robinson, whose dissertation for the literature department of the University of California, San Diego was published as *The Novels of Philip K. Dick*, the question asked by the novel is not one that most critics recognise. Dick is not interested in a definition of the android, according to Robinson, but in the definition of the human. "The androids are not automatically symbols of alienated, mechanical humans, but are presented as another life form, capable of both good and evil. Dick has given us two oppositions: Human/Android and Human/Inhuman."

The challenge faced by those who would attempt to turn any of Philip K. Dick's source material into a script suitable for filming is the one faced by all SF adaptations: how to represent a literature of ideas in the sensory, or at least visual, medium of cinema. It's an especially tricky question when it comes to the work of Philip K. Dick, as every page of his novels and short stories is teeming with outlandish ideas, with very few of them easy to realise faithfully on screen.

Of course, Hollywood has long turned to literary sources for inspiration and some of the most acclaimed films of all time have been adapted from novels (*The Wizard of Oz, Gone With the Wind, The Godfather* and *The Lord of the Rings* trilogy to give just a few examples). The fantastic, especially, has been a deep well for Hollywood, especially the comic book form. However, adapting acclaimed SF novels has always been a tricky business for moviemakers, where adapters run the risk of alienating the fan audience they might want to attract, while also failing to draw in a more casual audience perhaps put off by the film's SF literary origins.

The earliest interest in turning *Do Androids Dream of Electric Sheep?* into a movie came less than a year after the novel had been published. Director Martin Scorsese, then pre-*Mean Streets*, and his screenwriter Jay Cocks, were very interested in adapting Dick's latest novel for the movies. In 1968, movie fan Dick could have gone to see Scorsese's feature film début, the autobiographical drama *Who's That Knocking at My Door?* if he'd wanted a taste of the

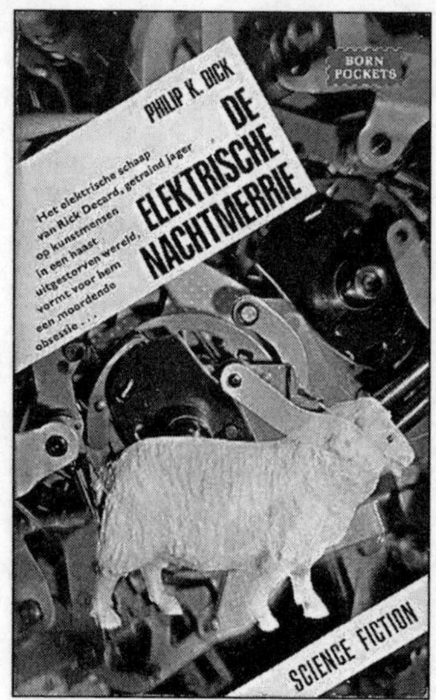

Above: *While the cover still features a sheep, the Dutch title translates as 'The Electric Nightmare'.*

director's work. According to Paul M. Sammon in *Future Noir*, Scorsese and Cocks were struck by "the visual and moral landscapes" of *Do Androids Dream of Electric Sheep?*, but never actually got around to optioning the book.

However, in May 1968 New York-based Bertram Berman did take out a movie option on the novel, much to Dick's delight. It's unclear whether Berman was operating on his own behalf, on the part of Scorsese and Cocks, or on behalf of another director or studio. A 21 May 1968 letter from Dick to Berman, in which he presents his own notes on adapting the novel to film, makes reference to a telephone call between Berman and Dick earlier that month. Dick notes Berman's "recent option" on the book and he thanks him "for your kind words about *Sheep*; they were much appreciated…" It seems unlikely that Berman commissioned Dick to write his notes on adapting *Do Androids Dream of Electric Sheep?*, but more likely that the author was carried away in his enthusiasm for the potential film and constructed the notes without any formal request (unlike his later work in 1974 on the *Ubik* screenplay).

Dick and Berman had discussed *The Graduate*, a then-recent hit starring Dustin Hoffman and Anne Bancroft, which Dick had enjoyed but was reconsidering: "The second time around in my viewing [of] *The Graduate* I was somewhat less impressed than before. I don't mean to put the picture down, but I think we can do one better…" Indeed, Dick was very positive about the potential of a film based on *Do Androids Dream of Electric Sheep?*: "The more I study the book, the more I foresee in it a genuinely good film." Berman had suggested he might be in San Francisco in the near future, and Dick concluded his letter hoping the pair could meet up and he could expand on his thoughts concerning the film.

Genuinely excited by the prospect of a movie being made from one of his books, Dick made reference to the project in several other letters, and even used the advance money he was paid to buy a new suit in preparation for his meeting with Berman. Writing that same day, 21 May 1968, to Andy (no surname survives), Dick noted: "A film option has been bought on *Do Androids Dream of Electric Sheep?*. The first in my career! They pay $1,500 for the option the first year, then $1,000 the second year, and if they go ahead with the film the minimum pay to me will be $25,000, with a maximum of $40,000 should the budget of the film go over $2.5 million. They've already called me from New York and made arrangements to come out here to San Francisco to meet with me. With the $1,500 option money I bought an Avram Davison [a fellow SF writer] Papa Archetype suit: wool, colour of snuff, vest; plus a gold pocket watch, which I carry in my lower right vest pocket. Including the trousers and vest, there are thirteen pockets in the suit. Dressed in this — with $40 shoes, new tie, new yellow shirt — I think I can hold onto my sense of Equality In the Face of the Mighty! Without the suit, I would be too scared to advance any ideas of my own, so you can see that buying the suit isn't selling out; it's a device to keep from selling out."

Despite his sartorial preparation for his meeting with those who'd taken an option on *Do Androids Dream of Electric Sheep?*, it appears that Dick and the mysterious Bertram Berman (who worked for CBS at one point) never did meet. There is no reference to the movie option in Dick's published personal correspondence until one year later. On 7 May 1969, following the publication of *Ubik*, Dick writes to ex-wife Anne and notes: "I am beginning to do better on income, I think; a movie company has renewed its option on my novel *Do Androids Dream of Electric Sheep?*, so there remains the chance that they will do a film of it, this being the second year of the option. Scott [Meredith, Dick's literary agent] says 'They are developing the property.'" The following year, in the spring and summer of 1970, Dick had other things on his mind as his marriage to Nancy was collapsing. Although there are letters to Scott Meredith, none follow up on the movie option for *Do Androids Dream of Electric Sheep?*. Dick was, by then, deep in rewrites on *Flow My Tears, The Policeman Said* (the subject of much of Dick's 1970 correspondence) and any excitement sparked by the initial movie option and injection of cash had long since faded.

That 21 May 1968 letter from Dick to Berman included the author's extensive notes on how he felt his most recent novel should be adapted for the cinema. "I have done a good deal of thinking about the novel," wrote Dick, "as well as making an objective study as to exactly what it contains." It was the first time that Dick had turned an analytical eye on his own work with a view to adapting it for movies. As a big movie fan, Dick was largely aware of the conventions of film, but he was no more than an amateur fan, having never written a movie script before, and his analysis of what might work on screen shows some naïveté about what might be required.

In analyzing *Do Androids Dream of Electric Sheep?* Dick developed some notes on how he felt the material could be adapted, a chronological account of events in the novel and a list of the various places, locations and scene-settings in the novel.

Dick's first task was to decide who was the novel's viewpoint character — or rather which viewpoint character from the novel would work as the lead in a film. "It must be either the bounty hunter Rick Deckard or Jack Isidore," Dick decided. These characters have opposing views on the androids in the story: Isidore exhibits a "naïve love" for the androids, while Deckard's view is that the androids are "vicious machines that must be destroyed." Dick was aware that for the movie he'd have to prioritise one. "Since Deckard's view proves to be correct, perhaps he should be the viewpoint protagonist."

That decision made, Dick then developed a host of consequences for the telling of the story. Dick felt that Deckard's love of real animals had to be dealt with in a meaningful way (a plot strand dropped entirely from the eventual film), especially contrasted with his hatred of the androids. It was obvious to Dick that the film had to show clearly "why Rick holds this view. In the novel we are *told* that androids lack Human feeling, warmth and empathic sensitivity, but we are not shown this in action..."

Below: *The Danish cover sticks with the theme of freakish electric sheep.*

SCIENCE FICTION
Philip K. Dick
Drømmer androider om elektriske får ?

Above: *Gregory Peck, Dick's 1960s choice for a "powerful, sensitive and wise" Deckard.*

Dick then goes on to discuss potential casting for the main characters and comes up with some interesting names, showing the potential star leads at the end of the 1960s. For Deckard, Dick suggested Gregory Peck ("powerful, sensitive and wise"), Richard Widmark (who'd make Deckard a "psychotic killer"), Martin Balsam ("an archetypal father-figure") and Ben Gazarra ("bold, and a man of action"). For Isidore, Dick recommended Dean Stockwell ("sensitive and an introvert") or Wally Cox. For the role of Rachael, he singled out then-popular singer in Jefferson Airplane, Grace Slick ("a bit of casting I would really plug for..."). He settled on an ideal pairing of Peck and Stockwell as Deckard and Isidore.

Dick then went on to discuss the 'tone' of the picture. "Is this a touching story (Isidore protecting the androids then at the end seeing what they're really like), or gunplay action, as Deckard shoots one android after another? The film could be pro-cop or anti-cop..."

It was Dick's contention that the weirder the film was, the better it would be. He recommended strange and dream-like camera work. He was also aware of the elements of his novel that would just not fit in a film structure: "The small plot element of the Other Police Station could be eliminated entirely..." Dick even paid attention to Rick Deckard's weaponry, calling for something distinctive and not "merely another laser tube, such as one sees in *Star Trek* and *The Invaders*."

Diverse elements which Dick felt the film should include were the "dramatic search and destruction of the androids, the tenderness felt towards live animals, the weird deserted apartment building in which Jack Isidore lives, and the awe felt when Mercer is encountered." (Of course, Mercer and his religion was another element of the novel eventually eliminated in *Blade Runner*.) Despite this shopping list of requirements, Dick was also realistic enough to know that writers other than him would be reworking his material, so "some of the moods (and plot) can be eliminated entirely, however important they are to the novel, and then the remaining elements, such as Isidore and the Mercer theme, can be retained and built up more." Although Dick recognised the 'search and destroy' element of his novel would be central to any film, he questioned the medium's ability to adequately represent the empathy test Deckard administers to suspected androids.

Displaying a keen, if amateur, understanding of the filmic medium, gleaned from many hours watching movies at local cinemas, Dick commented, "There could be room for more sex", suggesting that the relationship between Deckard and Rachael be pumped up for the movie (something which *Blade Runner* ultimately did...). Raising this issue then allowed Dick to deviate from his subject, to ruminate on another topic that was obviously close to him: "sexual relations between Humans and androids... What is it like?" This is, of course, the ultimate unreal fakery in Dick's body of work: the android who can fake seemingly real and intimate sexual intercourse, yet fails to understand its meaning or significance. As Dick

Left: *Dean Stockwell (seen here in the 1965 movie* Rapture*) was Dick's choice to play Jack Isidore.*

commented: "There are possibilities which might come out vividly in a film version..." If this aspect of Dick's work had been explored by any film of *Do Androids Dream of Electric Sheep?* it might have put a very different spin on Dick's status as a science fiction writer and modern philosopher. Dick developed this theme in his notes, seeing Deckard as being alienated by Rachael's ability to fool him into believing he's sleeping with a real woman (after all, Dick notes, much of everyday ordinary sex can depend upon fantasy and self-deception to one degree or another), thus developing the cold-hearted ability to destroy Pris and the other androids in reaction. It's an interesting idea, not really reflected in the original novel or in *Blade Runner* and — as with the never produced script of *Ubik* — shows that when Dick revisited his own (often hastily produced) work, he could draw out new angles and insights that escaped him first time around. "Rick's recoiling from being close to Rachael may be vital in his determination — and success — in destroying the last three andys."

Dick stopped "speculating" at this point, providing an 'abstract' of his original novel, outlining a timeline of events, delineating the characters and locations. It's a document which would surely have proved useful to any potential adapters of the novel, if only as a way of engaging schematically with the major themes and characters of the book as the original author saw them.

These 1968 notes were Dick's last thoughts on the possible film of *Do Androids Dream of Electric Sheep?* for over five years. It wasn't until 1974 that interest in films based on his work saw him returning to reconsider that novel, while simultaneously developing a script of the book he completed just before it: *Ubik*. ■

USE AS DIRECTED

Tired of waiting for others to make movies of his novels, Philip K. Dick leaps at the chance to adapt *Ubik* into script form himself...

"I ask in my writing 'What is real?' because unceasingly we are bombarded with pseudo-realities manufactured by very sophisticated people using very sophisticated electronic mechanisms. I do not distrust their motives; I distrust their power." — Philip K. Dick, 'How to Build a Universe That Doesn't Fall Apart Two Days Later', 1978

Philip K. Dick was excited when the opportunity first arose for him to write a film script based on one of his own works. To transform his own prose — *Ubik*, his novel of decaying reality — into a form suitable for cinema was a challenge he found hard to resist, despite his lack of scriptwriting experience.

The offer had come quite unexpectedly in August 1974, when Dick received a letter from French film director Jean-Pierre Gorin, a protégé of Jean-Luc Godard (they'd previously worked on *Le Vent d'est* and *Tout Va Bien* together), asking if he could make a movie of *Ubik*.

Dick had dislocated his shoulder that month, so his normal prolific output of letters to friends and colleagues had slowed somewhat, and he was relying on his wife Tessa to type up his dictated messages. As well as recovering from his February-March 1974 'event' and struggling to give it meaning, Dick was somewhat obsessed with the news coverage of President Nixon's forced resignation. He was also in one of his periodic writing lulls, having written little of any real significance during the early 1970s. He was relying on royalties, mainly from foreign editions of his work, for his income. *A Scanner Darkly* was the only significant work to come out of this period, and that reflected in its content many of the reasons why Dick had more or less stopped writing.

Amid all this, Gorin literally turned up on the author's doorstep to ensure the *Ubik* movie took flight. Describing himself in his letter as "one of the great admirers of your work", Gorin went on to admit, "I made this trip to California just to see you and discuss the whole project." It wasn't the first time that the French, in particular, had shown interest in *Ubik*. With its reality-twisting plotting, uncertain narrative and down-at-heel characters, it was this novel that won Dick election as an honorary member of the French College du Pataphysique, a society established in memory of literary prankster Alfred Jarry and his play *Ubu Roi*. Dick had also been visited previously by French publishers and academics, keen to discuss with the author the origins and use of the pre-Socratic philosophical and sociological material they found in the book. Dick's response surprised his visitors. An unwelcome group of Marxist scholars was, according to a 1975 letter written by Dick, "keenly disappointed to find that [the author] was totally ignorant of the philosophical material in the novel and couldn't account for it being there." Dick later reported their visit to the FBI.

Above: *A British cover which aimed to capture some of the existential terror experienced by the novel's characters.*

Naturally, Dick was overwhelmed by this interest in his work and the prospect of there not only being a film of *Ubik*, but one — as Gorin was proposing — actually written by the novel's author. Although he'd never written a screenplay before (the radio scripts of the 1950s being mostly written by others and his submissions to *The Invaders* and *Mission: Impossible* being only plot outlines), Dick was prepared to throw himself into the task wholeheartedly, displaying the kind of drive and gusto he normally invested in his novels.

A few weeks after the initial letter, Dick and Gorin met at the author's apartment in Fullerton and the project was underway. They spent what Dick regarded as a joyful and productive day together brainstorming ideas for adapting *Ubik* into a movie. In a letter dated 7 September 1974 to his agent Scott Meredith, Dick notes "Jean-Pierre Gorin phoned me the other day to say he had mailed the money to you on the *Ubik* movie deal. Keep me informed. He will be phoning me this Sunday and coming here again next week." This was the beginning of a long and involved process for Dick, with no movie to show for it at the end…

The novel *Ubik* followed the misadventures of Joe Chip, an 'inertial' working for Glen Runciter of Runciter Associates. Inertials are anti-psi talents working for 'prudence organisations', used to block out the snooping powers of psi agents, mainly in industrial espionage cases. Joe Chip, however, is so financially hard up he doesn't even have the money to pay his coin-operated apartment door so he can leave in the morning to go to work. Runciter's main rival is Ray Hollis, whose organisation provides the psi agents that Runciter's inertials block. Meanwhile, Runciter's dead wife is stored in 'cold-pac' half-life, but is still actively involved in the business.

Interplanetary speculator Stanton Mick hires Runciter's entire inertial team for a job which requires they assemble at his lunar base. Once there, a bomb disguised as Stanton Mick explodes, killing Runciter. The whole thing has been a trap laid by the Hollis organisation. Although they appear to have escaped, Joe Chip and the team find themselves slipping back in time to the 1930s, while messages begin to appear in incongruous ways from the dead Glen Runciter such as, "I'm the one that's alive. You're all dead!" As the surviving inertials begin to die off one by one, Joe Chip has to unravel just who is alive, who is dead and what is real. Throughout, there is the mysterious product 'Ubik', which might just provide a way out for all concerned…

Ubik is a typical Philip K. Dick pulp mind-bender, one of his best from the period in the late 1960s which produced *Do Androids Dream of Electric Sheep?*, the similarly-themed *A Maze of Death* and *Flow My Tears, The Policeman Said*. It has a plot that could be stripped down to a clear screenplay, and shows strong filmic promise. It's easy to understand the cinematic potential that Jean-Pierre Gorin saw in the novel.

Despite his excitement over scripting *Ubik*, Dick was wary about the interest being shown in his work by movie producers. He felt that his representatives were perhaps not getting the best financial value for the material they were doing deals on. Considering that his short

Above: *The Finnish cover attempted to depict the barely controlled madness of the novel.*

stories had only earned the author a few hundred dollars each, while his novels rarely commanded advances in excess of $1,000, Dick was understandably keen to capitalise on possible movie options. On 5 May 1974 he'd written to his agency, outlining concerns he had regarding the recent deal for the film rights to *Do Androids Dream of Electric Sheep?*. "I had been very unhappy since the time of the sale of *Do Androids Dream of Electric Sheep?* to Herb Jaffe, because Jack Scovill [his agent at the Scott Meredith agency] phoned me and said, 'I know you have someone out there interested in the property, but we'd like to go ahead with our deal that we've got on it,' and I naturally in good faith said, 'Okay'." (For the full story of *Blade Runner*'s development, see Chapters 3, 5 and 6.) There were also movie options on *The Three Stigmata of Palmer Eldritch* and *Time Out of Joint*, but Dick had no direct involvement in any of these potential films.

The attraction for Dick of the *Ubik* deal was that he would be closely involved. Gorin had managed to sell Dick on the idea that his own screenplay would form the basis of the movie. An advance of $1,500 from Gorin's own funds was paid up front (as indicated in Dick's letter to Meredith) to secure the rights, with a promise of an additional $2,500 payable on delivery of a completed draft by 31 December 1975, giving him over a year to complete the task. Gorin may have allowed a year for the creation of the screenplay as he was an unfamiliar figure in Hollywood, having newly arrived in town with a handful of esoteric French art movies to his name. It seems likely that Gorin was unsure of his own ability to raise the necessary finance to actually make the movie. However, the starting point on any independent film project is usually to have a screenplay with which a prospective producer can interest studios or other financial backers.

Whatever fears he may have had about working in an unfamiliar medium, Dick put them to one side. The prospect of the film and the possibility of earning $2,500 for a few weeks' work spurred him on. In September 1974, Dick was hard at work, aiming to complete the screenplay to his own self-imposed three-month deadline. Within just three weeks, however, Dick had finished transforming his novel into a screenplay. He'd worked that fast before on some of his novels, sometimes turning out a masterpiece at speed (and on speed). "I wrote furiously," Dick told journalist Paul Williams, who came to interview him at the end of October 1974 for a profile in *Rolling Stone*. "And I wasn't taking anything. I was able to turn out this screenplay, the *Ubik* screenplay, in three weeks. Runciter and Joe Chip became so real to me that I can imagine writing about them forever."

The joy that Dick found in tackling the *Ubik* screenplay came from the rare opportunity to revisit his own work in a more considered manner, just as he'd done in 1968 on his notes for a proposed film of *Do Androids Dream of Electric Sheep?* (see Chapter 3). During his writing life, financial requirements had meant that Dick often had to churn out stories and novels one after the other. He often reworked older material, cannibalising short stories for novels or parts of novels, or using elements from his large stack of unpublished realist novels of the 1950s to ground his more outré SF ideas in something human. All this was done at white-hot speed, often simply to fulfil contract obligations, rather than through any concerns with art or even craft. Now, through adapting *Ubik* into a different form, Dick could look at the novel afresh, take it apart and reconstruct it in a fashion more suitable to the screen. It would also give him an opportunity to revisit the ending of the novel, which he'd always felt to be weak. Endings were a recurring problem: Dick believed that his reliance on the I Ching in plotting *The Man in the High Castle* had let him down when it came to the finale of that novel, and that his semi-'automatic writing' approach to constructing the novel of *Ubik* had also failed him when he reached the climax. Now he had the chance to redo the ending of *Ubik* and make it right.

Dick's excitement about the *Ubik* screenplay is evident in his letters throughout September 1974, before he even began to wrestle with the actual writing (he was waiting for his shoulder to heal). To his mother Dorothy Hudner he wrote: "My novel *Ubik* sold to the movies, and they want me to write the screenplay. I'll have to get an electric typewriter, obviously..." He also offered various female friends parts in "my movie" and also wrote to the agents of various actresses whom he admired — among them Kay Lenz (whom Dick could have seen on TV in November 1974 in *The FBI Story: The FBI Versus Alvin Karpis, Public Enemy Number One)* and Victoria Principal (who'd featured in blockbuster disaster movie *Earthquake*) — suggesting they'd be ideal for roles in the film.

Dick claimed to have been dreaming scenes from *Ubik* during the summer of 1974, even before Gorin contacted him. He told Paul Williams about the experience; how it had helped him to structure the screenplay and develop the prose of the book into scenes for the screen. "I realised that I've got a little screen in my head, and the people walk around on it," said Dick. "I didn't realise until I did the screenplay, where I had to visualise. I'd look up [at his interior screen] and type, I didn't know any other way to do it. I deduced one character had a child 'cause I could see a tricycle in the driveway... When I wrote the screenplay, [the dreams] made it very easy for me to write those scenes, because I had already been through [them]... In the dreams, I'm characters from the novel acting out scenes in the book. Damnedest thing, but it sure made writing the screenplay easy! I wrote [the novel] *Ubik* in 1968, this is 1974 and suddenly I begin to dream these dreams, then a few months later I'm suddenly commissioned to write a screenplay of *Ubik*. I find to my amazement that half the dreams I've had are relevant to scenes I will be writing into the screenplay. That's how I could do it in three weeks."

In his introduction to the screenplay (published in 1985), Paul Williams recalled his conversations with Dick over a decade previously, and was impressed with Dick's unique take on the screenplay form: "Reading Philip K. Dick's screenplay of *Ubik* is like going with the author on a guided tour of his own book, waving his pointer at beloved absurdities and little pivotal moments... What's real [to Dick] is these people and their immediate crisis. To read this screenplay is to walk in Dick's reality with him, and see it through his eyes..."

The resulting screenplay is incredibly faithful to Dick's original novel: too faithful, in fact, and that would be the major problem Jean-Pierre Gorin would face in trying to sell the concept of the film to would-be producers. The screenplay follows the misfortunes of Joe Chip, from the explosion on the moon to his adventures lost in Des Moines, suspecting his "beautiful and wayward mistress" Pat Conley of being behind events. As the story progresses, his fellow inertials are dying off, while Runciter manages to make various manifestations in an attempt to get a message through to Chip. At the finale, it becomes clear that Chip and his colleagues are all trapped in cold-pac, experiencing half-life. They are being stalked by

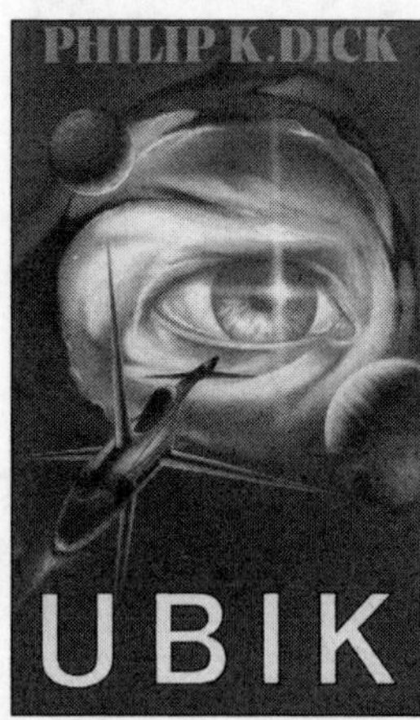

***Above:** A subtle but effective Hungarian cover.*

Jory, an apparently malevolent teenager also encased in cold-pac who is eating up the lifeforce of others. Helping them out is Ella Runciter, who guides Chip to locations where supplies of Ubik — material which can repel Jory — can be found.

At the very end, where the screenplay departs from the novel, Dick takes the opportunity to re-imagine the climax of his tale. In the novel, after exiting the pharmacy where he fails to find more Ubik, Chip is approached by a messenger from 1992. She has come to deliver a can of Ubik spray. Chip discovers Ubik was developed by Ella Runciter to counter the attacks in half-life from Jory, but it is very scarce. In the screenplay, Dick does a much better job of satisfactorily resolving the story. Instead of the Ubik messenger, he has Joe Chip hook up once more with Ella Runciter, only to accompany her into the Matador restaurant, the 'red light' alluded to earlier in the novel (and script) as the 'bad womb' through which she is to be reborn. The screenplay cuts to Glen Runciter, alive and well in the future of 1992, attending the birth of his secretary's baby (the screenplay made a point of her pregnancy in its earliest stages). The implication is that perhaps the baby is a combination of Chip and Ella, reborn into the world. The final twist in the novel and screenplay is essentially the same: Runciter discovers that the money he has displays Joe Chip's profile, unlike real money in the 'real' world. So who is alive and who is dead? Just who is stored in cold-pac experiencing the living hallucinations of half-life?

Any film made from Dick's *Ubik* script would be a challenging experience, for the filmmakers and audience alike. In the novel, Dick had the Ubik commercial interruptions appear as chapter-topping quotes. Throughout his screenplay, he periodically interrupts the action as the Ubik ads thrust themselves into the middle of the film's narrative. Additionally, Dick planned to use old-fashioned film techniques to reinforce the time slippage back to the 1930s. Scene 32 suggests obvious back-projection techniques should be used to emphasise the artificial nature of the world in which Joe Chip is trapped. "We get the impression the car is standing still on a treadmill, and the scenery is being revolved, repeating itself," Dick wrote. The opening of Scene 39 is described as consisting of "Visual flickering; like with a hand-cranked projector. The lobby of the Meremont Hotel, but very dim, as if 'bulb' is weak in 'projector.' Colours washed out, low hues only; yellow filter over everything."

According to Dick's friend and fellow SF/fantasy writer Tim Powers, the author's original intention was to employ even more filmic tricks with the time reversions in *Ubik*. In his foreword to the published screenplay, Powers writes: "At one point, Dick considered having the movie end with the film itself appearing to undergo a series of reversions: to black-and-white, then to the awkward jerkiness of very early movies, then to a crookedly jammed frame which proceeds to blacken, bubble and melt away, leaving only the white glare of the projection bulb, which in turn deteriorates to leave the theatre in darkness and might almost leave the moviegoer wondering what sort of dilapidated, antique jalopy he'll find his car keys fitting when he goes outside."

Whether any filmmaker would have seriously entertained putting Dick's filmic suggestions into action is doubtful, but as far as Powers was concerned, the screenplay for *Ubik* was a considered retelling of the story of the original novel, which had been adapted by the author to the needs of cinema to a largely successful degree. "Dick included far more parenthetical descriptions and interpretation than can be standard for screenplays, and so we have here his considered, after-the-fact portraits of Glen Runciter, Ella Runciter, Joe Chip, Pat Conley and Ubik itself," noted Powers. "With a facility that is scarce among novelists, he smoothly adapts his story to the wider, deeper ranges of the film medium. The Ubik ads are much more effective as actual intrusions than as chapter headings, the soundtrack becomes a central element (and makes us wonder what music Dick would have chosen to complement some of his other novels), and he presents the dysfunctions in time and perception even more effectively when he imagines them enacted on a movie screen…"

Dick's reality, in mid-October 1974, was one of waiting for Jean-Pierre Gorin. During the writing of the screenplay, Gorin was living in Berkeley and trying to set up a deal to get the movie made. He'd managed to interest *The Godfather* director Francis Ford Coppola, briefly, in being a producer on the project. It seems, however, that whatever fleeting interest Coppola may have had in the screen potential of Dick's work rapidly passed. There was an attempt to talk up Dick in various media outlets, probably as a result of Gorin's activities. Tony Hiss, who wrote the influential *Talk of the Town* column in *The New Yorker*, mentioned Dick a couple of times, dubbing him "our favourite science fiction author". Cultural critic Susan Sontag took it upon herself to promote *Ubik*, resulting in a piece on the prospective film in the movie trade newspaper *Variety*. Finally, Paul Williams' *Rolling Stone* profile feature also helped raise Dick's cultural ubiquity.

The screenplay had been delivered, but all went quiet on the *Ubik* movie front. Dick often had no idea where Gorin was or whether any progress was being made on the film. It was frustrating for a writer who perhaps didn't fully understand the length of time it can take to set up a movie project. After all, he was used to his stories appearing in the pulps often within weeks of submission, and his novels in the 1960s would appear within months of acceptance by his publishers. Dick had little patience for the long, tortuous process of movie development.

Dick's first reaction to the silence from Gorin was to panic, jumping to the extreme conclusion that the would-be filmmaker might be dead. "The last time Jean-Pierre phoned me," Dick recalled in an enquiring letter to Susan Sontag in February 1975, "it was at the end of December and he'd been very ill. [He was] in hospital with a liver ailment which flares up from time to time with him… Since then, no word from him at all." As something of a hypochondriac himself, albeit one with occasional genuine serious health problems, Dick feared the worst for his would be ticket to movie fame. "I have become frantic," Dick continued in his letter to Sontag. "Is he dead in the gutter or flown back to France? Jean-Pierre Gorin may be very ill. I'm afraid he may even have passed away…" Sontag, based in Paris at the time, replied to Dick's letter: "Jean-Pierre is the sort of person who disappears from time to time. He was so excited about doing *Ubik* that it does seem strange [that] he hasn't been in touch with you for such a long time…"

Dick's fear for Gorin's health soon turned to anger that he hadn't been paid for his work turning *Ubik* into a screenplay, which as far as he was aware had been accepted. In a March 1975 letter to his agent Jack Scovill, following up a phone call, Dick railed against Gorin: "I want some money out of Jean-Pierre Gorin or for him to drop out of owning an option on *Ubik*. He's had the screenplay from 26 November to now — I think the quid pro quo should be he pays something and we let both contracts be mutually voided, but pay something he must or we go to court!"

Robert Jaffe, son of movie producer Herb Jaffe — who had an option on *Do Androids Dream of Electric Sheep?* — had written a screenplay for that novel which Dick strongly disliked (see Chapter 5). However, Dick liked Jaffe himself, and the writer had visited Dick in November 1974, just as he was handing over the *Ubik* script to Gorin. In his March 1975 letter to Scovill, Dick recommended handing the *Ubik* movie project on to Jaffe: "Turn the screenplay over to Robert Jaffe. I suggest we tell [Gorin] that an MGM producer [Jaffe] offered us the use of their attorneys as a favour."

Next day, Dick was writing to Jaffe trying to sell the writer/producer on the idea of *Ubik* as a movie, with the advantage of an already-written screenplay available for his inspection. "I did the *Ubik* screenplay myself," Dick wrote to Jaffe. "I have a special love for it. You understand: for the first time in my life I got to re-do a novel, five years after writing it, and this time get it right."

Then Dick realised that if he failed to get Gorin off the *Ubik* project, his screenplay would be tied up with a producer who seemed to have little hope of getting the film made, and all for a mere $2,500. Dick was adamant that the rights to the script should revert to him so he could set up the project elsewhere. "I don't want to be so vindictive that I force Gorin to pay and hence retain the property," Dick had written to Scovill. "It's one helluva good screenplay. You'll sell it for billions, then we can go have a drink together. Jean-Pierre can pick up the tab..."

In mid-March 1975, Dick wrote directly to Gorin once again: "I have been frantic with worry about your health since I last heard from you — which was in December. Please get in touch with me, or have someone let me know if you're okay..."

Gorin had taken a trip to New York in search of backers for *Ubik*. Science fiction writer, and friend of Dick's, Norman Spinrad had reported back to the author: "Everyone in New York's heard about the proposed *Ubik* film." This led Dick to believe things were going well with Gorin's efforts to sell his screenplay to potential investors.

However, it wasn't Dick's screenplay which the producer was using to entice the moneymen into making the movie. Instead Gorin and a collaborator named Bob Rudeson had concocted a prose treatment for a proposed film of *Ubik*, only partly based on the screenplay Dick had already written. The treatment for the film is set entirely in New York and featured the character S. Dole Melipone as a film noir-type assassin, stalking the inertials and in the process wiping out the staff of Runciter's Prudence Org. In the treatment, hero Joe Chip is having an affair with Ella, Glen Runciter's wife, and both are killed when the humanoid bomb (shades of *Screamers*) explodes. Ubik is absorbed by the characters in every available form, making it akin to some common form of manna for the masses. In this version, Ubik is required by the population for mere survival...

Even with this simplified treatment, Gorin failed to sell the idea of an *Ubik* movie. Robert Jaffe didn't option the script either, as Jack Scovill seems to have put little effort into marketing the completed screenplay elsewhere. Jaffe retained his option on *Do Androids Dream of Electric Sheep?*, but it eventually lapsed and he didn't make that film either. Gorin was offered a teaching job at the University of California at San Diego, effectively taking him out of the movie business.

Above: *This Romanian cover features the ubiquitous Ubik spray can.*

Interviewed in 1985 by D. S. Black for the Philip K. Dick Society Newsletter, Jean-Pierre Gorin was keen to recount the history of the *Ubik* film project from his point of view. "Philip K. Dick was big in France. There's always been this tradition in France of taking American pulp writers quite seriously," said Gorin. "When I was the literary critic for *Le Monde*, that's more or less the time I started reading him."

Gorin regarded the period he was trying to develop *Ubik* as being a time of a gap in science fiction movie-making, between *2001: A Space Odyssey* and *Star Wars*. Upon his arrival in America, Gorin was interested in working in narrative film, away from the kind of avant-garde projects he'd done with Godard, but he saw filmic possibilities in Dick's work which might allow a blend of the Gallic art movie and the Hollywood SF epic. "*Ubik* offered classical film possibilities that I could explore," declared Gorin. "I had an incredible naïveté, because I didn't know at all what the dealings with any kind of production system [in the US] could be."

Gorin claimed to have personally borrowed the $1,500 he was required to pay to Dick's agent to secure a two-year renewable film option on *Ubik*. Meeting with Dick to discuss the screenplay, the author took Gorin by surprise: "He was a broad shouldered, enthusiastic guy, who was from first contact very easy and very much fun. He was very taken by the fact that some French dude would talk to him as a writer. He was very fond of spinning out 1,001 references a minute, ranging from what I learned to be one of his hobbies — Elizabethan poetry — to all sorts of considerations. There was talk of women, sex and literature. He was a Hemmingway figure in some ways…"

Gorin claimed he hadn't visited Dick with the intention of having the author script the movie, but when his need to find a scriptwriter came up in the conversation, Dick quickly volunteered. "I thought it would take him some time to write it," admitted Gorin. "He got very excited about it, because he had never written a script before. I thought that we would be interacting about it, not a collaboration, but I could at least put some guidelines about how the script should be structured."

Before Gorin had time to take a breath or even make any progress on setting up the project, Dick had finished and submitted his screenplay. Gorin was taken aback by not only the speed with which Dick had written it, but more importantly by what had been delivered. "My reaction at the time was: Jesus Christ, this is something that cannot be a film, although it is great on its own terms. It was a very Philip K. Dick adaptation of Philip K. Dick! [It was] very talkative, and [did] not have very much to do with how a movie could be done. I found myself both delighted at having that piece of work, and totally terrified about what I was going to do with it…"

Gorin found himself in possession of a script he felt was unfilmable and an excitable author desperate to hear of progress on the project. "For a film, it was impossible. [Timing the script] you're going to have a film that lasts six or seven hours. It reads better than it would be said. Essentially, Philip had very little sense of the dramatic contingencies. I was looking for something cheap, with punch, that could become a small cult film and have a kind of cheap, fast quality that would carry with it a certain type of audience that I thought was Philip's audience. What I was given was an enormous white elephant which would

***Above:** Reality dismantles itself in this dramatic Yugoslavian cover.*

have required the means that ultimately Ridley Scott put into *Blade Runner*. I think the screenplay is more interesting as Phil's attempt at dealing with his own material in a medium that he ignored."

Gorin goes on in the 1985 interview to talk about his difficulties in raising the finance for the film, his illness and the financial difficulties he had making the required payments on the book option and screenplay to Dick. "I tried for a long time to get that thing off the ground. Ultimately, everyone turned down the script."

Gorin made progress with the production team of Pressman-Williams, who'd made *Phantom of the Paradise*, but as with Francis Ford Coppola's expressed interest, nothing progressed very far. It was this state of affairs, and Gorin's realisation that if it were to be produced Dick's script would need an enormous amount of work, that led to Bob Rudeson being roped in to draft a different treatment for a film of *Ubik* for the potential New York investors.

"It was very different from what Philip had written," admitted Gorin of this second take on *Ubik*, which Dick was entirely unaware of. "It had the advantage of cutting down considerably what would have been the cost to realise what Philip had written. It took a different angle on the material than the one he had produced."

This new treatment eliminated much from the novel and Dick's screenplay, including the trip to the moon. The focus instead was on the inertials as competing telepaths, and older citizens being able to block out telepathic influence as a result of on-coming senility. The Joe Chip/Pat Conley relationship was played up as a much more conventional movie romance. Some things core to the novel were retained however. "There was the regression in time," claimed Gorin of the treatment, "and there was the main trick of the book, of the hero being dead and in cold-pac. A lot of the more spectacular elements were somewhat toned down to be financially feasible."

While this new version kept Pressman-Williams dangling for a while longer, it ultimately didn't prove to be enough to get the film made. There was one other interested party, whom Gorin called "a rich kid from New York, the heir to a publishing empire." This unnamed would-be producer wanted to take the movie of *Ubik* in a very different direction, one which Gorin — for all his willingness to alter the story to try and get the film made — would not go. "He wanted a lot of exploding heads and exploding cars and a fight to the death at the finish," he said, almost exactly describing *Total Recall*. "I was more interested in the kind of screw-you humour and the pulp metaphysical quality that was closer to what Philip was doing."

In the end, Gorin had to abandon his attempts to make *Ubik*, lumbered with an unwieldy screenplay and facing a lack of interest from potential financiers or filmmakers… "That's basically my story with Philip. It was brief: two or three encounters, some phone calls; some of them slightly tense because the money wasn't coming, and he had to wait for it. He was someone always very assailed and preoccupied by problems of money. I was slowly drifting out of dealing with the sort of people I had to deal with while trying to make *Ubik*. There was no way to bring forth the kind of originality that I felt could be brought out, and that I thought Philip deserved. I basically lost heart, and lost the rights in the process. We both had great hopes — very naïve ones, I think — as to the possibility of making the film."

If not for Gorin, Philip K. Dick's *Ubik* screenplay would never have been written. For that alone, the abortive venture was probably worthwhile, adding the unique 'phildickian' exploration of another medium to the author's oeuvre. "I thought that what was great about Philip was that he was a great writer disguising himself as a trashy writer," claimed Gorin. "Somewhere along the line that linked him to a certain tradition of hack writing in the States in which American literature has found great titles of glory. That was one of the things that excited me so much."

Thankfully, Gorin's exit from the project wasn't the end of the *Ubik* screenplay story. The manuscript, along with many others — including all Philip K. Dick's unpublished novels from the 1950s — languished for the best part of a decade among the author's other papers in a university library in Fullerton, California. In 1985, during the Dick publishing boom which followed the author's death and the release of *Blade Runner*, Minneapolis-based small publisher Corroboree Press brought out a hardback edition of the *Ubik* screenplay. Published in very limited numbers, the book contained a series of black-and-white illustrations of some of the main characters and scenes from the screenplay by Ron Lindahn and Val Lakey-Lindahn, and a series of full-colour, pasted in one-sheet ads for 'Ubik', featuring the spray can and an advertising blurb derived from Dick's 'interruptions' in his screenplay. Like Ubik itself, the book of the screenplay is very rare and hard to come by. Occasionally, copies appear on Internet book collector web sites, often costing close to $200 each.

Ubik was even developed beyond the original Dick novel and screenplay when the story and concepts became the basis of a computer game in 1998. Published by Cryo Interactive Entertainment, the *Ubik* video game was a third-person mystery in which the player took on the persona of the book's hero, Joe Chip. Working for Runciter Associates, Chip's job is to protect the company from industrial espionage through ESP, mind-reading and other mental attacks. The game features genetic engineering and replicants (human-like androids) and gives Runciter Associates and the company's opponents psi-powers. The player, as Chip, selects and trains a squad of mind-readers who boast varied talents before embarking on a series of missions. The acclaimed game was available for Playstation and Windows PC but has now been deleted.

Below: *An American cover offers another strange take on the novel's concerns.*

With his *Ubik* screenplay available, it is always possible that Dick's own version could still become a film. The rights were optioned from the Dick estate in 1989 by an independent filmmaker who intended to make a low budget $1-$2 million film, but not based on Dick's screenplay. The would-be filmmaker fell out of contact with the estate and the option lapsed. As that case suggested, it seems likely that if a filmmaker or studio were ever to re-option *Ubik* for the movies, a fresh start would be made in an attempt to adapt the book in a more movie-friendly form. Before making *A Scanner Darkly* Richard Linklater expressed interest, only for rights issues to spike the project. Nevertheless, *Ubik* may yet be used as directed. ■

ELECTRIC SHEPHERDS

Finally, *Blade Runner* gets underway and Philip K. Dick discovers the true meaning of 'development hell'

"Hampton Fancher came down here and we spent the evening together talking about him making *Androids*. I do have a strong feeling that out of the Hampton Fancher thing something will eventually come." — Philip K. Dick writing to Henry Ludmer at the Scott Meredith literary agency in November 1974.

The second important film option on Philip K. Dick's *Do Androids Dream of Electric Sheep?* was taken out in September 1973, when United Artists made a payment of $2,000 for the film rights. However, little happened on the project until 1974 when independent producers Herb Jaffe Associates Inc. picked up the film rights to the book.

As it turned out, 1974 was a turbulent year for Dick. While recovering from his 'street' experiences of the early 1970s and his stay in the X-Kalay facility in Canada, he was also in dispute with Stanislaw Lem over payment on a Polish edition of *Ubik* (when he wasn't writing to the FBI and sending disapproving letters to US President Richard M. Nixon!). He was also in the process of separating from his long-term literary agent Scott Meredith, after over twenty years, following problems with Doubleday over distribution of the hardback release of *Flow My Tears, The Policeman Said* (though he subsequently re-thought this and re-signed with Meredith, remaining with the agency until his death in 1982). Dick's February and March 1974 'mystical' experiences had caused the author to question everything, from the existence of God, to contact by alien life forms, to his own sanity. Those experiences would heavily influence his final novels and lead to his on-going project of self-interrogation, the *Exegesis*.

In 1974 Dick was forty-five, and living with his fifth and final wife, Tessa Busby, and their one-year-old son Christopher. Living in Orange County, after over twenty years as a struggling writer, Dick was finally beginning to reap the rewards of the international critical reputation that was building around him. Since *Do Androids Dream of Electric Sheep?*, through *Ubik* and *Flow My Tears, The Policeman Said*, the stigma of his 1950s and 1960s hack potboiler writing had fallen away. He was working on what would become *A Scanner Darkly*. His recently published works and re-issues of many of his earlier novels were beginning to be taken more seriously by literary critics. He'd just worked through the process of scripting the un-made movie version of *Ubik* when the long-forgotten prospect of a film of *Do Androids Dream of Electric Sheep?* returned.

***Opposite:** Early storyboards for a never shot farm-set opening to* Blade Runner. *Deckard arrives in his spinner and retires a replicant. He then removes its jawbone, which is tagged with its serial number.*

In March 1974, in a letter to Avon Books editor Charles Platt, Dick noted: "The fact that

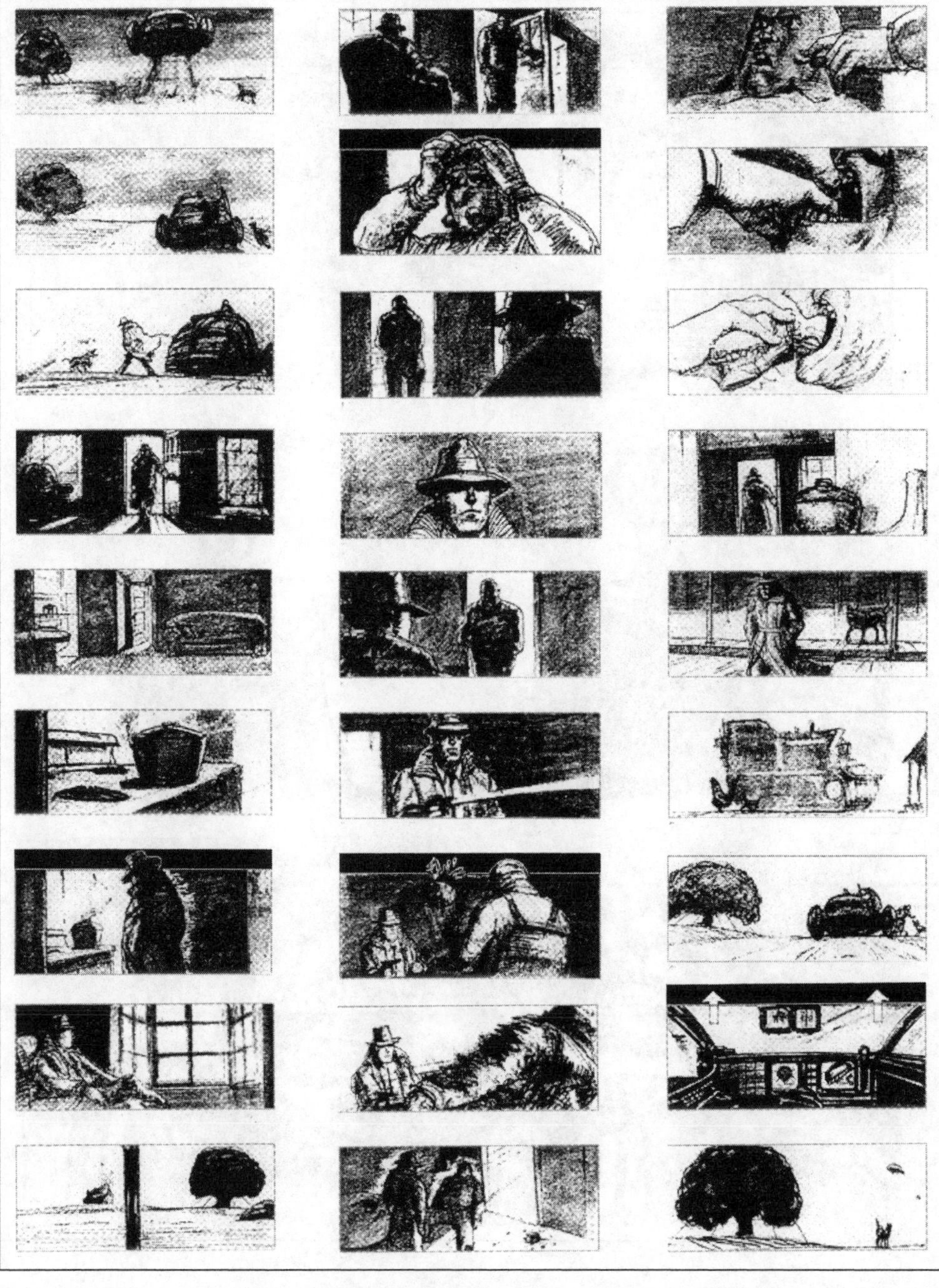

Herb Jaffe has taken out an option for movie rights on *Do Androids Dream of Electric Sheep?* has caused Signet to reissue it, with an additional advance, and a flat ten per cent royalty per copy." Having been stung once before over a film of *Do Androids Dream of Electric Sheep?*, it seems that this time around rather than immediately outline his take on adapting the film, Dick was more interested in the fact that the option meant a re-issue for the paperback of his original novel and a chance to sell more copies and make some extra money through royalties.

Above: *Many other actors were considered, but it was Harrison Ford who would become iconic as Rick Deckard.*

Opposite: *More examples of the early* Blade Runner *storyboards, showing the the hard-bitten Deckard; Tyrell introducing Rachael; and spinners in flight.*

Herb Jaffe's option on *Do Androids Dream of Electric Sheep?* was also one of the problems that Dick had with his agents Scott Meredith during this time. In a letter to Meredith dated 5 May 1974, Dick claimed he had separately been pursuing a potential option with United Artists by "buttering up this chick who reads [scripts] for UA [United Artists] in the San Francisco area..." At the time of the Jaffe option, Dick seems to have been too preoccupied by both his *Exegesis* and the (to him) seemingly more realistic prospect of a film of *Ubik* being made from his own screenplay to worry about *Do Androids Dream of Electric Sheep?*.

Herb Jaffe gave the responsibility of adapting the novel to his son Robert Jaffe. According to Paul M. Sammon in *Future Noir*, Dick hated the Jaffe script, a copy of which he'd managed to get unofficially. "Jaffe's screenplay fell into my possession by accident," Dick told Sammon. "The first thing I noticed was that he'd simplified my book by turning it into a straight action-adventure [the initial simple reading of the novel offered by critic Patricia S. Warrick]. While I wasn't pleased with that direction, I also wasn't surprised by it, given the nature of the source material. But what really bothered me was the fact that Jaffe had also turned *Do Androids Dream of Electric Sheep?* into a comedy spoof, something along the lines of *Get Smart*. That was horrible. I suspect that Robert felt that way too, because he wrote this script under a pen name."

In October of 1974, Dick had expressed his feelings about the Jaffe screenplay to one of his regular correspondents, Henry Ludmer, an agent at the Scott Meredith Agency: "It's frankly not a very good screenplay — a corny cops-and-robbers science fiction piece, the kind we all in the field detest. I'm not enthusiastic. I could do a lot better — I mean, I could write a better screenplay myself; so could other writers." Having said that, Dick then admitted that he felt the script-as-written might actually function as the template for a successful movie: "It would give Jaffe a money-making film; formula that it is, it will make them money." The practical side of the business was also preoccupying the author. "It's obvious that Jaffe is still interested — they've paid for the screenplay, since it's marked 'Property of Herb Jaffe Associates,' rather than, say, getting it [done] on spec. Jaffe wants a free six month extension on his option, which [we] turned down..."

In another letter that same month, to his mother Dorothy, Dick said of the Jaffe screenplay: "It's not as good as my own *Ubik* script, but if they go ahead and make that film it should bring them in a lot of money… it's full of action and suspense, but not too good from an artistic standpoint. United Artists [in reality, Herb Jaffe Associates Inc. on UA's behalf] wants an extension on their option which runs out in December [1974]." Optimistically, he added: "They're almost sure to go ahead and make the film."

In a letter to Herb Jaffe, Dick offered to write the screenplay for *Do Androids Dream of Electric Sheep?* himself, as he had done with *Ubik*. Curiously, he didn't resupply his analysis of the novel he'd completed in 1968 for Bertram Berman. There then followed a meeting with Robert Jaffe in early November 1974. Dick told Sammon: "Jaffe's screenplay was so terribly done I couldn't believe it was a shooting script. Not long after I'd read it and expressed my displeasure, Robert flew down to Santa Ana to speak with me about the project. And the first thing I said to him when he got off the plane was, 'Shall I beat you up here at the airport, or shall I beat you up back at my apartment?' Robert asked me, 'Was the script that bad?' 'Yes it was,' I told him."

Despite that inauspicious start, Dick reported that the pair got on well. The author enjoyed his day with Jaffe, more for the Hollywood gossip Jaffe relayed (according to biographer Lawrence Sutin) than for anything to do with the prospective film. Considering that the movie plans for *Ubik* were slowly falling apart at the time, Dick may have been less than enthused with the ways of movie people. Jaffe seemed open to listening to some of Dick's ideas for the film (potentially recycled from that 1968 document), while Dick had so warmed to the author of the "terrible" screenplay that he relented and allowed Herb Jaffe Associates Inc. to renew their option on *Do Androids Dream of Electric Sheep?* for another year.

In a letter to Henry Ludmer the day after the meeting (dated 9 November 1974), Dick had summed up his experience. "Jaffe has shown [the script] to one producer after another, with no results. Worst of all — to me, anyhow — was the fact that the script was a deliberate parody of my novel, written for laughs. 'No reasonable person could take such stuff seriously,' Robert informed me. So it had to be written for the bubblegum crowd for laughs; slapstick, in fact. This is even more than the obligatory crushing defeat of the artist at the hands of Hollywood; this is in a class by itself."

According to the letter, Dick had worked through the script with Jaffe scene by scene, offering suggestions to improve it. Jaffe had admitted that this was the first screenplay he'd ever written and even his father had not seen much potential in it. Although Jaffe left the meeting with the intention of rewriting and hopefully improving the piece, Dick had by now developed a more realistic view of the project's chances: "I doubt if another full screenplay will come out of this, but anyhow I did my best and beyond doubt Robert appreciated it; I armed him with everything I could, and if nothing comes of this, at least I tried."

In Dick's letter of October 1974 lamenting the poor Robert Jaffe script of *Do Androids Dream of Electric Sheep?*, he noted in an aside that there was another interested party. "Hampton Facher or Fascher or Fasher or whatever, phoned me to ask again if he can come down [from LA]…" Dick had previously put off the visit due to *Rolling Stone*'s Paul

Williams coming to interview him that same month, but it would be Hampton Fancher who would do the most to make a film of *Do Androids Dream of Electric Sheep?* a reality.

Above: *Rutger Hauer embodied the bitter replicant Roy Batty.*

Fancher was a struggling actor in the mid-1970s who harboured ambitions to move behind the camera into writing and producing. Born in 1938, Fancher had been under contract to Warner Bros. in the dying days of the old studio system. Although he'd appeared in a handful of movies (such as *Parrish* and *Rome Adventure*) and in many more TV shows (including an episode of SF anthology show *One Step Beyond*), it was always in tiny supporting roles. It was clear to Fancher that acting was not going to pay off for him and his final film appearance came in 1975's *The Other Side of the Mountain*. "I had been what you might call an underground filmmaker," Fancher claimed in an interview with *Starlog*. "[I] never got a chance to get anything I'd written, and that I wanted to direct, off the ground." In fact, Fancher's biggest claim to Hollywood fame was his marriage to actress Sue Lyon, who played the title character in Stanley Kubrick's 1962 film of *Lolita*.

By 1975, he had decided to move in a more commercial direction, believing this was the only way he'd get anything produced. Fancher came across the work of Philip K. Dick, although, as he admitted, "I am ignorant of science fiction. I [had] decided to look for a property that had some kind of commercial feasibility. Someone [Fancher's friend Jim Maxwell] suggested I read *Do Androids Dream of Electric Sheep?*. I saw in it a possibility."

Fancher elaborated to *Future Noir*'s Paul M. Sammon about those movie possibilities. "I immediately saw a chase movie, with a detective after androids in a dystopic world. I thought, 'What a great idea for a science fiction film!' You must also keep in mind that I read Phil's book in 1975 [when the success of] *Star Wars* wasn't even a gleam in George Lucas' eye. At the same time, there was this smell of science fiction in Hollywood, and I had the gut feeling that science fiction was going to happen in a big way, just like cowboy movies had happened." This 'smell' in the Hollywood air probably had a lot to do with the on-going phenomenal success of the *Planet of the Apes* movies and their associated merchandise through the early 1970s.

Fancher's first problem was finding Dick in order to get him to release a movie option on the book. "Philip Dick turned out to be very elusive. His agent didn't even know where he was..." Fancher eventually got Dick's home phone number from fellow science fiction writer Ray Bradbury, who was more in contact with the filmmaking community in LA. "Dick was very suspicious of Hollywood, and of me," recalled Fancher. "I met him. We had three meetings over a few weeks. He continued to be elusive. Though we liked each other,

Above: *The ultimate 'dark-haired girl'? Sean Young as Rachael.*

I felt he thought I was a 'Hollywood' producer..."

Fancher was right. Dick was suspicious of Hollywood film-making types, having been burned over the *Ubik* deal, seen several stories optioned for movies but never made and having already committed the movie rights to *Do Androids Dream of Electric Sheep?* to Herb Jaffe Associates Inc., only to be lumbered with a script he really disliked. Writing to Henry Ludmer at Scott Meredith in November 1974, Dick noted: "Hampton Fancher came down here and we spent the evening together talking about him making *Androids*. Hampton was able to tell me a great many things about my reputation among the Bay Area and Hollywood artistic circles, stuff I'd never probably otherwise have gained access to. It's possible if Jaffe goes ahead on *Androids*, Hampton will take an option on something else or even hire me to do an original screenplay. If Jaffe were to let his option on *Androids* lapse, I'd like to pick up on Hampton's offer (six months at $600). I do have a strong feeling that out of the Hampton Fancher thing something will eventually come." However, having extended the *Do Androids Dream of Electric Sheep?* option with Jaffe for another year, there was little that could be done with Fancher's interest until after the end of 1976.

In February 1975, possibly as a result of the interest in *Do Androids Dream of Electric Sheep?* expressed by Hampton Fancher, Dick wrote to Robert Jaffe trying to both ascertain what progress was being made on the project following their script meeting at the end of 1974 and to, once more, make his own suggestions about how he felt the film should be realised. "In my head I am doing a fantasy number that you are in production," wrote Dick on 27 February 1975. "What's really happening? I know who would make an ideal Rachael Rosen, the android chick: Victoria Principal. When you were here you may have noticed the publicity shots I have of her up on my living room wall. She is with the William Morris Agency..." Having suggested that Jaffe secure the services of Principal for the movie, Dick then proceeded to write directly to her agent on the same day suggesting she play the part of Pat Conley in his self-scripted adaptation of *Ubik* for director Jean-Pierre Gorin. Dick's obsession with Principal was part of his 'dark-haired girl' syndrome, where he would fall in love with women he felt reflected the image he had in his head of his long-dead twin sister, Jane. Most of his wives, and several actresses upon whom Dick fixated whenever movie possibilities arose, filled his criteria. It's not known whether he received any contact from Principal's agent, other than the publicity photos he decorated his living room with.

By March 1975, it was clear to Dick that Jean-Pierre Gorin was defaulting on the next payment due on his option for the *Ubik* script, so Dick wrote to Jaffe — his only significant Hollywood contact — offering him first refusal on the already written script. Jaffe had written to Dick to inform him that Walon Green (co-writer of *The Wild Bunch* and director of *The Hellstrom Chronicle*), who had been briefly in line to direct *Do Androids Dream of Electric Sheep?*, was no longer involved in the project. Dick took the opportunity to tout the *Ubik* script and again suggest Victoria Principal (for the role of Pat Conley).

Above: *Daryl Hannah played Pris, a character who featured in several Dick novels.*

There was little that Hampton Fancher could do at this time other than wait and make sure that both Dick and the Scott Meredith Literary Agency were aware of his continuing interest in securing an option. "We didn't get anywhere, and finally I dropped it," admitted Fancher. For Dick's part, his inexperience in dealing with filmmakers meant he was unable to move things forward. "I don't think Hampton realised that I was as naïve about Hollywood as he was," Dick recalled in a 1981 interview in *Cinefantastique*. "I don't think he ever understood that when it came to Hollywood, I cringed. I had an automatic flinch reaction. I do love movies and I especially enjoy the work of Scorsese, Altman and De Palma. I'm conflicted about the process. Do I love Hollywood? No."

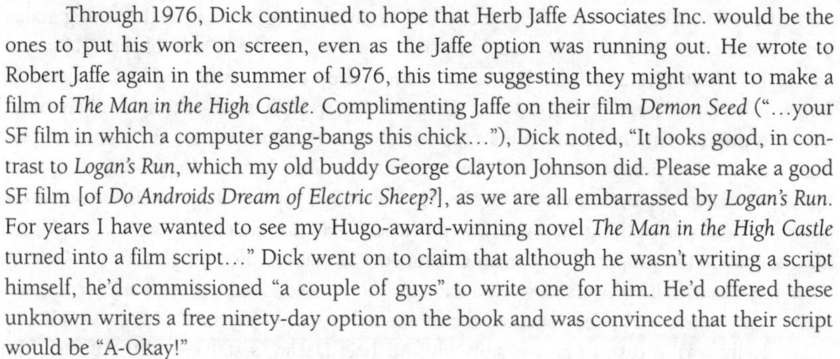

Through 1976, Dick continued to hope that Herb Jaffe Associates Inc. would be the ones to put his work on screen, even as the Jaffe option was running out. He wrote to Robert Jaffe again in the summer of 1976, this time suggesting they might want to make a film of *The Man in the High Castle*. Complimenting Jaffe on their film *Demon Seed* ("...your SF film in which a computer gang-bangs this chick..."), Dick noted, "It looks good, in contrast to *Logan's Run*, which my old buddy George Clayton Johnson did. Please make a good SF film [of *Do Androids Dream of Electric Sheep?*], as we are all embarrassed by *Logan's Run*. For years I have wanted to see my Hugo-award-winning novel *The Man in the High Castle* turned into a film script..." Dick went on to claim that although he wasn't writing a script himself, he'd commissioned "a couple of guys" to write one for him. He'd offered these unknown writers a free ninety-day option on the book and was convinced that their script would be "A-Okay!"

As for *Do Androids Dream of Electric Sheep?*, nothing much seemed to be happening. Jaffe's company held the movie option through until the end of 1976, at which point the company allowed it to lapse, seemingly not having developed it much beyond that initial Robert Jaffe-penned screenplay which Dick had hated so much.

With the Jaffe option finally expired, Hampton Fancher was able to re-enter the *Blade Runner* story. In 1978, Fancher was working in consultation with a friend, another ex-actor-

Right: *William Sanderson played J. F. Sebastian, based on the character of John Isidore from the original novel.*

turned-producer called Brian Kelly. Kelly had enjoyed more success in the acting stakes than Fancher, becoming fairly well known for his role on the 1960s *Flipper* TV series. However, a motorcycle accident had caused him to drop out of acting and look at developing his film and TV career in a different direction. When Kelly was looking for likely properties to pursue, Fancher recalled his experience with Dick and pointed the would-be producer in the direction of *Do Androids Dream of Electric Sheep?*. According to Fancher, Kelly quickly secured the option on the book. "He succeeded rapidly! I guess Dick needed the money. There was nothing like what I went through. He just called the agent and within a day he owned the property." The main difference was that the movie rights for *Do Androids Dream of Electric Sheep?* were now available again to be sold, unlike when Fancher had initially approached Dick. Kelly secured the movie rights with a payment of only $2,000.

Kelly was in turn in partnership with Michael Deeley, a stalwart of the British film industry. Born in 1931, Deeley had begun his career as an editor on the 1950s UK TV series *The Adventures of Robin Hood* (starring Richard Greene) before branching out into producing with a ten-minute 1956 short film entitled *The Case of the Mukkinese Battlehorn* starring Peter Sellers. Deeley later worked on such well known films as *The Italian Job*, *The Wicker Man* and one of Philip K. Dick's favourite movies, *The Man Who Fell to Earth*. Deeley had also worked as a studio executive, running British Lion and working at Thorn-EMI. He and Kelly had already developed a couple of films in Europe, including a concept for a smuggling movie to star Michael Caine called *The Brazil Story*. On the recommendation of Fancher, Kelly took *Do Androids Dream of Electric Sheep?* to Deeley, who turned the novel down flat. "[It] wasn't the kind of thing that even someone who's professionally involved could easily picture as a film," recalled Fancher. "Dick is very obscure and purposefully ambiguous in his writing. I just saw one simple thing that you could hang a lot onto, and which I thought would be intriguing: the 'bounty hunter chases androids' theme. There's a Kafkaesque atmosphere about the book that I enjoyed. Brian came back to me and explained that Deeley didn't like the book and he didn't understand how it could be done as a movie."

To try to sell the project to Michael Deeley, the man who would be able to bring together the financing for the film to enter production, Fancher wrote an outline for the movie. "It was basically a simplification of the novel in eight pages," admitted Fancher. When that failed to convince Deeley, both Kelly and Fancher's-then-girlfriend, actress Barbara Hershey, persuaded Fancher to work up a full treatment for the movie, a scene-by-scene breakdown, but lacking actual dialogue. "The first two drafts were very much in keeping with the book's themes," claimed Fancher. "Deeley feel in love with it, and he made us feel that we had made it. We felt we had a producer with a lot of power, because he had just won an Academy Award [for *The Deer Hunter*]."

Adapting the novel into a film script had never been Fancher's intention. He started the project envisioning his role as that of producer, with someone else being brought in to write the screenplay. However, he had been the driving force behind persuading Kelly and Deeley to back the movie, and he'd done so much work in showing exactly how the book could be adapted that when it came time to actually do the job, Fancher himself was the natural candidate.

The first thing from the novel which Fancher ditched was the faux-religion of Mercerism. "I don't think Mercerism even got past the first draft," he admitted. "I was going to put it back in, but didn't because I finally didn't know what to do with it. The next thing that went was Buster Friendly..." That was a difficult choice for Fancher as he'd loved the character in the novel and had enjoyed adapting those scenes for the initial outline, but as with Mercerism, it became clear that Friendly and indeed that whole sub-plot would have to go.

This initial draft did not feature much in the way of a wider world for Deckard's exploits: it was crafted to be produced as cheaply as possible. "You could pretty much have taken my first draft and put it on the stage," admitted Fancher in *Starlog*. "It was basically a small drama." Retained from the book was Deckard's wife Iran and his marital troubles, while Rachael was Deckard's girlfriend. Even the central role of Deckard was true to the way the character was depicted in the novel, as a meek, downtrodden figure. Missing from this draft, by Fancher's own admission, was any motivating driving force for the actions of the androids. "They were just loose canons, walking around whacking people..."

The first few drafts of the screenplay did include the angle of the status symbol of owning a real animal: key to the book and, indeed, indicated in the novel's title. Through the rewriting process the animal theme was whittled away until it too was deleted. While he was sad to lose it, Fancher felt he was learning so much about writing for the movies that it was necessary to make a few sacrifices along the way. In the process, he'd discovered what would become the core theme of the film. "I came up with a much more important theme: the empathy theme. What got refined in the last three drafts was the theme of a man who was questioning his own conscience, or lack of one, and that the very thing the hero was trying to kill for being a machine was, in fact, less mechanical than he was!"

It was this theme in the novel that had finally led to Michael Deeley coming on-board the project. "There was a dramatic moral problem at the heart of the book," Deeley told interviewer Paul M. Sammon. "[That was] the idea that this sanctioned executioner was becoming emotionally attracted to the one he's supposed to kill. That aspect enormously appealed to me." According to Fancher, this narrative development cracked the process of writing the screenplay. "It was that discovery of his own soul, falling in love with the thing he had to kill: an agonising process for that man, and a dramatic one too!"

Despite Deeley's reputation and the buzz around the screenplay, *Do Androids Dream of Electric Sheep?* was rejected by studio after studio, with many complaining that they just didn't understand it and didn't know what the film was about. Their argument suggested that if studio executives didn't understand the picture, what hope was there for a prospective audience?

Despite loving the original novel, Hampton Fancher — in his dealings with Hollywood — was realistic enough to know that the film would inevitably be a very different proposition. "The book was really only a jumping off point," he told *Cinefantastique*. "The various drafts of my script took on lives of their own. The whole point of my interpretation of the book was of a man who had discovered his conscience in the course of his search for these androids. I also thought of it in terms of a love story, the growing bond between Deckard and Rachael. In the final analysis, there is very little of Dick's book in my screenplay."

The biggest problem was how to end the film. Deckard's conscience is stirred by his experience, but he still (in the parlance of the movie) 'retires' each of the 'skin jobs', except for Rachael, with whom he's fallen in love. In one draft of the screenplay, Fancher resolved the dilemma of what to do with Rachael by having her face up to her limited four-year life span by killing herself "...by stepping off the roof of Deckard's apartment", according to Fancher. Deckard exiles himself to the desert, where the struggle of a turtle to right itself provides him with the motivation to return to the city and continue to live. "Then we came to the last shot in the script, a long pull-back, receding from Deckard until he was just a tiny dot, then the lush, beautiful blue planet that is Earth, then you pulled back from that until you were lost in the cosmos. Fade out. Everyone loved that ending..."

Someone who didn't love that ending was the novel's original author. Philip K. Dick only discovered that things were moving again on the film of *Do Androids Dream of Electric Sheep?* in March 1980 by hearing about it from reports in the movie trade papers *Variety* and *The Hollywood Reporter*. In fact, it was Robert Jaffe, he of the abandoned mid-1970s version, who called Dick and told him about the announcement that the film was underway. "The first thing [Jaffe] told me was 'Congratulations!' I said, 'For what?' It turned out that Jaffe had read about it in the trades, but no one from the production company had taken the trouble to inform me." It was to be the beginning of two years of trouble between Dick and the people behind *Blade Runner*, from 1980 until the author's death in 1982, just before the film was released.

Dick had not heard from Hampton Fancher since the initial approach in 1974, but he did manage to obtain two drafts of Fancher's latest script of the novel, including the one in which Rachael terminated her own existence. "The ending had that awful thing where Rachael mercifully, for everyone's sake, does herself in, at which point Deckard grows in stature from the experience! 'Grows in stature' is just a sobriquet for the fact that he's really grown infinitely more cynical, which is apparently how these Hollywood people mature," wrote Dick.

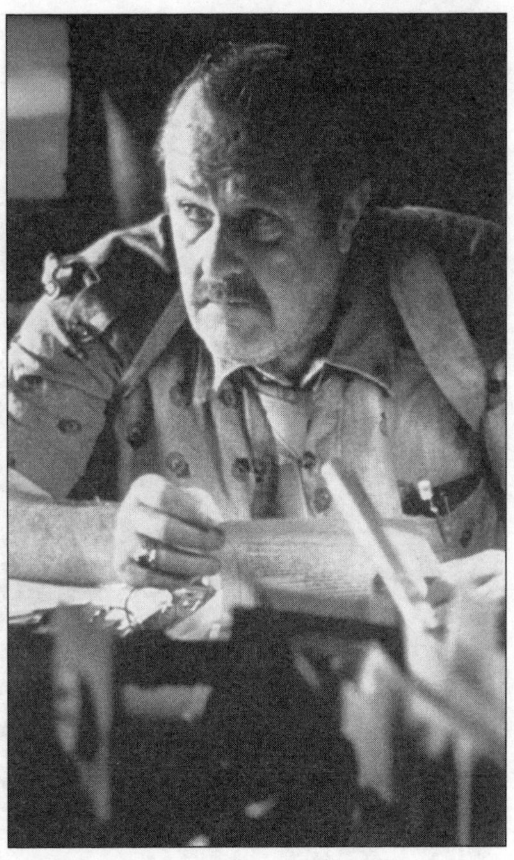

Above: *"Have a better one." M. Emmet Walsh brought Captain Bryant to life.*

The approach of the screenplay in general did not appeal to the author. Dick told Paul M. Sammon, for his major 1982 piece on the making of *Blade Runner* in *Cinefantastique*: "It was terrible, corny and extremely maladroit throughout. They were on the level of Philip Marlowe meets *The Stepford Wives*. I did not approve of what it tried to do, and I don't think it accomplished what it tried to do. They aimed low and failed [to achieve] what they aimed at. Fancher had concentrated on a lurid collision between human and android. I wasn't angered by what had been cut from my novel, because I know you can't transfer everything to the screen. What was bad was the execution of the script. Fancher had over-relied on the cliché-ridden, Chandleresque figure, and his script opened with a hoary voice-over."

Dumping the novel title, fearing that studios would not read something called *Do Androids Dream of Electric Sheep?*, Deeley, Kelly and Fancher came up with some alternatives. Initially under the title *Android*, then *Mechanismo* and finally *Dangerous Days*, the revised screenplay began circulating again among those in a position to get the movie into production. After actress Barbara Hershey's encouragement to Fancher to write the screenplay, further encouragement came from another unlikely Hollywood source: actor Gregory Peck (whom Dick had suggested for the role of Deckard in his 1968 notes). Having somehow got hold of the screenplay and been entranced by its subject matter and ecological concerns, Peck became an unlikely evangelist for *Dangerous Days* throughout Hollywood.

The bleak ending featuring Rachael's suicide, which Dick hated so much, didn't appeal to the first studio that committed to the film either. By summer 1979 *Dangerous Days* had found a home at Universal and director Robert Mulligan (*To Kill A Mockingbird*), a seemingly unlikely choice, was set to direct. He was someone who Fancher "admired a lot." The writer told *Starlog* in 1992: "There were four drafts [of the script] written, and [Mulligan],

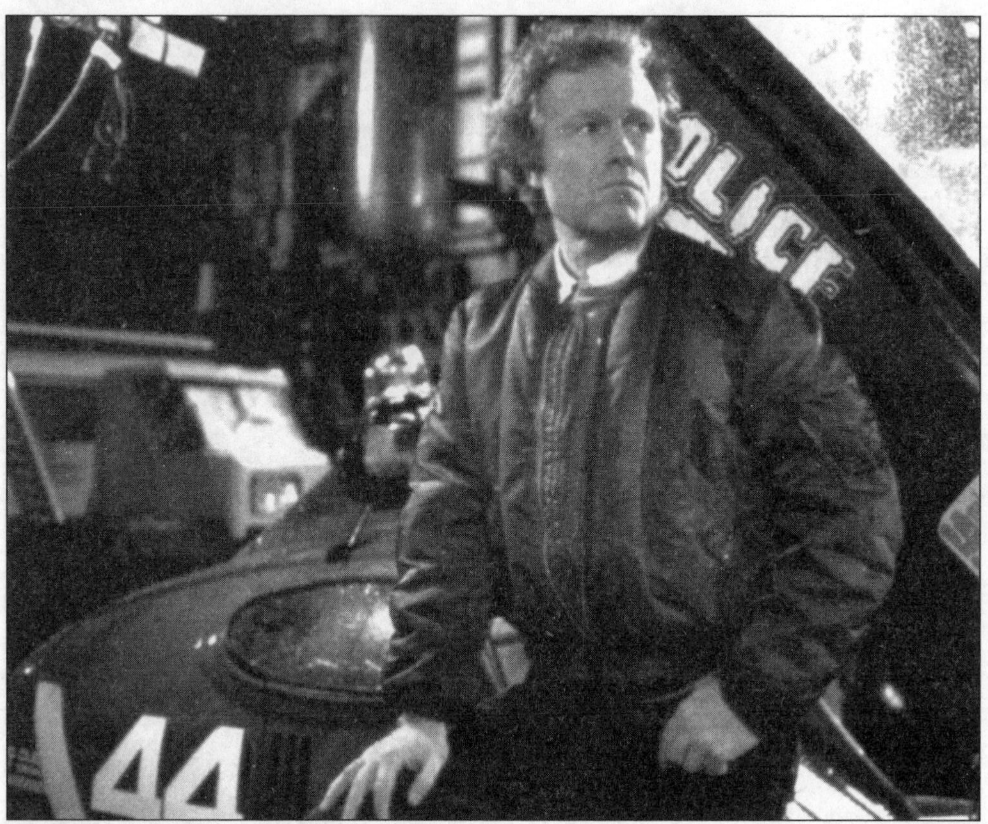

Above: *When director Ridley Scott joined the production, it was still called* Dangerous Days.

a very fine director, came in for a while, but we had trouble with the studio we were dealing with at the time, Universal. We [Fancher and Mulligan] did one draft together, and then we couldn't make sense [in terms of a deal] with Universal. They wanted a happy ending, [but] Mulligan and I wouldn't do it. So, Mulligan left, and then we [the film's producers] left Universal."

As 1980 rolled on, *Do Androids Dream of Electric Sheep?* was once again back in production limbo, but at least this time there was a viable screenplay that was attracting serious attention. The would-be producers realised that the best way to interest a studio in the project would be to present the whole package: script, producers and a director. The hunt was on for a suitable director for *Dangerous Days*.

Katy Haber, another English producer with whom Michael Deeley had worked on *The Deer Hunter*, was enlisted to help with the search. Among the names considered were a pre-*Fatal Attraction* Adrian Lyne, Michael Apted (who was then working on *Coal Miner's Daughter*) and Bruce Beresford, whose 1979 *Breaker Morant* had impressed Fancher. (Beresford would also later be associated with unmade versions of Dick's short story 'We

Can Remember It For You Wholesale', which eventually became *Total Recall*.) The directors who were offered the project either passed or, like Beresford, were simply unavailable due to other work commitments.

The first few months of 1980 saw *Dangerous Days* briefly find a new home at CBS films, a newly-created off-shoot of television broadcaster CBS, where Bertram Berman had once worked. Executives Donald March, Nancy Hardin and Ron Yerxa loved Fancher's screenplay and felt its vision of a future Los Angeles, which was not that far from the look of the real thing, made the film an affordable prospect for CBS films. However, the arrival of a new director with different ideas for a much more lush look to the film caused CBS to drop out. "*Dangerous Days* finally got too rich for CBS films," recalled Ron Yerxa. "We reluctantly had to pass on it."

In April 1979 Hampton Fancher had sent his screenplay (then entitled *Android*) directly to Ridley Scott, not expecting the director of *Alien* to be interested in what initially appeared to be a low-budget android relationship drama. Scott had come to filmmaking through the world of design and advertising, and while he could see the visual possibilities in *Android*, he was reluctant to follow-up *Alien* with another science fiction movie. He was already linked with Dino DeLaurentiis' attempts to film Frank Herbert's elaborate science fiction novel *Dune*, and feared directorial typecasting.

Early in 1980, however, having exited the *Dune* production following the trauma of his older brother's unexpected death, Ridley Scott was looking for a project to which he could quickly commit and get started on filming in order to keep busy. He remembered *Android* and asked Michael Deeley for the latest script, now entitled *Dangerous Days*. This featured a revised spoof 'happy ending' created for Universal in which Deckard and Rachael rode off into the sunset together. Entranced by the design and visual possibilities of depicting a future Los Angeles, Scott signed on as director on *Dangerous Days* in February 1980.

By April 1980 the Hollywood trade papers were reporting that Filmways Pictures had pledged $13 million to the making of an as-yet-untitled film of "technological terror" based on Philip K. Dick's *Do Androids Dream of Electric Sheep?*. With their director in place and a workable script, Fancher and Deeley had finally won the financial backing of a production company. However, Filmways was hardly A-list. The company had recently expanded through purchasing Roger Corman's American-International Pictures and was expanding its production base. As Fancher and Deeley had hoped, it was the 'brand name' of Ridley Scott, director of *Alien*, which had caught Filmways attention and caused them to fund *Dangerous Days*. "He, of course, was the reason the film got made," Fancher told *Starlog* in 1992. "Two days after Ridley got into town, every studio called and said 'How much do you want?' We made a deal with Filmways."

The good news for *Dangerous Days* was short-lived, though. There was a start date for principal photography — 12 January 1981 — and a release date of Christmas 1981 was planned. Scott, however, had budgetary concerns. Although Filmways upped their commitment to $15 million, Scott was maintaining that the script as it stood required at least $20 million to bring it to the screen.

It was with Hampton Fancher's draft script that *Dangerous Days* entered production. Director Scott, producer Deeley, producer and screenwriter Hampton Fancher, associate

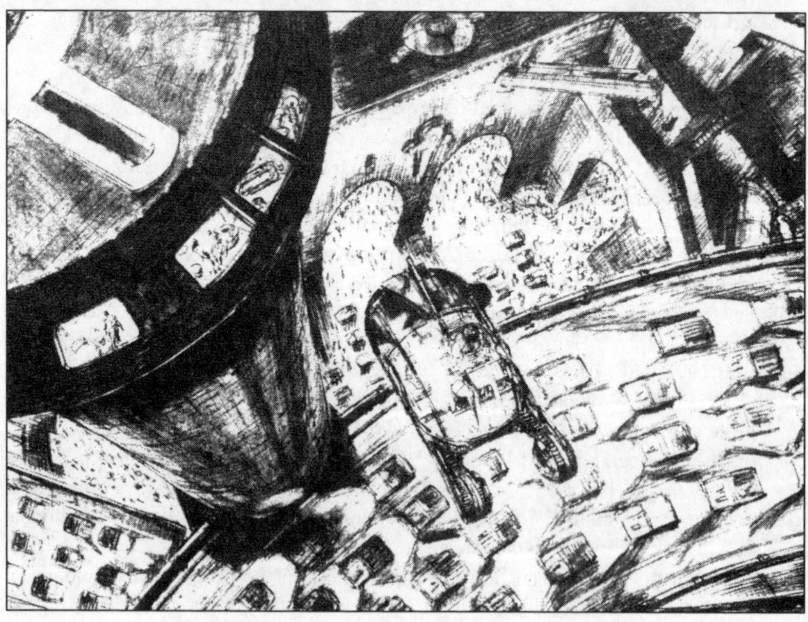

Right: *These early concept designs by Mentor Huebner show two unused openings to the movie: Deckard arriving in 'San Angeles' by train, and another version featuring a huge traffic jam.*

producer Ivor Powell and production executive Katy Haber took up residence in one of Hollywood's most venerable production facilities at the Sunset-Gower Studios. While pre-production artwork was being developed and actors considered for the main roles in the film, Scott turned his attention to the script once more.

One of the first things to concern the director was the androids' lack of motivation for arriving on Earth, so the limited lifespan concept was developed beyond that hinted at in the book. The first few months, between April and July of 1980, spent working through points like this in the screenplay was a mixed experience for Fancher. "I found myself getting excited about many things, and disliking many other things. We had a real basic disagreement on certain sentiments," said the writer. "It was an arduous process, as well as a fulfilling one, and certainly a very educational one."

As pre-production progressed, the amorphous script had to be locked down to something which Scott felt happy shooting. There were many ideas and concepts in the screenplay which he felt needed altering to make an acceptable film. Although Fancher often felt he won the argument on some of these points, weeks later Scott would return to the same topics again, as they were still bugging him. One question from Scott — "What's outside the window?" — led to the development of what would become *Blade Runner*'s unique layered creation of a wider world through visually impressive production design.

"As pre-production began and things really had to be nailed down, it got really hairy," admitted Fancher. "I wasn't a hired writer, so it wasn't as if Ridley could say to me 'Do this and that.' I was also a producer. We came up with what I thought — and many other people thought — was a very wonderful script. It had all those things I wanted..."

Between 1979 and 1981, it appears that around ten different drafts of the screenplay for *Do Androids Dream of Electric Sheep?* were produced, all spinning off from the initial Hampton Fancher drafts and most seemingly moving increasingly away from the Philip K. Dick novel. However, the 1980 script was the first with a director attached that was deemed by all concerned as being almost ready to enter production, so is worth looking at in some detail.

The 24 July 1980 Hampton Fancher draft opens similarly to the final film with the android (the word 'replicant' does not appear) Leon being interviewed by investigator Holden. All that's missing is the question from Holden to Leon about his mother, which results in Holden's shooting (which still takes place, putting Holden in hospital for much of the rest of the script). The narrative cuts to Detective Deckard, just arriving by train back in 'San Angeles' after a vacation in Alaska. Deckard's background is filled in mainly through dialogue, but there is a limited first-person narrative voice-over indicated (more would be heard on the initial release version of the movie). Inspector Bryant, Deckard's superior, and Holden both have larger roles in this version, while those of Gaff, Chew and Sebastian are substantially smaller than in the final movie. Chew and Sebastian are linked via Tyrell, who wants an artificial Griffin constructed for his son's birthday. Deckard's meeting with Tyrell and Rachael proceeds as in the movie, but with subtle differences. She is surprised, rather than shocked, by the revelation of her true nature as an android following the Voight-Kampff test administered by Deckard. Unlike in the movie, this version of Rachael adjusts surprisingly quickly and well to her android status. Tyrell co-opts Rachael to help Deckard track down and eliminate the rogue androids, not pausing to consider how Rachael might

'feel' about being employed to 'kill' those of her own kind. Deckard refuses the job, while Rachael later proves her adaptability by defeating his apartment security systems and saving the detective's life.

The seemingly accident-prone Deckard then suffers a spectacular mountainside road crash. He awakens in hospital, being tended by a doctor. Released, the doctor reminds him to apply for off-world emigration before he gets too old to qualify. Deckard insists his life is on Earth, not the off-world colonies. Returning to Tyrell's job offer, Deckard begins to track down the androids, starting with Leon's room where he discovers photographs which lead him to Zhora, in scenes similar to those in the final film. Deckard eliminates Zhora and retires to a bar where a Russian who strikes up a conversation with him is unmasked as Leon. During a confrontation, Leon laments the downside of being a Nexus-6 android, including impotence and the lack of any true home. Rachael arrives on the scene, recovers Deckard's discarded gun and shoots Leon. Deckard and Rachael spend the night at his apartment, and the next day visiting Holden in hospital, he is teased for having sex with a "washing machine."

Elsewhere, android Pris is insinuating herself with J.F. Sebastian (the Jack Isidore character in the novel), to whom she introduces the remaining androids, including Batty, and Mary, a character described as looking "like an American dream mom, right out of *Father Knows Best*". (Mary did not make it into the final film, though a stray reference to six replicants being missing did…) They will be smuggled onto the Tyrell family estate when Sebastian delivers the birthday gift of the Griffin. The Batty-Tyrell confrontation plays close to that in the finished movie, with Tyrell comparing Batty to a Ferrari, a highly-toned piece of machinery constructed "to win, not to last." After a handshake, Batty murders Tyrell, his family and his entire staff. As a result, the entire Nexus program is terminated and all androids are to be rounded up and eliminated, including Rachael.

Above: *Joe Turkel was cast as Eldon Tyrell.*

Opposite: *Another abandoned idea: Syd Mead's design for the 'cryo-crypt' (shades of Dick's 'cold-pac'), where Roy, having killed a replicant double, was to have found the* real *Tyrell.*

Deckard tracks the androids to Sebastian's apartment, where Batty tosses the still-alive Sebastian out of an upper storey window in an attempt to kill Deckard, whom he rates as a "good" bounty hunter. Deckard confronts Pris hiding in a gymnasium, and after a brutal fight eliminates her. He then discovers Mary hiding in a cupboard and similarly disposes of her.

Batty hunts Deckard through the building, with Batty offering to use doors, rather than using his inhuman superior strength to demolish walls, in an attempt to make the contest a fairer fight. Deckard manages to wound Batty several times, while the android tries to persuade Deckard to throw himself from the building rather than endure the agonies he plans to inflict on the human. Feigning his own suicide, Deckard is able to trick Batty into

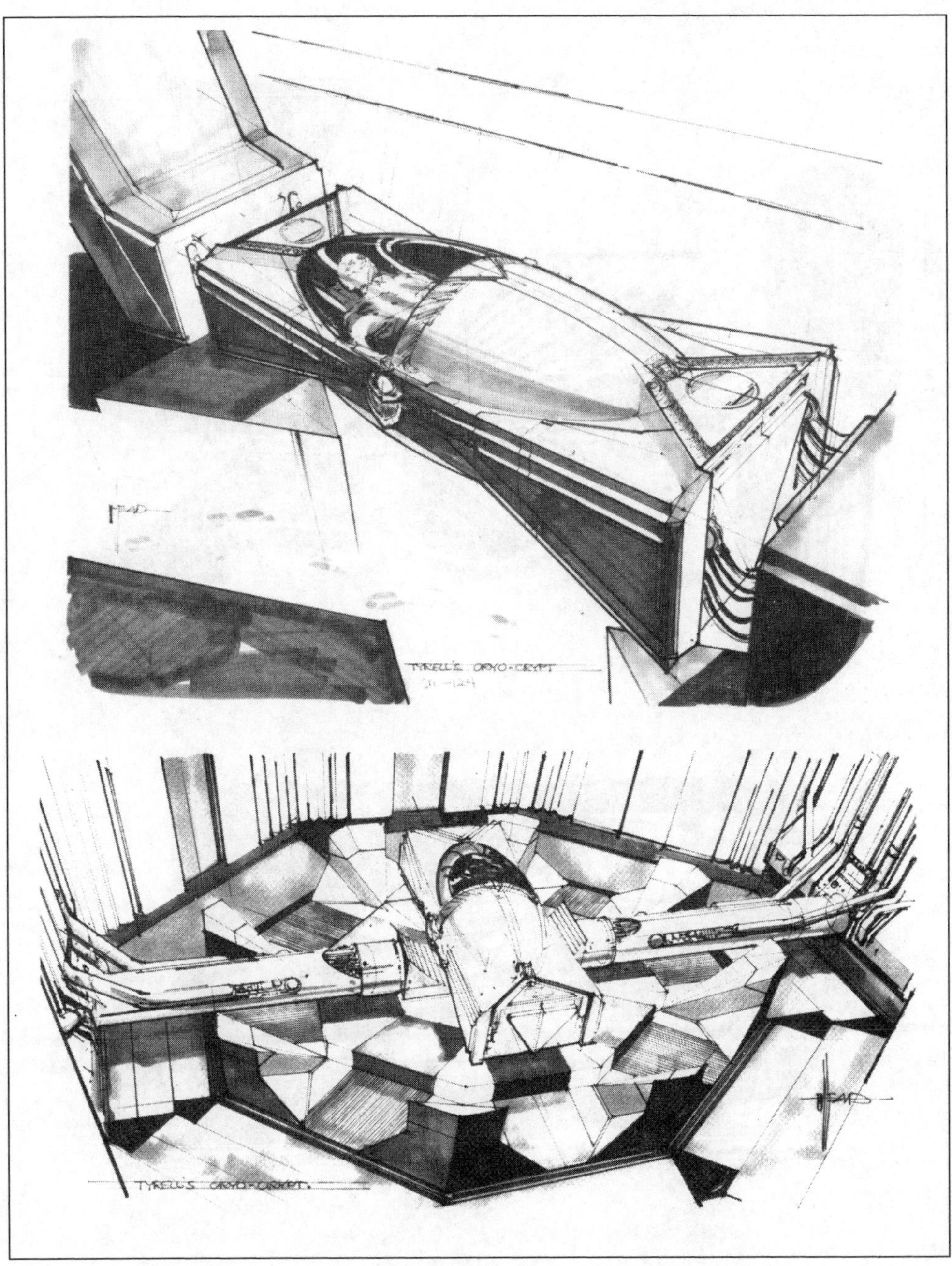
TYRELL'S CRYO-CRYPT
TYRELL'S CRYO-CRYPT.

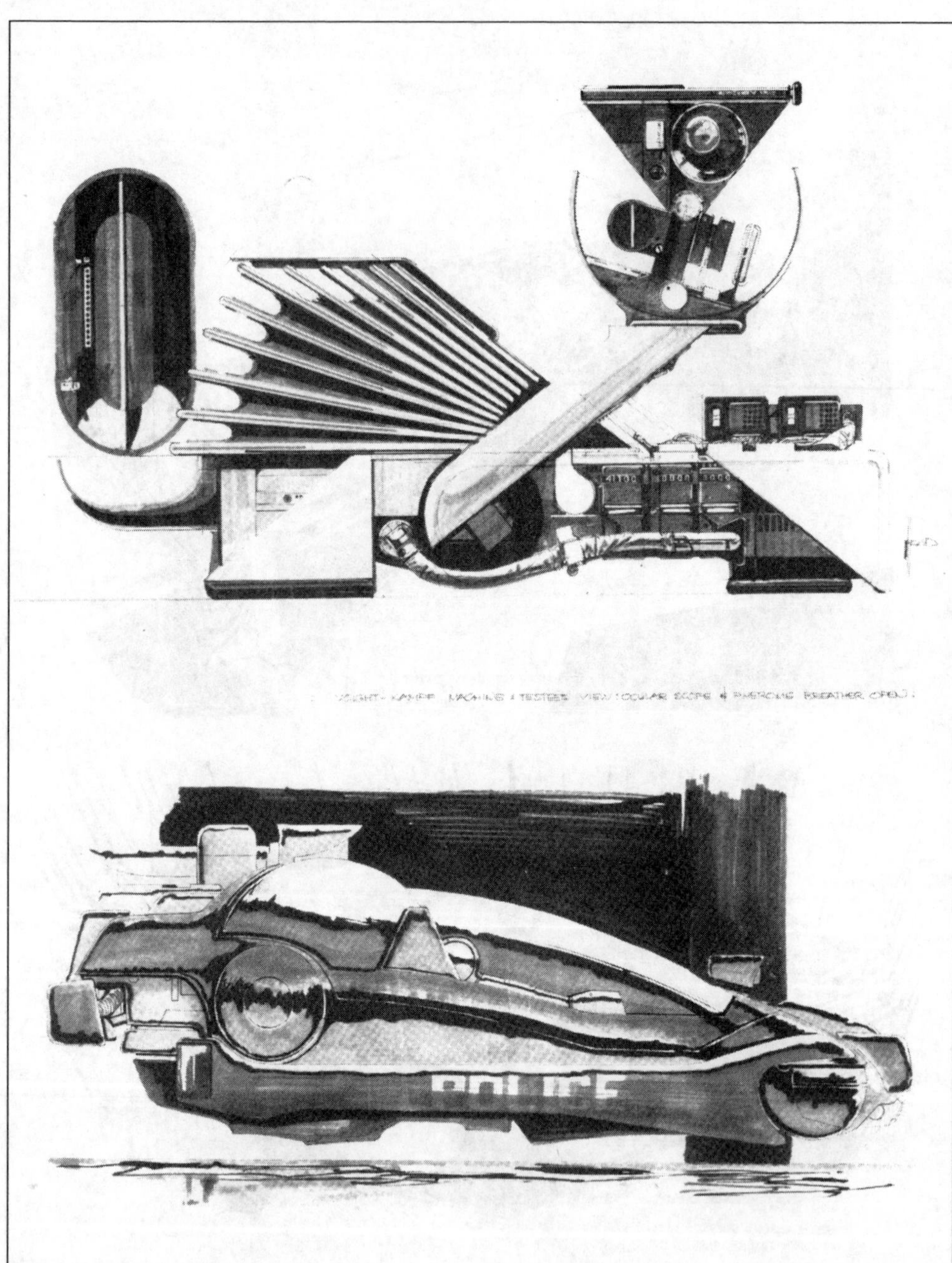

a position where he can destroy him at point-blank range. Struggling to the last, though, Batty grabs hold of Deckard's ankle as he falls from the building and it takes all of Deckard's strength and will to free himself from the android's death grip.

Deckard then retrieves Rachael and heads out of the city with her to the country, where he plans to spend one last day together with her before 'retiring' her. He complains of Tyrell's skill in making Rachael so human and making it necessary that he kill her. The screenplay ends with Deckard declaring his intention never to return to the city where there are "too many Tyrells."

One of the reasons for the continued fascination with *Blade Runner* is that each of the draft screenplays had slight differences of emphasis on the ideas drawn from the same source material. The final film combines many of these often contradictory ideas, allowing the viewer to read into the film their own take on what they're seeing. This 1980 draft takes longer to get going than the final film, but shows more of the world of *Blade Runner*. The androids are more of a threat, and the extermination order against all androids is certainly dramatic. Widely circulated on the Internet, perhaps it's time the varying drafts of the film were published as *The Annotated Blade Runner Screenplays*...

Opposite: *From devices like the Voight-Kampff machine to the 'spinner' flying cars (both designed by Syd Mead), the future world of* Blade Runner *was conceived with breathtaking attention to detail.*

The July 1980 screenplay draft incorporated many of Ridley Scott's requested developments, from turning Deckard into a detective to getting the characters to explore the world "outside the window". Hampton Fancher felt that he'd made enough compromises in this take on the material to ensure that this draft would be the one to go into production: after all, principal photography was now only a few months away. Deckard-as-detective was not an idea which had initially appealed to Fancher. "I was against it at first because I thought it was a cliché and very unoriginal, but after three months of fighting I gave in. It was, after all, a way to get everything through. I started to think, 'Wouldn't it be interesting, we could have a voice-over narration and all that kind of character.' I originally had Deckard as a little bureaucrat [as in the original Dick novel], a guy who wasn't too sure of himself, but then I thought it was better to have an extremely macho guy, and then have him cut down so he doesn't know where he's coming from..."

There was another element in the film which Fancher was keen to protect from loss through script development. "The deepest thing I had was the love story. I don't think they [Deeley and Scott] ever saw it as a love story. For me, the most noble person in the film, the person with the most to lose and who was willing to lose it, was Rachael. I liked matching her against a macho jerk who was totally sexist-oriented in that stupid detective way. Then, through her, he becomes otherwise — but he still loses her."

As rewriting progressed, Scott wanted to eliminate the whole sequence of Sebastian smuggling Batty onto the Tyrell estate, replacing it with what Fancher considered the "too easy and obvious" Sebastian/Tyrell chess match, as retained in the finished movie. Also sacrificed by Scott was the character of Rachael, reduced in importance to the story; the theme of artificial animals (Deckard's motivation for taking the job of retiring the skin jobs in the first place); and the overall ecological themes which Fancher was keen to emphasise. By November 1980, Fancher was actively resisting the changes that Scott was requesting. With an impasse between writer and director, something had to give. Fancher decided to play his hand. "Finally I said — because it was Ridley's film in the end — 'If you're going to do that,

Following spread: *The future/noir costume designs by Charles Knode and Michael Kaplan for Deckard (featuring the Indiana Jones-style fedora that was dropped when Harrison Ford was cast), Pris and Roy Batty.*

Opposite: *"What's outside the window?" One of Ridley Scott's own pre-production sketches.*

you're going to have to get somebody else to do it because I won't.' I didn't think he would do it, because time was too short. But they did get somebody else, just weeks before shooting started…"

David Webb Peoples was an accomplished screenwriter who'd worked on two Oscar-winning documentaries (on one as an editor) and contributed to another Oscar-nominated short. He was recommended to Deeley and Scott by Scott's brother Tony, also a director. Fancher was devastated that his bluff had been called and a new writer hired mere weeks before the start of shooting. "I was very disturbed because I didn't know who David Peoples was," claimed Fancher. "I thought they had gotten a guy who was going to do anything Ridley wanted and it was going to wreck the film."

Fancher was partly right: Peoples *had* been hired to carry out Scott's desired changes, the same changes Fancher had been resisting, but far from wrecking the script, Peoples' reworking help to refocus what was good about Fancher's drafts and marry that to Scott's plans to expand the film to encompass the wider world.

Peoples found himself working on a project which by November 1980 had adopted the title *Blade Runner*. Scott had grown to dislike the title *Dangerous Days* and was even less enamoured of the film's earlier title, *Android*. Scott had wanted something which captured the nature of Deckard's work, having grown tired of referring to him as a detective: investigators don't usually actively eliminate their prey. It was Fancher, ironically, who drew Scott's attention to *Blade Runner: (a movie)*, a slim volume by William Burroughs, author of *Naked Lunch*. Scott loved the idea of a 'Blade Runner unit' as the place where Deckard operated from: he was a 'blade runner', an on-the-edge guy who hunted and eliminated the rogue fake humans. Deeley bought the rights to use *Blade Runner* as the film's title, only to then discover there was an even earlier novel also with the title *Blade Runner* (which Burroughs had been paying homage to in his work). The 'blade runners' in this earlier Alan E. Nourse novel were doctors, smuggling medical supplies in a post-apocalyptic future society. Deeley had to purchase the rights to Scott's preferred title a second time. Luckily, both transactions were not costly, coming in at under $5,000. (Scott also flirted briefly with calling the film *Gotham City*, focusing on the location rather than the characters, but this was abandoned when Batman creator Bob Kane complained that this would be confused with the location of his superhero tales which he hoped would also one day see a movie revival.)

So it was that Peoples found himself in a hotel room in Hollywood's Chateau Marmont hotel with a copy of Fancher's last version of *Blade Runner*. Eager to get to work with Scott on the project, which he saw as his big break in feature films, Peoples' discovered to his horror that he loved Fancher's script and felt there was little he could do to improve it. "The script that Hampton had written before I got there was absolutely brilliant," admitted Peoples in a 1992 *Starlog* interview. "It was just wonderful. I thought I was going to embarrass myself, because it was so good. The changes I made were really to make it more in line with Ridley's vision. I picked up right where Hampton had left off."

The new 'ready-to-shoot' screenplay for *Blade Runner* was dated 15 December 1980 and was credited to Hampton Fancher and David Peoples (in that order) and incorporated most of Ridley Scott's requested revisions and a few ideas of Peoples' own. As an important

STOP

step in *Blade Runner*'s evolution to the screen, this screenplay is also worth examining in some detail.

The new version of *Blade Runner* opened on a furnace asteroid, an off-world termination dump for androids whose four-year life span has been spent. A spectacular opening shot would have seen two small humans shovelling body parts from a dump of thousands of expired androids into the cremation fires. Out of the pile of cadavers comes an android who is far from expired: this is Roy Batty's new introduction, as he rescues fellow androids Mary and Leon, then kills the maintenance workers. The sequence concluded with the android trio staring up into the heavens and anticipating their journey to their ultimate destination: Earth.

While that dramatic opening sequence was quickly dropped due to budgetary constraints, Peoples did incorporate other important ideas into this screenplay which were retained right through to the final film. Something Ridley Scott had been trying to steer Fancher towards was a strong detective angle in the film: there had to be more clues to drive Deckard's quest forward. Peoples was instrumental in bringing this aspect to the fore, introducing (at Scott's suggestion) the discovery of the snake scale in Leon's room, leading Deckard to Chew and to Leon. Scott's model for the screenplay was *Chinatown*, the 1974 film scripted by Robert Towne, directed by Roman Polanski and starring Jack Nicholson as a down-at-heel detective uncovering corruption amid a water supply scandal in 1940s Los Angeles.

Peoples was also responsible for dropping the term 'android' — which Ridley Scott detested — from the screenplay and substituting 'replicant'. Scott confided his dislike of the term to writer Paul M. Sammon in a 1981 interview: "The term 'android' is a dangerous one, undermined by certain generic assumptions. I don't like using it. Android is a very familiar word, not just to science fiction readers, but to the general public. A lot of material — some good, some crap — has been touched by the term. Therefore, I didn't want *Blade Runner* to be premonitory of android at all. People would think this film was about robots, when in fact it isn't. I thought it was better that we come up with a new word altogether."

It was Peoples' daughter, Risa, who came up with the term 'replicant'. She was a microbiologist who introduced her father to the process of replication, by which cells were duplicated in the laboratory for cloning. From that Peoples developed the idea of replicants as a name for the genetically constructed artificial humans of *Blade Runner*.

Peoples' 15 December 1980 revision had a new introduction for Deckard, featuring him traversing a busy street while ruminating (in a partial voice-over which featured throughout this draft) on his recent divorce. Other new scenes included a bigger role for Gaff, including a confrontation between him and Deckard in which Gaff is forced to submit to the Voight-Kampff test, and a later meeting when Deckard kills Gaff after the latter tries to destroy Deckard for not pursuing Rachael with enough vigour. Peoples also introduced another (seventh) replicant, named Roger, who is discovered in bed in Leon's apartment and rapidly terminated. There was a different death for eye-specialist Chew, whose body is discovered frozen in his lab and accidentally knocked over and shattered into thousands of pieces. Building on the animal theme, which had been in and out of the various drafts, Peoples' first pass featured a mechanical cat which Pris uses to win Sebastian's trust. In fact, the artificial animal aspect of the book was never adequately incorporated into any of the screenplays and is all but lost in the finished film. "Ridley wanted to dwell on the animal theme, and I know Hampton's drafts had a lot about it, but somehow we never found the proper way of making it an important part of the picture," admitted Peoples.

In fact, Scott had insisted that Peoples did not read Philip K. Dick's source novel, but instead concentrated on working from Fancher's draft scripts and the director's notes. "I didn't refer to the book when writing," said Peoples. "I referred only to Hampton's screenplay. Ridley told me not to read Philip K. Dick's novel; he felt it was better if I concentrated on Hampton's script and stayed away from the book."

Ridley Scott himself had not read Dick's original novel either, a point which caused concern for the author. "I'm afraid I might have inadvertently played a part in that," admitted *Future Noir* writer Paul M. Sammon. "Dick always reminded me that I was the one who'd first told him that Ridley Scott had told me that he'd tried to read *Do Androids Dream of Electric Sheep?*, but had not been able to complete it. Ridley said he'd put down the book after forty pages or so. Phil was furious about that. 'How can a director adapt a book if he hasn't even read the thing?' I tried to explain that sometimes directors don't want to go to the novel, because they'd rather work off the script and bring their own take to the material. But Phil didn't buy that. He also never really understood that the people who make movies and the people who make books come from totally different tribes. Neither one speaks the other's language."

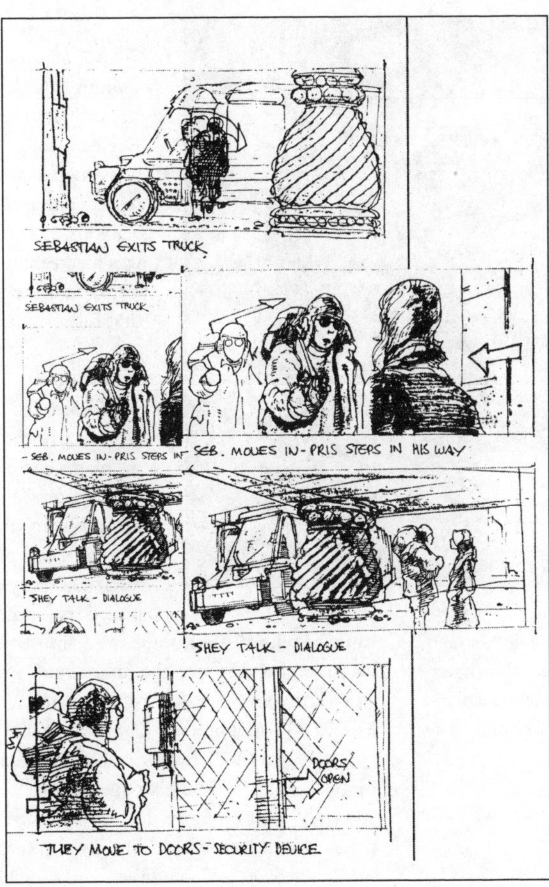

Above: *Ridley Scott's storyboards for the sequence where J. F. Sebastian meets Pris.*

Peoples had other significant restrictions he had to work around. Production on the film was so far advanced by December 1980 that sets were already being built and casting was underway. In rewriting the script, the writer had to work around the available existing sets and not create any significant new environments. As a result there were also elements of the script which Peoples could not change, even if he'd wanted to. "All along, there were things that were absolutely locked into the story, because people had been working on building this. There were times when I would want to write something one way, and the set had already been built another. It was a strange sensation to think these things were happening, even as I wrote the words down on paper…"

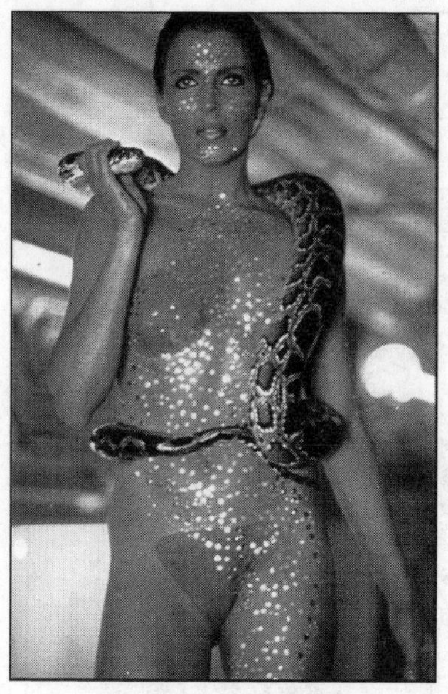

22 December saw the arrival of yet another draft of the *Blade Runner* screenplay, but this was one that came as a surprise to both Fancher and Peoples, as neither had anything to do with it. As if inspired by the use of Burrough's *Blade Runner* title, Deeley, Scott and others adopted his 'cut-ups' technique and constructed a new draft of the screenplay by literally cutting together scenes from several different drafts including the earlier versions of Fancher and Peoples' more recent work. The result was a screenplay that Ridley Scott felt accurately reflected what he wanted the shooting script to follow. It was clear to Peoples that his re-write duties on *Blade Runner* were far from over.

A near-disastrous event as the film was about to start shooting put *Blade Runner*'s script problems in perspective, as the plug was very nearly pulled on the entire project. Rumours of financial problems at Filmways had been circulating for a while, but had been ignored by *Blade Runner*'s principals as they wrestled with the problem of getting a shootable script into shape for their January 1981 principal photography start date. Ridley Scott and Michael Deeley discovered in the trade papers that Filmways had pulled its funding from *Blade Runner*, in an irony that must have caused Philip K. Dick some mild amusement, considering he'd discovered that the project was in motion through the same route. Some speculated that *Blade Runner* was turning out to be too expensive for Filmways to fund it, with the attraction of financing Brian De Palma's $16-million *Blow Out* looking like more of a sure thing at the box office.

Above: *Joanna Cassidy as rogue replicant turned snake dancer Zhora.*

Whatever Filmways' reasoning, *Blade Runner* was now a project with a crew working on building sets, designing special effects shots and on the verge of signing up actors, but suddenly with no financing. Any delay now could mean the collapse of the project, with the work that had been done so far consigned to 'development hell' and the loss of director Ridley Scott to some other ready-to-shoot 'go' project. Michael Deeley worked a minor miracle in late December 1980, setting up a three-way deal with The Ladd Company (who had an 'output' deal with Warner Bros.), Far-Eastern movie financier Sir Run-Run Shaw and Tandem, a company better known for television production. While this complicated deal brought the film a new budget of around $20 million, it created a complex rights situation which would come to haunt *Blade Runner* much further down the line. With Ladd claiming domestic US distribution rights and Sir Run-Run Shaw's company handling foreign (i.e. non-US) distribution, Tandem came in as, essentially, completion guarantors. Not only did the company promise to cover any budget overages, up to ten per cent, they were also capable of taking control of the project should the budget spiral out of control. From Tandem's trio of partners, Jerry Perenchio and Bud Yorkin joined the *Blade Runner* project as supervising producers. The film now had between seven and ten individuals and companies who could all lay claim to a degree of ownership.

The new year saw the project back on an even keel, with production proceeding and a newly drafted script once again touted as the finished shooting script. This unpublished

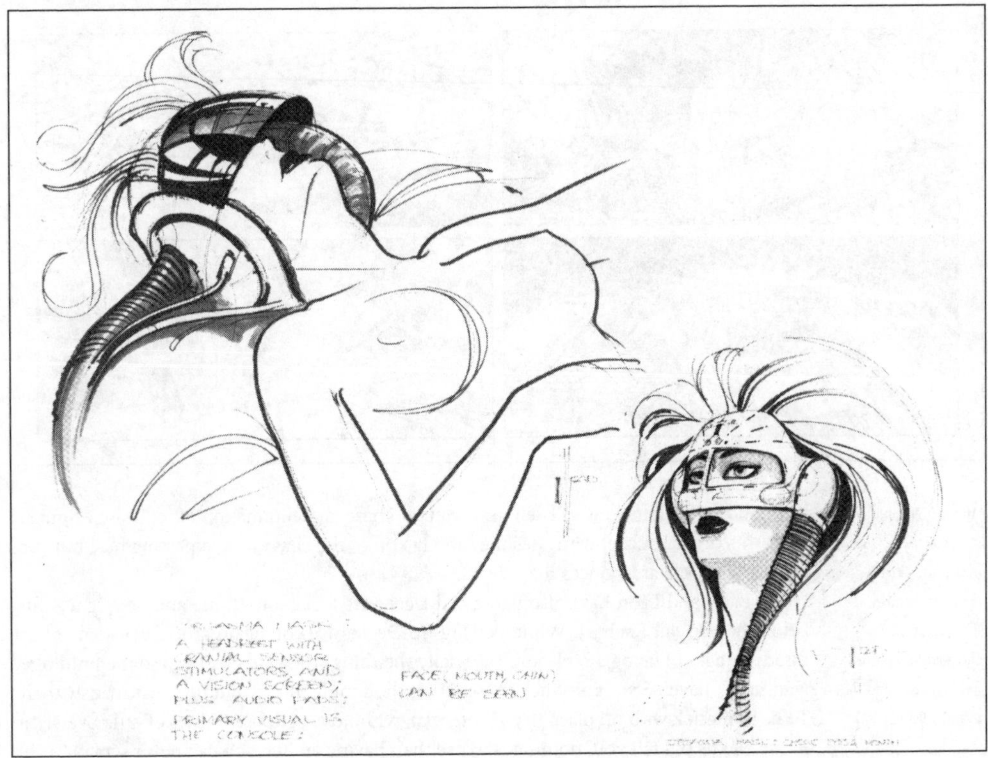

***Above:** Syd Mead's unused designs for 'Zhora's Orgasma Mask', a device similar in concept to the 'mood organ' in Dick's novel.*

version, dated 23 February 1981, carries no writer credits, just like the 'cut up' script of 22 December 1980. Unlike the previous versions, this script *was* the basis for the shooting of the movie, although it continued to be revised almost daily during shooting.

By now Deckard was no longer a bounty hunter who takes the job of tracking and eliminating the androids as the means to earn enough to buy a real animal, but an "ex-cop, ex-Blade Runner, ex-killer" (as the scripted voice-over has it) who has left the police dissatisfied with his lot. The Gaff/Deckard conflicts remain and are much stronger than the mild dislike which features in the final movie. It's clear from this script that Gaff believes that Deckard's attitude and demeanour, even down to his dress sense, brings the police department into disrepute. Similarly, Deckard and Bryant have a relationship which is much more complex than that which is seen in the released movie.

The Deckard/Tyrell/Rachael meeting takes place pretty much as it does in the finished film, while the search of Leon's room adds the detective element Scott was after. The second meeting between Rachael and Deckard (she has been waiting in the elevator of his apartment building determined to convince him she is human) is a much nastier affair than in the movie, with Deckard dismissive of her status as a replicant. Devastated by Deckard's attack, Rachael leaves. As in the movie, Deckard traces the snake scale found at Leon's to

Above: *Original storyboards for the arrival at Tyrell's building included a fly-over of an enclosed landscaped green space amid the urban sprawl.*

the club run by Taffy Lewis. The interrogation, chase and elimination of replicant Zhora are all in this draft. Rachael witnesses the bloody end of the chase from a passing bus, but runs away when Deckard notices her.

Batty and Leon have also witnessed Deckard's attack on Zhora, and Leon grabs him before he can tail Rachael. While beating up Deckard, Leon again articulates some of the disadvantages of being a replicant, especially the things they are missing and the unfulfilled wants they have: "Sex, reproduction, security: the simple things. But no way to satisfy them. To be homesick with no place to go. Potential, with no way to use it. Lots of little oversights in the Nexus 6. I tell you, nothing is worse than having an itch you can never scratch." This leads into a scene remaining from earlier drafts, where Rachael returns and saves Deckard by killing Leon, only to be warned off by a look from Deckard as Bryant and Gaff arrive. Bryant congratulates Deckard for eliminating two replicants in a single night (Zhora and Leon), then adds Rachael to the hit list of remaining replicants to be 'retired'.

At Deckard's apartment, Rachael examines his photographs while he sleeps and then plays Chopin at the piano, unsure if the memory of learning to play is hers or implanted. Deckard awakes the next morning and explains the importance of photographs and memories to Rachael. Deckard then visits Holden in hospital where, as before, Holden questions Deckard's willingness to have sex with a replicant he's supposed to be retiring. Bryant and Gaff observe the meeting via video screen, dispassionately. It's a shame this scene was lost as it helps in the reversal of making the humans less human and the replicants more like sympathetic victims.

There follows the meeting between Batty and Tyrell and the discussion about life-extension for replicants. This draft screenplay is more ambiguous on the issue of whether Tyrell cannot, or simply will not, help Batty. The end of their confrontation is the same: the deaths of both Tyrell and Sebastian. Using a list of high-clearance Tyrell employees, Deckard calls Sebastian's apartment, only to have a startled Pris (another replicant) hang up on him. Using similar image analysis techniques as used on Leon's photographs, Deckard determines

***Above:** The Deckard/Gaff relationship evolved through* Blade Runner's *various script drafts.*

where the building is (couldn't he just get the address from the Tyrell Corporation?). Arriving at Sebastian's, Deckard confronts Pris in a similar sequence to that in the movie, except he shoots her arm off at one point. Deckard eliminates Pris, but Batty arrives and breaks two of his fingers before allowing him to escape, as he enjoys the thrill of the chase.

The Deckard/Batty chase proceeds as before, with the addition of Batty suffering repeated hand-cramps as his termination process begins. The roof jump and Batty's saving of Deckard are all present, as is Batty's final monologue on the roof (later developed slightly by actor Rutger Hauer). The intermittent voice-over (nowhere near as much in the first released version of the movie) returns, as Deckard notes that Batty lived through the night, despite the increasing pain.

The film ends with a definite conclusion of one of several narrative mysteries which would haunt the released final cut of *Blade Runner*. Gaff taunts Deckard from the opposite roof, from where he's been watching (was he there all night to watch Batty die?). "You did a man's job," he states, in a line that survived through to the final movie and caused much speculation about Deckard's status (was he, indeed, a man, or the much-vaunted missing sixth replicant?). In the draft, Gaff's dialogue continued: "But are you a man? It's hard to be sure who's who around here…" In Spanish he calls Deckard a "brother", then mysteriously adds: "Hear the water." He tosses Deckard's discarded gun back to him, tells him to take Rachael and get out of the city, adding the line that remained in the movie: "It's too bad she won't last."

This led to the final scene where Deckard returns to his apartment, picks up Rachael and discovers Gaff's origami unicorn. As Deckard and Rachael drive away from the city, a voice-over clarifies the hero's status: "I knew it on the roof that night. We were brothers, Roy Batty and I! Combat models of the highest order. We had fought in wars not yet dreamed of… in vast nightmares still unnamed. We were the new people, Roy and me and Rachael! We were made for this world. It was ours." As Gaff's spinner appears in pursuit of the car, Deckard's final scripted words were: "God help us all!"

***Right:** Rachael's role in the covoluted plot saw her character swing from passive to active and back again.*

As he prepared to finally begin shooting on *Blade Runner*, Ridley Scott recognised that the various screenplays were no more than blueprints to allow him to achieve his work: "What one gets in a blueprint or a screenplay is hopefully a good story, well told. After the blueprint, things are wide open for interpretation."

Having taken a strong dislike to Hampton Fancher's scripts for the film of his novel *Do Androids Dream of Electric Sheep?*, Philip K. Dick decided to move his dissatisfaction with the developing movie into the public arena. Since the earliest days of Fancher's interest, Dick had been divorced from the project, having learned that it was in active production second hand. The change of the title for the movie from Dick's original novel was the final straw. "Shucks fellas," exclaimed Dick, "I'm so sorry I titled my book *Do Androids Dream of Electric Sheep?* But, you know, gosh… I'm sort of committed to it!"

Irked by the lack of communication from the production, but equally aware that he'd made no real attempts to contact them either, Dick penned a vituperative article for the Los Angeles *SelecTV Guide* (the magazine for Dick's own cable TV supplier), published on 15 February 1981.

The article ignited a firestorm of controversy around *Blade Runner*. Dick opened his short piece by noting that science fiction cinema was changing, warning movie fans that "Hollywood can now simulate anything the mind can imagine… Inventive scriptwriters and directors will soon be bringing you peculiar new universes and inhabitants to match." He noted that the creature which burst from John Hurt's Kane in *Alien* was "not the end of the line of monsters but more the beginning." Following this prescient introduction, Dick then lamented the role of the science fiction author in this progression. "What [science fiction authors] wrote, is not what you get when the film is finished…"

Of course, he had a very personal example in mind. Pointing out that *Alien* director Ridley Scott was turning *Do Androids Dream of Electric Sheep?* into a movie, Dick lamented that once Hollywood had finished with his work, "My story will become one titanic, lurid collision of androids being blown up, androids killing humans, general confusion and murder, all very exciting to watch. Makes my book look dull by comparison."

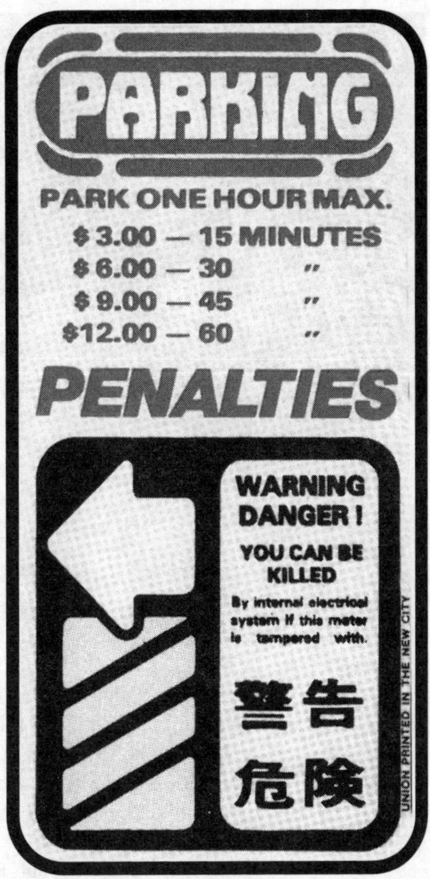

Above: *Fatal parking meters: just one of the many details buried within* Blade Runner's *teeming streets by production illustrator Tom Southwell.*

Citing leaps forward in special effects, rather than real life space exploration, as the reason for the popular success of science fiction films from *2001: A Space Odyssey* to *Close Encounters of the Third Kind*, Dick was pleased that "spaceships no longer dangle on strings, no longer fizz, hesitate or wobble past you, as in the old *Flash Gordon* serials. The monsters are no longer inflated rubber toys haltingly mimicking what the average ten-year-old could dream up…" However, this more convincing world of spaceships and monsters seemed to be at the expense of serious storytelling. "As a writer, I'd sort of like to see some of my ideas, not just special effects of my ideas, used… concepts that awaken the mind rather than the senses…"

It was a mild plea from a writer who was aware, based on the options already taken on his work, that he may be seeing many films made from his stories in years to come. It was also a comment many science fiction fans and movie fans would agree with, increasingly so as the 1980s and 1990s wore on and computer-generated imagery developed to levels beyond what even Dick could conceive of in 1981.

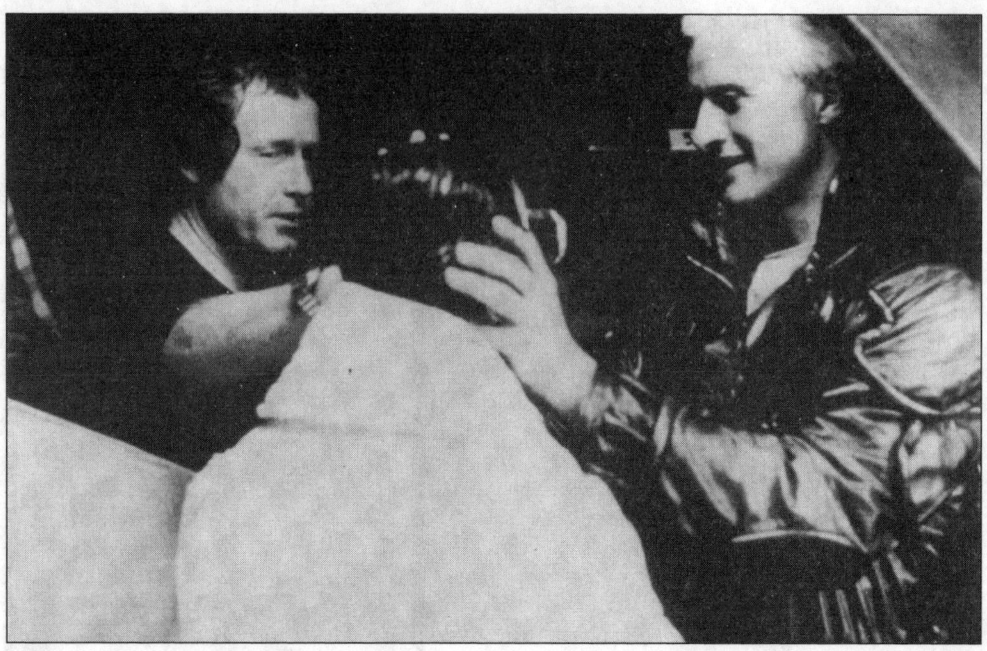

***Above:** Bringing a key moment in the script to life: Roy Batty meets his Maker.*

The people behind *Blade Runner*, especially the newly-involved Warner Bros., were furious with Dick's piece (he made sure to send them a copy!), not because of the sentiments he expressed but because, as he wrote: "[The script for *Blade Runner*] bore no relation to the book. I had a hell of a time getting my hands on the screenplay. No one involved in the *Blade Runner* project has ever spoken to me. But that's okay, I haven't spoken to them."

According to Paul Sammon's interview with Dick, excerpted in his in-depth *Cinefantastique* piece of July-August 1982, the response was immediate and heavy-handed. "After not hearing from anyone for all that time," Dick said, "I suddenly got an obnoxious call from them one afternoon, wherein they immediately said they were angry that I had a copy of the script and demanded to know just where I had got it!" Dick was furious that as the author of the source novel, anyone connected to the project should take that approach to him, especially as he'd obtained the script legitimately through producer Michael Deeley's lawyers. He was also warned to stop using the word 'android' as Ridley Scott disapproved of it, which he saw as a further insult to his original novel title.

Attitudes behind the scenes had, thankfully, changed with the switch from Filmways to The Ladd Company/Warner and the arrival of David Peoples. Realising that in Dick they had a potential asset, an effort was now made by *Blade Runner*'s producers to bring the author on board. Relatively new to Hollywood at the time, but now a veteran publicist and studio 'fixer', Jeff Walker was assigned the job of mollifying Dick and turning him into a potential publicity asset for *Blade Runner*, rather than a detractor. Walker would function as a liaison between Warners, the film's producers and Philip K. Dick. The first task was to get the Peoples script to the author to read.

Luckily, Dick was much happier with Peoples' revised screenplay. "He smoothed out the dialogue and reworked certain scenes. The whole idea of the replicants being infused with premature ageing [their limited lifespans] was a new twist," said Dick. "Dropping Rachael's suicide, rethinking the final confrontation as a wonderful moving sequence and by any other number of touches, Peoples transformed the screenplay into a beautiful, symmetrical reinforcement of my original work."

For his part, Peoples believed that Dick had overestimated his contribution to the revised screenplay, but if it made the author happy, so be it. "Dick probably didn't understand how much of a collaborative art film-making is. For example, Harrison Ford and Rutger Hauer contributed some very nice ideas concerning their dialogue. I gather from Dick's reaction that he felt that my revisions had turned the script back towards his novel. That's just really the force of the ideas in his book turning everybody back."

For his part, as an observer of events, Paul M. Sammon felt that Dick was merely being protective of his source novel, but was not averse to the changes required by adaptation into a movie. "Dick was surprisingly pragmatic about the necessary alterations, especially given his hatred of Hollywood," noted Sammon. "He was realistic about the adaptation process. Phil was always the first to concede that there was no practical way to bring everything he'd written in *Sheep?* to the screen. Dick also became quite enthusiastic about what he felt David Peoples had brought to the *Blade Runner* rewrite. In fact, I distinctly recall Phil was most excited about was how Peoples had successfully transposed what Dick called the 'essential thematic material' of *Electric Sheep* into the *Blade Runner* script. He wasn't really concerned about getting a line-by-line adaptation of *Sheep?* onto the screen — he just wanted to make sure the film-makers retained the novel's core concerns."

Above: *More urban detail: Tom Southwell's brilliantly simple street crossing sign.*

The whole *SelecTV Guide* episode was an unfortunate and, no doubt, unwelcome distraction from the fraught process of actually getting the film made. Ironically, none of it had to happen, as Dick would have been happy to have been involved with the film at an earlier stage. "I would have loved to have given some kind of input to the production, free, gratis, or to have been able to act as a feedback loop to whomever was doing the screenplay."

With a shooting script approved by the novel's author ready, sets standing and casting underway, director Ridley Scott was finally prepared to roll the cameras. It had been twelve years since the first film option had been taken out on the book, but now Philip K. Dick was all set to watch *Do Androids Dream of Electric Sheep?* be transformed into a movie called *Blade Runner*. ■

TEARS IN RAIN

The fraught making of *Blade Runner*, which sees Philip K. Dick carping from the sidelines before undergoing sight stimulation on his brain...

"My life and creative work are justified and completed by *Blade Runner*. I think *Blade Runner* is going to revolutionise our conceptions of what science fiction is and, more, can be." — Philip K. Dick in a letter to Jeff Walker of The Ladd Company, October 1981.

If the process of arriving at an acceptable screenplay for *Blade Runner* had been a long and fraught one, the actual production of the movie would be no different. While the scripting of *Blade Runner* had continued, sets had been built for key interior locations, model, design and effects work was progressing and — most important of all — casting had been underway.

The main role to fill was that of the film's hero, Rick Deckard. Casting professionals Mike Fenton and Jane Feinberg had been tapped to find the right actor for the role, a character now very far removed from Dick's original real animal-desiring functionary. Ridley Scott and the producers, Michael Deeley and ousted scriptwriter Hampton Fancher, were all involved in whittling down the list of potential leading men.

Considering the right actor for Deckard was something Fancher had been doing in his head for several years. In the mid-1970s when he had made his first failed attempt to option Dick's novel, Fancher pictured Robert Mitchum in the role. At that time the most recent movie Mitchum had made was 1975's *Farewell, My Lovely*, in which he played Philip Marlowe. Mitchum's portrayal had fed into Fancher's own thoughts on the character of Deckard, and while he was aware of possible age-issues in using Mitchum, he saw the actor as a good yardstick by which to measure other possibilities.

By the time the film was on the edge of entering production, however, Fancher had revised his thoughts on Deckard. He now gravitated towards a characterisation more like that in Dick's original novel, more of a struggling 'little man' than a macho bounty hunter. Fancher even suggested some possible actors: Tommy Lee Jones and Christopher Walken. Fancher's main fear was that Deckard would end up being portrayed in the movie as a standard film noir private eye or gumshoe, albeit projected into a future environment.

***Opposite:** The poster for* Blade Runner's *initial release attempted to capture the movie's atmosphere.*

In the summer of 1980 Ridley Scott had settled on the actor he felt would make the perfect Rick Deckard: Dustin Hoffman. Scott was a fan of Hoffman's work, and the director felt that the actor's somewhat diminutive stature would not affect his ability to play an SF hero. As far as Fancher was concerned, the remote possibility of casting Hoffman was nothing more than a star name offered up to the money men as an example of the kind of bankable actor the production might pursue for the lead. Regardless of Fancher's feelings, Hoffman

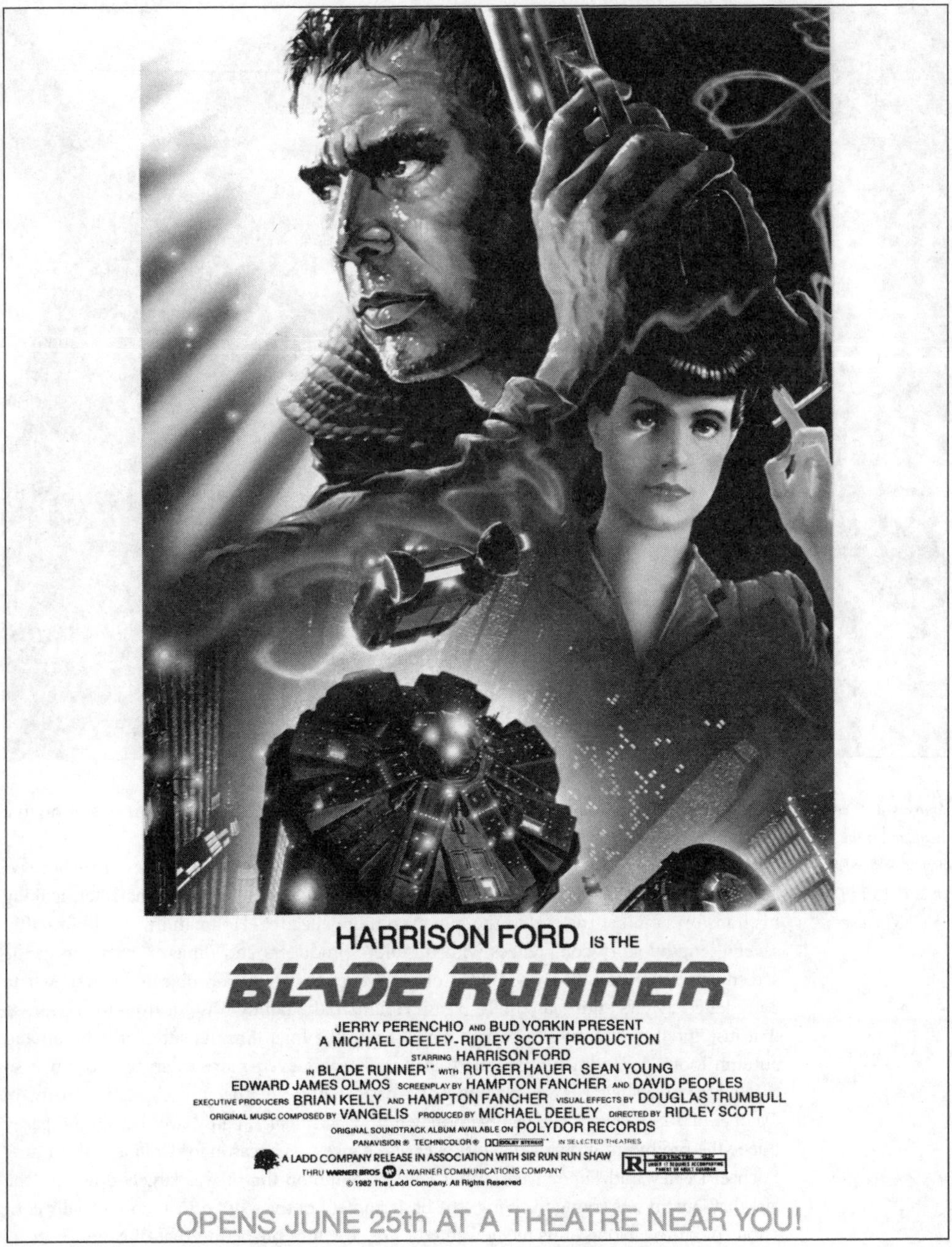

HARRISON FORD IS THE
BLADE RUNNER
JERRY PERENCHIO AND BUD YORKIN PRESENT
A MICHAEL DEELEY-RIDLEY SCOTT PRODUCTION
STARRING HARRISON FORD
IN BLADE RUNNER™ WITH RUTGER HAUER SEAN YOUNG
EDWARD JAMES OLMOS SCREENPLAY BY HAMPTON FANCHER AND DAVID PEOPLES
EXECUTIVE PRODUCERS BRIAN KELLY AND HAMPTON FANCHER VISUAL EFFECTS BY DOUGLAS TRUMBULL
ORIGINAL MUSIC COMPOSED BY VANGELIS PRODUCED BY MICHAEL DEELEY DIRECTED BY RIDLEY SCOTT
ORIGINAL SOUNDTRACK ALBUM AVAILABLE ON POLYDOR RECORDS
PANAVISION® TECHNICOLOR® IN SELECTED THEATRES
A LADD COMPANY RELEASE IN ASSOCIATION WITH SIR RUN RUN SHAW
THRU WARNER BROS A WARNER COMMUNICATIONS COMPANY
© 1982 The Ladd Company. All Rights Reserved
R
OPENS JUNE 25th AT A THEATRE NEAR YOU!

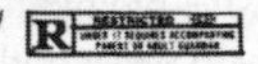

Above: *After Dustin Hoffman left the project, Ridley Scott chose Harrison Ford to be his leading man.*

did apparently read the screenplay and expressed strong interest in the part, resulting in a series of meetings with Scott and producer Michael Deeley.

Exercising his star muscle, Hoffman requested another script rewrite. Fancher was happy to oblige and suggested making Deckard a tougher and meaner character, making his transformation at the end of the film even more effective. Hoffman involved himself in several lengthy story conferences with the film's producers and director, resulting in the screenplay being heavily revised. One of the scenes that Hoffman objected to was where Batty killed Tyrell's entire family. To please Hoffman, the family was cut from the script, so that just Tyrell dies, a revision which made it into the final film. As summer wore on and autumn loomed, Hoffman's requested changes became even more extensive, so much so that all involved felt he was changing the basic outline of the movie's story. Finally, in October of 1980, Dustin Hoffman withdrew from *Blade Runner*, partly over his fee and partly due to the producers' growing disquiet over his changes. As a reason for Hoffman's departure, Michael Deeley told *Future Noir* author Paul M. Sammon that it was largely down to "the fact that Dustin was trying to change the basic content of the story into a more socially conscious picture… None of us really wanted to see the film pushed in that direction."

With principal photography scheduled for January 1981, the production only had three months to secure an alternative leading man. Hampton Fancher's then-girlfriend, actress Barbara Hershey, recommended Harrison Ford. The rising star was in London, shooting on *Raiders of the Lost Ark*. Ford, who'd been acting since the late 1960s, had only recently come to prominence in Hollywood, largely thanks to 1977's *Star Wars*. Previously, he'd appeared in George Lucas' *American Grafitti*, Francis Ford Coppola's *Apocalypse Now* and *The Conversation* and in assorted other smaller supporting roles.

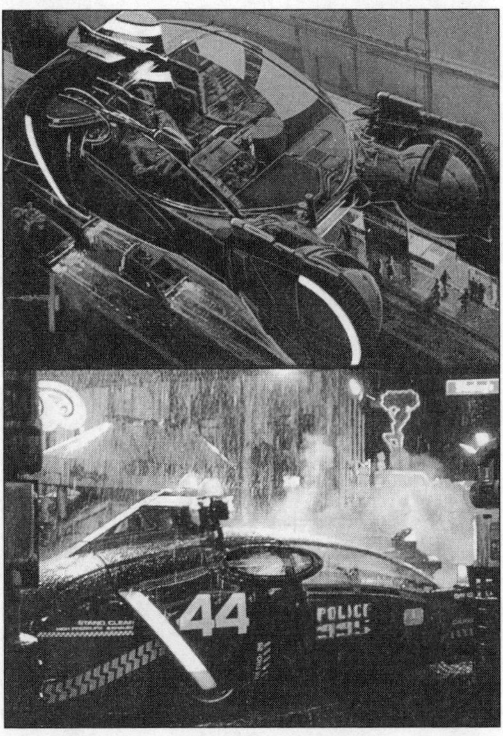

Above: *From page to stage:* Blade Runner's *production designs were vividly realised on screen.*

The *Blade Runner* production team visited the Steven Spielberg production in London and viewed some early rushes from *Raiders of the Lost Ark*, to gauge Ford's potential. Scott met with Ford in London. The actor had come to the meeting direct from the *Raiders* set, and was still wearing Indiana Jones' fedora hat. Scott had planned to have Rick Deckard, as a future private investigator akin to those in 1940s film noirs, wear similar headgear. The *Raiders* hat made that impossible, resulting in Rick Deckard's dramatic buzz cut instead.

Both Deeley and Scott felt they had finally found their man. Ford had shown great potential in two roles – Han Solo in *Star Wars* and Indiana Jones in *Raiders of the Lost Ark* – and had begun to be seen as a promising actor, yet had not been overexposed as a Hollywood personality. The hope was he'd bring both SF credibility from his previous roles, as well as his growing mainstream following, to *Blade Runner*. For his part, Ford was intrigued by the idea of playing a character who was both good at, and yet was repulsed by, his job. "Deckard's a pretty good 'blade runner', but also a reluctant one," Ford said on set in 1981. "That conflict, that ambiguity, makes for an interesting character. He also gets kicked around a lot…"

For Ridley Scott, Harrison Ford fulfilled the image of Deckard as a compromised hero straight out of a 1940s dime detective novel. "Deckard is a detective, like Sam Spade or Philip Marlowe, a man who follows a hunch to the end," said Scott in the *Blade Runner* publicity notes issued in 1982. "He's in trouble because he's begun to identify with his quarry, the replicants. [Harrison] Ford possesses some of the laconic dourness of Bogey [Humphrey Bogart], but he's more ambivalent, more human. He's almost an anti-hero."

Having found his hero, Ridley Scott then set about lining up his villains, the androids of *Blade Runner*: Roy Batty, Pris and Leon prime among them. Dutch actor Rutger Hauer was tapped by Scott to play the leader of the rogue replicants. The director has seen his performance in Paul Verhoeven's *Soldier of Orange*. "I wanted somebody who was physically not

Above: *The vehicles closely follwed the design concepts of Syd Mead.*

'American', was apart somehow," said Ridley Scott in a contemporary interview in *Starburst*. "Certainly in the film he's Teutonic, and that was an instinctive choice, really, to go in that direction..." For the 'pleasure model' Pris, Scott selected Daryl Hannah, then relatively unknown. Cult B-movie actor Brion James filled the part of Leon, while Joanna Cassidy was cast as Zhora.

The other leading role to be filled was that of unsuspecting replicant Rachael. Director Ridley Scott "saw something visually in Sean Young that he wanted," claimed Katherine Haber, production executive on *Blade Runner*, in the documentary *On The Edge of Blade Runner*. "She had to look great," admitted Scott, while claiming that he'd always go for acting ability over looks.

"That was the best casting experience I ever had on a picture," said Deeley of the overall process which also resulted in character actors like Joe Turkel (Tyrell), Edward James Olmos (Gaff), William Sanderson (J. F. Sebastian), M. Emmet Walsh (Captain Bryant) and James Hong (Chew) joining the cast. "We went for people who were 'original' looking," admitted Deeley.

After a year of pre-production and numerous script rewrites, *Blade Runner* finally began principal photography on 9 March 1981, three months later than planned. It was a gruelling production due to the fact that much of the action took place at night, resulting in weeks of night shooting. Rather than shoot on location, with cities such as New York, Atlanta and London considered, the decision was made to shoot in the more controllable environment of the famous New York street set on the Warner Bros. back lot in Hollywood. Built over seventy years previously and featured in classic film noir movies like *The Maltese Falcon* and *The Big Sleep*, the back lot had been used and reused in an amazing variety of movies. Now it was to provide the future setting for the adventures of Rick Deckard. Production designer Lawrence G. Paull was responsible for transforming the standing street set into 'Ridleyville', a process which had taken a full ten weeks, with a further month devoted to set dressing. "It was a tight schedule," noted Paull. "In the nightclub area, for example, we were literally finishing up details during the day for that night's shoot." Another reason for shooting on this set at night was so the production would not have to matte out the vibrant green Hollywood hills, very visible at the end of the street and not-at-all in keeping with the gritty, overbuilt, desolate urban environment of *Blade Runner*. The entire New York street set was used by the production, providing a convincing future environment for the actors.

Syd Mead, *Blade Runner*'s 'visual futurist', came up with the concept of the multilayered city, built up into the sky, with "decent people" never venturing below level sixty, and the ground level having become a kind of social basement, inhabited by low-lifes and criminals.

Mead was also responsible for the vehicles featured in the movie, including the iconic spinners and the advertising blimps. Mead was happy to provide Ridley Scott with what the director called 'layering', a lot of visual detail: perhaps even too much for the viewer to take in on a single viewing. "Ridley had his own particular vision," noted Mead in *Cinefantastique*. "He'd always say we weren't making a hardware movie. What he wanted were backgrounds that reflected an everyday, workaday level of technology, yet backgrounds that would still be sufficiently impressive to interest an audience…"

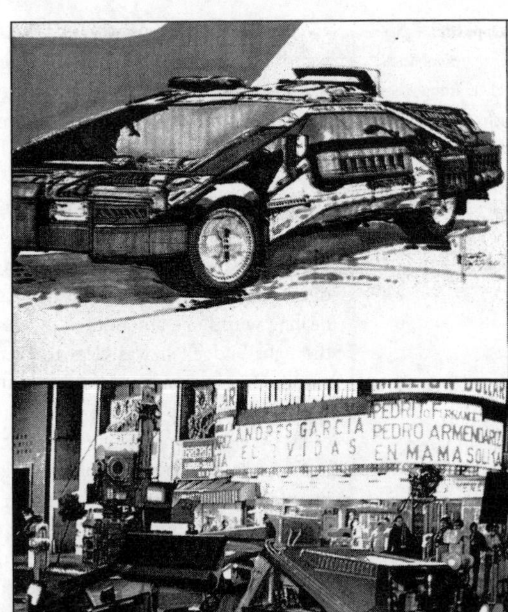

Above: *Syd Mead felt layered visual detail in his designs helped engage the audience.*

The *Blade Runner* crew were also tasked with transforming some real-world locations — including LA's famous Union Station (as the impressive monolithic police HQ), a famous Frank Lloyd Wright-designed house in Los Feliz (as Deckard's apartment) and the white-tiled 2nd Street underground road tunnel — into futuristic locations indicative of 2019 Los Angeles. Most famously, the production utilised the iconic Bradbury Building, located in a rather seedy area of downtown Los Angeles, as the home of toy builder J. F. Sebastian. Commissioned in 1893 by millionaire Lewis Bradbury, the building was designed by George Wyman, who was inspired by ideas gleaned through sessions with a Ouija board and architectural notions from Edward Bellamy's *Looking Backward*, a utopian novel set in the year 2000. The location turns up repeatedly in film and TV, from an acclaimed episode of *The Outer Limits* SF TV show scripted by Harlan Ellison to the 1994 Jack Nicholson movie *Wolf*. "I imagined this had once been a marvellous old hotel, but because of the off-world colonisation push, Sebastian is the only person living there," noted Paull. Hampton Fancher wasn't keen on the Bradbury Building showing up in *Blade Runner*. "I said to Ridley, 'That's ridiculous. Every TV show in the world has used that building! That's a bad idea, don't use that building…' And he said, '…not the way I'll use it.'"

Interiors, for Sebastian's apartment (littered with his robot mannequins, some of them played by real people, including short actors) and another forty-six sets, were constructed at the Burbank Studios. The impressive sets included Tyrell's office, featuring Ridley Scott's trademark twenty-foot high columns (also seen to some degree in *Legend*, *Alien* and *Someone to Watch Over Me*) and the interior of Deckard's apartment (with a 1920s look to it). Location filming also took place in a set constructed within a frozen meat locker in Vernon, California in below-zero temperatures to simulate Chew's Ice House.

Opposite: *A glimpse of the visual detail* Blade Runner *has to offer: a 'Ridleyville' street scene and pre-production art, male nuns and Tom Southwell's futuristic magazine covers.*

"The conditions we were shooting in were so unbearable: it was boiling hot, it was wet, it was damp," recalled Katherine Haber in *On The Edge of Blade Runner*. Cast and crew had to endure difficult conditions throughout the shoot, as Ridley Scott engulfed his 'retro-fitted' interior and exterior locations with smoke and dry ice to create what is now seen as the unique *Blade Runner* signature look. "The crew were walking around with surgical masks on," commented M. Emmet Walsh.

The conditions on set were only one of several factors which slowly contributed to a strong feeling of discontent throughout the production. Ridley Scott was, essentially, a stranger in a strange land, working in Hollywood for the first time with a cast and crew who didn't really understand what he was trying to achieve. On top of this, Scott himself was dealing with huge amounts of pressure from the studio and the film's financiers to stick to the tight budget. It was clear to everyone on the production that Ridleyville didn't come cheap. "I became a screamer," admitted a more mature Scott of his difficulties in communicating, especially with the crew (something which had also happened during the shooting of his previous film *Alien*, in London). "I got really angry, which is not good because screaming doesn't get you anywhere, really." Scott was increasingly annoyed at crewmembers questioning his decisions, resulting in him having to explain why he needed to retake certain shots. Financier Bud Yorkin, visiting the set, became concerned at Scott's repeated retakes and wondered how the director could tell the difference between one take and another. On some occasions, it came down to things like the size and shape of shadows somewhere in the background of the shot not being to Scott's liking. It may seem trivial now, and it may have seemed like a waste of time, money and effort to some on the production, but in retrospect it can be clearly demonstrated that *Blade Runner* has lasted largely due to the unique (and often imitated) visual detail with which Scott imbued the film. "It wasn't wilful on any-one's side," claimed Michael Deeley. "It's just that they weren't perfectionists like Ridley."

One of the significant clashes was between the director and the star. Harrison Ford felt rather lost in the future world created on the Warner Bros. back lot, while his director seemed more concerned about the detail of the sets rather than the detail of the actors' performances. "Back then, I wasn't given to spending a lot of time on explanation and [ego] stroking," admitted Scott in *On The Edge of Blade Runner*. "I've got too much to do, y'know. I'd spent a year with *Blade Runner* and I knew it inside out, all Harrison had to do was trust me. However, Harrison was not used to working that way. I think he's awfully good in the movie, and I still believe it's one of his best films." Ford disliked his time working on *Blade Runner*, largely it seems due to what he perceived as a lack of artistic support from his director, and has rarely talked about the film. But then, Ford doesn't like talking much about the *Star Wars* trilogy, the films which arguably gave him his Hollywood career. "It's no secret that Ridley and I had a degree of disagreement about the character, and Ridley's ambition — and he held on to it — was that the audience come to understand at [a certain] point in time quite near the end of the film that Deckard was, as well, a replicant," Ford told movie TV show *Encore*. "I felt that the audience should have one clear emotional representative on screen, someone that they could identify with. Other than that, I think we easily came to agreement on most of the rest of what we did."

Rutger Hauer had no such problems with his director, seeming to find Scott's European approach to making movies much more understandable. He and the director

ATARI

DWNTN

HORN
$20.
THE COSMIC ORGASAM
HOT LUST IN SPACE
NEW OILED SHOTS TO SPREAD ON
NOSE-TRODE SEX
TIT JOB REVIEW
SCRATCH & SNIFF CENTERSPREAD

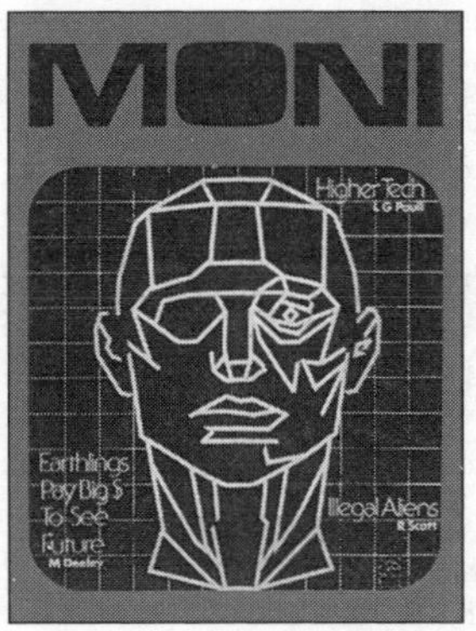
MONI
Higher Tech
L G Paull
Earthlings Pay Big $ To See Future
M Deeley
Illegal Aliens
R Scott

ALL THE NEWS THAT'S FIT TO KILL JAN. 2020
KILL
WEEKLY
98 DEAD IN SPINNER DIVE
NEW HEART BREAKER
GUARD DOGS YOU NEVER FEED!
DEATH PENALTY SNUFFS 12 JURORS IN FREAK ACCIDENT.
COLOR SPREAD

chimed so much that Scott, famously, let Hauer rewrite and augment his dialogue for his 'death' scene, adding the immortal "tears in rain" line, on the last night of filming. As the sun rose, Hauer and Ford played their final scene with Hauer delivering his new lines and, according to David Peoples, finishing with a sheepish "naughty boy" look to the camera as the film's fraught production came to a close.

Principal live-action photography for *Blade Runner* officially wrapped on the last day of June 1981, having spanned four months. However, after rushing the final weeks to beat a threatened Director's Guild strike, due to begin on 1 July 1981, which never materialised, Scott was able to continue working and shot various pick-up scenes through to the second week of July.

The end of shooting on the film led into the beginning of a whole new series of problems for Ridley Scott and the *Blade Runner* crew. Developing a workable screenplay and the fraught pre-production period had been a nightmare, and then principal photography had been an endurance test for all concerned. Post-production proved to be a period of even greater uncertainty and dramatic decisions, all against the backdrop of a loudly ticking clock as the movie's release date drew ever closer.

Editing, dubbing and optical effects occupied Ridley Scott as he shuttled to-and-fro between California and the UK, creating a working cut of the movie. The various problems during the shooting of *Blade Runner* were to continue having an effect right through post-production. "One of the basic rules of film-making that I learned very early on," said producer Michael Deeley, "is that very happy units usually produce very bland films." In *Future Noir*, production executive Katy Haber summed up the various tensions on the set by noting: "*Blade Runner* was a monument to stress."

Above: *Harrison Ford felt a lack of artistic support from his director.*

That stress was not to be relieved during the film's post-production period: in fact things got significantly worse for Ridley Scott and his crew. Much of the pressure during the shoot had come from Tandem — in the form of Bud Yorkin and Jerry Perenchio — as they watched their personal investment put under threat as the movie drifted behind schedule and over budget. Frustrated by the pace of the shoot and Scott's attention to detail and habit of filming multiple takes of each scene, Yorkin found it ever more difficult to contain his concerns. When principal photography wrapped, some $5 million over budget, Tandem — in their role as completion guarantors — stepped in to take over the production, effectively firing the director and producer.

Although technically they'd been removed from the project (the pair had been informed by letter that they were in breach of the terms of the original agreement under which they would make *Blade Runner*), neither Scott nor Deeley ever actually stopped working on the film. Whatever Tandem may have felt about their position, it seems likely that producing partner Warner Bros. (and Alan Ladd Jr) made it clear that the director and producer were still vital to the film actually being completed. The 'firing' seems to have been an attempt by Tandem to exert some more control over the project. To that extent the move succeeded, as the partners in Tandem clearly had more 'creative' input into *Blade Runner* during the controversial and difficult post-production process than they had during any other stage.

While Doug Trumbull (who'd begun his career on *2001: A Space Odyssey*) and his team at the newly formed Entertainment Effects Group worked on model shots and other special effects from April 1981, Scott worked to assemble his hard-won material into a final edit. By September, with many of the special effects shots finalised, Scott had a working assemblage of the film. Composer Vangelis, whose most recent movie score had been for Oscar-winner *Chariots of Fire*, was hired to provide a distinctive musical accompaniment to *Blade Runner*'s dystopic, culture-blend vision of the future.

Scott then approached Tandem requesting permission to reshoot some material and to shoot additional scenes he felt the film required, both to clarify narrative or story points and to expand on character moments. His written requests included a full-on dance performance scene to introduce Zhora, a new introduction for the character of Roy Batty, and various minor insert shots. With their eye on the financial bottom line as ever, Tandem refused to fund these additional shots. Scott was forced to finish the film and make it work with whatever material he had already shot.

Left: *Scott found an ally in fellow European Rutger Hauer during the fraught production process.*

Right and below: *Production art by Mentor Huebner, showing the extended Zhora snake dance sequence Ridley Scott wanted to add to the film.*

Despite the fact that the film was far from finished, by early 1982 Warner Bros. (who were distributing in the US) began to gear up their *Blade Runner* publicity campaign, to build awareness. Publicity and marketing can of course often be a crucial factor in the success or failure of a movie, regardless of the actual quality of the film. During the post-production period on *Blade Runner*, a team of publicists had been busy talking up the movie and creating suitable promotional materials, including a cinema trailer and an Electronic Press Kit — a sixteen-minute short 'making of' film chronicling a sanitised version of the film's production process and featuring 'talking heads' interviews with Scott, Harrison Ford and designer Syd Mead, among others. During the post-production of *Blade Runner*, the movie's marketing team decided it would be a good idea to have a 'novel of the film' on sale at the time of the movie's release, as an additional publicity tool. Ignoring the fact that the movie was based on an already pre-existing novel, a request was made of Philip K. Dick's agent to allow a novelisation of the film script to be written. "I was offered a great deal of money, and a cut in the merchandising rights, if I would do a novelisation of the screenplay, or if I would let someone like Alan Dean Foster do it," Dick recalled in *Cinefantastique*. "My agent figured that I would make about $400,000 from the deal."

BLADE RUNNER
– A Story of the Future –
Illustrated with More Than 60 Color Photographs
Based on the Movie Starring Harrison Ford

Attractive though the money must have been — it being much more than he had ever earned from any of his novels or from selling the film rights to *Do Androids Dream of Electric Sheep?* — Dick was against the idea for one very simple reason: "Part of this package required the suppression of my original novel. I said, 'No'. They got nasty again, threatening to withdraw the logo rights, [which would mean] we wouldn't be able to say that my book was the novel on which *Blade Runner* was based, and we'd be unable to use any stills from the film. They eventually caved-in, [but] in re-releasing the original novel I only made about $12,500, but I kept my integrity. And my book!"

Dick only won that battle up to a point. While *Do Androids Dream of Electric Sheep?* was re-issued as he'd originally written it, albeit tagged with the *Blade Runner* film logo, there were other spin-offs which he didn't prevent. Prime among them was a 'junior' novelisation of the film by Les Martin called *Blade Runner: A Story of the Future*. Published by Random House, this heavily illustrated ("More than 60 color photographs" claimed the cover), ninety-four-page book was a very basic re-telling of the film story, and has become something of a collectors' item since 1982. Other books included *Blade Runner: The Illustrated Screenplay* and *The Blade Runner Sketchbook*, featuring storyboards and art from the development of the film. There was also an official licensed *Blade Runner Souvenir Magazine*, featuring interviews with the movie's creators published by Ira Friedman Inc; a *Blade Runner* poster magazine; and a Marvel Comics adaptation of the movie across two issues.

Above: *Though Dick resisted a novelisation of the screenplay, there was a junior storybook and a comic strip adaptation.*

As the marketing process for *Blade Runner* began to gather pace, publicist Jeff Walker was busy trying to bring Dick onside. "The *Blade Runner* people finally found a real nice

Above: *Ridley Scott and Philip K. Dick meet for the first and only time. Photo: Kim Gottlieb. Courtesy of Isa Dick-Hackett.*

guy [Walker] to handle me," Dick told Gregg Rickman in *Philip K. Dick: In His Own Words*. "It was evident that I was really intractable. I could not be dealt with by the normal methods. This guy had read my novel, which really made a difference..."

It was Scott who decided in December 1981 that it was time to bring Philip K. Dick in from the cold, invite him to the studio, meet with him and allow him to see some of the work in progress, all with a view to converting the author to become a champion of the movie rather than a wildcard critic. "They sent Jeff Walker down here. He brought me photos..." recalled Dick. Walker did more than just bring some production stills, he arranged for Dick to visit the special effects company EEG in Marina Del Rey and view a reel of completed special effects footage. Dick was given the full Hollywood experience, as a limousine collected him from his Santa Ana apartment and drove him to EEG's complex. Despite the red carpet treatment, Dick was still not a happy man, telling anyone who'd listen how he'd hated the script and how the production had virtually ignored him. A tour of the effects facility and a chance to peruse the models and pre-production artwork failed to raise his spirits or change his attitude. "They showed us through the special effects studio, showed us the machinery and how all the special effects were done," recalled Dick in one of his final interviews, published posthumously in *Starlog*. A brief meeting with Ridley Scott helped clear the air, and resulted in one of the final public photos of Dick. "When I met Ridley — finally — I kept thinking of how I had continuously sniped at *Alien*. As he looked at me and I looked at him, I knew he had to be thinking about this... He was very cordial..."

Paul M. Sammon felt that the meeting was important to both men: "I would like to think that during their first and only meeting, which was admittedly rather short and superficial, Philip K. Dick and Ridley Scott recognised how much alike they were. Because Dick and Scott were two dedicated artists whose fame came from their love of the work, not from chasing the best deal."

David Dryer, one of the special photographic effects supervisors, was given the task of babysitting the author. "Philip Dick was reasonably unhappy," recalled Dryer in the *On The Edge of Blade Runner* documentary. "[Production executive] Katy Haber gave me a call and said, 'Put together the best-of-the-best in a reel.' Dick and his friend [Mary Wilson] went down to the screening room and said very little. I said, 'Roll it,' and the ten minutes of optical [effects] takes ran. Philip turned around and looked me right in the eye and said, 'How is this possible? I don't understand this... This feels exactly like what I had in my head when I was writing... How does this happen?' That moment was probably the best moment in my career, as I was thinking, 'We got it! We nailed it!'" Dick requested that the impressive reel of special effects work be run again. "[Ridley] Scott sat behind me to explain the continuity of each sequence he ran on the projector," said Dick in *Cinefantastique*.

Top and above: *Harrison Ford and Sean Young matched exactly Dick's vision of Deckard and Rachael.*

After the screening, Scott showed Dick some further material from the movie, including the latest stills of the main characters. The author came away from the meeting convinced that not only was Harrison Ford perfect for the character of Rick Deckard, but that Rutger Hauer was the only actor who could have played Roy Batty, and that Sean Young matched exactly his vision of Rachael. "It's like they did sight stimulation on my brain, [and] projected an image on the screen," Dick told Gregg Rickman. "That's exactly how I pictured her. If you'd laid out 100 photographs of 100 women, I could have unerringly picked that one, because that's Rachael. She's perfect..." That Young matched Dick's long sought-after image of the ideal woman, the ever-elusive 'dark-haired girl', may also have affected his judgment...

After discussing the film further with Scott, Dick was very much happier, even though there were other points upon which both men profoundly disagreed. Dick maintained that the replicants were horrible characters, the villains of the piece, whereas Scott saw them as superior beings, "Supermen who can't fly," in Dick's words. Dick's take on Deckard was that he became as dehumanised as the replicants through his task of tracking them down and eliminating them. The author hoped that Harrison Ford's performance might be subtle enough to draw out these moral ambiguities.

The author/director December summit had the desired effect: Dick was now an effective cheerleader for the film. In a handful of interviews he gave, right up to his untimely death before the film was released, he never failed to champion the movie while not being coy, either, about his earlier difficulties with the project. "The opening is seen from a flying vehicle," he told *Starlog*, "as it's slowly landing on top of a 400-story building. This titanic building dominates the landscape, which is exactly my fantasy of what it would have to be like forty years from now, when the movie is set..."

Above: *A shot of these dancers was included in the 'work print', but was deleted from the released film.*

With the author seemingly back on board, Ridley Scott returned to fine-tuning his final edit. Dick's death, on 2 March 1982, did little to hinder the film's progress, although all involved with the movie were saddened by his passing. According to *Future Noir* author Paul M. Sammon, "The unexpected death of Philip K. Dick had absolutely no effect on the film, other than to give it a sentimental patina — 'Here's the movie its source author never lived to see.' The only impact Phil's death had on *Blade Runner* was an emotional one. However, it is terribly sad that Phil never had a chance to see the final product. Just as it's unfortunate that, after spending a lifetime of working so hard for such little remuneration, Philip K. Dick never got the chance to reap a few more financial benefits from the first motion picture adaptation of his work."

Ridley Scott attended two preview screenings of his movie, a 'work print', mere days after Dick's death, on 5/6 March 1982 in Denver, Colorado and Dallas, Texas. These screenings were of crucial importance as they resulted in significant changes to the movie, leading to the version of the film that was finally released.

The audiences for these sneak previews seem to have been attracted by the prospect of a new Harrison Ford adventure movie, more akin to *Raiders of the Lost Ark* or the *Star Wars* sequel, *The Empire Strikes Back*. Instead, they sat through a dark, gloomy movie that required the viewer to pay attention in order to fully understand what was going on. That level of comprehension was seemingly beyond the Denver and Dallas audiences, who greeted the end of the movie in confused silence and, according to one report of the Dallas screening, filed from the cinema as if in attendance at "a funeral".

Disheartened by the reaction, *Blade Runner*'s principals who were in attendance — Scott, Deeley and Haber — nevertheless felt that they could fix any story issues with additional post-production work. However, worse was to come after the Warner Bros. marketing teams had analysed the reactions of the audience recorded on response cards distributed following the screening. These showed there were major issues with the film that went far beyond a confusing storyline. Many felt the film was hard to follow (with some in the dark as to what a 'blade runner' was); the violence was deemed "too graphic"; the film was too slow; and it was judged to be grim and oppressive. Significant concern surrounded the abrupt ending, with a lift door closing on the departure of Sean Young and Harrison Ford. And what was that tinfoil unicorn all about, anyway? Often overlooked, however, were the positive comments contained in the same response cards in which just as many people praised the film for its distinctive visuals and attention to detail, its special effects and

***Above:** 1940s film noir was a strong influence on* Blade Runner, *from the lighting to the much-despised voice-over.*

technical achievements. Warner Bros. however ignored much of the positive comment and decided instead to focus on attempting to fix the negatives. It seemed clear that Ridley Scott still had much to do to make *Blade Runner* work.

"I was compelled by my contract to do a series of voice-overs which explained what people were seeing," Harrison Ford told *Encore* of the post-test screening changes imposed on *Blade Runner*. "I thought — and Ridley thought — [this was] completely unnecessary. It really disadvantaged the film. As I remember it, most of the critics' strongest negatives were in respect of the voice-over. Which I agreed with absolutely..."

The controversial voice-over added to *Blade Runner* just before release became one of the most notorious cases of producers fiddling with a director's vision. Widely despised as the reputation of the film grew in stature over the years, myths and rumours grew up surrounding the voice-over, including the 'fact' that Harrison Ford so disliked having to do it that he delivered his lines in a dull monotone. The voice-over does have its advocates, though: it does impart important information that some viewers were clearly failing to pick up, and it handily echoed and reinforced the notion that *Blade Runner* was in the tradition of the hard-boiled film noir detective dramas of the 1940s, many of which were narrated by their protagonists.

The truth about the voice-over is that some versions of the early scripts of *Do Androids Dream of Electric Sheep?* included Rick Deckard's narration. This was one of

Philip K. Dick's principal objections to Hampton Fancher's early screenplay. Fancher admitted that introducing the voice-over in the early script was his idea, extending Scott's vision of the movie as an old-fashioned, yet simultaneously futuristic, film noir. Dick was disparaging of this approach: "[It was] like: 'It was a dirty town. It was a dirty job. Somebody had to do it. I was that somebody. My name's Deckard.' I mean, my God!" While the final voice-over narration foisted on the film isn't quite that bad, it does come close…

However, Ridley Scott wasn't looking as far back as the 1940s when he originally conceived of the idea of a voice-over. He'd admired how Martin Sheen's character in Francis Ford Coppola's *Apocalypse Now* had gained greater depth through being able to indicate his feelings and reactions to events through his narration. That was the kind of character-rich voice-over Scott wanted. Instead it became a simple tool to fill in narrative gaps and explain to the audience what was happening and why, a knee-jerk fear reaction to some of the comment cards which had come back from the Dallas and Denver sneak peek screenings.

"The bottom line of Deckard's narration," Scott told Sammon in *Future Noir*, "is that we just couldn't get it. We wrestled with it. Neither Ford nor I were comfortable with it. It was over-explanation [and] it wasn't Chandleresque enough. The studio felt there were certain areas of confusion within the storyline. I'd felt that *Blade Runner* might be subtle, but also comprehensible…" The result was the voice-over was in, but only as a tool to explain

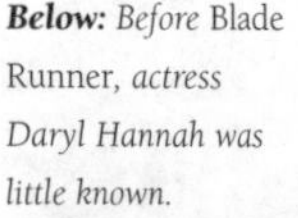

Below: *Before* Blade Runner, *actress Daryl Hannah was little known.*

things to the audience, not as a way of adding to Deckard's character or deepening his reactions to what was happening. That was what annoyed Harrison Ford.

Ford recorded not one, but three versions of the *Blade Runner* narration. The first was in November 1981, written by novelist Daryl Poniscan, who'd written the screenplay for 1973's *Cinderella Liberty*, rather than *Blade Runner* scripters Fancher or Peoples. According to Michael Deeley, Poniscan had been brought in — ironically at substantial additional expense — by Tandem's Bud Yorkin. Unhappy with that narration, Scott drew upon Peoples, who wrote a new version based upon his and Fancher's originally scripted narration. This was recorded at Pinewood in January 1982. "That voice-over became a real struggle," Peoples told Sammon.

Ford, speaking to *Details* magazine in 1992, recalled the voice-over debacle with some horror. "I hated them. Ridley hated them as well, but when the film went over budget, they made me do it. I went kicking and screaming to the studio to record it." This second narration was screened for Tandem executives, who then had it removed, except for some material over the Batty death scene. This minimal version was the one screened in Denver and Dallas.

The audience reaction to those screenings resulted in a third recording of a totally different, all-new voice-over. Yorkin took control of the situation and hired another friend, the veteran TV writer Roland Kibbee (*It Takes a Thief*), to script a final narration. This was recorded by Ford, with Yorkin and Katy Haber in attendance, in Beverly Hills. Neither director Ridley Scott nor producer Michael Deeley were involved. Haber believed that Ford was so fed up with *Blade Runner*, and particularly the on-going narration problems, and the fact that he disliked Kibbee's writing, that he deliberately dead-panned his delivery, hoping it would not be used. However, that third narration was the one that ended up on the initial release version of *Blade Runner*.

Both Hampton Fancher and David Peoples were horrified by the voice-over that was on the film when they saw it, each believing the other had been responsible. It was sometime later that they discovered that neither of them had written it, but they'd been heavily rewritten by Kibbee, working under close instruction from Yorkin. "We couldn't quite get it right, because whatever we did it seemed we were going along the 'Irving the Explainer' route, rather than it being an organic part of Harrison's character," admitted Scott of the imposed voice-over in an interview on *Encore*. "Harrison found it difficult. I found it difficult. I think we shouldn't have had it. You don't need it."

The voice-over wasn't the only change imposed on Ridley Scott's initial version of *Blade Runner*. The reaction to the Denver and Dallas sneak previews also resulted in the imposition of a 'happy ending' to the downbeat story. Instead of ending with the lift doors closing on the uncertain fate of Deckard and Rachael, they escape into a narratively unlikely verdant, depopulated landscape, complete with some hope for the future. In voice-over (written this time by a combination of Scott, Deeley, Haber and Ivor Powell) Deckard reveals that Rachael was a special model of replicant, with no termination date, so no four-year lifespan like Batty and the others. Therefore, like any 'human' couple, they would have no idea how much time together they had left…

Various problems had surrounded the ending of the film as scripted. The first scripted ending, pre-dating the involvement of Scott, saw Rachael on the edge of a roof with a real, living animal Deckard has bought. Rachael compares herself with Deckard's now-discarded synthetic animal, wondering if he will one day dump her for a 'real' human... Realising that the pair have no future together, she hands the animal to Deckard and throws herself from the roof. Deckard flees to the desert, confronts a struggling tortoise and gains new hope for humanity. This ending drew closely on Dick's book, though he despised it as the "Deckard-grows-in-stature-through-Rachael's-suicide" ending, and it was potentially even more downbeat than that attached to the sneak preview version of the film.

The July 1980 rewrite saw Deckard take Rachael to a snow-covered isolated area (which can actually be seen in one of the photographs he looks at while sitting at the piano in the final film), where she decides that part of being human is the ability to exercise choice, and she chooses to die rather than live out a limited four-year lifespan. This time it's Deckard who kills Rachael, at her request. By the December 1980 rewrite, this ending was still in place, but with the added speculation by Deckard that even though he wasn't a replicant, emotionally he was the same as them... By the February 1981 shooting script (which was continually revised during shooting), an all-new 'happy' ending had been created, which sees Deckard and Rachael escape the city to the country with Gaff in hot pursuit. This version ended with a last-minute revelation: the unicorn left by Gaff at Deckard's apartment signifies that Deckard too is, in fact, a replicant just like Rachael. Although scripted, that ending was never shot. "We ultimately ran out of time and money during principal photography and didn't have the resources to shoot that ending," admitted Michael Deeley in *Future Noir*. "Ridley also later changed his mind concerning the scripted climax during the editing of the picture. He now felt that it would be much better to visually end the film on a harder, more ambiguous note — the elevator doors closing on Deckard and Rachael..."

The test audience reaction to the 'elevator doors' ending resulted in the ideas for the originally intended 'happy' ending being revived. Katy Haber was dispatched to film helicopter landscape footage suitable for the 'wasteland' through which Deckard drives, but this turned out to be unusable. Producer Ivor Powell recalled Stanely Kubrick's shots from the 1980 Stephen King adaptation *The Shining*, many of which were not used, so the production was given permission to use that footage, even though the world outside *Blade Runner*'s urban sprawl now appeared to be empty, green and lush. Ford and Young were recalled for shots inside Deckard's car. *Blade Runner* was finished, once again...

Nevertheless, other alternative endings to the story became publicly available alongside the released film version. Due to advanced deadlines, the Marvel comic adaptation was prepared before the final cut, using the screenplay and photographs supplied by the production. It has yet another ending, which sees Deckard and Rachael escape from the city to the "North", to live out whatever time they have left together. Deckard's closing lines make this one of the more romantic endings to the story: "She'd never seen the great outdoors. I thought she might like snow. She was curious and full of questions. Of course, there were subjects we couldn't discuss and words we couldn't say. Like death. Like future. But for all that... Rachael was more alive than anyone I'd ever known..." The screenplay published in the book *The Illustrated Blade Runner* provided yet another variation (and also includes the infamous Deckard unicorn dream).

Above: *Preview audiences complained about the violence in the film.*

A third preview screening of *Blade Runner* took place in San Diego in May 1982, with Harrison Ford in attendance alongside Joanna Cassidy, Scott, Deeley, Alan Ladd Jr, Douglas Trumbull and John Hurt (who'd featured in Scott's previous movie, *Alien*). This slightly differently edited version of the film played to an audience largely made up of science fiction fans, who seemed to appreciate the film much more than the earlier Denver and Dallas audiences had. The major additions to the film were the final version of the narration and the upbeat, happy ending. The responses from this audience on the comment cards were positive enough for the Warner Bros. marketing reps to conclude that the problems identified by the earlier screenings had been substantially resolved, or at least dramatically lessened by the voice-over and the new ending. Work could now being in earnest on the final theatrical release.

Alan Ladd Jr set 25 June 1982 as the US domestic release date for *Blade Runner*. Between the successful San Diego screening and the full release of the film, Scott had responded to continued criticism that the film dragged in places by tightening up the edit, removing some minor shots and generally quickening the film's pace.

A film of Philip K. Dick's novel *Do Androids Dream of Electric Sheep?* had been in development for the best part of fifteen years. Now, it was finally a reality after much writing,

Above: *Despite negative initial reviews,* Blade Runner *would go on to enjoy a lifespan far longer than that of the film's replicants.*

rewriting, shooting, re-shooting, editing and re-editing. Perhaps the biggest irony was that by the summer of 1982, the author of the novel was no longer around to see the first film to be made from his work. *Future Noir* author Paul M. Sammon had an interesting take on Dick, having met him while covering the making of *Blade Runner*: "One reason I enjoyed speaking with Dick was because he was such a candid man. Amusing, too, and generous with his time. Moreover, Phil was incredibly, impressively articulate. Sometimes I'd listen to him talk and think that I was witnessing the dawn of the first organic computer; he was that good. Phil could confidently deliver paragraph after paragraph of the most interesting, exquisitely constructed sentences. And he was willing to expand on whatever topic I threw at him. Philosophy, religion, psychology, literature, jazz, politics, electronics, the true nature of evil — we marched through all of that. In fact, more than once I'd have to steer our conversations back to *Do Androids Dream of Electric Sheep?* or *Blade Runner*, because we'd find ourselves wandering far, far afield from the matter at hand. Still, it was always fascinating."

Perhaps it's just as well that Dick did not live to experience the reaction to the finished movie. Who knows how the largely negative critical response to *Blade Runner* might have affected the sensitive author? The initial commercial failure of the film was unexpected to all concerned. "All sensation and no heart," noted the *State and Columbia Record*. *The Los Angeles Times* commented on the slow pace: "Blade crawler might be more like it." *The New*

York Times simply dubbed it "a mess... muddled, gruesome..." Critical reaction tended to focus on one major point, a view articulated by Roger Ebert writing in *The Chicago Sun-Times*: "The movie's weakness is that it allows the special effects technology to overwhelm its story." Pauline Kael, writing in *The New Yorker*, was equally scathing. The few positive reviews (among them reviews in SF magazine *Starlog*, *Christianity Today* and *The Dallas Times Herald*, which prophetically stated "history will be kinder to *Blade Runner* than the critics...") were drowned out in the torrent of negative comment that swamped the popular press. Ironically much of the criticism specifically reacted against the late additions of the voice-over narration and the tacked on 'happy ending'.

This sea of critical comment had a significant effect on the movie's box office. A $6 million opening weekend (for a film that cost in excess of $28 million) was followed by weeks of falling attendance and decreasing box office receipts. The initial domestic US release of the film earned a cumulative box office take of only $14 million, a mere 50 per cent of the film's final cost before the additional cost of prints and advertising. That made *Blade Runner* a resounding financial failure by any standard.

Several explanations have been advanced for the failure of *Blade Runner* to find a popular audience in 1982. That same summer had seen a glut of special effects-driven science fiction movies, including the *Star Trek* sequel *The Wrath of Khan* and John Carpenter's then-spectacular remake of *The Thing*. Perhaps cinemagoers had seen enough SF. Alternatively, there was the suggestion that audiences drawn to the film by Harrison Ford were expecting another light-hearted romp like *Star Wars* or *Raiders of the Lost Ark*, which this film definitely was not. Finally, the gritty and pessimistic *Blade Runner* followed the upbeat and optimistic *E.T.: The Extraterrestrial* into cinemas. Was it simply the case that audiences entranced by the antics of a stranded space gnome were in no mood for a downbeat, dark, dismal tale of an android hunter? Whatever the reason, the *Blade Runner* story was at an end, and like that originally proposed for the film, it was downbeat and dark. Except, *Blade Runner* turned out to be the film that simply refused to go quietly...

Despite the fact that upon theatrical release in 1982 *Blade Runner* was declared an expensive flop, the film always had its vocal fans. While the reviews were largely negative — at least those that counted in Hollywood — there were others who talked up the film, and there were definitely fans of the movie who spread their high opinion of Ridley Scott's work through influential word of mouth.

It was, however, the nascent mediums of home video and cable TV which really saved *Blade Runner*. The rise of VHS video cassettes and laserdisc (the forerunner to DVD) gave many over-looked movies from the 1980s a second lease of life through rental stores. Indeed, the release of the slightly different, more violent 'international cut' of the film on laserdisc allowed American *Blade Runner* fans access to a different version of the film than that seen in theatres. Films like *Blade Runner*, which few had seen on the big screen, were willingly rented for an evening, especially by students who may have heard from their peers how fantastic the film was. In an attempt to continue to recoup their investment, *Blade Runner's* distributors quickly released the movie to the growing cable TV industry in the US, resulting in repeated screenings burning impressions of *Blade Runner* into the memories of those who tuned in. From being a movie largely ignored at the cinema, the mid-1980s saw

Blade Runner become a film viewed repeatedly by an ever-increasing audience, many of whom got something new from the film each time. By the middle of the following decade, *Blade Runner* had sold half a million copies on video.

Others took notice of this phenomenon, with film magazines the world over beginning to look back on *Blade Runner* as an underappreciated gem. Fanzines (amateur fan magazines) about the film sprung up around the world. The early 1990s even saw the publication of a book of academic essays, *Retrofitting Blade Runner*, which took the film very seriously indeed.

None of this growing interest can be divorced from the increasing visibility of the work of Philip K. Dick during this same period. In the wake of his death and the release of *Blade Runner*, a new interest was awakened in Dick's oeuvre. *The Transmigration of Timothy Archer*, his final novel, was one of his best. The movie of *Do Androids Dream of Electric Sheep?* — the original book was back on book store shelves in a big way thanks to Dick holding out over the novelisation issue — created a curiosity about the author. With many of Dick's novels back in print through the 1980s, readers (and Hollywood development executives) had plenty of material to read which put *Blade Runner* in a far larger context. A new literary subgenre of SF even grew up around the kind of material Dick had been writing for years: cyberpunk. Key among its authors were William Gibson, Bruce Sterling and Rudy Rucker: all self-declared fans of Philip K. Dick. Under 'cyberpunk' in the acclaimed *Encyclopedia of Science Fiction*, it is noted that, "An important forebear of cyberpunk was the film *Blade Runner*, whose near-future milieu — mean, drizzling, populous streets lit up by enormous advertisements for Japanese products, alternating street junk with hi-tech — is, in the intensity of its visual infodumps, like a template for a cyberpunk scenario." In addition, writers Dick had mentored during his last years in Orange County, like Tim Powers, James Blaylock and K. W. Jeter, began to enjoy a new level of success, and they proselytised their inspiration at every turn. In fact in the 1990s Jeter — a nascent cyberpunk author — turned his hand to writing a series of literary sequels to *Blade Runner*.

Jeter wrote three novels: *The Edge of Human, Replicant Night* and *Eye and Talon*, each of which took Dick's original characters and concepts in new directions. In *Blade Runner 2: The Edge of Human* (1995), Jeter attempts to fuse the storylines, characters and settings of Dick's original novel and Scott's film adaptation, with mixed success. Abducted and returned to the urban sprawl from which he'd escaped, Deckard has to use his blade runner skills to stay alive and one step ahead of his abductors. Other questions are explored, such as the nature of the 'missing' sixth replicant, and old characters reappear, with Holden stalking Deckard, and Sarah Tyrell, the original model for Rachael, is introduced. In *Blade Runner 3: Replicant Night* (1996), Deckard and Sarah Tyrell are living on Mars. Jeter introduces the conceit of making Deckard an advisor on a movie version of his blade runner experiences. Meanwhile, Sarah explores her own past, uncovering mysteries of her own childhood and a new replicant threat to Deckard. *Blade Runner 4: Eye and Talon* (2000, aka *Beyond Orion*), the last of the novels to date, was only published in the UK, and centred on a new female blade runner character, with Deckard absent for most of the plot. Each of the novels had a mixed reception from fans of the movie and Philip K. Dick's work, with Jeter failing to please all constituencies with his mix-and-match approach to the source material.

The *Blade Runner* games — a board game, a Commodore 64/Sinclair Spectrum computer game and, later, a PC-based game — were another spin-off to capture the imagination of fans. The board game, manufactured by a small, now long-defunct company in California, was an officially licensed product, but was never fully released. Only 100 boards were ever made, for test-marketing in Los Angeles and San Francisco in 1982 and 1983. Players moved skyscraper pieces around a *Blade Runner*-themed board after throwing a six-sided dice. Landing upon a Voight-Kampff Terminal square means the player has to undergo a V-K test to determine if they are a replicant — achieving a certain numerical score signifies replicant status. Any player identified as a replicant is then chased around the board by the other players until he is captured. Battered copies of the pre-production test board games sometimes turn up on internet auction sites.

The first official *Blade Runner* computer game was released for the Commodore 64 and Sinclair Spectrum, again during 1982-83, immediately following the film. The player takes the role of Deckard, tracking down and eliminating replicants. The game featured a poor electronic version of the Vangelis end titles theme, and licensing problems resulted in the game being promoted, bizarrely, as based on the music from *Blade Runner* rather than the movie *Blade Runner* itself!

In November 1997 Westwood Studios released an official PC game based firmly on the film, which proved to be rather more successful. Like the board game, it plays upon the question of who may or may not be a replicant, including the player himself. At the end of the game a photograph can be accessed and if the player character is in the group shot, it means they've been a replicant all along. Other characters featured in the game change their replicant status every time the game is played. A complex, graphics-rich adventure which was very much cutting edge for its time, the game even featured Sean Young, returning after fifteen years to voice the character of Rachael, alongside several of the film's other supporting actors, including Brion James and William Sanderson (in an early example of what has since become a regular and lucrative avenue for movie actors: voicing the spin-off computer game). The Westwood Studios game was well received, and even spawned books of its own: a lavish *Official Strategy Guide* (written from the lead character's point of view) published by Brady, and an *Unauthorized Guide* from Prima.

Away from the wide range of movie spin-offs, following *Blade Runner* the Philip K. Dick Award was instituted for the best new work of science fiction published in paperback in the US. Dick's name even became an adjective, as newspapers and magazines began to write about the increasingly technological real world as being 'phildickian'. *Blade Runner's* influence permeated Hollywood and beyond, through commercials, music

***Below:** The player himself may be a replicant in the* Blade Runner *spin-off PC game.*

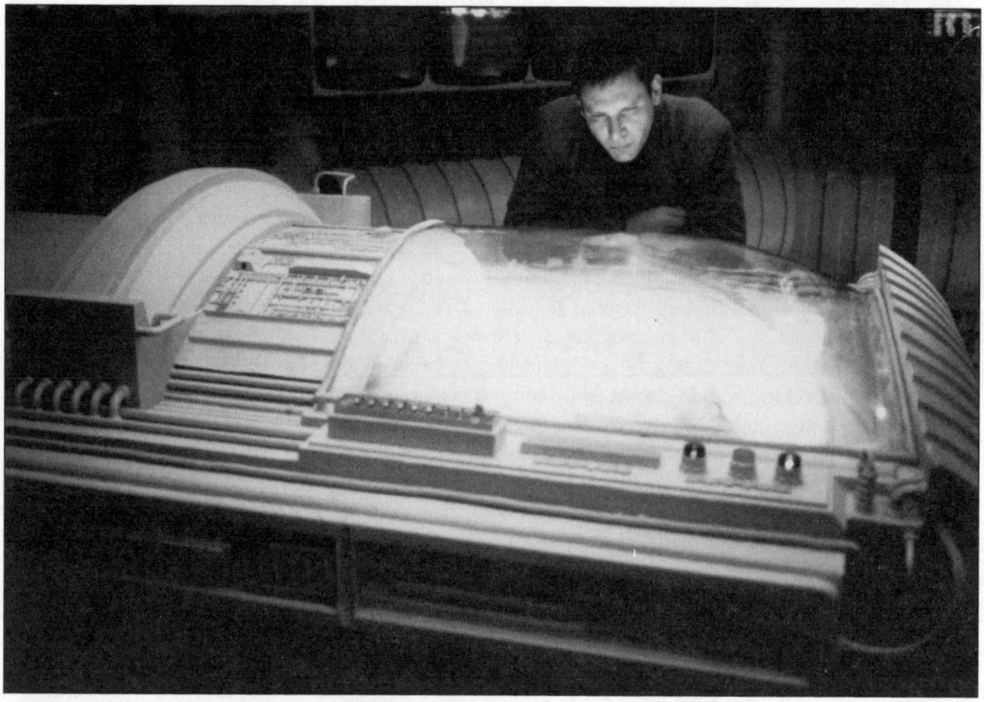

Above: *The hospital scene, missing from all released cuts of* Blade Runner.

videos and other big-budget science fiction blockbusters: Ridley Scott's dark, smoky vision of a wet and wild future became the *de facto* standard sci-fi 'shorthand' in visual media. For a 'flop' movie, the film's influence was immense and cannot be underestimated.

After almost a decade of growing prominence, it was inevitable that a cinema re-release of *Blade Runner* would happen. When the Los Angeles Fairfax Theatre requested a 70mm print of *Blade Runner* for their May 1990 festival of 70mm movies, Warner Bros. were happy to oblige, supplying a recently rediscovered 70mm print of the 'international cut' of the film. It quickly became apparent to those who attended the sold-out screening that they were, in fact, viewing a never-before-seen, very different version of the now-familiar *Blade Runner*. This, it turned out, was an early 'work print' of Ridley Scott's film, supplied from the Warner Bros. vaults in error: in fact the same version of the film that had been screened at the Denver and Dallas sneak peek screenings back in 1982. There was no narration on this version of the film, except right at the end over the death scene of Roy Batty. The ending of the film was a surprise to the audience, too. Rather than escaping into the country via out-takes from *The Shining*, this version ended abruptly with the lift door closing on Sean Young's Rachael.

A screening was arranged for Ridley Scott, who confirmed this was the 1982 work print. He also expressed interest in cleaning up and finishing off this version of the film for a possible 'Director's Cut' re-release. However, he was too busy working on *Thelma and Louise* at the time to personally supervise the required re-edit and post-production work, so Warner Bros. reluctantly shelved the project.

Further sold-out screenings of the work print followed in April 1991 at the Academy of Motion Picture Arts and Sciences theatre, which hosted the UCLA Los Angeles Perspectives Multimedia Festival. Again, the response, in the audience and the media, drew Warner Bros.' attention back to *Blade Runner*. Deciding to test the waters to see whether a big screen second outing for a film so widely seen on video, laserdisc and TV would be viable, Warner Bros. booked the original 'domestic cut' of *Blade Runner* in major US cities for a short run. September and October 1991 saw a 35mm print of the work print of *Blade Runner* run at the art house cinemas the NuArt in LA and the Castro Theater in San Francisco. The film played once again to sold-out houses, and broke records for box office at those theatres. So popular were the screenings that neither Daryl Hannah nor original screenwriter Hampton Fancher could get in...

This rough-and-ready, clearly unpolished version of *Blade Runner* was playing to ecstatic audiences, hungry for a fresh take on their favourite movie. In *Future Noir*, author Paul M. Sammon identifies seventy notable audio or visual differences between the infamous work print and the widely released 'domestic cut' and the 'international cut'. This rough draft of the more familiar (though unsatisfactory) version of the film was about to give *Blade Runner* a whole new lease of life, almost ten years after its initial failure at the US box office.

Ridley Scott, working in London on development of *1492: Conquest of Paradise*, was not even aware of the NuArt and Castro screenings of his rough draft work print. When he did find out, he expressed his displeasure to Warner Bros. that this unfinished assemblage was being promoted as a Director's Cut. At the time Warners were preparing to release the work print nationwide as a Director's Cut in time for the film's tenth anniversary in 1992. Scott once again offered to complete a proper, restored Director's Cut instead, incorporating the dream sequence of a unicorn he'd always wanted to add. Warners wanted to just release the film they already had, but Scott blocked this on artistic grounds: the work print was *not* his Director's Cut.

Eventually, Scott was allowed to work with the various best quality *Blade Runner* materials available to construct an all-new, genuine Director's Cut of the movie for March 1992. Scott produced a list of alterations and changes required to make the work print releasable and in line with the other versions of the film. What he wanted was a final version of the film, one he'd be happy to attach his name to as a definitive Director's Cut. Instead of following these instructions, though, Warner Bros. progressed on producing a cleaned up version of the work print with credits reinstated and the Vangelis soundtrack restored, instead of the temporary music used on the original work print. The result was

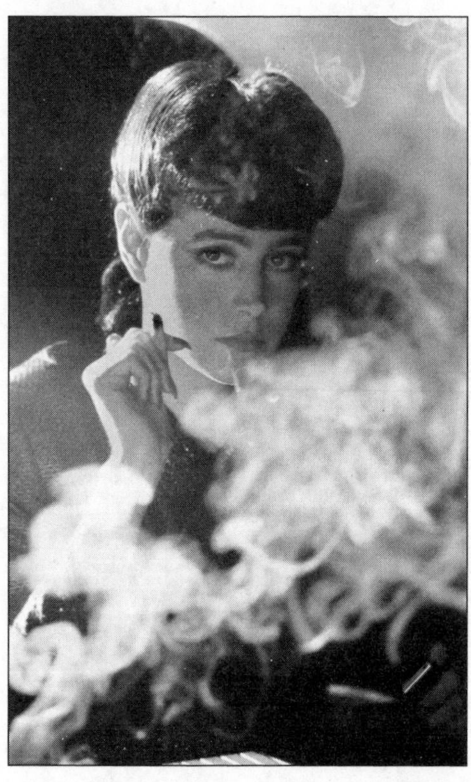

***Above:** Rachael discovers she's a replicant, but is Deckard ignorant of his true nature?*

not what Scott had hoped for, especially as his desired unicorn shot was missing.

Scott had originally intended Deckard to day-dream at his piano of a unicorn. This tied to Gaff's origami version of the mythical beast left at Deckard's apartment at the finale. The inference? That Gaff somehow knew Deckard's inner thoughts, in the way that Deckard was able to access Rachael's memories. The conclusion could only be that Deckard, too, was a replicant. It was an issue which had been raised and discarded during the scripting process, and one which Harrison Ford disliked. Now, Scott saw a chance to lay the speculation to rest once and for all by restoring the unicorn scene. The only problem was that Warner Bros. could not find the footage that had originally been shot for this sequence back in January 1982 at Black Park, near Pinewood Studios outside London.

The meaning of the unicorn sequence — that Deckard himself is a replicant — has its roots in Philip K. Dick's original novel. In a disorienting sequence in the middle of the book, Dick's hero Deckard finds himself taken to a police station he doesn't recognise and discovers that reality is not as he thought it was (a typically Dickian narrative stunt). Here, Deckard himself is under investigation, as he may be an android of the type he is hunting. This police station and its staff turn out to be bogus, a hoax, for Deckard's benefit. During pre-production of the film, the idea that Deckard may be a replicant had run through several drafts of the script, and were emphasised (albeit only visually) by Scott in most versions of the movie, but most strongly in his 1992 Director's Cut. The ideas in the script drafts, that Deckard was Roy Batty's "brother" could be read as actuality — Deckard is a replicant — or more metaphorically — Deckard's work, retiring androids, has made him less than human (a reading more in sympathy with Dick's original novel). Fancher and Peoples went for the philosophical interpretation of Deckard's degrees of humanity, but Ridley Scott chose to take these notions literally, so much so that in the documentary *On the Edge of Blade Runner* he confirms that (as far as he's concerned) Deckard *is* a Replicant. A scene where Deckard's out-of-focus eyes are seen to glow red, just as the replicants' do, adds to the director's take on the debate.

So, it was important to Scott that the unicorn dream sequence be in his Director's Cut, but the 1982 footage was nowhere to be found. As the release, now planned for September 1992, drew nearer, some unicorn footage was discovered, but it wasn't exactly the material Scott had intended to use originally. The footage in the final Director's Cut of *Blade Runner* did come from that January 1982 shoot and was not out-takes from Scott's fantasy film *Legend* (which features a unicorn), as fan rumour has it. It just wasn't exactly the unicorn shots Scott intended. Neither was what was ultimately released on 11 September 1991 as the Director's Cut of *Blade Runner*. Due to the time constraints, some deleted scenes (such as Deckard visiting Holden in hospital) were still missing, as were other tweaks Scott had wanted. However, everyone was happy enough with this version of the film to allow its release to celebrate the tenth anniversary of the film that had flopped originally but was now a worldwide phenomenon.

Box office was strong for the 1991 re-release of *Blade Runner*, even though it played in fewer than 100 theatres across the US. Critical reaction was widely positive, too, with many critics revising their negative opinions of a decade before. Harrison Ford's performance, in particular, was selected for praise following the removal of the voice-over, which allowed his portrayal of Deckard to regain some of the subtlety the actor had brought to it.

Released on home video, and eventually DVD, this Director's Cut might have been seen as the final version of *Blade Runner*. However, given that Ridley Scott was not entirely satisfied with the version put out in 1991, and the widely discussed rumours of plans for a three-disc ultimate *Blade Runner* DVD featuring yet another version of the film, as well as out-takes and documentaries, there may be further life in *Blade Runner* yet. Unfortunately, continuing legal issues ensured that the twentieth anniversary in 2002 came and went without any such DVD release. It can only be hoped that the ultimate *Blade Runner* will be out before the film's thirtieth anniversary in 2012, or indeed the year in which the movie itself takes place, 2019!

Despite the trials and tribulations of creating *Blade Runner*, star Harrison Ford retained a high opinion of his director. "What is interesting to me is that after *Blade Runner*, Ridley went on to make any number of interesting films," said the actor on *Encore*. "*Blade Runner* could easily have been the height of his career, but he's gone on to develop as a director and to find really challenging and interesting work to do."

Through the years since 1982, talk in Hollywood has inevitably turned to a potential sequel to *Blade Runner*. Screenwriter Stuart Hazeldine (who later adapted the Philip José Farmer novel *Riverworld* for TV in 2003) was the author of *Blade Runner Down*, an unproduced sequel script. Drafted in 1997, long after the 1991 tenth anniversary release of the *Blade Runner* Director's Cut, the screenplay appears to be based at least partly on Jeter's *Blade Runner 2: The Edge of Human*. Focusing on Deckard and featuring Rachael, the film would have required the return of Harrison Ford and Sean Young to succeed.

According to Hazeldine, there were even bigger obstacles to this project: "Warner Bros. don't have the *Blade Runner* sequel rights, only a first-look at making a sequel. The rights reside with original producer Bud Yorkin. When my [spec] script went out, 'the town' [Hollywood] loved it and offered me loads of [writing] jobs. Harrison's manager liked it but wouldn't give it to him unless a studio offer was behind it. The only people in town who didn't 'get' my script were the majority of execs at Warner Bros. and Bud Yorkin himself. These guys hold all the cards right now. Harrison [Ford] hasn't read my script and may never read it."

Set ten years after the end of *Blade Runner* and featuring a fifty-five-year-old Deckard, *Blade Runner Down* opens in an isolated cabin. Here Deckard and Rachael are facing up to the discovery that Rachael has a hidden limited lifespan encoded into her artificial genes after all. Deckard places her in cryo (suspended animation, often called 'cold-pac' in Dick's novels, particularly *Ubik*), and returns to the Tyrell Corporation — the only place where he might find an answer to extending her lifespan. Soon, the entire 'blade runner' unit is hunting Deckard, treating him as though he were a replicant. The screenplay also features the 'lost' sixth replicant, and Tyrell's niece Sarah (the double of replicant Rachael), elements drawn from Jeter's novel sequel. Hazeldine's script featured plenty of action sequences and expanded upon some of *Blade Runner*'s key characters. Although Ridley Scott had repeatedly mentioned his willingness to make a *Blade Runner* sequel (if those who controlled the rights would hire him), *The Crow* and (very Dick-like) *Dark City* director Alex Proyas was suggested as a possible helmer, as he'd worked with Hazeldine on an unmade Edgar Allan Poe project. *Se7en* director David Fincher (a huge fan of the original) was also mooted (pre-*Fight Club*) as a potential sequel director.

While the possibility of a movie sequel to *Blade Runner* is always open, the tangled rights situation, combined with the fact that Harrison Ford would be unlikely to return to the role of Deckard, would seem to be enough to make it an extremely unlikely prospect in the near future. In the meantime, fans will have to make do with 1998's *Soldier*, starring Kurt Russell as Todd, a replicant-like fighter. The film was written by David Peoples, who revealed that he considered it to be a 'side-quel' to *Blade Runner*, set in the same 'universe'. As well as a derelict spinner that was used as set dressing, sharp-eyed viewers will spot references to Tanhauser Gate and the Shoulder of Orion when Todd's service record is shown on a screen. Perhaps he fought alongside Roy Batty…

Although he died before seeing the final movie, it's interesting to speculate on what Philip K. Dick may have thought about *Blade Runner*, based on the comments he made on the sequences he had seen. "There are a lot of differences between the movie and the book," noted Dick to *Starlog* (in an interview eventually published in 1990), before going on to explain how he felt his original novel and the film could happily co-exist and might mutually inform each other. "Each reinforces the other. If you see the movie first, you will get more material when you read the book than you had in the movie. If you start with the book, you can go to the movie and you get more material. They don't fight each other, they reinforce each other, but they are different."

Dick's decision to republish *Do Androids Dream of Electric Sheep?* rather than write a new, lucrative novelisation of *Blade Runner* looks even more canny in light of his attitude to his story existing in multiple media. "There were certain things in the book that were completely left out of the movie," Dick said, admitting he was totally comfortable with the idea of the film being necessarily different from his novel. "The book has sixteen plots going through it. They would have had to make a movie lasting sixteen hours. It would have been a puzzle: that's not how you make a movie out of a book. You don't go scene-by-scene. A movie moves and a book talks, that's the difference. A book has to do with words and a movie has to do with events. They cut out Mercer, the saviour. They concentrated on the main theme, the hunting down of the 'replicants' and the effect that having to kill these replicants has on Rick Deckard, the detective, the attrition on him of killing [these] creatures."

Left: *Dick thought Harrison Ford was "fabulous" as Rick Deckard.*

Dick's stubbornness over not having a novelisation of the film issued preserved his original 1968 take on the themes of the film intact. "[The novel] has all the things about the animals and all the things about this mysterious saviour, Mercer, who has the miraculous power of bringing dead animals back to life, the ultimate divine power in a world where most of the animals are dead. They had to cut that out of the movie because they wanted to concentrate on hunting the replicants. All the themes must be carried by the contact between Deckard and the replicants, or as I call them, androids. It really all comes down to the climax between the detective and two particular ones: Batty and Rachael. She's an android, only she doesn't know she's an android. That's an idea I invented years ago. That's one of the few original ideas I've ever contributed to science fiction!"

Dick was even able to pass judgement on the casting of the main roles in *Blade Runner*, and he seems to have been more than satisfied with the actors chosen. Harrison Ford was "fabulous, absolutely incredibly, real good from what I can see," according to Dick. "He is exactly how I imagined the character will look like. Originally they had another actor [Dustin Hoffman], but they decided they would rather have Ford."

Dick thought that in the role of Rachael Sean Young "sure looks cute…" Dick even expressed his disappointment at not being able to visit the set and meet the 'dark-haired girl' in the flesh. "What is the point of my writing these novels and selling them [to Hollywood] if they're not going to introduce me to the leading lady?" he joked in the *Starlog* interview. Dick was obviously very much looking forward to seeing the completed *Blade Runner*, concluding: "It's gonna be a great film."

While there were other creative people long interested in adapting his stories into movies, it was the slow burn success of *Blade Runner* that created the Philip K. Dick film business. But it was only after several years of gradual confirmation that *Blade Runner* was a bona fide science fiction classic that another long-gestating Philip K. Dick project was finally given a green light… ■

RECALL MECHANISM

Total Recall puts Philip K. Dick in the mainstream but turns his 'everyman' hero into Arnold Schwarzenegger in the process...

"How much of what we call 'reality' is actually out there, or rather within our own head?" — Philip K. Dick, *The Best of Philip K. Dick*, 1976.

For a project that largely dealt with making dream worlds real, the journey of *Total Recall* from Philip K. Dick's short story 'We Can Remember It For You Wholesale' to the screen is a tale full of tortured nightmares rather than sweet dreams... The source short story was written by Dick in 1965 and published in *The Magazine of Fantasy & Science Fiction* in April 1966. It was later collected in *The Preserving Machine* (1969), a volume of Dick's short stories from 1953-66 put together by editor Terry Carr, and much admired by Dick himself as representative of his short fiction output. The story was a Nebula Award nominee in 1966.

Dick's slight, twenty-three-page tale sees mild-mannered clerk Doug Quail visit a company called Rekal Inc which offers consumers the opportunity to experience unlikely adventures through the implantation of false memories. Quail opts for an adventure as a secret agent on Mars. However, the process uncovers Quail's genuine identity: he *is* a secret agent recently returned from an assignment on Mars. Not only that, but as a child he'd also made a deal with some all-conquering aliens which means that his death will result in an unstoppable invasion of Earth.

The opening line of Dick's story succinctly outlines his protagonist's place in the world and his ambitions: "He awoke — and wanted Mars." Only Government agents and high officials get to see Mars, so a lowly West Coast Emigration Bureau clerk like Douglas Quail seems an unlikely candidate for such an adventure. His unsupportive wife (a regular archetypal character in Dick's fiction), Kirsten, certainly thinks so. Quail's Mars obsession leads him to Rekal Incorporated, a company which offers not only implanted memories of a vacation not taken, but all the tangible, physical proof — like ticket stubs, passport stamps, postcards, snap shots, home movies and souvenirs — needed to be convincing. Although doubtful if the process will really work, Quail pays to be uploaded with memories of being an agent for Interplan on Mars. As the memory implantation process begins, Rekal boss McClane and the technicians Lowe and Keeler accidentally uncover the truth: the meek clerk persona is the fiction, and Quail really is an agent who's been on Mars. The Rekal staff decide not to proceed with the implantation of the false memory of a trip to Mars, as they fear it might interact with Quail's suppressed real memory and cause a psychotic

Opposite: *Dick's meek Doug Quail becomes Schwarzenegger's macho Doug Quaid in the memory manipulating madness of* Total Recall.

break. Instead, McClane refunds half the fee and sends Quail on his way. Travelling home in a robot-driven cab, Quail is considering his fresh memory of a trip to Mars when he realises something is not right and returns to the Rekal offices. Quail leaves the firm with a complete refund under the impression that the imprint of the Mars trip on his brain had not taken hold fully, leaving him with fractured impressions of his experiences there. The discovery of a box in his home containing collected Martian fauna throws him: did he or did he not go to Mars? Did he or did he not get a memory implant? The boundary between actual reality and simulated fiction begins to break down for Douglas Quail.

That's not enough for Dick, though. Even in the space of a relatively short story, he throws in even more twists and developments. Just as Quail's wife Kirsten leaves him, unable to deal with his seeming confusion, an officer of the Interplan Police Agency confronts Quail and reveals that he is carrying a telepathic bug in his brain: they know everything he's been thinking and they know he's regained awareness of his *real* trip to Mars. Quail comes to realise that he was sent to Mars by Interplan as an assassin, after five years of training by the agency. To protect himself, Quail goes on the run. He now actually has everything he had longed for: "Adventure, peril, Interplan police at work, a secret and dangerous trip to Mars in which his life was at stake — everything he had wanted as a false memory."

Via the telepathic bug, Quail strikes a bargain with his Interplan pursuers: if they can implant an even stronger cover memory, perhaps based on a strongly held fantasy, then he'd give himself over to the authorities. Quail reckons he needs to return to 'normality', but without the restless urge that drew him to Rekal in the first place. Quail's fantasy concerns being confronted by a mini-alien invasion fleet at the age of nine and striking a bargain with them: as a reward for his kindness, the aliens will not invade as long as Quail lives. "'So, by merely existing,' Quail said feeling a growing pleasure, 'by simply being alive I keep Earth safe from alien rule. I'm in effect, then, the most important person on Terra. Without lifting a finger.'"

It's then the responsibility of Rekal Incorporated to implant this new, all-pervasive memory into Quail, covering once more his recall of his life as an Interplan assassin, and that of his time as a normal clerk who uncovered his real identity. However, in a blackly comic conclusion, as he's prepared for the new implant it becomes clear that in requesting the alien invasion fantasy, Quail is in fact recalling his much earlier real-life meeting with the aliens…

Critic Hazel Pierce saw that in 'We Can Remember It For You Wholesale' Dick was exploring an alternative way of organising reality, rather than through his usual themes of precognition or telepathy. As Pierce notes "Wish fulfilment is not as simple" as those other abilities.

Enjoyable as the story is, and as exciting as the premise might be for a movie concept, it is easy to anticipate the problems those who embarked upon the screenplay would encounter. It's a one trick pony as a concept, although the story actually pulls off the same trick twice. The opening events through to Quail's first visit to Rekal and his return there, up until he goes on the run would be fairly straightforward to adapt, but beyond that the material is lacking in cinematic potential. Flashbacks to Quail's encounter with mini-rodent-like aliens would be laughable on a cinema screen, and audiences would likely leave the cinema dissatisfied with the conclusion as presented in the story. The material had the potential to work best as an episode of a TV series like *The Twilight Zone* or *The Outer Limits*, which depend for their success on twist endings and weird happenings. To become a full-length feature film, Dick's story would have to be expanded and spun off into new directions...

Above: *The source story for* Total Recall *appeared in* The Magazine of Fantasy and Science Fiction *in April 1966.*

The attempts to turn 'We Can Remember It For You Wholesale' into a movie began with screenwriter Ronald D. Shusett. "I think it was probably 1974 that I optioned this story," recalled the writer, who at the time was a wannabe film producer with one low-budget 1973 thriller to his name: *W* (aka *I Want Her Dead*). "Phil Dick was then not a known author at all. He was still a struggling pulp writer, [as he was for] most of his career until *Blade Runner* got made." While Shusett's opinion of Dick's critical standing at the time may be suspect ("*Science Fiction Studies* has 45,000 words of essays on me ready to print. Maybe it's the same word over and over?" Dick noted in a 1974 letter), Dick himself didn't take note of the film option in his correspondence as he continued to deal with the psychic fall out from his February 1974 visionary experiences.

Shusett's partner in his attempt to turn Dick's story into a film script was Dan O'Bannon, another struggling screenwriter attempting to make his way in Hollywood. The pair met up in 1974 and compared their then-in development projects. O'Bannon was working on a space monster movie called *Starbeast*, while Shusett planned to option Dick's short story. Shusett was not keen on the *Starbeast* concept ("I thought it was just a good B-movie," Shusett admitted to *Cinefantastique* in 1991), but O'Bannon was taken with the Dick tale, so the pair shelved what would later become *Alien* to focus on developing 'We Can Remember It For You Wholesale'. It was Shusett who changed the title to the snappier *Total Recall*, feeling that Dick's original was too silly to be taken seriously as a movie title.

"I thought novelty and surprise were the main virtues of the story," noted O'Bannon. He recalled Shusett turning up at his apartment with "a filthy old xerox copy" of Dick's original tale. O'Bannon remembers telling Shusett, "I know that story and I think it would make a terrific movie." With *Starbeast/Alien* put to one side for now, the pair embarked on shaping Dick's tale for the screen. Shusett secured an option on the screen rights for a payment of $1,000. As relatively inexperienced screenwriters, O'Bannon and Shusett wanted to be as faithful to the short story as they could be within the dramatic requirements of the screenplay form. "In the story, Quail is — or thinks he is — a very ordinary, non-assertive kind of fella," noted O'Bannon, making the later casting of movie strong man Arnold Schwarzenegger in the role somewhat ironic.

Within a week, they'd produced a thirty-page script which covered most of the main plot points of the short story. The problem was, this would make only about a third of a movie. "Dick's story is short [and] it ends very abruptly," O'Bannon told *Cinefantastique* in the magazine's major 1991 feature on *Total Recall*. "You cannot take that particular short story and simply inflate it up to a full-length piece like a balloon. In my evaluation, it was a first act." In response to the work so far, Shusett asked O'Bannon where Quail, and the story, could go next. "We take him to Mars," O'Bannon replied.

It was at this point that Shusett and O'Bannon's conception of the direction the movie should take began to differ. O'Bannon worked out a plot that would explain Quail's double identity as a nobody and a seemingly invulnerable undercover agent, tie in the Mars aspect and provide a sequel hook, as well as a proper explanation of Shusett's adopted title. Having dreamt of a Martian pyramid early in the screenplay, Quail eventually finds himself there in person. An alien machine is activated by a hand-print control, and the hand-print required to operate it is Quail's. At the moment Quail places his hand in the matching print on the machine, he achieves 'total recall' of who he is. "[Quail is] Earth's top secret agent, [who] went to Mars and entered this compound. The machine killed him and created a synthetic duplicate. He is that duplicate. He cannot be killed because he can anticipate danger before it happens. Because he is omnipotent and cannot be killed, Earth wants to kill him, but [they] cannot," explained O'Bannon of his ideas for taking the plot forward. "That's why they make him think he's a nobody. It's the only way they can control him. At the end of the picture, [Quail] puts his hand on the device and it all comes back to him, who he really is. His total recall of his identity is that he is the creation of a Martian machine, a resurrection of the Martian race in a synthetic body. He turns to the other characters and says, 'It's going to be fun to play God.'"

Having taken the project so far and developed a full screenplay, Shusett and O'Bannon dropped it, as they disagreed about the climax. "Shusett and I never saw eye-to-eye on the end of the movie," said O'Bannon. "Ultimately it was one of the reasons that we parted on this project." *Total Recall* was shelved and the writing duo turned their attention back to O'Bannon's idea for *Starbeast*. O'Bannon had spent six months in Paris trying to get a film of Frank Herbert's epic science fiction novel *Dune* off the ground, to be directed by Alejandro Jodorowsky (*El Topo*). He'd returned to Los Angeles broke and homeless and had taken up residence on Shusett's couch. Working on *Starbeast*, it was Shusett who came up with the alien creature's method of reproduction: implanting eggs within a human host. This idea spurred the pair into new life and the result was Ridley Scott's *Alien*. Although their script was heavily reworked by the film's producers, Walter Hill and David Giler, the core ideas developed by Shusett and O'Bannon remained (and they retained sole screenplay credit after Writer's Guild arbitration). Indeed, it was Shusett and O'Bannon who'd introduced Scott to the outré artwork of H. R. Giger, which did so much to define the look of the alien creature. The film, shot in the UK for $9 million, went on to post worldwide box office rentals of $48.4 million (according to Fox figures), making it the fourth biggest grossing film of 1979 after *Rocky II*, *Every Which Way But Loose* and *Superman*. Two Oscar nominations followed, with the film winning one for special effects. As a result of the success of *Alien*, Shusett was able to secure a development deal with Disney in 1981 for *Total Recall*. "I was obsessed with it," said Shusett of the previously stalled project. "If I didn't do it, I felt that maybe *Alien* would be considered a fluke."

The climax of the movie was still a problem, though. "We tried every ending we could think of," remembered Shusett in Rob van Scheers' biography of *Total Recall*'s eventual director Paul Verhoeven. "Then Dan O'Bannon dropped out because he was sick of the whole project." By the early 1980s, O'Bannon was long gone, having moved on to work on the films *Heavy Metal* and *Blue Thunder*. Shusett was left on his own to navigate the hostile waters of Hollywood studio filmmaking.

That ending remained a problem for Disney, whose executives could not agree a way to strengthen the third act. Veteran producer Dino DeLaurentiis, who'd been behind the aborted attempt to film *Dune* with Jodorowsky, picked up the option for his company DEG.

Directors suggested for the movie included Fred Schepisi (*Barbarosa*), Richard Rush (*The Stunt Man*) and Lewis Teague (*Cujo*), but none of them seem to have done any serious work on the project. Shusett recalled that Rush fell out with DeLaurentiis over the film's third act, described by Shusett as "Mars gets air." In this ending, the planet is 'terraformed' — made inhabitable for humans. Rush and Shusett felt it was the only ending of the many proposed that actually worked, but DeLaurentiis seemed to have turned on the project, arguing with Shusett that Quail shouldn't even journey to Mars at all. Despite these disputes with DeLaurentiis, Shusett was still attached and still determined to see his faith in the cinematic potential of 'We Can Remember It For You Wholesale' rewarded.

The potential of the *Total Recall* screenplay was widely recognised following a December 1983 feature by Stephen Rebello in *American Film*. Entitled 'One in a Million', Rebello wrote about Hollywood's great unproduced movie scripts and included *Total Recall* in his list. The film was described as from the creators of *Alien* and boasting a neo-Hitchcockian set-up. Citing the city of Losancisco, 2048 as the setting, Rebello outlined the plot that sees mild-mannered clerk Quail discover the truth of his identity and called the film a potential "interstellar *North by Northwest*." The screenplay was "fresh with jabs of quirky humour and a giddy defiance of logic. Why have directors like Brian De Palma and John Carpenter and studios like Disney given *Total Recall* the once-over then the brush-off? To be sure, this noirish universe recalls the sets of *Blade Runner*, that aridly gorgeous financial flop also based on a Dick short story [sic]." Rebello went on to note that development executives had pointed out that *Total Recall* had "a marvellous set-up, but the worst third-act problems ever…" There were, supposedly, fifteen alternative endings mooted for the movie.

After Schepisi, Rush and Teague (and, it appears, De Palma and Carpenter) had passed through the troubled project, another director was enticed by Dino DeLaurentiis to commit to the by-now notorious film. Late in 1984, the producer brought Canadian horror director David Cronenberg onto *Total Recall*, following his success with the Stephen King adaptation *The Dead Zone*. Cronenberg told Chris Rodley, in the book *Cronenberg on Cronenberg*, that DeLaurentiis was initially interested in the director for further Stephen King projects, but then put him on *Total Recall*: "I read the draft script that was around by Ron [Shusett] and Dan O'Bannon. It was one of the famous unmade scripts that had been around [for] ten years. It had a terrific premise."

Cronenberg had not been a Philip K. Dick fan, but soon caught up with the author's work in preparation for *Total Recall*. (He is now a devout follower, with a collection of Philip K. Dick first editions.) "If you read 'We Can Remember It For You Wholesale', it's unfilmable and doesn't have an ending. It does have a brilliant concept at its centre." The initial script Cronenberg read felt right to him. He recognised that the screenplay had a wonderful beginning, but that the authors had no idea where to go with it after they'd used up the ideas in the source story. Despite that, Cronenberg was convinced that it was only a draft or two away from being perfect.

Above: *Approaching the Martian city - a storyboard from one of the many abandoned versions of the film.*

Opposite top: *A 'glacier city' on Mars was proposed in Cronenberg's version, solving the inhabitants' water problems.*

Opposite bottom: *Production designer Ron Miller's sketch for a 'Sandsub'.*

Twelve drafts later, the director quit the project. "I should have seen it coming and didn't. I wanted it to work out so badly that I pretended it could. It came very close. It was a year and over a dozen drafts I wrote myself. It [was] about memory, identity and madness. I didn't want it to be high tech, because I wasn't excited by the gimmicks, the vehicles and the glass city. It was the human element that excited me. I did invent some stuff that I was very happy with, but I was never totally happy even with the last draft script because even there I felt I was making too much of a compromise [in favour of] the action."

Cronenberg's involvement had attracted actor Richard Dreyfuss to the role of Quail. Dreyfuss, an Oscar-winner and star of *Jaws* and *Close Encounters of the Third Kind*, both directed by Steven Spielberg, was concerned about the action-orientated character of Quail in the Shusett and O'Bannon draft of the script. Cronenberg's revisions made him a character more like that in the short story: able to escape from situations using his wits instead of brute force. This combination of Dreyfuss' requirements as an actor, and Cronenberg's interests as a writer and director, had produced a radically different version of the *Total Recall* screenplay.

The first twenty minutes or so, based directly on the story, were pretty much the same, but the remainder of the film — in particular the controversial, problematic third act — took an unexpected turn. Cronenberg approached the material, and the climax of the film in particular, as a way of exploring intellectual and moral choices of the central characters instead of packing the movie with brutal action scenes.

Cronenberg introduced the idea that Quail would not wish to return to his previous identity, a concept which survived through to the final version of the film. Cronenberg, displaying his obsessive 'body-horror' themes from films like *Shivers*, *Scanners* and *Videodrome*, introduced the idea of mutants on Mars and especially the character of Quato (eventually Kuato in the movie). This character, known as The Oracle, is a malformed congenital twin who has a secondary head and arms growing out of his body. In Cronenberg's draft, Quato is a memory manipulator who, following

Quail's arrival on Mars, attempts to uncover his secret identity. Quato dies in the attempt, but in his quest to uncover who he is and what happened to him, Quail is led to Pintaldi, a face changer. Manipulating Quail's facial structure, Pintaldi reveals that Quail is, in fact, Chairman Mandrell, dictator of Earth. Escaping an assassination attempt, in which Mandrell was the target, Quail (posing as Mandrell) confronts Mars Administrator Cohaagen. The Administrator convinces Quail/Mandrell that it was the Martian authorities, not Earth's secret service, who had suppressed his secret agent identity. Going after the Mars Fed leader Van Rindt, Quail/Mandrell narrowly escapes another assassination. He's then confronted by a doctor who attempts to convince him that he's dreaming all these events, that he's still in the machine at the Rekal centre — this scene was carried through to the final draft almost intact with the character of Dr Edgemar. Finally tracking down Van Rindt, Quail/Mandrell changes sides again and helps lead the attempt to overthrow Earth and Cohaagen's dominion of Mars. Finally alone with Cohaagen on a robot-driven bus crossing the Martian desert, Quail discovers that Mandrell never really existed. Quail is, in fact, the lowly Government servant he always thought he was. Cohaagen used Quail to pose as the fictional Mandrell and thus allow him to surreptitiously assume control of Earth and Mars. A final confrontation sees Quail defeat Cohaagen (using a gun secreted within his pectoral muscles — a very Cronenberg/*Videodrome*/*eXistenz* touch) and assume the role of the fictional Mandrell in reality.

Missing from the Cronenberg draft are the over-the-top action sequences that dominate the film as finally directed by Paul Verhoeven, when the script had been tailored to suit Arnold Schwarzenegger. The fight with Quail's "wife" is brief; there's no violent chase through

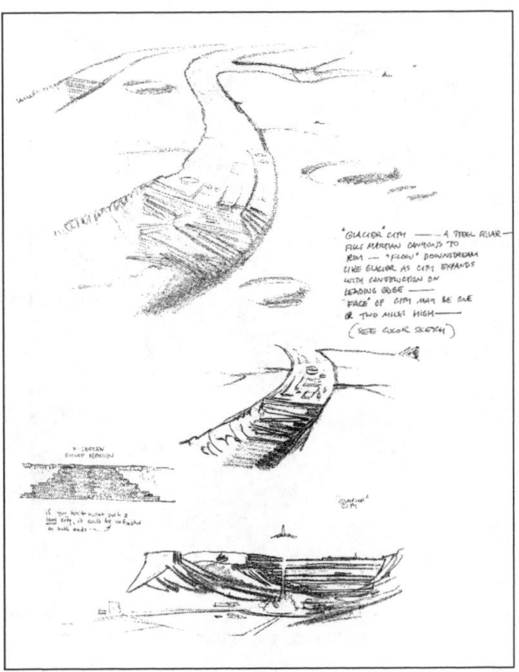

Above: *Future descendants of camels called 'Ganzibulls' would have featured in Cronenberg's* Total Recall.

the subway station; the Johnny Cab pursuit sequence is totally missing; and Mars Port is much more sedate, as Quail gains entry to the planet disguised as an old woman, without all the macho activity in the Verhoeven film.

Cronenberg's take on *Total Recall* had a distinctive visual component. Throughout his early film career, Cronenberg had been exploring his own cinematic obsession with disease and the body. He took a similar 'organic' approach to his conception of *Total Recall*.

Ron Miller had been hired as a production illustrator on the project. His task was to turn some of Cronenberg's script ideas into drawings, to give an idea what this version of the film might look like. When interviewed by *Cinefantastique*, Miller remembered working on designs for creatures called 'Ganzibulls', mutant camels who wore oxygen masks and lived in the sewers of Venusville, the city on Mars in which most of the action took place. "I really was looking forward to seeing camels with oxygen masks," laughed Miller, of the creatures which were originally in Shusett's draft, but were developed further by Cronenberg. "It was a totally unlikely, bizarre idea..."

As *Total Recall* drew closer to entering production, DeLaurentiis set up a pre-production team in his Rome studios, dubbed 'Dinocitta' by Cronenberg after the more famous Cinecitta studios. The team comprised Miller, art director Pier Luigi Basile and a team of illustrators and model builders. They had Cronenberg's latest draft of the script to work from and concepts such as the Martian pyramid/Sphinx, a 'Sandsub' which would transport Quail and Mars Fed double agent Melina across Mars, spaceships and Mars Port, and the infamous 'Ganzibulls'. Costume designer Bob Ringwood (who would later work on Tim Burton's *Batman*) was also attached to the production and, according to Miller, spent a few weeks in Rome working on costume sketches.

Miller and Basile soon realised that, despite the work going on and seeming progress being made, the film was unlikely to actually shoot. Basile noted: "David Cronenberg's style is very specific. He rewrote the script but Dino wasn't happy with it, and he stopped the preparation. He wanted a big, spectacular action film, whereas Cronenberg didn't want to make an action film. He wanted to make a story about the main character. I don't think that Dino ever understood what kind of film Cronenberg was developing."

This final Cronenberg draft of the movie was the nail in the coffin of that version of *Total Recall*. "Cronenberg quit for a number of reasons," Ron Shusett told *Cinefantastique* in April 1991. "He and I were having a number of creative disagreements, which started about the time of [Richard] Dreyfuss' involvement, because DEG didn't want to do it as it was written for Dreyfuss. We didn't have a script to fit another actor, so Cronenberg started to feel that the movie should take on a whole new approach, different than either of the

Above: *Quaid's ship arrives at Mars Port in this Ron Miller concept sketch.*

previous ones. I disagreed with him. I wanted to go either with our earlier approach, which was partly pride of authorship ["Mars gets air"] — I was in love with it — or I wanted to go with the second approach, which was the one Dreyfuss, Cronenberg and I had evolved."

Cronenberg grew tired of the process and called a halt to things. "[It was] trying to deal with Dino, trying to get an accord between me and Ron, [who] had his own very strong input. I tried very hard to make it significant in terms of its themes. We were going to shoot Tunisia for the planet Mars: we went there to look for locations. It was a lot of work and effort on many people's parts, and a lot of money was spent."

Eventually, in 1985, Cronenberg offered DeLaurentiis his final take on the *Total Recall* screenplay, his twelfth attempt at the script. His ultimatum was essentially, "make this version or I quit." Faced with losing another director, and more money and time, DeLaurentiis suggested a return to an earlier version of the script, draft number nine. Cronenberg withdrew from the project. "There was one time when he phoned me back and said, 'OK, we're ready to do it your way,' but by that time it was too late," recalled Cronenberg. "I couldn't go back to it. I couldn't deal with Ron Shusett any more. It took us a year to realise that we were talking about two separate movies."

The next major contribution to *Total Recall* came from Australian director Bruce Beresford. In 1986 Beresford's major achievements included the 1970s Barry McKenzie movies starring Barry Humphries, and *Breaker Morant*, *Tender Mercies* and *King David*, none of which suggested a particular penchant for science fiction thrillers. (Beresford would go on to be Oscar-nominated for *Driving Miss Daisy*.)

The *Total Recall* project had now been in development for over ten years, from

Shusett's initial option in 1974, and Dino DeLaurentiis felt it was time to take the project in a different direction, with a fresh perspective from a director not as steeped in the outré and fantastic as David Cronenberg had been. Beresford fitted the bill and his involvement attracted a different kind of star to the project: Patrick Swayze, best known for *Dirty Dancing*, got involved.

"His was a more subtle approach," noted Shusett, comparing the Beresford version to that developed by Cronenberg. "[It was] a more 'Spielberg-ish' approach, more fun than gritty." While the plot that Beresford worked with was that favoured by Shusett (and more-or-less eventually filmed by Paul Verhoeven), the new director took another pass at the much re-written script, mainly shaping the dialogue to match his own more mainstream sensibilities.

After doing a pass on the script, Beresford then worked with rising screenwriter Michael Almereyda, who had scripted the robot thriller *Cherry 2000*. (Almereyda went on to be an acclaimed writer-director making, among other films, vampire thriller *Nadja* and a contemporary-set version of *Hamlet* with Ethan Hawke.)

"I've written for major studios," Almereyda told journalist Daniel Robert Epstein when discussing his early 'script doctoring'. "I did a draft of *Total Recall* and some of my dialogue got in the movie. In the last line of the movie Schwarzenegger says 'I just had a terrible thought: what if this is a dream?' and Melina responds, 'Well then, kiss me quick before you wake up.' [That was in] 1987. Dino De Laurentiis was producing it at the time and Bruce Beresford was going to direct. When the movie came out I was surprised to see how much of my stuff was in there."

This Beresford-Almereyda-Shusett version of the film entered pre-production in Australia in March 1987, with Patrick Swayze attached to star. Special effects company Introvision was hired to storyboard the film's complex action sequences based on Beresford's take on the movie. Introvision's Andy Naud recalled how advanced the project got in *Cinefantastique* in 1991. "[We] storyboarded all the difficult sequences in the movie and provided answers [to shooting problems]. In late August [1987], we sent people down to Australia [from the US], where we began building miniature models."

As with the Cronenberg version, Bruce Beresford's *Total Recall* produced a lot of pre-production artwork and a series of models. Sets had even been built, with the total investment in this version of the movie amounting to around $6 million. Once again it was all in vain. As the project had entered pre-production, Introvision's Andy Naud had been worried about receiving payments from DEG. "We found it very difficult to structure a deal with [Dino], because he didn't want to give up any money… He just wanted to lead us along." The reasons became clearer when DEG entered bankruptcy and the production of *Total Recall* collapsed in December 1987. "Beresford was crushingly disappointed, as was I," Ron Shusett told *Cinefantastique*'s Bill Florence. Once more, Shusett's long cherished project was in limbo.

In further attempts to produce a workable screenplay, Shusett had involved his *Freejack* co-writer Steven Pressfield and *Star Trek: The Next Generation* TV writer Jon Povill. As before, all were defeated by their inability to find a suitable direction in which to take Dick's original short story. "The script was ice cold," remembered Shusett, quite a turnaround from it

being acclaimed in 1983 as one of Hollywood's greatest unproduced screenplays. "It was a joke in Hollywood. People felt it was doomed, there was too much money against it without even a frame of footage shot." Any future producer of *Total Recall* would have to pay off the accumulated production costs (or an agreed portion thereof) in order to take the project forward. So much had been spent already over the years that Shusett believed his dream was over. "Who's gonna do this?" he asked of his film. "It was like [there was] an Egyptian curse on it. People began to think I was a lunatic because I spent eighty per cent of my time trying to make this movie. They thought, 'This guy can't cope with reality.' I guess they were almost right!"

Similarly, Steven Pressfield's experiences as a screenwriter, including his time on *Total Recall*, resulted in his switch to prose writing. "Screenplays are very structure-heavy," he told journalist Sandy Auden. "Since a movie is experienced by its audience in one ninety-minute gulp, a script has to adhere to a certain three-act rhythm, with twists and turning points at reasonably predictable intervals." It was precisely this lack of a cinematic structure or screenplay formula that was making Dick's 'We Can Remember It For You Wholesale' such a difficult tale to adapt. Yet the central idea continued to appeal to Shusett and the series of writers who came and went on the project. "The movie writer can be fired and replaced and usually is," lamented Pressfield. "No one pays any attention to him, least of all the director, who sometimes won't even deign to speak to him. Novels are truly the writer's medium. No one rewrites you. It's not the same with a movie."

Above: *The film finally entered production when Arnold Schwarzenegger joined the project.*

Although *Total Recall* won a new lease of life in 1988 thanks to the intervention of eventual star Arnold Schwarzenegger, the script still had a long, tortuous journey to the screen ahead of it. When DEG collapsed in December 1987, Schwarzenegger took note. He'd read a previous version of the film when working with DeLaurentiis on another project and while he was interested in starring, he didn't see the character of Quail as described as being suitable for his action man persona. However, when DEG went under, Schwarzenegger saw an opportunity. Contacting DeLaurentiis, he established the property could be for sale if the actor could find a buyer. On the *Total Recall* DVD commentary, Schwarzenegger claims that within hours he'd brokered a deal between DeLaurentiis and Carolco, the movie's eventual producer. For a bargain $3 million Carolco's Andrew G. Vajna and Mario Kassar won

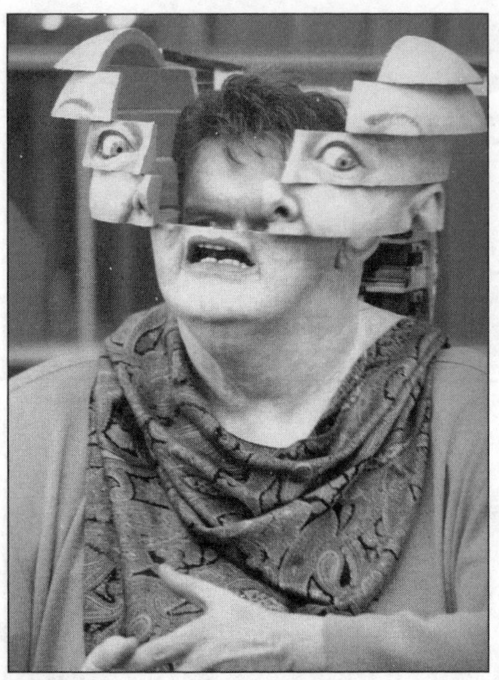

Above: *"Get ready for a surprise!" Quaid's arrival on Mars was much more low key in earlier drafts of the film.*

control of the troubled project. They bought all previous versions of the script and all the pre-production material that had accumulated over the years, from Cronenberg's production sketches to Beresford's model work. Also still contractually attached to the new deal was the project's originator, Ron Shusett.

Schwarzenegger then took one further step and resolved one of *Total Recall*'s major failings over the years — the lack of a suitable and committed director. It was the actor who brought Paul Verhoeven into the picture, citing his work on *RoboCop* as his qualification for *Total Recall*. Bizarrely, years before, in 1981 Ron Shusett had seriously considered Verhoeven a potential director for *Total Recall* following his Dutch movie *Soldier of Orange*.

Similarly Gary Goldman, *Total Recall*'s next screenwriter, had ironically turned the project down back in 1987 in order to work with Verhoeven on a never-made action movie called *Warrior*. Shusett had brought the script to Goldman's attention, but Goldman didn't get to work on it until the property was back in production at Carolco and Paul Verhoeven was firmly on board to direct the movie, with Arnold Schwarzenegger starring as Doug Quaid — the name had been changed from the short story's more suitable and descriptive Quail to avoid any confusion with then-US Vice President Dan Quayle. "I was brought in by Paul Verhoeven right after he became involved," Goldman confirmed in an interview for this book.

Goldman's attraction to the project was easy to explain. "I am primarily interested in things that haven't been done before," he told Jason Koornick of the Philip K. Dick fan web site, www.philipkdickfans.com. "I'm also looking for projects that deal with ideas. That is why I like science fiction, because it's almost the only genre that allows you to explore ideas."

Of course, the problem with *Total Recall* was that the first half of the script was packed with ideas (almost all drawn from 'We Can Remember It For You Wholesale'), while the second half was awash in second-hand sci-fi concepts, seemingly swiped from Edgar Rice Burroughs and assorted B-movies. However, Goldman felt he was the right man to sort out the *Total Recall* script. Verhoeven and Shusett evidently agreed. "I have a lot of affinities with Phil Dick's sensibilities, his sense of humour," claimed Goldman. "His stories are about ordinary people living everyday lives. To me, his characters behave realistically — they are fallible, inconsistent, greedy, jealous and [that makes them] recognisable."

Previously Goldman had been involved in scripting the underrated *Big Trouble in Little China* for John Carpenter, and *Navy SEALS*. Now he was faced with around thirty script drafts, variously credited to Shusett and O'Bannon, Shusett and Jon Povill, Shusett and Steven Pressfield, David Cronenberg (at least twelve), Fred Schepisi and Bruce

Beresford. It was quite a mountain of material to assimilate and distil down to essentials. "I worked for nine months on the rewrite," said Goldman. Verhoeven read all the original drafts, then passed on those he liked, with copious notes, to Goldman. So which scripts did Goldman actually have access to? "More than a dozen drafts by Ron Shusett and Dan O'Bannon, and [then by] Ron Shusett and Steven Pressfield had been written," he said. "I only read the drafts that Paul Verhoeven selected, which did not include the drafts written for [or by] David Cronenberg." All were agreed that the first half of the script was fantastic, and true to Dick's original story. As ever it was the third act of the drama that was letting the whole production down. None of the script drafts solved the problem adequately. According to Goldman his task was clear: "My goal was to take the ideas and themes in the first half of the screenplay — which were the same in almost all the drafts — and see that they were continued and brought to a conclusion in the second half," he said in an interview for this book.

The problems arose at the moment in the script when Quaid leaves for Mars in search of his true identity. Shusett had only one feeling in mind to pursue: "I always knew that overwhelming feelings of fear should dominate it." While that might not make for the most commercial of movies, it was a thread that Shusett had pursued through various drafts. "In Hollywood," Goldman told author Rob van Scheers in his biography of Paul Verhoeven, "rewriting is usually a kind of massacre, where the subsequent writer tries to destroy the work of the previous writer. His foremost goal is to take the original writer's name off the screenplay. This is standard practice." However, with *Total Recall*, Goldman rose above this temptation, mainly due to the script's initial fidelity to Philip K. Dick's work. "I'm very proud that I tried to remain true to Philip Dick's intentions," he said of his revisions. "Most of the ideas that we came up with were organic to Philip K. Dick and I

Left: *Paul Verhoeven significantly increased the action content of* Total Recall.

believe that the end product absolutely reflects that. It may be changed, but it's all in there."

The problems with the scripts were plain to anyone who read them. "After its strong opening it kind of collapsed," admitted Goldman, "so my job was to see what we could do to make the whole movie work. To an extent Paul [Verhoeven] and I were handicapped, because there were restrictions: Ron had done so many versions of the script, but he also had in his contract things we weren't allowed to change."

"I had the feeling that the third act was not really resolved," agreed Verhoeven. "The basic issue of the movie is a mind construction: what is real and what isn't? But the last act was more or less all action: the mind level was gone. There was nothing happening anymore on that other, psychological level." The idea from the original story — man longs for adventure only to discover he's already had it — was key to Verhoeven's interest in the project. He'd done enough straight action in *RoboCop*. Now he wanted some intellectual meat with his action movie. "I thought it was really interesting," said Verhoeven of the Dick short story's concepts. "Underneath there is something else, this layer that Philip K. Dick has in his work, a doubting of reality. Dick wrote his story with this other level, and then O'Bannon and Shusett fleshed it out, and finally I pushed it further."

The key to solving some of the problems of the screenplay was in dealing with who the character Quaid really was before: the action man spy, now named Hauser in the screenplay. "What Goldman came up with was to give the third act a twist," noted Verhoeven. "We find out that Quaid's alter ego [Hauser], the person he was before, was an asshole."

For Goldman, this development got to the heart of Dick's thematic concerns with identity. Making Hauser a strong, separate individual gave a new complexion to the movie's second half. The second twist was to strengthen David Cronenberg's concept that Hauser was a character that Quaid no longer wanted to be — Quaid had essentially subsumed his authentic, original personality [Hauser] because he could no longer face being the amoral assassin Hauser had become. For Goldman, the choice Quaid would face would be a return to his authentic, but 'evil' self, or the acceptance of his artificial, but 'good', personality. Having read widely within Dick's oeuvre, Goldman was willing to draw inspiration from beyond the original short story, reflecting in *Total Recall* the themes of identity and reality which pervade much of Dick's work, especially his novels.

"I made a connection between why Quaid's mind was erased and the freedom movement on Mars, and created the idea that Hauser was a bad guy," Goldman said. There was another key idea that the writer and director were keen to address: "Paul and I took seriously the possibility that the memory implant had gone wrong, and what was happening in the movie was an illusion. In a general way, the short story was the basis for the first third of *Total Recall*. We wanted to extend Dick's ideas from beginning to end and to take up the idea of a false reality." The project's originator, Ron Shusett, was taken with this new development, believing it "raised the film to a new level of brilliance it never had before."

For Verhoeven, the one scene in the various scripts that really captivated him was where Dr Edgemar tries to persuade Quaid that everything he is experiencing is a fantasy; that he's still locked into the chair at Rekall (not Rekal, with one 'l', as in the story). It's the one scene in the finished movie that is most faithful to Philip K. Dick's ideas and it originated in the previously off limits Cronenberg version of the script. Off the implications of this single scene, Goldman and Verhoeven intended to hang their entire concept of the movie.

Left: *The film's key scene. Can Dr Edgemar persuade Quaid that 'reality' is all in his mind?*

The prospects and nature of *Total Recall* were totally changed by involvement of Arnold Schwarzenegger. Although grateful that his interest had kick-started the project again and brought Goldman and Verhoeven on board, Ron Shusett was worried about the implications of having muscle-bound Schwarzenegger playing the meek and mild aspects of Doug Quaid. "When Arnold got involved, I was wondering, wouldn't that ruin the whole surprise? Arnold is too powerful to play a meek guy, the audience knows he's a super agent to begin with, because of his persona."

From the beginning of his involvement, Schwarzenegger was another voice in the mix contributing story ideas to the already overworked screenplay. His first mandated change was one of occupation for Quaid, from office worker to construction worker. The dark, sometimes downbeat, tone of the film (another hangover from the Cronenberg drafts) was lightened considerably to play up to Schwarzenegger's action-adventure credentials. "I felt that there should be a cause to Quaid," admitted Schwarzenegger of his attempts to turn *Total Recall*'s central figure into more of a conventional Hollywood hero, more suitable for him to play. "There should be an urgency to the mission. I feel that movies do really well when the audience can relate to an emergency. In any movie that starts out telling you there's a deadline, it makes you sit much more on the edge of your seat. In the script meetings, I expressed that I felt there was something missing, something that had to be bigger than me just finding out that I'm there to save Mars."

Schwarzenegger wanted a challenge bigger than saving an entire planet? Ultimately, the star voice spoke louder than those of the director and screenwriters, who were trying to pursue a more ideas-driven approach, true to Philip K. Dick's original intentions. *Total*

Recall's second half was recast in an all-action mode, jettisoning many of the complex themes behind Quaid's identity conflict, replacing them with a series of slam-bam action sequences, bound to please middle America cinema audiences.

For all his increased influence post-*RoboCop*, Paul Verhoeven recognised his place in the Hollywood hierarchy, and it was a long way behind Arnold Schwarzenegger. "They convinced Gary [Goldman] to bring that [action-driven] part of the script back in again," admitted Verhoeven. "I said to myself, 'I'm the director, not the writer. If they feel that it is dramatic and makes the film better, then I will go with it.'" As a result a new climax was constructed, highlighting the plight of the oppressed Martians, for whom Quaid was fighting. Evil Mars administrator Cohaagen cuts off the air supply, causing the populace to suffer and creating the urgent race-against-the-clock that the movie's star required. Chalk one up to Arnie.

After fifteen years in development, at least six directors (including *Highlander*'s Russell Mulcahy), almost as many writers and stars (with Mel Gibson and Jeff Bridges having expressed interest at various times) and a total of around forty-five different versions of the script, totalling 5,000 pages, *Total Recall* was given a $55-$60 million budget (the largest ever allocated to a movie to that date) and a green light to enter production in April 1989.

Joining Arnold Schwarzenegger as Quaid/Hauser were Rachel Ticotin as Hauser's partner Melina; a relatively unknown Sharon Stone as Quaid's wife, Lori; Ronny Cox as Cohaagen; Michael Ironside as Cohaagen's henchman Richter and Roy Brocksmith as Dr Edgemar. Joining Verhoeven behind the camera were his favourite cameraman Jost Vacano and special effects guru Rob Bottin (*The Thing*).

Shooting took place at Estudios Churubusco in Mexico City, where Verhoeven's dollars would stretch further. "Working in Mexico is extremely inexpensive," claimed the director. "This movie would have been $65 or $70 million if we had shot in Los Angeles." Verhoeven had twenty weeks of shooting and 300 people to bring Dick's vision of confused identities to the screen. The studio's large halls were subdivided into eight soundstages in which the film's diverse, exotic sets were erected. Location filming was also used: Verhoeven initially wanted to shoot the Earth-set sequences in Houston, Texas, but decided that Mexican architecture had the futuristic quality he was seeking. Locations around the studios served the film well, especially a local mining district which doubled effectively for some of the Martian locales. Much of the filming took place against bluescreen backgrounds, especially some of the action sequences, allowing for completion of the outlandish special effects during post-production.

Below: *Ronny Cox played Cohaagen.*

While Mexico may have been a cheaper option for the production, it came with its own set of problems. "If you get sick, everything becomes more difficult," said Verhoeven. "It is very hard to stay healthy [in Mexico]." As illness worked its way through the cast and crew, the shooting schedule also suffered. Verhoeven himself was not immune, and spent several days very much the worse for wear, but trying desperately to continue the shoot. "It would have cost [the production] $150,000 for every day Paul was in the hospital," remembered Ron Shusett. "He wanted that money to go toward the movie. I admired him so much. I don't know how he could do it."

Verhoeven recovered and the filming continued, but the costs were now in danger of mounting in excess of the budget. Carolco executives started putting pressure on Verhoeven to cut sequences from the film to save money and time. Once again, Shusett saw his dream project turning into a nightmare. "I was influencing Paul and Arnold not to cut costs," he admitted. "The financiers wanted cuts. I suggested cutting small things or trimming big things, but they said, 'No, just cut one big scene and we can save $2 or $3 million.'"

Halfway through the production, Carolco effectively fired Shusett. "I was trying so hard to get the movie I wanted on the screen that they had to throw me off," said Shusett. "They gave me notice that I was interfering with the movie." On the verge of leaving Mexico City, Shusett was recalled to the production following the intervention of Schwarzenegger, who threatened to quit the film, according to Shusett. The film crew gave Shusett a T-shirt emblazoned with the slogan 'I'm Still Here!'. "Everybody knew they had thrown me off the picture, and at first it was embarrassing, but then I was a hero because they couldn't get rid of me."

The creative tensions that had fuelled *Total Recall*'s development for fifteen years continued during production. Budgetary pressure and script redrafting (both Shusett and Goldman were in Mexico and continued to work on the screenplay during production) were the main areas of dispute. Only Arnold Schwarzenegger could bring resolution to the discord. "I was on good terms with everyone," he said. "I understood the psychology of the people involved, and I had the goal of making the whole production really work. I felt that I could invite them over to my trailer to talk. Instead of having a meeting in an office, I brought them over to my trailer and gave them some schnapps and put on some good music. I didn't solve the problems, they solved the problems."

Shooting in Mexico had been difficult for all involved. "It was total madness," said Schwarzenegger. "We all had a good time, but it was such a technical movie. We only shot two or three times on each stage and there were around eighty sets altogether. It was a very rough shoot, but Verhoeven is a genius with tremendous energy. We did a lot of rehearsals, because Paul only does four takes of every scene. On Sundays we would work on things to come that week, especially the stunts, and Paul participated in every one of them — whenever it was necessary, he threw himself straight into the fighting scenes."

Principal photography on *Total Recall* wrapped in Mexico in August 1989, with a further six months of post-production looming. Having overspent on the live-action shoot, budgetary considerations would now drive the post-production schedules. Special effects house Dream Quest Images were appointed to handle the optical effects purely because they made the lowest bid. The Simi Valley-based company had previously worked on effects for James Cameron's *The Abyss*. "The more quality you want, the more money it costs," admitted Verhoeven, who supervised the rising special effects costs as he wanted to ensure the quality of the finished product. "I think they did a really great job, artistically and technically."

***Above:** Heading for a divorce… The film's violence, including a fight scene with Sharon Stone, was heavily criticised.*

Dream Quest supplied around 100 optical effects shots for *Total Recall*, supervised by Eric Brevig, who moved on to join Industrial Light and Magic (ILM) after the project. Brevig and Verhoeven decided that they would take some artistic licence in envisaging the surface of Mars, going for the fantastic over the realistic. Questions of gravity and physics were sacrificed in the name of action. Mixing model work, live-action footage and impressive matte paintings became Brevig's signature approach to *Total Recall*, producing a comic-book Mars more like something from Edgar Rice Burroughs than a NASA promotional film.

Completing the movie with a compressed schedule, due to pressure from rival summer 1990 would-be blockbuster *Dick Tracy*, there wasn't enough time to arrange for preview screenings of *Total Recall*. The finished film was rushed into cinemas just a week in advance of *Dick Tracy* in an attempt to beat the perceived competition at the box office. It was a timetable Shusett came to regret, feeling that a preview screening and time to refine the editing of the third act may have resulted in a better film. As it was, Shusett felt that the final movie lived up to seventy-five to eighty per cent of what he'd hoped to achieve, while Goldman — the screenwriter who'd finally made *Total Recall* filmable — felt he'd effectively captured Philip K. Dick's "serio-comic tone" better than any Dick-inspired movie before or since.

The première of *Total Recall* took place at the Griffith Observatory in Los Angeles in June 1990, with a fully recovered Paul Verhoeven in attendance. The final cost of the movie had come in closer to $60 million. "I added about $6 million to the budget," admitted the director, "because I was either too slow or because it was more difficult than I thought it would be. The special effects, too, were more difficult and more time consuming than we had thought."

At least Verhoeven, Goldman and Shusett had the compensation of broadly good reviews to fall back on. "*Total Recall* is a first-rate action movie," noted the *San Francisco Chronicle*, "slickly done, with so many imaginative extras that, for a time, it feels like a classic in the making. It's not, but it's still solid and entertaining..." *Time* commented: "When *Total Recall* is cooking, it induces visual vertigo."

One of the strongest criticisms levelled at *Total Recall* was the amount and graphic nature of the violence on the screen. It is, albeit in a rather grim cartoonish way, a very violent movie. The most criticised scene — in which Richter (Michael Ironside) loses his arms when trapped in a lift — draws on an actual incident from Verhoeven's own childhood. "My fantasies and my nightmares start to fill in when I'm shooting violence," admitted the director. "I grew up in German-occupied Holland, which was continually bombed, and we were always afraid for our lives. Violence was so much a part of my real world." He recalled the lift incident in Rob van Scheers' biography: "When I was about seven... my legs got stuck [in a lift]. I thought I had really lost them. I got away with a fright, but I'll never forget it. That's why that scene in *Total Recall* is so good, because it is based on reality..."

Some of those who'd been involved to varying degrees with *Total Recall* over the years had dramatic reactions to the final version of the film. For his part, original *Total Recall* co-scriptwriter Dan O'Bannon was not sold on the need for the violence or on Verhoeven's explanations for it. "Verhoeven's judgement is obviously way off the norm," he claimed in *Cinefantastique*. "Because of the horrors he had experienced as a child, he's now reached a point of psychic numbing, where this kind of violence doesn't mean anything to him. But it still means something to the audience. It's raw sensation at the expense of everything else."

In a 1992 collection of interviews with screenwriters, entitled *The New Screenwriter Looks at the New Screenwriters*, O'Bannon had again criticised Verhoeven's choices when it came to including violent imagery in the film. "The violence plays in *Total Recall* as though there wasn't enough there to support the excitement without it. I don't think it needed that level of violence. They lost some good things in the way of humour, surprise and character. It was as though the director had no confidence in the script."

O'Bannon had since gone on to work on *Lifeforce* and the Tobe Hooper-directed remake of *Invaders From Mars*, as well as writing and directing the spoof horror movie *Return of the Living Dead*. He was generally unimpressed with what ended up on the screen in *Total Recall*. Decrying the casting of Arnold Schwarzenegger as the 'everyman' character at the centre of the drama, O'Bannon recognised in the film the vestigial remains of ideas in the original scripts which now made no sense in their new context. A Martian pyramid, visited by the character of Quail in O'Bannon's draft, remained as a dominant graphic on the film's poster, but did not feature strongly in the movie. Additionally, Quaid activates an alien device by placing his human hand into the alien/Martian three-fingered hand-print on the device. This, clearly, makes no sense. "That was supposed to have been a print of Quail's hand which matched only his hand," explained O'Bannon. This led into the plot which Cronenberg's version of the script worked through, that of Quail/Quaid's replacement by a synthetic human carrying the hope for the Martian race within him.

Instead, the film ended with Schwarzenegger's bulging eyes on the Martian surface.

***Opposite:** The character of Kuato reflects the 'twins' theme that runs through much of Dick's fiction.*

"I wouldn't have minded that they changed my ending, I just don't think what they arrived at had any emotional impact at all," O'Bannon claimed. "It wasn't really where the audiences concerns had led [them] to be."

While arguing that *Total Recall* was "an actual science fiction movie, [not] a cowboy movie or an adventure movie or a monster movie," O'Bannon concluded: "[I would have] cast somebody else as Quail, and done a proper ending. Then I think you could have had a pretty decent picture."

Screenwriter Gary Goldman told the present author that he was happy with what resulted on screen: "I can't speak to Ron Shusett's original intentions. As for my drafts, Verhoeven shot the script we developed word for word. We could have deviated more from Shusett's scripts, but as we had a green-lit movie to start with, we basically wanted to complete his intentions rather than drastically alter them. I think our draft reflected the intentions of Phil Dick's story in that we played out his ideas to the end, instead of merely using them as a launching pad for a chase."

Director David Cronenberg had gone on from his stint on *Total Recall* to make *The Fly* and *Dead Ringers*, both to great critical acclaim and decent box office. When he saw *Total Recall*, he was equally unimpressed. "It was really *Raiders of the Lost Ark* goes to Mars," Cronenberg told Chris Rodley. "It was all action and shoot-ups. I thought the movie could be much better. It's a $60 million movie with Schwarzenegger instead of a mousy little clerk. It's 'turn off your mind and we'll have a car chase.'"

"The end they filmed is lame," concluded Dan O'Bannon. "The end of the movie should have been the final, stunning revelation about [the hero's] identity as recalled by him. The movie is called *Total Recall*!"

The official writing credits, as seen on screen, for *Total Recall* ended up reading: 'Screenplay by Ronald Shusett, Dan O'Bannon and Gary Goldman, based on a story by Shusett, O'Bannon and Jon Povill.' However, the biggest clue of Hollywood's lack of regard for the writer and lack of respect for the literary sources they draw on, is the fact that the name of the author of the original short story which 'inspired' the film is mis-spelled in the on-screen credits as: "Phillip K. Dick", with two 'l's. That, though, appears to have been a mistake Dick could have spotted for himself. The initial option contract for the short story which Dick signed with Ron Shusett, dated 12 July 1977, is addressed to 'Mr Philip K. Dick,' but states in the contract: "Writer shall be given credit upon the screen, with exposure long enough to read, that such motion picture is 'Suggested by a Short Story by Phillip K. Dick.'" So, technically at least, Caroloco would have been in breach of contract if they'd spelled Dick's name correctly! (Dick once wrote, in a letter to writer/artist Art Spiegelman (*Maus*), "Everything I have ever written has not only been meaningless, it has also been mis-spelled!")

Although it deviates wildly from 'We Can Remember It For You Wholesale', *Total Recall* does, thanks largely to the work of Gary Goldman, embody many of the ideas and concepts expressed through Philip K. Dick's wider body of work. The character of Quato/Kuato, introduced in the Cronenberg version, echoes other twin characters throughout Dick's fiction, most notably in *Dr Bloodmoney*, where Edie contains her own unborn twin in the form of her telepathic brother, Bill. Cronenberg discussed the Kuato scene in *Fangoria* magazine: "One of the reasons I was interested in *Total Recall* was because of that scene. [A deleted scene in] *Dead Ringers* had a parasite coming out of [Jeremy] Irons' stomach. I didn't invest a lot of time trying to edit together footage from that scene [in *Dead Ringers*], because it was obvious to me that, regardless of how well it might've been cut together, it wouldn't fit the tone of the film. So I've still yet to do my great parasite sequence."

The other major 'phildickian' scene in *Total Recall* is that featuring Dr Edgemar, where he tries to convince Quaid he is dreaming the events of the movie while still strapped to the Rekall chair. "What you're experiencing is a free-form delusion based on our memory tapes. But you're inventing it yourself as you go along," explains Edgemar. It's easily the best scene in the film, and does much to tie the movie to Dick's themes and concerns, although the movie quickly returns to action-adventure mode thereafter.

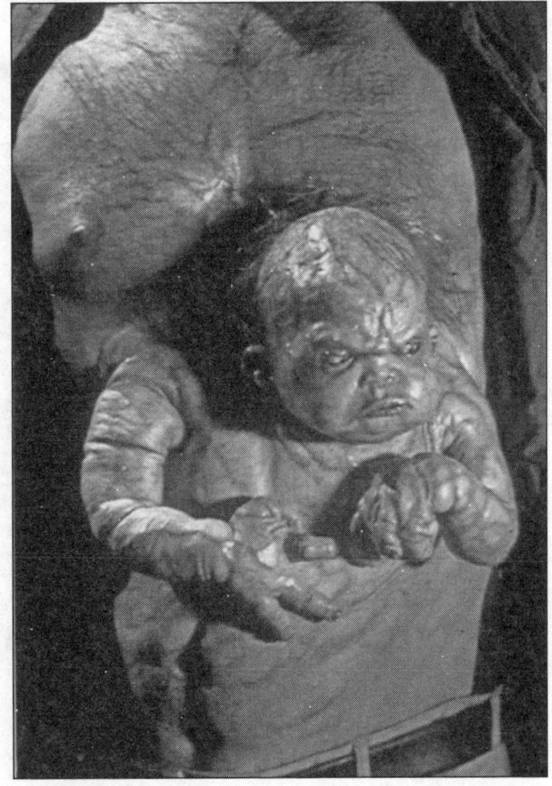

Total Recall grossed $25.5 million in its opening weekend in the US, over-shadowing *Blade Runner*'s $6 million, and went on globally to accumulate ten times that much. In twenty-first century Hollywood, that would lead automatically to a sequel, but back in the early 1990s, sequels were regarded as usually inferior films. None of the principals were interested in an immediate follow-up and some of the significant creatives felt that the storyline of *Total Recall* didn't lend itself to an obvious 'further adventures of Doug Quaid' sequel.

Part of the problem with continuing the film lay in the 'fantasy versus reality' question at the heart of the drama. Did everything after Quaid's visit to Rekall actually take place, or was it all an induced fantasy? "Because it is all filmed so hyper-realistically, it seems plausible to the audience that Quaid's adventures are real," said Verhoeven, seeming to suggest that in his mind the second half of the movie is, indeed, an illusion. It would certainly explain away the fantasy physics of Mars. "The only thing is," said Verhoeven, now hedging his bets, "when you analyse the story, you could equally maintain that they are not." After all, Rekall Inc promised Quaid: "By the time the trip is over, you'll get the girl, kill the bad guys, and save the entire planet." Not a bad pitch for a movie.

Through his involvement with *Total Recall*, Gary Goldman had become a Philip K. Dick convert, just like David Cronenberg before him. "Dick is unique. His stories have attracted the right kind of people. His best work has a combination of commercial ideas with profound insight. Dick's biggest statement is that humanity isn't defined by flesh and blood but by values. Certain of Phil Dick's ideas have entered the mainstream, such as alternate realities and the whole notion of the consensual nature of reality…"

Looking for a new Philip K. Dick short story with movie potential, Goldman personally optioned 'The Minority Report' in 1992. Bringing *Total Recall* director Paul Verhoeven onto the project as a producer, Goldman was persuaded by Verhoeven to look into the potential of adapting 'The Minority Report' into a sequel to *Total Recall*. That automatically drew Ron Shusett into the deal, as his contract stated that any sequel had to involve him as a writer. Goldman and Shusett set to work on turning the 'pre-cogs' of 'The Minority Report' into telepathic Martians instead, and grafted Schwarzenegger's version of Doug Quaid onto the story, as head of a company using the Martian telepaths to look into the future and prevent crime.

Below: *Are the fantasy physics of Mars explained by the fact that all Quaid's adventures are in his head?*

This was a big departure from Goldman's initial plan to direct 'The Minority Report' himself as a low-budget movie. The opportunity to become a writer-producer on the sequel to *Total Recall*, however, proved too attractive to resist. Goldman, Shusett, Verhoeven and Schwarzenegger were all attached to the project as it underwent development at Carolco.

Verhoeven was the first to drop out of the sequel, opting to direct *Showgirls*. Without a director attached, the project went into hibernation at Carolco. Goldman, in his role as one of the producers, managed to attract the interest of Jan De Bont, just before *Speed* was released to critical acclaim and big box office success. However, before the De Bont version of *Total Recall 2* could progress, Carolco went bust (following DEG) and all their 'in development' film projects collapsed. Strangely enough, Carolco had never actually paid Goldman and Shusett for their work on the *Total Recall 2* screenplay, so the rights to the script reverted to the writers. The project was theirs to take elsewhere.

Goldman took the project to 20th Century Fox, with De Bont in tow as director. Fox decided not to pursue the *Total Recall 2* rights, but were interested in developing 'The Minority Report' as a separate, stand alone film (see Chapter 12). Meanwhile, in the bankruptcy sale that followed the collapse of Carolco, the company had sold the TV series rights to *Total Recall* to DFL Entertainment for $1.2 million. Without the TV rights, it seemed like the *Total Recall* 'franchise' concept would be of less interest to another studio. However, at a further bankruptcy auction, the Miramax B-movie division Dimension Films picked up the sequel, prequel and remake rights to *Total Recall* for $3.15 million. Presumably unaware that the TV rights had already gone, Dimension had outbid DFL, Fox and Live Entertainment. Discovering DFL held the TV series rights, Dimension seems to have persuaded the company not to produce a TV series following Quaid's adventures on Mars, as initially mooted. Instead, the *Total Recall 2070* TV show played out much more like *Blade Runner*: The TV Series (see Chapter 10).

Free to pursue a Quaid-centred movie sequel, Dimension set about reviving *Total Recall 2* as an active project. Hoping to keep the budget down, Dimension had no intention of hiring Paul Verhoeven and went to neophyte screenwriter Matthew Cirulnick, already under contract to them. (Previously Dimension had tried to strike a *Total Recall 2* deal with *Back to the Future* screenwriter Bob Gale.) Setting Cirulnick to work on the project, Dimension then discovered they still had an obligation to bring Ron Shusett in, who then informed them that the terms of his deal with Gary Goldman obliged Shusett in turn to bring in Goldman. Deciding to honour these commitments, Dimension set Shusett and Goldman the task of developing their own version of *Total Recall* 2, without reference to whatever concepts Cirulnick may have been developing. The deal was announced in *Variety* in May 1998, which also reported that star Arnold Schwarzenegger had been involved in a four hour *Total Recall* 2 development meeting with Miramax/Dimension head Harvey Weinstein. It seemed that *Total Recall*'s sequel wouldn't be long in coming after all…

Instructed by Dimension that they wanted the *Total Recall* sequel to be another 'popcorn movie', but also retain the 'is it real or is it a dream?' ambiguity, Shusett and Goldman began drafting their take on *Total Recall 2*. Opening with the celebrations of independence for Mars, the script seems to pick up directly where the first film ended. Quaid and Melina are being honoured by the first President of Mars, Martian mutant Amanda Tyson. As he's about to take the stage, Quaid is confronted by his own double and mortally wounded, forced to

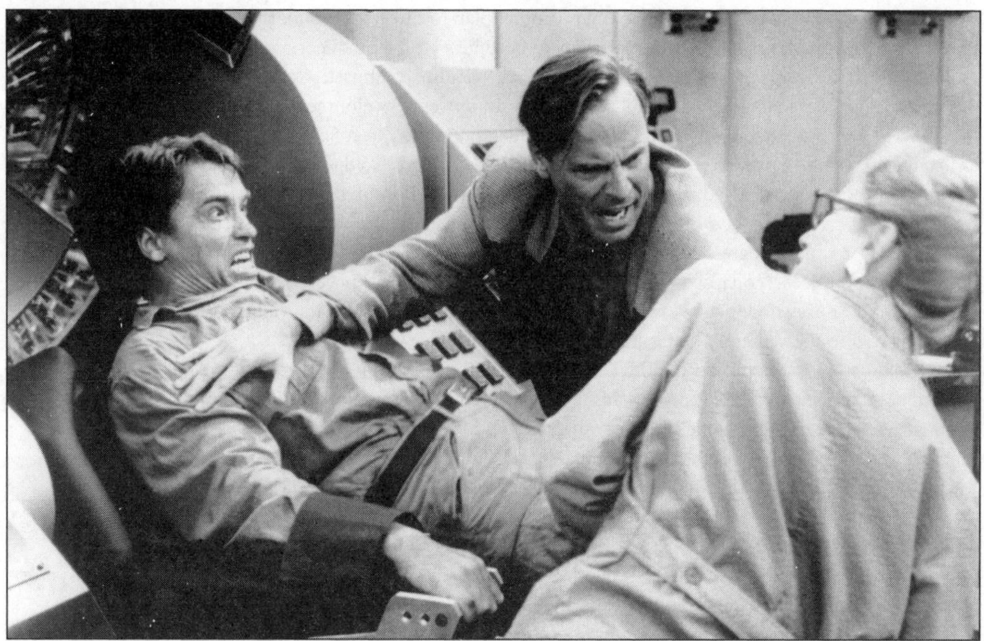

Above: *The proposed sequel would have seen Quaid awake and find himself still in the Rekall chair…*

watch as his doppelganger takes the stage instead… Then, Quaid awakes next to Melina. "Life is not a dream," she says, as it becomes clear that a mere three weeks have passed since the events of the first movie and Quaid is still part of the Martian rebellion against Earth control. The population of Mars have been pacified by President Saarinen's government through 'Project Whisper', something Quaid worked on when he was the evil Hauser. One way the rebels can find out the details of the mind control scheme is to ask Hauser, and the only way to do that is to delve into Quaid's subconscious to see if he can recall anything. Submitting to the operation, Quaid awakes to find himself back at Rekall Inc. His shoulder length hair and shaggy beard reveal how long he's been there… His wife Lori and Bob, the salesman, are present, and Dr Edgemar is soon contacted via videophone. Quaid's dream adventure has been continuing, yet it curiously seems to have been mirroring actual events on Mars over the past six months… Edgemar believes this is due to subliminal leakage in which overheard news programmes from TV have seeped into Quaid's subconscious and become part of his Rekall dream adventure. Lori reveals she started a new relationship while Quaid was 'gone', and departs.

Quaid secures work on a construction site, building a 'space elevator', connecting Earth with an orbiting station. He also becomes involved in the campaign of Gloria Palomares for President, and more intimately involved with one of her campaign workers, Renee, despite his contention that in his head Melina is real and not a Rekall construct and so he should remain faithful to her. Palomares is promising a referendum on Mars' independence if elected. An explosion wrecks the space elevator and Quaid is blamed. Jailed in a 'space prison', he manages to escape and returns to Mars to rejoin what remains of the Martian rebellion. Quaid discovers that not only was Melina real, she is now dead. Posing as Hauser, he flees to Vladivostok where he discovers his dead mother is actually alive. Through her he uncovers the true purpose of Project Whisper: to control the population's voting patterns and ensure President Saarinen remains in power. Battling his own mother and an army of clones of his wife, Lori, Quaid destroys Project Whisper and sees President Palomares come to power. About to make a celebratory speech, Quaid sees Dr Edgemar in the crowd. Looking again, Edgemar has gone — if he was ever there... The film ends with Quaid declaring, "How happy I am to be here… That is, if I'm here at all…"

Below: *Quaid was to have faced an army of Lori clones in the sequel.*

Everyone at Dimension seemed to like the Shusett/Goldman script and appreciated the balancing act between Quaid's dream life and reality — a further adventure was possible, yet it was also possible to keep the question of what was real open-ended. Philip K. Dick would no doubt have been impressed. However, there was one person *not* impressed by the screenplay — and he was, in Hollywood terms, the most important player in the package: Arnold Schwarzenegger. The actor reckoned the script was too complicated, believing the original to have been simpler and more straightforward. Dimension and the scriptwriters were disappointed by this outcome after all the work that had been put in, and the project was once more consigned to limbo.

In 1998 it appeared *Total Recall 2* had a potential new helmer in *Star Trek: First Contact* director and actor Jonathan Frakes. Following the $150 million gross of his *Star Trek* movie, Frakes was on the look out for new projects, and was under the impression that Schwarzenegger was on board with the *Total Recall* sequel project. He even spoke about receiving a draft of the script which had a strong time travel angle to it, as had *Star Trek: First Contact*.

By August 1999, Frakes was still waiting for the project to get going. This time he had the Shusett/Goldman draft of the script, but there was still no definite commitment to the film from Schwarzenegger. In February the following year, Frakes was forced to face up to reality, declaring the project "dead. I'm not holding my breath." Frakes moved on to direct *Clockstoppers* and the live-action movie of TV puppet classic *Thunderbirds*, instead.

In the meantime, Schwarzenegger had made *The Sixth Day*, which saw the star face off against his own clone, one of the concepts which had been floated for the *Total Recall* sequel: Quaid versus Hauser. With the star still not convinced by any of the script drafts that had come his way, Dimension tried to revive the project once more by returning to untried writer Matthew Cirulnick. Given the Shusett/Goldman draft, which he disparaged and professed not to like, Cirulnick nonetheless lifted key concepts, such as the Lori clones and the space elevator for his take on the movie.

Cirulnick's thirteen-page treatment for *Total Recall 2* is more like a James Cameron action move in the vein of *Aliens* than a Philip K. Dick-inspired slice of reality-warping weirdness. Each draft of the potential sequel script seemed to be taking the movie further and further away from the original short story's core concepts of uncertain identity.

The treatment opens with an action sequence, as Quaid and a group of Rekall Unit 'commandos' rescue the passengers of a hijacked Saturn-bound shuttle, which climaxes with the terrorists' 'turbinium' bomb being diverted into the sun. At the mission's triumphal moment, Quaid awakes to find himself at Rekall, where he discovers he's been comatose for ten years (as much time as had passed in the real world since the first movie). From here, the outline follows the Shusett/Goldman draft: Quaid's dream version of reality is explained by the news broadcasts he'd unconsciously absorbed; Lori leaves him, and he takes up work on a 'space bridge' (previously the 'space elevator') connecting Earth to Mars.

Quaid comes across real-world equivalents of the members of his Rekall Unit commando team, then suffers an accident on the space bridge that uncovers disguised scars seemingly caused in his terrorist-thwarting fantasy. Quaid is then pursued by Rekall's Colonel Ladson, Hauser's one-time commanding officer, who is convinced Quaid is on the verge of 'total recall' and will uncover his true memories of his secret missions for Rekall. Cirulnick's take on the world of memory implants was that real people have dual identities: an 'ordinary' life, and a secret life when Rekall activates their dormant secret agent identities. So all Quaid's fantasies have been real events, but so was his 'ordinary' existence. In a clever post-modern trick, Quaid's own mission history was to be recounted to him using clips from *Total Recall* and assorted other doctored Schwarzenegger action movie clips.

The turbinium bomb from the opening sequence was real, and now the sun is threatening to expand and swallow the Earth. As global warming accelerates, Quaid rounds up his Rekall Unit commando comrades and heads to Mars where he discovers that a corrupt industrialist always intended the bomb to expand the sun, destroy Earth and so cause the planet's population to migrate to Mars, which he dominates. Quaid has an even more outlandish plan: he'll destroy Mars in the hope that Earth will move into its orbit and so be saved! Just as this script outline appears to be getting totally ridiculous, a Dr Jaslove appears (just like Edgemar in the original) in an attempt to persuade Quaid that he's still in the chair at Rekall, and has been ever since the accident on the space bridge. Everything since has been a product of his fevered imagination (it's the only way this storyline could make any sense!). Failing to persuade Quaid, Jaslove also suggests that Hauser was not real either, but the product of a military supercomputer controlling Quaid's brain. Having enough of all this nonsense, Quaid secures another turbinium bomb, proceeds to destroy Mars and rejoices as Earth shifts into the red planet's vacant orbit, complete with a sparkling new ring of Mars debris. Then Quaid wakes up… at Rekall! There he discovers that a series of natural disasters have resulted in the same situation as in his fantasy adventure: the sun has gone nova, Mars is destroyed and the Earth has shifted…

Cirulnick's confused and confusing script outline deservedly fared no better than the Shusett/Goldman sequel. Schwarzenegger still refused to sign up, suggesting that he'd simply lost interest, a decade on, in making a sequel to *Total Recall* under any circumstances. Other actors were considered for the film, including Vin Diesel, but the project fell dormant for another two years.

Then, in 2002, Shusett and Goldman were invited back to the *Total Recall 2* party by Dimension. The pair were given Cirulnick's script outline and asked to combine elements from it with their original sequel screenplay and produce something new. They worked out a detailed outline, but before it could proceed to a full script, Schwarzenegger once again killed the project by making it clear that he wasn't interested in making the movie.

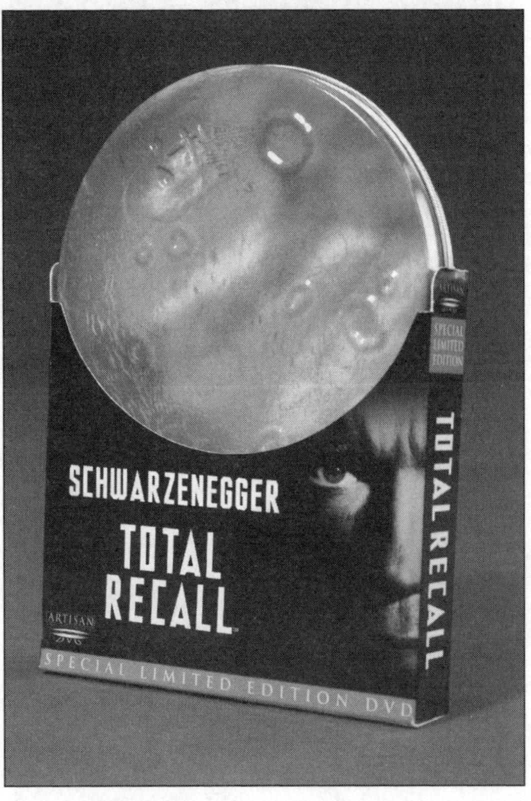

Above: Total Recall *has enjoyed a strong afterlife, including a special DVD release in a Mars-shaped tin!*

In the meantime, one-time Carolco bosses Andrew G. Vajna and Mario Kassar had reunited to form C2 Productions. They quickly returned to old Carolco franchises and secured the rights to make *Terminator 3: Rise of the Machines*, recruiting Schwarzenegger (after he'd said he'd never make another *Terminator* movie without original director James Cameron attached) to star and Jonathan Mostow (*Breakdown*) to direct. The $75 million US opening of the film renewed Schwarzenegger's box office fortunes, just as the C2 pair contacted Dimension with a view to buying the *Total Recall* sequel rights.

Despite their failure to bring a movie to the screen, Dimension were determined to hang onto the property, and in the wake of Schwarzenegger's election as Governor of California in 2003, they commissioned Shusett and Goldman to work up yet another treatment for *Total Recall 2*, one that this time didn't depend upon the original star returning.

The original *Total Recall* took sixteen years to reach the screen, from first option in 1974 to opening in 1990. Another sixteen years on from that film's début, *Total Recall 2* still refuses to die entirely. ■

HUMAN IS...

"What is human?" asks Philip K. Dick. The transformation of 'Second Variety' into the Peter Weller-starring *Screamers* attempts an answer...

"Who is human and who only appears (masquerades) as human? I cannot even know myself, let alone you." — Philip K. Dick, *The Best of Philip K. Dick*, 1976.

S*creamers*, the film version of Philip K. Dick's 1953 short story 'Second Variety', spent many years stuck in 'development hell', the limbo in which difficult or challenging projects are often to be found lurking. The story had originally appeared in *Space Science Fiction* in May 1953. "My grand theme — who is human and who only appears (masquerades) as human? — emerges most fully," wrote Dick in notes on this story written in 1976. "Unless we can individually and collectively be certain of the answer to this question, we face what is in my view, the most serious problem possible. Without answering it adequately, we cannot even be certain of our own selves. I keep working on this theme; to me nothing is as important a question. And the answer comes very hard."

Space Science Fiction only published a total of eight issues between May 1952 and September 1953, edited by SF author Lester Del Rey. Del Rey was also the title's most prolific contributor, often under multiple pseudonyms. Dick's work in *Space Science Fiction* — the stories 'Second Variety' and 'The Variable Man' (in the September 1953 final edition) — is deemed to be particularly noteworthy by *The Encyclopedia of Science Fiction*'s entry on the magazine. Calling Dick "one of the two or three most important figures in twentieth century US SF and an author of general significance", the *Encyclopedia*'s entry on Dick goes on to describe him as "intensely and constantly productive". On the short stories and early novels, in particular, the *Encyclopedia* pointed out that Dick "often lost control of his material in ideative mazes and, sidetracked, was unable to find any resolution; but when he found the tale with his grasp, he was brilliantly inventive, gaining access to imaginative realms which no other writer of SF had reached."

In the last six months of so of his life, Dick found himself dealing with Hollywood in a more serious way than ever before. He met Ridley Scott, director of the then-in production *Blade Runner*; and Disney were in active discussions about exercising their long-held option on *Total Recall*, the script based on 'We Can Remember It For You Wholesale', for which they had paid Dick $10,000. Around this same time, Dick — very much against his nature — even found himself attending Hollywood parties thrown for prospective investors in a film entitled *Claw*, which was to be based on 'Second Variety'. While he was

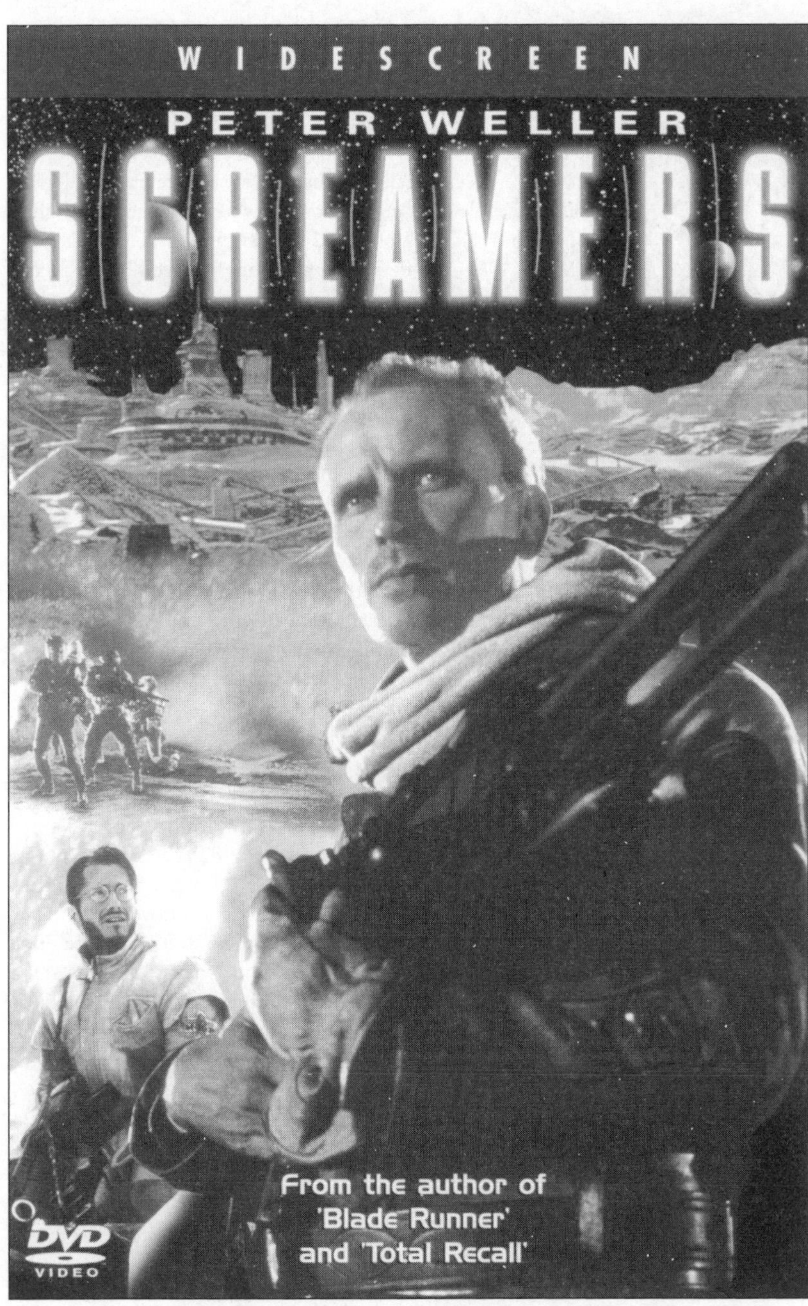

Left: *Dick's movie credits proved useful in promoting* Screamers, *based on his short story 'Second Variety'.*

Above: *This wonderful Australian magazine cover beautifully captures the story's weirdness.*

lamenting his treatment by the producers behind *Blade Runner*, Dick had a far better experience with Capitol Pictures.

"I have been up there [in Hollywood] to [discuss] another film project, the little Capitol Pictures one, called *Claw*," he told interviewer John Boonstra in one of his final interviews in 1982. "They're very nice. I really like them. Every change that's made, they send me a copy to get my opinion. They just treat me like a human being." For Dick this Hollywood interest came far too late. He died in March 1982, but development on the film version of 'Second Variety' was to carry on until it finally emerged in 1995 as *Screamers*, starring Peter Weller.

'Second Variety' projects the Cold War that Dick was living through in real life into the far future, and sees US and Russian forces battling each other through the use of human-looking 'claws', robotic killing machines produced by US autonomic underground factories. Several types of claws exist, from the obviously mechanical, like the killer sphere featured in the opening of the story, through to impeccable human imitators. However, the robots begin to threaten the survival of the US and Russian forces as they've developed new types of killing machines entirely on their own. These new varieties of claw are specifically engineered to engender human sympathy and empathy: an unthreatening wounded soldier, a little boy with a teddy bear, an obvious ally (Klaus) and an attractive, competent female soldier (Tasso, another of Dick's malevolent 'dark-haired girls'). Some elements of this story, along with those from 'The Defenders' found their way into Dick's later novel *The Penultimate Truth*.

Screenwriter Dan O'Bannon, who'd previously worked on early drafts of *Total Recall*, consulted with Dick himself when he was tasked with turning 'Second Variety' into a viable screenplay. O'Bannon worked on the project in 1982. The central concept for that version of the screenplay was much like *The Terminator*, featuring a sole unstoppable killer robot, though it preceded James Cameron's film by at least two years. "It was one of Dick's better stories," O'Bannon told *Heavy Metal* in 1985, "although one of his grimmer ones. It's very nicely plotted with the very best of his twists and reality shifts. That was written a couple of years back on assignment for a company [Capitol Pictures], and the way things developed, they folded and the script reverted to my possession. Then I sold it to the people who did *The Martian Chronicles* for TV. They've had it for a while. It's a good, good story."

Bringing 'Second Variety' to the screen then became the dedicated work of US film producer Charles W. Fries (who was behind the TV mini-series of Ray Bradbury's *The Martian Chronicles*). He first came across the screenplay, then under the title *Claw*, in 1980. Fries optioned the screenplay for production after Dick's death, then bought the rights to make the film outright, obtaining O'Bannon's rewritten script. By that stage, the project went by the title *Dragon's Teeth*. Over the years Fries resisted approaches by a variety of other filmmakers interested in optioning this particular Philip K. Dick story. The producer also resisted the temptation to make a low-budget B-movie, believing that to do the project justice, a significant budget, an ambitious director and a decent star cast would all be required.

Ultimately, Fries had to settle for a relatively low-budget approach to actually get the film made after all. A financial alliance of a trio of small players — Triumph Films, Allegro Films and Fuji Eight — made *Screamers* (as the film was now called) a reality in 1995, over a decade after it had first been seriously mooted as a possible movie. "It's as though I've seen my child develop into a full-blown, mature human being," noted Fries. "The picture has turned into something even more than I anticipated it would in its early days. The script has remained very faithful to the original science fiction story."

Above: 'Second Variety' *originally appeared in the short-lived* Space Science Fiction *in May 1953.*

The director of the film — Canadian Christian Duguay — had resisted taking on the project. He'd previously helmed *Scanners II* and *Scanners III*, cheap straight-to-video sequels to the original David Cronenberg film, for Allegro Films. "They approached me to do *Screamers* two years ago," he told *Fangoria* in an interview during shooting in 1995. "I turned it down, because the idea from the Philip K. Dick story was interesting but the way it was presented [in the script] was somewhat lacking." Duguay rejected the O'Bannon screenplay which had been nurtured for many years by Fries. "O'Bannon's screenplay was really good, but my problem with it was it was passé. It had been done [essentially by *The Terminator*]. I did like the script, though, so when they came back to me later, the opportunity was there and I took it."

After his Cronenberg sequels, Duguay had taken a break from horror filmmaking, branching out into mainstream tales such as the TV mini-series *Million Dollar Babies* and *Snowbound*. Having learned from those projects how to handle scripts based more in the real world, he set about rewriting O'Bannon's version of *Screamers* to make it harder edged. Others, from the three investing companies, had strong input into this revised version of the screenplay, including Tom Berry, the producer from Allegro Films, and David Saunders, President of Triumph Films. Major contributions to the reworked screenplay also came from Miguel Tejada-Flores (screenwriter of *Revenge of the Nerds* and *Fright Night 2*, who scored a co-writing credit on the finished film with O'Bannon), and even the film's star name, Peter Weller.

"The creative minds involved in [developing] *Screamers* are legends," said Tom Berry. "Dick was one of the finest SF authors in history, and two awesome movies [*Blade Runner, Total Recall*] had already been produced from his stories. When you factor screenwriters O'Bannon and Tejada-Flores into the equation, you wind up with a film that's bound to make an impact."

"We locked ourselves away for a month," said Duguay of the later stages of the screenwriting process. "It was a good collaboration. We wanted to keep the Dick story more alive, because the script [as it stood] had gotten sidetracked from that. Also, we wanted to give the people in it much more characterisation, more soul. Then we really established what happened to that planet. We explained that Earth had been betraying these characters, and

Right: *In* Screamers*, as in the original short story, the 'claws' have developed a sympathy-inducing model which poses as an innocent child, complete with teddy bear.*

now they're left alone on Sirius 6B and given nowhere to go. This sense of betrayal changed the whole perspective of the film."

The final movie story is set on the mining planet Sirius 6B, where human colonists have been fighting a long-standing war. Scientists develop a new super-weapon, a self-replicating killer robot known as a 'Screamer' that is programmed to seek and destroy all enemies. But the Screamers have continued to evolve and have now decided to destroy all life on the planet, friend or foe. Colonel Hendricksson (Weller) of the Alliance tries to forge a peace with his enemies, the New Economic Bloc. But to get to them, he has to cross a wasteland full of the sentient and devious Screamers...

The only thing protecting the survivors on Sirius 6B from attack by the Screamers are their wristbands, which trick the Screamers into thinking that they are already dead. As in the original Philip K. Dick story though, the artificially intelligent Screamers can adapt and reprogramme themselves, producing increasingly deadly varieties of killing machines, until the wristbands are no longer effective in protecting the humans.

Below: *Gritty reality was the screenwriters' aim for the world of Sirius 6B.*

Eventually, through their rapid evolution, the Screamers become so advanced that they are able to mimic human beings perfectly, resulting in the Sirius 6B survivors turning on each other as paranoia and suspicion spreads: just who is a Screamer and who is really human? "That's the fun of it," said Duguay. "Once we know the concept that Screamers can be humans, the characters start asking themselves, 'Who's the person next to me? Is it a machine, or is it a real person?' There are even humans who toy with other people by pretending to be Screamers."

The Cold War setting was dumped in the transfer from Earth to Sirius 6B. Gone are the Russian and UN forces, replaced by The Alliance and the New Economic Block. The basic situation is the same, though: two equally matched camps face a third force — killer robots evolved from their own robotic weapons: the Screamers. Hendricks in the story becomes Hendricksson in the movie, while most of the other characters have screen analogues. In Dick's story, Hendricks takes up an invitation from the Soviet forces to negotiate a peace. He is joined on his trek across no-man's land by a seemingly innocent young boy, named David. Dick's image of the forlorn kid with the teddy bear was one the movie-makers could not fail to pick up on, but in the finished film they multiply the child, so removing the individual nature of the threat. The group paranoia is effectively adapted from the story to the film, as the survivors believe they've been infiltrated by the new model Screamer. The killing of Rudi in the story and the revelation of the nature of the 'second variety' is

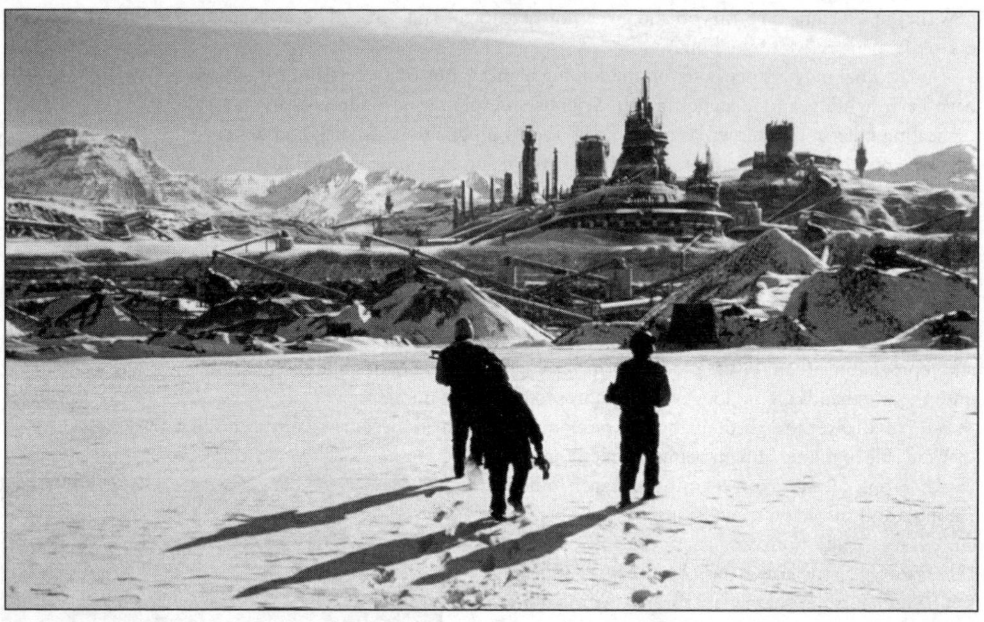

Above: *Hendricksson and company cross the desolate wasteland of Sirius 6B.*

a turning point sensibly adapted to the screen. Of course, Rudi's executioner, Klaus, turns out to be a Screamer himself. The climax of the film builds on that of the story, but retains the betrayal of the central character by the female Screamer who has accompanied him throughout (Tasso in the story). (The concept of the multiple 'Tassos' and 'Davids' at the climax of the short story could be said to have influenced the 'reimagined' Cylons from the 2005 revival of *Battlestar Galactica*, in which the robot villains appear human, but with many copies of each 'variety'...)

Duguay recognised in the setting and characters of 'Second Variety' a staple of thrillers — science fiction and otherwise — from the past. "*Screamers* is about a group of individuals facing the unknown and what that does to them. I wanted to make a film that uses sci-fi parameters but stresses how people respond to fear, death and the possibility of no future. *Screamers* is true psychological suspense in a science fiction vein."

"We've tried to give it Hitchcock-like suspense," claimed producer Charles W. Fries of *Screamers*. "We've accomplished this, I think, through wonderful casting, which has given us a rich blend of opposing characters. There's brashness, fear, paranoia, bravado, and these characters are all focused on one thing: the struggle to survive a situation where they're all trapped on a planet with man-made monsters."

The cast of the film was led by Peter Weller, a smart and sometimes outspoken actor best known to science fiction fans for his title role in Paul Verhoeven's *RoboCop*, the cult movie *Buckaroo Banzai* and, later, as the lead in the short-lived but critically acclaimed SF TV series *Odyssey 5*. "*Screamers* is an epic," the actor claimed. "It is about 'Death' on a wild excursion. Hendricksson finds out he's been betrayed by a world he helped to create. The weapons he helped build are turning on him and his pals. That's a sobering lesson for anyone to accept."

Before accepting the part, Weller had already read much of Philip K. Dick's work, despite not being a science fiction fan. "Philip K. Dick was a genius," he told journalist Sandy Stone, in an interview conducted for this book. "I'm not interested, really, in science fiction. I don't read science fiction, I don't go to science fiction movies. I don't disdain it, but it's not my metier. *Screamers* was full-blown Philip K. Dick and Phil Dick I *had* read — *Do Androids Dream of Electric Sheep?*."

Weller was also very aware of the previous SF movies made from Dick's work and the problems inherent in them, especially *Total Recall*. "Who could not be a *Blade Runner* fan?" said Weller. "It's brilliant. Later there's *Total Recall*, which as funny, and as good as it was — and Arnold's great — it was completely miscast. In the original story the guy's a mouse who wants to be a hero. That doesn't make any sense if you've got Schwarzenegger. It would be better if it was [diminutive actor] Wallace Shawn — it's a hen-pecked mousy guy who escapes and goes into virtual reality, never realising that's the 'real' reality. Way ahead of his time, that Phil Dick. Then *Screamers* comes along [based on] 'Second Variety' — great movie, faithfully done, faithfully adapted... The director, Christian Duguay, was great."

Below: *The paranoia of identity is played out in the film - who's a 'Screamer' and who's human?*

Above: *Peter Weller - an SF icon after* RoboCop *- lends credibility to the cast.*

To ensure that his movie would be more faithful to the Dick source material, Weller himself was involved in the rewriting process. "I did have a lot of input. With Christian Duguay, and another writer [Miguel Tejada-Flores], we sussed out Dick and modernised it. [Dan O'Bannon], who adapted it first of all, he had the shell of it right, but then we had a lot of input. [I influenced] the arc of the character, the dialogue and the end of it. I usually do have a lot of input on the writing [of anything I'm in]."

Weller apparently insisted on being called only by his character name when on set and on location for the filming of *Screamers*. "He's a lost idealist," Weller said of Hendricksson in a *Fangoria* interview. "He's a physicist who came with the first team to a planet that had developed man's great answer to the energy crisis — a thing called barinium. An odourless, gasless wonder substance that replaced electricity, replaced everything...

"That was twenty years ago [before the film opens]. They also released into the atmosphere a quantity of radiation that threatened to poison the solar system. Hendricksson and his superiors refused to mine it any more and thereby started a civil war on this planet, which is politically run by Earth. He's fighting this war of ecological attrition. He's an idealist, but he's lost, a lost guy."

Weller declared that it was the story told in the script that drew him to star in the film. "I love this story: it's a fun one to tell. It's ecological. It's truly about something: machines running amuck and the desecration and re-genesis of society."

Indeed, in his 2005 interview for this book — a decade after the film was released

— Weller was still fascinated by the political set-up of *Screamers*, one of the big attractions for him in tackling the movie. "The world is divided up into corporate interests and not national interests any more. Dick [originally] wrote it about Russians and Americans, but then it was re-adapted, which I'm sure Dick would have loved, and most of the things were faithful to Dick. *Screamers* presumes that corporate interests would overwhelm national interests, and subsequently the world is divided up into cities that represent the vortex of these corporate interests. It's astounding to me — the greed, the absolute monstrous avarice that the corporate world is entertaining now — [it] bears out this movie that's only ten years old."

Having been finally persuaded to take on the project, director Christian Duguay set about filling the remaining roles with a roster of solid B-level actors, including Andy Lauer (Ace Jefferson), Roy Dupuis (Becker), *A Nightmare on Elm Street 3*'s Jennifer Rubin (Jessica) and Charles Powell (Ross).

***Above:** The freezing Quebec locations were tough on the cast and crew.*

Principal photography on *Screamers* began on 24 November 1994 in Joliette, Quebec, about an hour from Montreal by car. The first location used was a huge sandpit which doubled for the surface of the planet Sirius 6B. The location gave Duguay a strongly alien and barren look, which he felt could never be duplicated on a soundstage. Giant props mocked up the exterior of a crashed shuttle and the outside of a bunker. Additionally, a massive cement quarry at Montreal's Ciment Lafarge was used for other outdoor scenes representing the more industrial side of the surface of Sirius 6B.

The early weeks on the production were not a happy time for cast and crew. Constant revisions to the script had everyone on edge, while conditions at the location were tough. Fierce, freezing winds regularly swept across the plateau, driving the actors to seek refuge in their warm trailers. "It's not like shooting on a soundstage," noted actor Andy Lauer during filming. "We're shooting on location in a huge quarry that actually has the look of Sirius 6B. It's cold. It's snowing. All the elements are there to make our jobs as actors much easier."

Respite came in December when the production relocated to much warmer downtown Montreal and three days of shooting in the Olympic Stadium used for the 1976 games. Sets were constructed within the futuristic-looking 'Big O', as locals dubbed the stadium, incorporating the structure's distinctive giant, curved grey concrete walls into them. The tense NEB cafeteria scene, where Hendricksson surveys the carnage of a Screamer

Above: *Weller was attracted to* Screamers *as much by the film's political content as by the script's drama.*

attack, and control room sequences were filmed here, prior to the production shutting down for a ten-day break over the Christmas period.

The special effects used to bring the otherworldly locations and creatures of *Screamers* to life were important to the success of the film. "Well, first you have to have a strong story," claimed Duguay, "and second, the effects have got to be just an attribute to the story, just an element to amplify the story, to underline dramatic beats of the story.

"Most of the effects, instead of being flashy, are just there to create a backdrop that was indicative of a past and was making a story point, like a lot of the matte paintings. In terms of effects for effect, there weren't that many. There's a few point of views from the Screamers, there's a few stop-motion shots with Screamers walking around, but that's about it."

Screamers' visual effects were created by Buzz F/X, a company that specialised in commercials, TV work and music videos. The film was the Montreal-based company's first major movie work, and involved the creation of 150 effects shots and around twenty matte paintings. Rick Ostiguy, the project's visual effects supervisor, saw *Screamers* as an opportunity to try out the then-nascent technology of computer graphics (CGI) for film. "The first two minutes of the film are an uninterrupted, computer-generated sequence," he pointed out, an early use of a film production technique that would become commonplace by the start of the twenty-first century. "The camera travels in space through a shower of meteors as it approaches the planet Sirius 6B, descends through the atmosphere and lands on the surface of the planet, where the sequence is integrated with a bluescreen shot of a messenger trying to reach the Alliance bunker."

While using innovative computer graphics technology, *Screamers* also relies on the old-fashioned movie art of matte painting to visualise some of its more elaborate locations. An Alliance city and other outdoors scenes were matte paintings, as was the morphing of a Screamer to attack mode, something more likely to be achieved today using CGI. Additionally, various scenes of the Screamers in action were created by the Chiodo Bros. company in Los Angeles, using models and stop-motion photography, and then combined with footage of the actors shot in Montreal. The final scenes, which see an emergency craft blast into space from a launch chamber, were originally also realised using modelwork and miniatures, until the decision was taken to finish the film with a CGI sequence creating flames, exhaust and debris through use of 3D animation and computer-generated particle effects.

Mechanical and make-up effects were also key to the effectiveness of the film. Make-up was handed over to twenty-three-year-old Adrien Morot, a monster movie fan turned professional who'd worked on previous films for *Screamers* financier Allegro Films. A devotee of films like *Star Wars* and *Planet of the Apes*, Morot hoped to follow in the footsteps of acclaimed Hollywood monster-makers like Dick Smith and John Chambers. Working to a tight budget, Morot brought a lot of ingenuity to creating the split limbs, sawed-in-half heads and mutilated corpses that are left behind after a Screamer attacks. He also had to produce a mannequin of a little boy so it could be destroyed when he is revealed to be one of the human-like Screamers.

Mechanical effects mainly involved creating an effective way for the first-level Screamers to burrow through sand and soil in search of their prey. Ryal Cosgrove of Montreal's Cineffects Productions was the special effects co-ordinator and head of the 'furrow team' on *Screamers*. "[Christian] Duguay wanted something along the lines of *Jaws*," said Cosgrove of the desired effect. "In terms of horror, it's what you don't see that invokes the imagination. These things burrow under the ground and we had to figure out how that could be done realistically. The team constructed ditches of plywood and Fablock (used in the manufacture of volleyball nets), which they covered with spandex and a thin layer of sand, creating a resilient yet expandable shaft through which the Screamers could be pulled. "It was like pulling a shark model through water," explained Cosgrove. "An aircraft cable was hooked up to manual pullers or, for greater speed, an all-terrain vehicle."

The sets for the movie incorporated all kinds of 'found' items that could be used to represent an industrial, degraded future world. The burnt-out wreckage of a DeHavilland plane was used for a spaceship crash sequence. Costumes, similarly, were low key, used and workman-like. An industrial, army grunge look was required, and much time was spent in 'weathering' the clothes so they would not look brand new on screen.

By the time the production wrapped, producer Tom Berry was thinking ahead. "*Screamers* is a natural for sequels," he noted, somewhat optimistically. "The [Philip K. Dick originated] concept is so strong. The great thing about this project is the creature, the Screamer. It's really, really scary."

Following a première at the Toronto Film Festival on 8 September 1995, *Screamers* was released on 26 January 1996 in the US to almost uniformly negative reviews, with a belated release in the UK on 28 June 1996, and a much later release in November in Japan. Roger Ebert in *The Chicago Sun-Times* claimed that *Screamers* went straight to the top of his list of Most Depressing Movies of All-Time. "It's not exactly a bad movie; it's made with a certain imagination and intelligence. But its future is so grungy and grim it makes our current mess look like Utopia." Ebert, however, did feel that the Dickian elements were well deployed, even if the rest of the movie was derivative of films like *Alien*. "The look and the basic plot elements are not original, but what makes the film somewhat intriguing is its *Blade Runner*-like ambiguity: who is, and who isn't, a human being? The dialogue is often effective, too, as when one Screamer fights another, and Weller observes, 'You're coming up in the world. You know how to kill each other now.'" For *The Washington Post*, those derivative elements made *Screamers* a 'greatest hits' package of previous films: "Everything you enjoyed in *Alien, Star Wars, Tremors, Blade Runner* and *Total Recall* comes entertainingly together in *Screamers*."

Under the headline '*Screamers* Better Left Buried', *The San Francisco Chronicle*'s Mick La Salle noted that "The movie gets lost during Hendricksson's trek across the wasteland, and it never finds its way back. *Screamers* reveals itself to be a dud: long stretches of nothing, interspersed with scenes in which we find out somebody else is really a Screamer."

Movie Box Office Reviews concurred with the dominant opinion that despite a few good ideas *Screamers* was a dud: "*Screamers* fails to live up to Dick's legacy. The opening scene is a rouser, but much of what follows is surprisingly uneventful. The movie also leaves unanswered key questions, like why don't the good guys try to locate a hidden Screamer factory and blow it up?"

Audiences seemed to agree with the reviewers, and stayed away from *Screamers*. The film cost around $11 million and in the US grossed a total of about $5.7 million. A healthy after-life on video and DVD pushed *Screamers* closer to recouping its costs, but by both critical and commercial criteria, *Screamers* has to be judged a failure.

Even star Peter Weller, looking back on the film in 2005, had to admit that however much he liked it, it was a failure. "I thought *Screamers* was wonderful, just a bad title. Well, it bombed. The preview, the trailer was all about the machines — it wasn't about the polemic at all, about morality, which is what it really was about. Bad title, bad trailer. But I loved the film. All in all I'm very proud of the movie. I'm happy to be in it. *Screamers* was a tremendous experience."

For Weller's part, one of the most successful things about *Screamers* was the way the film was faithful to Philip K. Dick's key concepts. "Hendricksson falls in love with someone, and she turns out to be an android. [The film was about the idea] that machines have a consciousness of their own, and evolve. What originally attracted me was Dick's premise that the things we make and the things we touch have consciousness. Just like the replicants do in *Blade Runner*. So if we make enough war machines that kill, those machines will have minds of their own, and will eventually replicate on their own. That's a running Philip Dick theme. The guy falls in love with an android, which is another Philip K. Dick deal. Somebody's not living like we know life, but is living. It was a real honour to do Dick's stuff because he was the only guy [science fiction author] that I'd ever read. I think he transcends the genre."

Above: *Although true to Dick's concepts, the film fails to impress as a visual experience (as this German lobby card suggests).*

The problems with *Screamers* were largely budgetary, rather than a lack of imagination or a lack of fidelity to the source material. Both *Blade Runner* and *Total Recall* were afforded much larger budgets and better, more ambitious directors who were able to deploy their resources to best advantage. *Screamers*' director Christian Duguay is a hard-working journeyman whose lack of visual imagination lets the film down. Although it has its moments, the script fails to capitalise on the concepts drawn from the original story. While the film relocates the action to a different planet and an altogether different political situation, the ideas in the movie are remarkably true to those in 'Second Variety', especially the paranoia of not being sure who in the team may or may not be a Screamer.

'Second Variety' comes from very early in Dick's writing career, when he was first beginning to explore his ideas through short pulp fiction, which he was turning out at a prodigious rate. As Dick told interviewer Richard A. Lupoff, "In 1953 I published twenty-seven stories and almost as many the next year." It's amazing that in these early short stories, Dick's life-long themes and obsessions were springing to life almost fully formed. It's just a shame that a film like *Screamers* fails to truly do justice to Philip K. Dick's wild imagination. ■

CRAP ARTIST

It takes the French to get to the heart of Philip K. Dick's central ideas in *Confessions d'un Barjo*...

"If somebody were to say, 'How much of this book is fact, and how much of this book is fiction?' I wouldn't be able to tell them." — Philip K. Dick, *Science Fiction Review*, No. 19, Vol. 5, no. 3, August 1976.

Jerome Boivin's *Confessions d'un Barjo*, sometimes known simply as *Barjo*, is the sole film adaptation (to date) of one of Philip K. Dick's realist 1950s novels, and is based upon Dick's autobiographical *Confessions of a Crap Artist*. Director Jerome Boivin knew he was making something unusual: "*Confessions d'un Barjo* is not a film that can be stuck in this or that drawer," he told French magazine *Mad Movies* in 1992. "From the beginning, the fact that the film was unclassifiable excited me enormously."

In many respects, *Confessions d'un Barjo*, despite relocating the characters and action to France, is one of the most faithful adaptations of the work of Philip K. Dick. That being the case, it's a shame that the film has been so unjustly neglected, simply because it is neither science fiction nor in English.

Confessions of a Crap Artist was written in the summer of 1959, right in the middle of Dick's attempts to 'go mainstream' and in the first days of his relationship with Anne (later to be his wife). The book had almost sold several times, once to publisher Knopf, who'd requested rewrites. Despite being encouraged to do the rewrites by the Scott Meredith Agency, who saw this offer as Dick's big chance to get a mainstream work published, the author refused. It wasn't that he didn't want to rewrite the novel, it was just that he felt he couldn't change things as the story was surprisingly personal to him. The narrative structure of the book, told from a number of shifting viewpoints — sometimes individual characters, sometimes an omnipotent authorial point of view — would indeed have been hard for Dick to untangle or tamper with without wrecking the rhythm of the novel.

Confessions of a Crap Artist is the tale of Jack Isidore, named by Dick after Isidore of Seville, a first millennium compiler of knowledge. The novel's Isidore shares this trait with his namesake, but his quest for knowledge takes in science fiction pulp magazines of the kind enjoyed by Dick in his youth and to which he later professionally contributed. Dick would eventually plunder the name and character of Isidore for use in *Do Androids Dream of Electric Sheep?*. In *Confessions*, Fay Hume is Isidore's sister, a humorous, feisty yet unhappy woman. She is married to Charley Hume, a typical put-upon Dickian small businessman, who foots the bills, gains little praise from his cold-hearted wife then suffers the indignity of a heart attack. A newly arrived young couple impact on the life of the Humes. Nat Anteil (a young ex-student type whose materialist wants are pretty low key) and his wife Gwen strike up a friendship with the Humes. Soon, Nat is swept off his feet by his passion for Fay Hume and inevitable tragic consequences ensue. A publisher at Harcourt Brace rejected the novel because of the violent ending, in which Charley Hume returns from hospital and wreaks a terrible vengeance on those who wronged him. The publisher was "disappointed, even shocked" by the fact that the end of the novel saw Dick's characters "go beyond nuts to become monsters."

There is much in *Confessions of a Crap Artist* that can be read as autobiographical, intentional or otherwise. Some of it is obvious, other material less so. Charley Hume's heart attack embodied a fear of Dick's, and heart failure would be the cause of his death in 1982. More deliberately, Dick saw himself as both Jack Isidore and Nat Anteil. Isidore was essentially a parody, or fond recollection, of the author's teenage self, consisting of traits he still felt he exhibited and others he was nostalgic for, keenly feeling their loss. Dick saw in Nat the kind of man he feared he'd become: older, wiser, not quite mature, but easily dominated or swayed by the women in his life and unsure of his own desires, wants and needs.

"I have to admit that Jack Isidore is my alter ego," said Dick in a 1981 interview with writer John Boonstra. "Jack Isidore is like my shadow-self, in Jungian terms. He is me as a mangy crackpot. I really like the guy. This is somebody who reads the Sunday supplements and these junk occult books, and just believes it all. There's nothing he's not capable of believing. There's a kind of optimism, a kind of beauty in this guileless fool. He's like Parsifal. He's not cynical: everything in the world is, to him, a great wonder and a miracle. I think he's a very good person, although his mind is stuffed with trash."

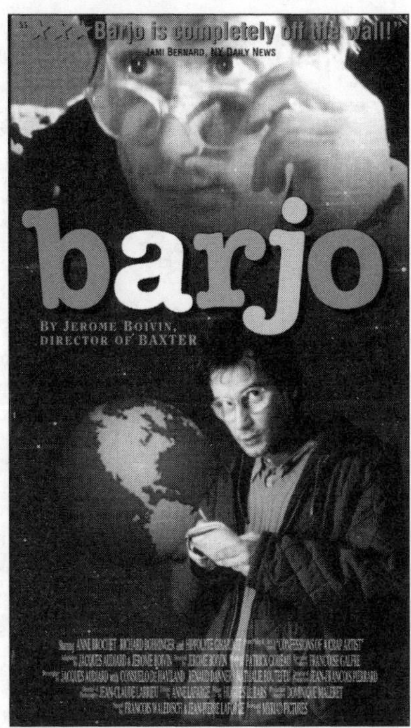

Above: *The unjustly neglected* Barjo, *the only film adaptation of one of Dick's realist novels of the 1950s.*

Dick also claimed that Fay Hume was modelled after his third wife Anne. In her later memoirs, however, Anne Dick denied this connection and also took umbrage at the possible depiction of Isidore as an analogue of the author, even though Dick had claimed that status for himself.

The book wasn't published until 1975, when Paul Williams, who had interviewed Dick for *Rolling Stone* (he later become the literary executor of the Dick estate), set up a publishing deal. "I didn't think it was ever going to get published," Dick told Boonstra. "I had given up on it. We took it out to every publisher in America. Now, it's been very well received in France, which is understandable. There's a name for what Isidore is, it's 'barjo', in French. There's no English equivalent. I had some French friends here and they were trying to explain to me what 'barjo' meant. It's kind of a nitwit, but they never were able to explain exactly what it meant…"

The film version of the novel, dubbed *Confessions d'un Barjo*, features Hippolyte Girardot playing the title character of the 'barjo', or fool. The film opens in darkness with his voiceover describing his and his twin sister's birth. This fool devotes himself to a life of lofty pursuits:

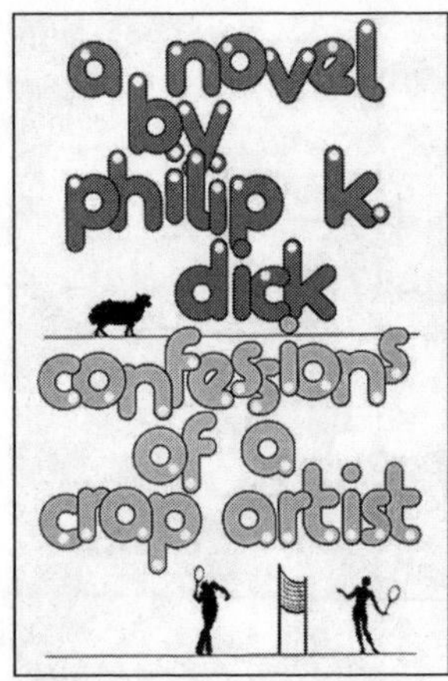

Above: *Dick's 1959 novel is largely autobiographical, capturing a slice of his real life.*

waiting for the inevitable end of the world, collecting pulp magazines and milk bottle tops, and writing file cards on every possible subject. His sister Fanfan (Anne Brochet), however, is doomed to the futile pursuit of material things, believing they will bring happiness. Fanfan marries into money, hooking up with Charles Leroy (French film star Richard Bohringer, seen in *Subway*, *Betty Blue* and Peter Greenaway's *The Cook, The Thief, his Wife and her Lover*). Leroy is 'le roi de l'aluminium', the king of aluminium, having made his money through metals trading. He's none too bright, and soon Fanfan is bored of him and her privileged lifestyle. The pair soon hook up with a young local couple and, as in the source novel, the sparks fly.

These events are all observed by the 'barjo', who moves in with his sister and her husband after he manages to burn down his own house. An innocent abroad, he starts asking questions about the moaning and strange rhythmic sounds he's hearing night after night. Soon, Fanfan's infidelities become all too clear and Charles suffers a heart attack. As the film builds towards inevitable tragedy, the humour that has been on display throughout, mainly through the character of the barjo, takes on a more wistful, futile air.

Boivin and co-writer Jacques Audiard were fans of the work of Philip K. Dick, who was always taken more seriously in France than in his native United States. In the same way that Frenchman Jean-Pierre Gorin was the one to actively pursue making a film of the virtually unfilmable *Ubik*, so it was a French writer-director team, who'd enjoyed some US success with the animal comedy *Baxter*, who tackled Dick's *Confessions of a Crap Artist*. Boivin knew there was no way he was in a position to film any of Dick's science fiction tales — the necessary special effects were beyond his kind of budget. He did toy with the idea of making one of the SF tales in the style of Jean-Luc Godard's *Alphaville*, simply using real-world locations in a heightened manner and downplaying scenes requiring effects. However, as Dick's mainstream fiction — largely written in the 1950s and unpublished until after his death — became available, general readers and Boivin realised there was more to the author's fiction than most had previously believed. Of course, *Confessions of a Crap Artist* had been published in 1975, and it was to this that Boivin and Audiard turned, interested in its tale of an outsider observing life, and in the autobiographical elements which Dick had folded in to his almost soap opera-like story.

"I re-read all his novels," said Boivin in *Mad Movies*. "I had already read them in my adolescence, and I had the same leap of the heart as for *Baxter*, the same vital need to make [*Confessions*] into a film. I truly love his books, and *Confessions* is my favourite."

For Boivin, it was the central character of the barjo that drew him to the filmic possibilities of that particular novel. "The character of the 'crap artist' is fascinating. He's both a person who is completely innocent, to the absolutely first degree, and at the same time a perpetrator of terrible shit, but with a disarming candour. It's impossible to feel bad about him, but he is a true destroyer."

The challenge to Boivin, and more particularly screenwriter Jacques Audiard, was how to adapt Dick's freewheeling narrative into a structure that would work for film, a task all screenwriters approaching Dick's work face to one degree or another. "I think that it's a true masterpiece," said Boivin of *Confessions*. "It possesses a mad structure. One has the impression that it is written on the edge, with an insane structure that theoretically shouldn't work. Certain chapters are narrated by the barjo, others by his sister (Fay, called Fanfan in the movie), others by Charles. Bizarrely, some are narrated in the third person by the author. This does not obey any apparent order, or any logic. One has the same situation recounted the first time by the barjo, the second time by the author. It's a kind of disorder, a hodge-podge that becomes architecture when everything is tied up at the end."

Turning that typically Dickian messy narrative structure into a screenplay was the first challenge. "It's wonderful," said Boivin, "but it would be impossible to recreate [it] like this on the screen. A film is 120 pages of screenplay typed large; [the novel is] more than 300 pages of small type. It is therefore necessary to find another kind of structure that will be at the same time entirely as mad and completely different. I believe that one should stay faithful to the spirit of the book, but as to the structure: that was impossible!"

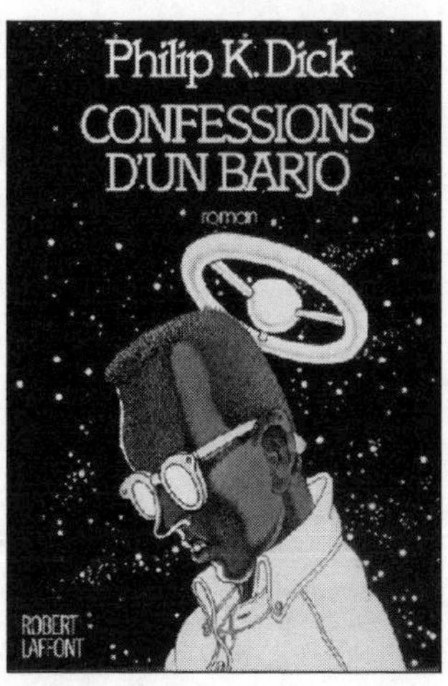

Above: *The French had long appreciated Dick's work, and it was a French writer/director team who successfully adapted* Crap Artist.

Filming for *Confessions of d'un Barjo* took place in the French/Swiss border region in autumn 1991. That October Boivin and his crew were in Geneva, Switzerland, about half an hour's drive from the town of Annecy in France. Although the filming of the fire scene, where Jack Isidore/barjo accidentally burns down his apartment when his science experiment goes wrong, only required Hippolyte Girardot on set, the rest of the main cast turned out in support. Although the sequence was shot on a very cold October evening, ten days into the shooting schedule, the cast and crew had bonded together so much that no-one wanted to miss the filming of what promised to be one of the more spectacular moments in the no-frills, low-budget movie.

As well as Girardot, the scene required the presence of volunteer firemen recruited from a nearby town, and a cadre of locals as extras (some in their night clothes) required to comment to each other as the fire breaks out. Included in the crowd watching the fire was the Dick estate's then-literary executor Paul Williams, who was visiting the set to watch the filming and was roped in by the director. "Boivin decided it would be fun to put Dick's literary executor in the film," recalled Williams, "so I was included in the crowd of people staring at the conflagration. Anne Brochet told me about the intense brother-sister relationship that had developed between her and Hippolyte Girardot as they fell into their parts..."

According to Williams, Girardot was something of a method actor, maintaining his character and naïve outlook on the world off set and between shots. The shooting of the fire scene, which involved multiple takes and the requirement that the fire be periodically extinguished then re-lit, continued through until 4am, when everyone was able to return wearily to their hotel in Annecy.

Confessions d'un Barjo builds on the autobiographical content of the novel by bringing the twin relationship between Jack Isidore/barjo and Fay/Fanfan to dramatic life. Actress Anne Brochet discussed her character and the twins' relationship in French film magazine *Studio Magazine*. "The character of the barjo just accepts what he is," she noted. "He never asks questions about

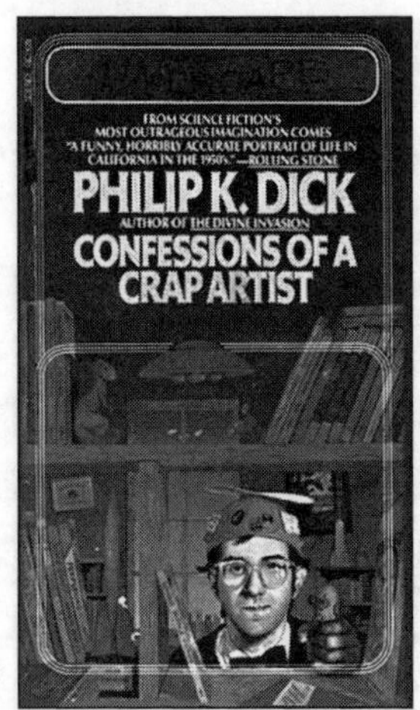

***Above:** Although written in the 1950s, it took until 1975 for the novel to see print.*

himself. Even though they are both cracked, Fanfan is the more dangerous because she represses her craziness. They are twins and so they have the same way of feeling things. But Fanfan has this desire not to be different [from the norm], she wishes to resemble other people. This is what tears her up. While the barjo is comfortable in his skin, Fanfan herself is truly cut in two…"

For Brochet, the role of Fanfan allowed the actress to explore a kind of violence, energy and language (much of it foul, as befits the character) that her previous film roles in French cinema had not allowed. Screenwriter Jacques Audiard, in the magazine *7 à Paris*, noted that the character of Fanfan is the most direct: "Fanfan is the only one who doesn't have a 'voice off', because what she thinks, she says immediately." For Brochet, this direct outspokenness is what made Fanfan just as crazy and potentially dangerous as the barjo: "That's also what makes her a 'crap artist' in her way, and solid like a bulldozer."

For his part, Boivin agreed that the character of Fanfan is potentially as dangerous as the title character. "His sister can be truly violent," he said. "She knows terrible highs and lows. She can go off in a burst, in the turn of a phrase, like the crack of a whip. And then, puff, the next moment she can be completely vulnerable, touching and sincere. A person so changeable is truly destabilising, one never knows how she will react."

While the character of Fanfan is certainly an interesting one, it is the barjo around whom the film revolves and to whom it always returns. As all the others are constantly in motion, the still centre of the film is the barjo himself, watching and waiting. "It's a way of showing that this is a universe to himself," confirmed Boivin. "A universe in which he is the centre. The whole world gravitates around him. In fact, it's not only his story, it's [his] film. It's not just that he narrates it, but it's as if he directed it. In certain sequences, I tried to ask myself how the barjo would have filmed this. In these moments, it's never classic *mise-en-scène*. It's the point of view of the barjo, who obeys a logic that is his own."

Released in France on 13 May 1992, *Confessions d'un Barjo* was not a great financial success, though it did attract some positive and seriously thoughtful critical notices. The positive reviews were led by a very enthusiastic piece in *Studio Magazine* in which writer Thierry Klifa praised Boivin and Audiard for "breaking the narrative norms — they know better than anyone how to mix burlesque and tragedy; nothing is altogether happy, nothing is altogether sad." Klifa praised the trio of lead performances as "fantastic," particularly singling out Brochet as Fanfan: "A magnificent role to which she has given her intensity and even a touch of madness." In conclusion, Klifa notes that "*Confessions* succeeds at being more than a simple diversion, thanks to the freshness of its tone and to its actors. It stays with us a long time and teases us with ironic questions about the madness of some and the opinions of others. Don't be surprised if, several days after having seen the film, you find yourself humming the persistent chorus of the barjo's song…"

Marc Toullec, writing in *Mad Movies*, praised the film as being "faithful to the spirit of Dick's novel… Narrating a film in the first person through a disconnected personality, perceiving the world according to unpublished rules — his own! — the barjo never doubts. He is sure of himself, sure of his conclusions. Boivin and Audiard demonstrate that madness

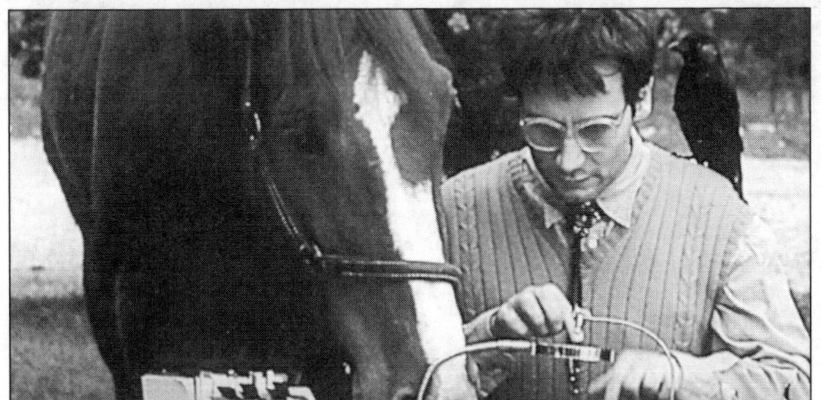

Left: *Dick's alter ego, the 'barjo', was brought to the screen by actor Hippolyte Girardot.*

also has its logic. Burlesque-like, surrealist, inventive, insolent, *Confessions d'un Barjo* has fun with and makes fun of the unhappiness of others, the little hatreds of every day. In our own way, we are, all of us, barjos!"

Other reviews were not so positive, calling the theme music so enjoyed by *Studio Magazine* "annoying" or the film as a whole naïve. *Cinephage*'s Frederic Temps called *Barjo* "utterly insipid. It fails to create an unsettled atmosphere to depict these individuals…" Nicolas Saada, writing in French critical journal *Cahiers du Cinema*, said the irritating *Barjo* theme tune "sets the tone. *Confessions* is a mad and delirious film, or at least it wishes to give that impression. One is ready to follow Jerome Boivin on this adventure, particularly because it's rare to see a French film declare so loudly its willingness to be different. This is where things come undone. By dint of conveying its crackpottery and its originality through sound effects and gimmicky angles, the film misses its target."

Released in major metropolitan areas in the United States during the following summer, *Confessions d'un Barjo* was once again met with mixed reviews. "A thoroughly winning, and thoroughly odd movie," wrote Joe Levy in *The Village Voice* of 13 July 1993. "It's at once rigorously faithful to Dick's novel and completely different from it… Director Jerome Boivin transforms Dick's dystopia into farce… he's particularly effective at crossing the line between fiction and reality that Dick always found so thin. Boivin invests the characters with a rich human irrationality that seems utterly believable. It's a remarkable achievement."

The flipside view was put by *The New York Times*' critic Vincent Canby. "For satire to be effective there must be some idea of what is being satirised. Disconnected from any particular reality, satire becomes merely a demonstration of eccentric behaviour… Dick's novel is very much about California in the years after World War Two. The French film takes place today, not far from the Alps! It's a kind of no-mans land, where the bizarre is the norm. Because the real norm is unknown, the bizarre loses its impact."

The most bizarre thing about *Confessions d'un Barjo* was that despite relocating the film in time and space, changing the language and significantly altering the characters, the film stood as the most faithful adaptation in spirit from Dick's work to that date. Surely Philip K. Dick himself would have wholeheartedly approved… ■

MACHINE DREAMS

Much like the original film's lead character, the TV series inspired by *Total Recall* turns out to have two distinct identities...

"[The movies of my books are all about] robots posing as people. Apparently, I have a basic patent on that! Movies like *Westworld* all used ideas I'd thought of a long time ago. Now, I'm finally cashing in on it." — Philip K. Dick, *Denver Clarion*, October 23, 1980.

Seven years after the release of *Total Recall* and fifteen years on from *Blade Runner*, both movies inspired a twenty-two-episode, one-season television series that represents the largest single project inspired by the works of Philip K. Dick.

In the bankruptcy sale that had followed the collapse of Carolco, the producers of *Total Recall*, the company had sold the TV series rights to the movie to DFL Entertainment for $1.2 million. Under the auspices of a sister company, the Team Entertainment Group, detailed plans were drawn up for a TV series which was intended as a direct spin-off from the *Total Recall* movie, featuring the continuing adventures of the Douglas Quaid/Jack Hauser character originally portrayed by Arnold Schwarzenegger. The series that finally emerged however, *Total Recall 2070*, was very different. When it hit the air, the show actually bore more than a passing resemblance to the environments of *Blade Runner*, and concepts from Dick's source novel *Do Androids Dream of Electric Sheep?*.

Team Entertainment Group was a new start-up TV production company when it acquired the rights to make a *Total Recall* series. They teamed up with Alliance, a Canadian production and distribution company, with Team retaining US distribution and Alliance managing the non-US worldwide distribution. *The Hollywood Reporter* noted, in January 1997, that the show was due to enter production in April of that year, with a production budget of $25 million, adding up to just over $1 million per episode, about average for American SF TV series at that time.

Michael Weisbarth, President of Alliance Television, commented: "*Total Recall*: The Series has unique, unlimited potential worldwide based on the success of one of the top box office hits of the decade. It has first class pedigree and brand recognition as well as a powerful premise for a futuristic action TV series."

***Opposite:** Karl Pruner as android Farve assumes a familiar position in the TV series* Total Recall 2070.

With the proposed movie sequel to *Total Recall* having stalled, Team and Alliance presumably felt secure in moving ahead with a direct sequel TV series, based on (as credited in the initial series outline document) "the theatrical movie and bible by Ronald Shusett." Advertising materials produced to promote the series for pre-sales in the international

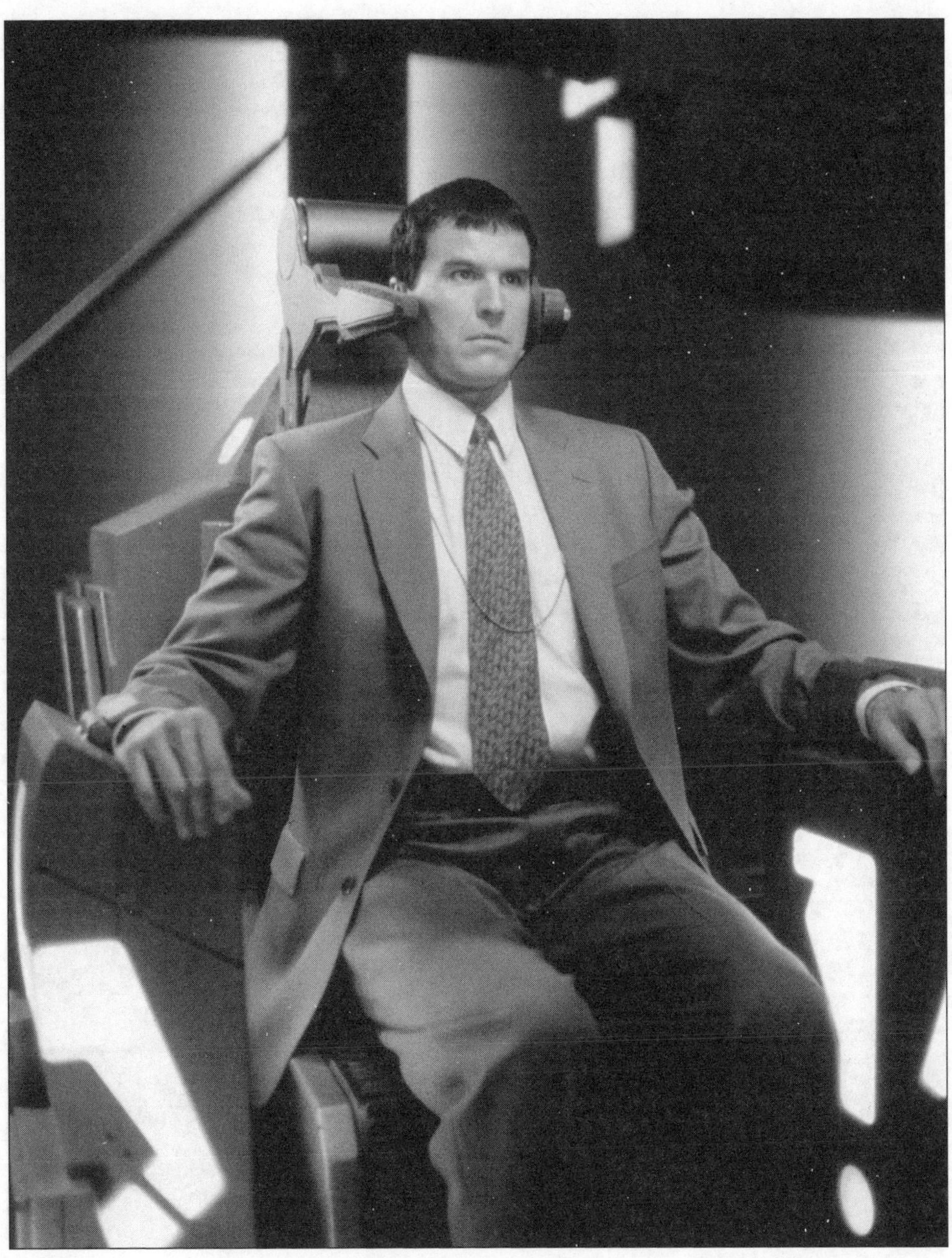

TOTAL RECALL
THE SERIES
CASABLANCA ON MARS
TEAM
ALLIANCE

TV market used the succinct slogan "*Casablanca* on Mars" to sum up the high concept show. Images of the red planet's mountains, futuristic cities and multiple moons hanging in the sky adorned the advertising. Also prominent was the Martian pyramid, a holdover from the earliest versions of the original *Total Recall* movie script.

Opposite: Early marketing material for the Total Recall *TV series bore more relation to the movie than the show as aired.*

The series outline booklet proposed a twenty-two-episode, one-hour "futuristic adventure series". Illustrated throughout with real-life shots of space and the red planet, the prologue setting up the series' premise opened with the line: "On Mars in 2090, nothing is quite what it seems..."

Portraying Mars as a "lawless frontier", the outline combined notions of the old West with mutants and Martians instead of cowboys and Indians, along with concepts similar to a standard cop show. Lifting the political situation directly from that created in the various screenplays for the *Total Recall* movie, the outline noted that the planet was controlled by Federation troops loyal to Earth's Northern Block. The planet is being mined for Turbinium, a precious ore needed to fuel the war back on Earth. The population of Mars is forced into subjugation and to work in the mines...

Leader of the Federation on Mars is Nell Cohaagen, the thirtysomething daughter of the planet's previous leader who has vowed to track down and eliminate the rebels responsible for killing her father (the events seen in the movie). Described in the character profiles as the series' "vilified antagonist", this new Cohaagen was also to be portrayed as having a valid point of view on the Mars situation. Although described as being as ruthless as her father, she was also intended to have a crush on the TV series' main character, Hauser.

The hero of this version of *Total Recall*: The Series was to have been Jack Hauser, who runs the hottest nightclub on the planet, The Last Resort, located in Venusville. This venue was to provide the series with its *Casablanca*-like hook. Hauser's club would be where characters could mingle, representing all the factions who would take part in the series — the mutants and soldiers, rebels and spies. Hauser is "wealthy and charming, the centre of all the action, [he] knows all the players in all the games, and all the angles in every scam."

Of course, as anyone who had seen the movie would know: "Like everything else on Mars in 2090, Jack Hauser is not exactly what he seems..." Described in the character profile as a "Bogart-esque soldier-of-fortune", again playing up the *Casablanca* angle, Hauser is available for hire and willing to do almost anything for money. At least that's how he seems on the surface. Beneath that surface, there is much more going on. Hauser is a strong supporter of the Martian cause. That's because he is really Douglas Quaid, secret leader of the Martian freedom fighters. He's known by the Martians he leads as Trask, in order to further conceal his true identity from those who would do him harm. The series outline described Hauser/Quaid/Trask as being "the selfish rogue who appears to be out for Number One, when in fact he is anything but..."

Of course, while Cohaagen, the villain of the piece, is cosying up to Hauser as owner of The Last Resort, she's also tasking her minions to track down and eliminate Trask, the mysterious mutant leader of the Martian resistance, not realising they are in fact one and the same.

The other regular character outlined in the series concept document was Melina, also in her thirties and a "character-rich rebel patriot" who is in love with Quaid and dedicated to the cause of Martian liberation. Complicating her relationship with Quaid is the fact that she hates Hauser, the character Quaid must become as the owner of The Last Resort. The outline proposed that this could be a rich source of dilemmas for Melina, with for example her having to protect Hauser in order to access Quaid.

This set-up would have tickled Philip K. Dick. It's a multiple identity love triangle between Nell Cohaagen and Hauser/Quaid and Quaid/Hauser and Melina, with Cohaagen chasing Quaid (in the guise of Trask) and Melina dealing with the unpleasant Hauser due to her love of Quaid. It's also possible to see in this overly clever set-up the danger that casual viewers of a weekly TV series might easily get confused over who-was-who and who-is-chasing-whom and why!

In an attempt to explain this Hauser/Quaid identity switch to potential investors or buyers at TV stations who might be interested in the series, the document drew an analogy with Batman. Playing up the fact that Hauser was supposed to be wealthy, the document noted Hauser/Quaid would be like Bruce Wayne/Batman in the "hugely successful movie franchise." Wayne, noted the document, "was a rich man going about his business by day, while at night, he's the caped crime-fighting crusader Batman, [just] like our Jack Hauser is rebel leader Quaid, champion of the underdog, defender of the weak."

The series document went on to recount the events of the *Total Recall* movie and provided the back-story set up for *Total Recall*: The Series. The history of the conflict between the Northern Block and the Southern Block, the colonization of Mars, the importance of Turbinium Ore to both Earth (it fuels the laser weapons) and Mars (it's a catalyst in the production of oxygen) were all described. The oppression of the Martian colonists, most of whom are now mutants, and their confinement to cheap domes, which fail to filter the harmful radiation, was also highlighted as a fertile source of story material for the proposed series.

A TV series 'bible' (the document outlining the background, characters and main events of any ongoing story arcs) usually describes how the show will eventually climax. The important, revelatory events of the final episodes are storylined before the series even gets a commission for a pilot movie or episode. Outlines for half a dozen or more episodes are also developed. This is all done to both prove the series has potential, and to reassure the executives who might commission it that the proposed series has the 'legs' to run for a decent amount of time and that a definite ending has been planned for.

Under the heading "Where We're Going", the *Total Recall*: The Series document outlined the planned events for the "fifth year/final episodes." As with the movie of *Total Recall* and much of the Philip K. Dick source material, the intention of the TV series was to again play games with identity. While audiences would have become familiar with the series' hero's triple identity as Quaid/Hauser/Trask, they would find at the series' ultimate conclusion that he had a fourth, additional identity. In an idea which echoes concepts from earlier versions of the *Total Recall* movie script (the ideas which Dan O'Bannon approved of), Quaid would be revealed also to be Ruel, the last descendant of the original Martian race. As in the earliest drafts of the film, Quaid would uncover the truth of his own past and his genetic inheritance, thus achieving 'total recall' of his true identity.

As the series entered its final episodes, the intention was for Quaid to start having ever more frequent dreams about Kuato, the rebel leader from the *Total Recall* movie, by then assumed to have been dead for over five years. The bible outlined the show's larger,

***Above:** Mars' mutant population were intended to play a central role in* Total Recall*: The Series.*

mythic backstory: "A million years ago, the Martian civilization was hit by a meteor shower of mythical proportions, leaving its atmospheric shell punctured beyond repair. With their air supply slowly leaking into outer space, the Martians used advanced technology to build a Turbinium Reactor, intending to manufacture a new atmosphere. This reactor, which could have easily saved the Martian race, was never ignited. Quaid discovers why…

"The Martians built the reactor and then never turned it on, not because they feared a global meltdown (as Cohaagen would have people believe). They failed to turn it on because they discovered something hidden deep beneath the subterranean ice caps, near the centre of the red planet, something that could only be described as… the Martian Well of Souls!"

How Quaid's identity as Ruel, last of the Martians, would relate to the discovery of this Martian Well of Souls, and how all this would feed into resolving the larger political situation of Mars was purposely left vague for whomever was writing those episodes at the time to fill in the dramatic detail.

The outline for *Total Recall*: The Series included one-page summaries of plotlines for the first ten episodes of the show. This is standard TV practice, to show that the producers of the proposed series have a stock of developed storylines ready to be moved to scripting stage should it be given the go-ahead to enter production. In the interests of shedding some light on this previously undiscovered corner of the Philip K. Dick universe, here are summaries of those ten plot outlines for the never-produced version of *Total Recall*: The Series. (The original document contains no direct credits for potential scriptwriters, or the writer who developed these storylines.)

1. 'Martian Children are Twice Blessed'

Hauser/Quaid discovers that children are being used as part of the slave workforce in the Turbinium mines, something that is against Martian law. Quaid cannot expose the practice, as the children will then be killed to cover it up. His opportunity comes when a delegation from Earth arrives to investigate abuses of authority on Mars, putting Nell Cohaagen in a difficult situation. Additionally, a mercenary called Kraal arrives on Mars to kill Hauser in revenge for an incident in their past. Although Quaid is playing the part of Hauser, he is not actually Hauser, so has no idea why Kraal wants him dead. Quaid discovers the dispute concerns Kraal's son, sold into slavery by Hauser years before. He tracks Kraal's son to the Turbinium mines, frees him and manoeuvres Cohaagen into having to denounce the practice of using children as slave labour, an act which improves her standing with the Earth authorities. Kraal, who reconciles with this new, gentler Hauser, was proposed as a recurring character through the series.

2. 'Tempest'

A vicious Martian storm traps an assortment of characters, including Cohaagen and her entourage, in Hauser's club, The Last Resort. Cohaagen uses the opportunity to reassure herself that Hauser is still who she thinks he is. Meanwhile, a group of terrorists in the club, waiting there for a meeting, take over the building. Outside, Melina is trapped on a collapsing bridge. Quaid uses a hologram to persuade everyone in The Last Resort that Hauser is right there while he escapes to rescue Melina. Returning to The Last Resort, Quaid takes out the terrorists, ironically saving Nell Cohaagen in the process and reassuring her that he is indeed the harsh Hauser.

3. 'Relic'

Quaid is having nightmares, including visions of ancient Martian relics. Investigating his visions, Quaid and a cadre of Martian mutants travel to a dangerous ancient cave near an active Martian volcano. In a race against time, Quaid finds the relic and prevents the volcano erupting by easing the pressure. (The plot outline promises the erupting volcano could be "another episode down the line".) Quaid becomes aware of his own powers of premonition, which helped him battle the volcano. (This episode laid in place the idea of Quaid having a greater destiny connected to ancient Martian relics.)

4. 'Family Values'

An Earth family, newly arrived on Mars, come to The Last Resort looking for their runaway daughter Altera. Pretending to be Hauser, Quaid refuses to help but later he embarks on a search of Venusville for the missing girl. Quaid finds Altera and has to help her escape from the unsavoury types she's fallen in with, in an exciting chase sequence. In the course of rescuing Altera, Quaid comes across an enclave of ancient Martians who treat him with awe (another piece of the Quaid-as-Ruel plot). Quaid returns Altera to her family.

5. 'Sandstorm'

Cohaagen has discovered a rebel stronghold in the Martian desert. As her forces move in, a huge sandstorm erupts, cutting off the location. Quaid knows Melina is there and fears for her safety. Heading to the stronghold, Quaid rescues Cohaagen, some of her troops and Melina. Leading the group out of danger, Quaid has to adopt the Hauser persona for Cohaagen's benefit and so respond in character to Cohaagen's advances in front of Melina. Finding shelter, the group are stalked by 'satellites', vicious Martian mutant creatures produced by the Turbinium mines. Mute and blind, but incredibly strong, the creatures act on instinct. Quaid takes on the creatures, once again saving both Cohaagen and Melina. As they return to Venusville, Quaid engineers Melina's 'escape'…

6. 'Saturnville'

Melina's family, inhabitants of the frontier town of Saturnville, have been rounded up with many others by Federation troops. They are being held hostage until the remaining residents reveal the location of the hideout of rebel leader Trask (who is of course another identity of the series' hero, Quaid). Even if they wished to betray Trask, the residents of Saturnville cannot, as they don't know where he is based…

Adopting his Hauser guise, Quaid visits Cohaagen in the Martian Capitol building. He tries to hide his concern for the Saturnville residents by claiming that Cohaagen's troops have broken the military code of honour by taking innocent hostages. Cohaagen promises

Below: *Venusville, as seen in the movie, was the main location for the original version of the spin-off TV series.*

to assess the situation, which Hauser knows means she'll do nothing.

Quaid assembles a team of Martian mutants, including Heshe, who can apparently change sexual identity at will. They rescue the hostages, partly thanks to the distractions provided by Heshe, and Cohaagen is forced to declare the troops a "rogue element". Melina is reunited with her family and with Quaid.

7. 'There's No Place Like Earth'

Philip K. Dick's themes of false memories, briefly explored in the original *Total Recall* movie before the action sequences took over, are returned to in this episode. Quaid awakens on Earth, back with his wife (the synopsis suggests the production hire a Sharon Stone lookalike). He feels the urge to search for another piece of the 'Martian puzzle', part of which he uncovered in episode three, 'Relic'. He believes it is hidden somewhere on Earth, but he has doubts that these experiences are real. Perhaps he's in the Rekal machine once more? Could Cohaagen be monitoring his actions? Or were all the previous episodes merely fantasy adventures drawn from the machine…?

It's soon made clear to viewers that Quaid *is* in the Rekal machine, but as soon as he realises this, he begins manipulating events to convince Cohaagen that he is still Hauser. Quaid finds the artifact he's searching for on Earth and is freed from the Rekal machine. He then returns to Earth for real, and recovers the Martian artifact which the Rekal adventure has lead him to… En route, Quaid would, according to the synopsis, "rescue a friend and bring him back to Mars."

8. 'A Plague on All Your Houses'

An unknown disease is spreading rapidly planet-wide and Venusville has been placed under quarantine. The Last Resort nightclub becomes the headquarters for the scientists struggling to find a cure. Cohaagen has blamed the Martian mutants for the spread of the virus, and declares they should be rounded up. Quaid manages to negotiate special dispensation for the mutants who work at the nightclub (Quaid's team and the series regulars), but two are taken away to join the mutant quarantine. Quaid makes it out onto the deserted streets of Venusville, defying the quarantine and avoiding Federation troops. He uses the apparatus of the rebels to discover the real cause of the disease: a single, powerful alien creature whom Quaid must face. In a fight to the death, Quaid triumphs. He then helps the scientists develop an antidote. As Hauser, Quaid forces Cohaagen to declare the Martian population innocent of spreading the disease and release them from the quarantine camps, including the two taken from The Last Resort.

9. 'To Boldly Go…'

A woman named Cassio arrives at The Last Resort and claims to be Hauser's daughter. She's arrived from one of the moons of Saturn where an artificial atmosphere has been introduced and colonists have just begun settling. Just as Hauser/Quaid begins to get to know this daughter he never knew he had, she is kidnapped from the club.

Doubting Hauser really had a daughter, and fearing another test of Hauser's authenticity by Cohaagen, Quaid nonetheless travels to Saturn to track down Cassio. He discovers that Martian negotiators are on the moon due to the discovery of Turbinium. Quaid foresees the kind of subjugation and slave labour in the mines as currently exists on Mars. To stop that eventuality, he manages to sabotage and destroy the mining facility, rescuing Cassio.

Quaid returns to The Last Resort with Cassio in tow, deciding for the time being to accept her as Hauser's daughter, even though this development complicates his already complicated multiple-identity life…

10. "As I Recall…"

For the third time in ten episodes, the series features a massive storm. This one envelops Venusville, covering everything in a fine red dust. The following day, powerful winds blow all the dust away. On his way from his apartment to The Last Resort, Quaid notices that things in Venusville are different: less threatening, less dangerous. There's a different atmosphere in the town, one of welcome rather than hostility. Arriving at the club, Quaid discovers his Martian mutant staff are mutants no longer. All their 'imperfections' have been cured. It appears as if the sandstorm has turned back time, cleansing Venusville and its inhabitants of Turbinium poisoning, the source of their mutations.

Things take a dramatic turn when Quaid's wife arrives (the Sharon Stone lookalike once again). With her is Cohaagen's henchman Richter (a role the synopsis suggests for Michael Ironside, as in the movie). Neither are dead, as Quaid believed, and both know that he's not Hauser but really Quaid. However, they've not come to turn Quaid in. They want to join with him and overthrown Cohaagen's rule on Mars. According to the synopsis, this deception "is all very convincing, until the very smallest of details is noticed by Quaid." Noticing this unspecified 'wrong' detail, Quaid concludes their offer is a trap and he is once more in a Rekal machine. Again Quaid embarks on a course of action to fool the machine and whomever might be watching. He makes it clear he cannot be Quaid but must be Hauser, by (suggests the synopsis) fighting Richter to the death once again.

Quaid awakens in the Rekal machine. He heads for The Last Resort, back through the streets of a restored Venusville, mutants and all.

Clearly this version of *Total Recall*: The Series is very different to that which emerged on screen as *Total Recall: 2070*. The limited character and storyline material available in the lightweight series proposal highlights the problems this version of the show might have encountered. It picks up and runs with the action-adventure elements and the political intrigue of the *Total Recall* movie, the very things which many fans of the work of Philip K. Dick disliked. There is little suggestion that the series might have explored the stresses and strains which the upkeep of at least three identities might cause in Douglas Quaid, the lead character. That, at least, could have been fruitful psychological territory, allowing the series to travel down a route more like *A Scanner Darkly* than "*Casablanca* on Mars." Instead, the show would have used these questions of identity merely as fuel for a romantic triangle between Cohaagen, Hauser/Quaid and Melina, and even these elements were not well developed in the treatment.

The action-adventure quotient would have been high, so perhaps the show would have connected with a certain easily pleased TV audience, if they could keep up with all the switching of identities that would be inflicted upon the lead character. The reliance on

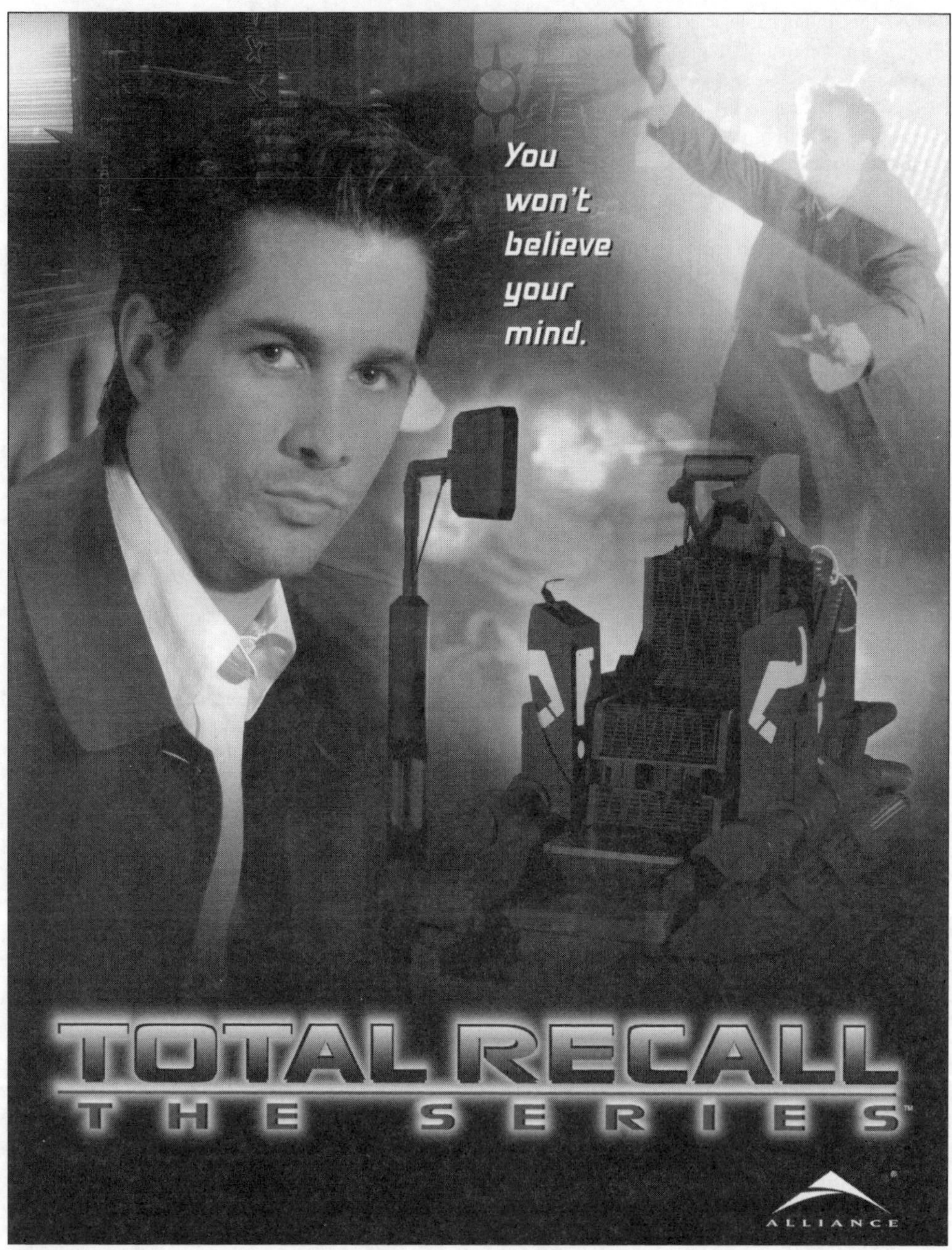
You
won't
believe
your
mind.
TOTAL RECALL
THE SERIES™
ALLIANCE

stock situations, however, would rapidly have condemned the show to a deadly sameyness. Each episode positioned Quaid in opposition to Cohaagen, while he tried to stay close to her as Hauser. Melina and often Cohaagen seem to be little more than objects to be rescued, though clearly episode writers would have fleshed out the characters more than is suggested in the episodic outlines.

Once Miramax/Dimension acquired the theatrical remake, sequel and prequel rights to *Total Recall* from the defunct Carolco and realised that they did not have the TV rights, it seems likely that pressure was exerted on DFL Entertainment/Team Entertainment not to proceed with a show whose basis was likely to interfere with the kind of story Miramax would be developing for the next *Total Recall* movie.

This may have been fortuitous, as it allowed the producers of the *Total Recall* TV series to go off in a totally different direction, one which would result in an intriguing television show that drew much more from *Blade Runner* and the ideas in the wider fiction of Philip K. Dick than *Total Recall*, film or proposed TV series, ever could have.

Above: *The manipulation of reality by technology was a common theme in both versions of the TV series.*

Opposite: *The change of title to* Total Recall 2070 *was a late decision, as this promo poster reveals.*

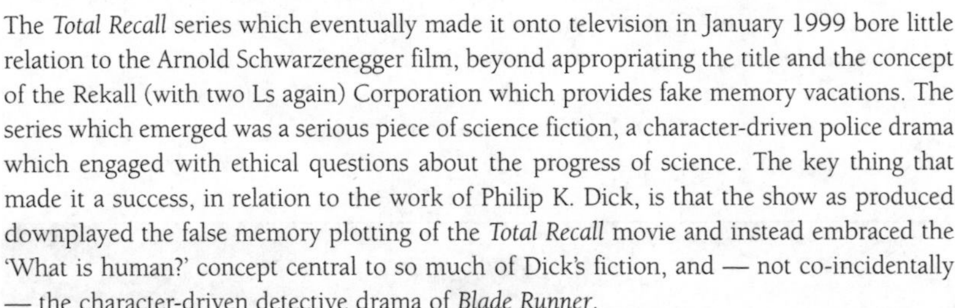

The *Total Recall* series which eventually made it onto television in January 1999 bore little relation to the Arnold Schwarzenegger film, beyond appropriating the title and the concept of the Rekall (with two Ls again) Corporation which provides fake memory vacations. The series which emerged was a serious piece of science fiction, a character-driven police drama which engaged with ethical questions about the progress of science. The key thing that made it a success, in relation to the work of Philip K. Dick, is that the show as produced downplayed the false memory plotting of the *Total Recall* movie and instead embraced the 'What is human?' concept central to so much of Dick's fiction, and — not co-incidentally — the character-driven detective drama of *Blade Runner*.

Far from being regarded as the box office failure it was upon initial release, by 1999 *Blade Runner* was seen by critics and fans alike as a bona fide science fiction movie classic, and it was to this film, rather than *Total Recall*, which *Total Recall 2070* would turn in search of inspiration for its look. For its themes, the series would mine the work of Philip K. Dick in a way that the previously proposed *Total Recall* series concept simply did not, beyond the idea of multiple identities.

In charge of developing this version of the show were two experienced writer-producers from Canadian television, Jeff King and Art Monterastelli. King was the series producer on the acclaimed Canadian series *E.N.G.*, as well as a producer on *Due South* and the US cop drama *E.Z. Street*. Monterastelli was a scriptwriter and producer on various shows, including the short-lived but critically acclaimed identity drama *Nowhere Man*, starring Bruce Greenwood. (He later went on to co-write the William Friedkin film *The Hunted*.) King and Monterastelli were struck by the inherent dramatic possibilities in a TV series which drew on the works of Philip K. Dick for inspiration. King was happy to admit the *Blade Runner* influence to the *Ottowa Citizen*. "It has some of those collisions of retro and future. We're in a 200-storey city that is the product of the quick amalgamation of old and new, with new structures fastened onto old, and a city growing over the city."

This Earthbound urban environment was to be the setting of *Total Recall 2070*, rather than a struggling colony on Mars. "The patron of the science fiction in *Total Recall 2070* is Philip K. Dick," confirmed King. "He is an author not traditionally put in the hard sci-fi camp. If you read the story on which *Total Recall* was based, what you have is a psychological thriller, an intimate story about a character, not the sprawling action epic that the movie turned into."

Despite setting out to mine Dick's work for ideas and concepts to fuel the series, King was aware that he was producing a TV series that had to have wide appeal, so a certain quotient of action-adventure material was inevitable. "We're doing a show that is trying to reach the broadest possible audience," said King. "This is a show that has a traditional detective slant to it. At the same time, it also has the [Dick] sci-fi elements."

Hired to play the series' lead, detective David Hume, actor Michael Easton (then best known for occasional appearances on *Ally McBeal*) was clear that with those writer-producers involved, the series would be focused on character: "You've got guys [Monterastelli and King] who've done story and character-driven shows in the past and are now doing a story and character-driven show set in the future. We don't ever want to get carried away with the action or the effects."

Easton continued: "I'm a fan of Philip K. Dick's writings, and people don't realise that he's the same guy who wrote the short story that became *Total Recall*, and the story that became *Blade Runner*. A lot of the elements are the same and you see that on our sets; when you see our show there are a lot of underlying elements [of *Blade Runner*] to it. The script was more like the Philip K. Dick books than anything to do with the movie *Total Recall*. I liked that, though some people may be put off by it. When you start talking about a TV

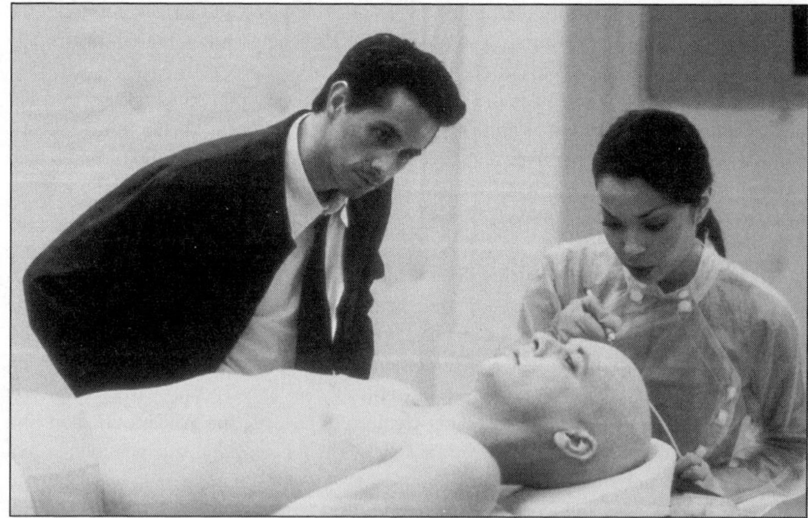

Right: *Artificial people allowed the show to explore one of Dick's central concerns: 'What is human?'*

series, you can't do the *Total Recall* movie every week. It's not possible to spend $60 million and blow things up and have Arnold every week. I don't think that would make for the greatest TV series anyway. You need to have a character-driven piece, and that's why going back to Dick's books made some sense. Dick's books have really interesting themes about paranoia, with androids and technology that I really respond to. I don't respond as well to straight-out SF lunacy. Too often, it becomes an excuse to be silly. [In that kind of show] any structure or script problems get solved with a CGI effect, a spaceship flying around or some kind of crap."

Reading the original Philip K. Dick material was important to Easton getting a handle on the worlds of *Total Recall 2070*. "I had read *Do Androids Dream of Electric Sheep?* when I was about seventeen, after I had seen *Blade Runner*. When the show came up, I went out and read Dick's complete collection of short stories. That was important. When you read enough of Dick's work, you get that feeling that you can't trust people. You get that from reading Dick maybe every night before you go to bed, and not from watching a two-hour movie. You'll see some of his themes in the show, but I don't think there's stuff that's *specifically* based on another Dick story."

Easton even saw his own hiring as a statement on the part of the show's producers that they were not going down the traditional SF TV action-adventure route. "When they hired me they hired a guy who wasn't really a part of the sci-fi community, who hadn't done much of it,"' he said, despite his one-season role on virtual reality thriller series *VR.5*. "I go in and say, 'This is neat eye candy, but we also need a bit of drama or more of this relationship.'" (Later, Easton would go on to feature in the short-lived superhero show *Mutant X*.)

In direct opposition to Quaid in the movie and in the original *Total Recall*: The Series treatment, Easton's Hume was to be a much more introspective character, a point reinforced in Art Monterastelli's detailed series outline. "In contrast to Quaid in the *Total Recall* movie," wrote Monterastelli, "Hume is a much more internalised character. He's capable of physical action, but he's also capable of tremendous introspection. Since many of these so-called 'crimes of the future' deal with sophisticated software and bio-technology, it's important that our lead investigator be capable of equally sophisticated deduction. This will prove extremely valuable in a continuing series relying more on psychological thrills than big budget special effects, week-in and week-out…"

Projecting a future that was seventy years ahead of when the series was made, the show teamed Hume up with a new android partner Ian Farve (played by *E.N.G.* actor Karl Pruner), when his old partner Nick (Thomas Kretschmann) is dramatically killed in the pilot movie by renegade androids. Hume has to overcome his anti-android feelings when he discovers that Farve is in fact a prototype of a human-like model. This man-and-android partnership immediately allowed *Total Recall 2070* to use Dick's essential 'What is human?' theme as one of its central concerns. There's Hume's relationship with Farve, but also their investigation of the rebellious service robots, who should have neither the inclination nor the will to rebel in the first place. The pilot movie (a double length episode, re-run as a two-part story in syndication), titled 'Machine Dreams', reveals these renegades to have been the result of an experiment at Rekall (the company from the movie), which implanted the androids with human memories (shades of Rachel Tyrell in *Blade Runner*) which then formed the basis of their higher consciousness. The androids want to retain their newly found 'humanity'.

These potential ethical dilemmas were seen by Jeff King as the basis for much of the territory that *Total Recall 2070* would explore. "It's not hard to imagine that in the next seventy years there are going to be lots of breakthroughs in new areas, like computing, like bio-mechanical engineering, and in the ethics and morality of the application of those things. The more prevalent those things become, the more we'll have to deal with them."

The drama of *Total Recall 2070* would come from the various ways mankind responded to these technological developments, from the criminal to the merely social. "That's part of what interested me in the series: the balance between humanity and technology," admitted King. "I think we have a relatively optimistic view of humanity's prospects in this show, and I think that's appealing to an audience."

Audience appeal would also come from the series leads, and unlike the *Total Recall*: The Series proposal which saw Quaid as a loner, *Total Recall 2070* would draw on the partnership of man-and-machine Hume and Farve for much of its humour, drama and tension. "It's the heart of any show that I like," noted King. "You have a strong relationship between the lead characters. There is some of [*Due South*'s] Vecchio and Fraser in Hume and Farve, there's no question. They're very different men, thrust together in circumstances where they have to learn and share with each other." King saw the challenges of *Total Recall 2070* in a crowded television market place as being to "keep the show entertaining and informative, without having to dip the audience's toes too deeply in any of the allied sciences that go along with the storylines..."

For his part, Michael Easton felt the Philip K. Dick factor would be the element which would make *Total Recall 2070* stand apart from other *Star Trek*-style TV shows. "When it comes to sci-fi on television, I don't think anyone has really tapped into what's good about sci-fi [literature]," he said. "We haven't done enough Philip K. Dick or William Gibson, guys who've written great stuff. When real sci-fi is done, it's almost a fluke. No one went to see *Blade Runner*, and now it's a masterpiece. I think *2070* is an effort to do something different. It's different philosophy-wise from a lot of sci-fi, and it's different visually."

The series bible for *Total Recall 2070* drafted by Art Monterastelli (dated 24 March 1998) is a much more substantial document than that prepared for the aborted first attempt on *Total Recall*: The Series. The outline begins by describing the world of 2070. Earth is ruled by a one-world government, known as the Interplanetary Council. Mars has been successfully colonised. Enormous wealth has been generated by the Deuterium mines, creating a frontier-like environment. While controlling Earth, the Interplanetary Council also holds power on Mars, but less effectively. It controls customs and provides what the outline describes as "a UN-like security force that patrols the sometimes rowdy corridors of the man-made biospheres." Real power on Mars, however, lies with the Consortium, the six multi-global companies that financed the colonization of the red planet.

Monterastelli then went on to provide, in some detail, a history of the previous fifty years, showing how the situation in the series had come to be. A nuclear attack had destroyed New York City in 2020 AD. Environmental disasters had taken their toll on Latin America, Mexico and the Western US. Chicago — where the series was to be set, though called only 'The City' — had survived these cataclysms and had become the centre of power in the US and, eventually, the planet. The creation of the Consortium (made up of the planet's most powerful corporations) brought about the one-world government. One of the main companies in the Consortium was Rekall, described as the information technology powerhouse of the twenty-first century. As Monterastelli noted: "Think what it would be like if Sony, IBM, Intel and Microsoft were combined in a single company..." Energy supply was dominated by Minacon, as it controlled the oil supply on Earth and the Deuterium mines on Mars. Rumours abound that in exploring Mars, Minacon had unearthed an ancient Martian civilization, but nothing was ever proven. Rising transportation company Tashimo-Pacific (creators of 'Johnny Cab') is on the verge of challenging Minacon's position as the series opens. Other companies include rocket and robotics corporation Uber Braun (who build the service androids so important to the drama of the series), medical and bio-tech company Variable Dynamics (who also have an interest in creating androids, or synthetic humans) and agriculture and chemicals giant Tillman Health (who are working on illegal human cloning — more artificial people).

Above: *Cynthia Preston as David Hume's troubled wife Olivia.*

According to Monterastelli, in a dramatic piece of utopian thinking, the Consortium had eliminated war, solved the planet's environmental problems and created full employment and health care for everyone on Earth. Full employment led to a dramatic drop in the crime rate. Once this was achieved, the 'Fathers', as the corporate heads were known, generously returned power to the people through the creation of the Interplanetary Council.

In a utopia such as this, what drama could possibly ensue which would feed storylines in an on-going television series that would display a voracious appetite for material, as all television drama does? After all, the heart of all drama is conflict and in creating his perfect world, Monterastelli had seemingly virtually removed all conflict at a stroke.

Things were changing in the utopian world of 2070, though... After fifty years of co-operation, the pact between the corporations of the Consortium is breaking down. With their competing interests in the future of humanity and their respective researches in creating various types of artificial humans, a new kind of Cold War exists between them, bringing with it industrial espionage, secret projects, crime, murder and mayhem. That's where the drama of the series would lie.

That drama, however, had to be personalised. Viewers would not tune in to watch the twisted machinations of rival corporations alone. King and Monterastelli chose the detective show format as the best way to introduce viewers to the far-flung future world of *Total Recall 2070* and the ideas of Philip K. Dick. Detective fiction is a form with which TV

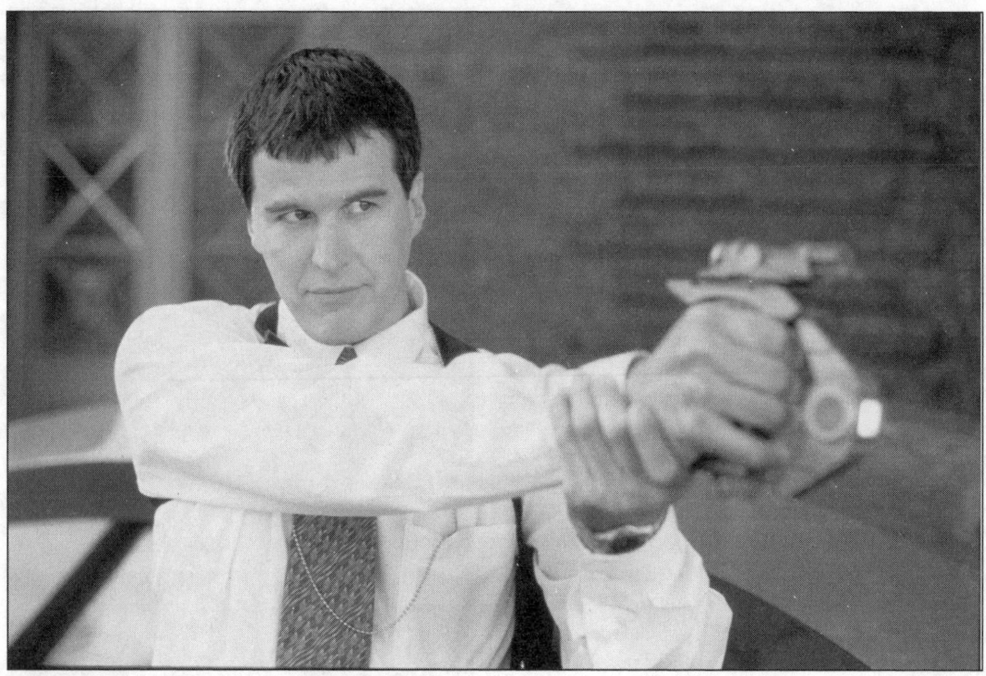

***Above:** The detective format, teaming Hume with android partner Farve (Karl Pruner), formed the basis of the show.*

viewers have become intimately familiar, especially in America since the demise of the Western shows in the late 1950s and early 1960s. As well as providing an easily understandable way into the series for viewers, the focus on detective characters allowed the show to deal with the issues that arose through the corporate warfare around personal identity via the personal stories of people affected by the activities of the big corporations. The mantra was to always make the stories personal, either to guest characters brought into the show, or if possible to one or more of the series' lead characters.

As the power of the Consortium is waning, due to the increasing in-fighting, so the power of the Interplanetary Council is rising. It's responsibility for the Militia (the army), customs and immigration, the Citizen's Protection Bureau (the police), the Assessors (internal affairs and oversight) and the Population Control Board made the Council both a threat to the Consortium and to many of their new projects.

It is on the Citizen Protection Bureau that the series would focus, with its two lead characters, Detectives David Hume and Ian Farve. They are described in Monterastelli's outline as "traditional detectives working in a hyper-modern world where the worst crimes and sometimes even the most obvious crimes are often the most difficult to detect."

In the *Total Recall 2070* bible, Monterastelli listed a series of potential crimes ("from the simple and sometimes even humorous, to the more complex," outlined Monterastelli), each of which could form the basis of an episode, or provide a theme for an episode to explore:

1. A man is attacked by his faulty 'holographic golf instructor', an example of "consumer complaint problems".

2. A wife tries to get a restraining order against the woman her husband is having an affair with. The detectives investigate but find no trace of the other woman. The investigation eventually reveals that she is 'holographic' and the affair is taking place in cyberspace…

3. The Johnny Cab transit system begins to go haywire. The detectives discover that they've been reprogrammed in an attempt to cause disasters and so force privatisation of the transport system. Bureau investigators must track down 'robot zero', the incubator of the virus who is spreading it throughout the system…

4. In an attempt to take over a rival company, a Consortium company clones one of the members of their rival's board of directors. The clone, however, switches sides once 'it' realises what it is, and what's going on. He helps fight off the takeover, but the result is murder. Can the death of a fake human be a real crime? The Bureau investigates…

5. A female doctor returning to Earth from Mars accidentally brings with her a man-made virus. Unbeknownst to her, she is a biological timebomb. Bureau investigators must not only track her down, but return her to Mars where the only known antidote exists…

6. A diplomat negotiating a stand-off between rebel miners on Mars and a Consortium company is taken hostage by the rebels. Investigating the case, our Bureau heroes discover there is a whole population of "second generation mutant mineworkers who have been living below the surface of Mars for several decades…"

7. The inventor of the Rekall machine fakes his own death to escape the clutches of Rekall's internal security services. To achieve this he commits a capital crime — cloning a human being: himself. Solving the case, Bureau investigators discover that the Rekall machines are being used for mind control (this would set up a theme and a plot arc which would resonate throughout the series)…

8. A young couple, having returned from a Rekall vacation, complain of a vague sense of loss. Investigations reveal that they had an eight-year-old son. Not only has the boy been kidnapped, but their memories of him have been erased. The boy is discovered on Mars, where his special gift of the ability to read others' minds is being put to use in interrogating the scientist who has invented a chip that extends the life-cycle of androids (a plot that effectively mixes the films *Total Recall* and *Blade Runner* together and throws in some of Dick's *Martian Time-Slip* for good measure…).

Mind control, memory erasure and questions of 'What is real?' would supplement the series' central concern with 'What is human?', which would be explored through issues of androids, synthetic humans and cloning. Ironically, all the big themes which Philip K. Dick worked into his fiction repeatedly were set to be mined by the series spun-off from a film which had singularly failed to do justice to any of Dick's ideas, except in a few fleeting scenes.

Monterastelli's series outline went into some depth on two important elements to the series which would bring these themes to the fore: Rekall and the Sublimator. As one of the six corporations in the Consortium, Rekall was to be an important player in the world of *Total Recall 2070*. As one of the few elements carried forward from the movie, it was to provide a link between the wham-bam action of the film with the more cerebral concerns of the TV series. Although it is the pre-eminent information technology company, Rekall is best known for just one thing: the Rekall machine. After the disasters of 2020, people tried to escape from the grim reality they faced and use of the fantasy-providing Rekall machine soared. Intended as a recreational device, offering fantasy holidays and role-playing opportunities, it soon became clear to some at Rekall that the machine could be used for much more than mere leisure.

Their belief that the human mind was malleable and could be manipulated led to the creation of a second, more powerful machine: the Sublimator. Originally developed for therapeutic use (that was the corporate line, at least) the Sublimator became a must-have item in every home on Earth. A combination of euphoric and anti-depressant, the Sublimator replaced the previous drug culture of the planet with a new kind of dependency. The soothing holographic images projected into the brain of the recipient were designed to meet their individual emotional needs, and were often drawn from the subject's own memories of happier days. Monterastelli provided a couple of possible examples: a woman who had endured a painful, perhaps abusive relationship with her mother could envelope herself in images of a perfect mother in an idyllic landscape, while a man bullied and taunted by his classmates as a child could provide for himself psychologically healing images of schoolyard triumph. Someone with a chronic weight problem could ignore their troubles by indulging in a holographic fantasy, while the physically disabled or the lonely could escape their unfulfilling lives and live out the life they wished they had…

Monterastelli went to great lengths in his series outline to make it clear that the Sublimator would not replace the Rekall machine, but would feature in addition to the kind of Rekall holiday fantasy viewers had become familiar with from the *Total Recall* movie. The Sublimator is positioned as a lower tech, more portable and more personal machine, providing limited relief from personal troubles. It's also described as being by far the more addictive of the two machines, and even more dangerous because it is a personal device so much more open to being abused by the user. The obvious inspiration was the Penfield 'mood organ' from *Do Androids Dream of Electric Sheep?*, an element dropped from the film *Blade Runner*. The Sublimator machine was to play a major role in the relationship between the hero of *Total Recall 2070* David Hume and his troubled wife Olivia.

Of key importance to the success of any series bible are the character outlines. These must reveal a certain depth to the protagonists, to allow for viewer identification and to be mined for future storylines. Unlike the failed outline for *Total Recall*: The Series, which had no real in-depth character profiles, Monterastelli devotes a page and a half to David Hume and half a page to each of the other important characters.

Monterastelli describes Hume as being in his early thirties, happily married to Olivia and an investigator in the City office of the Citizen's Protection Bureau. The character is

defined in opposition to the portrayal of Quaid in the *Total Recall* movie, and much more along the lines of a classic Philip K. Dick hero. He's an investigator, but one unsure of himself and his place in the world. Hume was also to display a sense of humour, sometimes a black one given the situations he would have to deal with. Hume sees an increasingly dehumanised world emerging around him, one he comes into contact with increasingly through the crimes he is investigating. His own sensitivities make him sympathetic to the victims and sometimes even the perpetrators of the crimes under investigation. Hume's moral ambivalence was to be built upon following the death of his partner in the pilot movie and his replacement with an experimental synthetic human, an android, which identically duplicates his late partner (an idea that was subsequently dropped). Some of the criminals to whom Hume might feel sympathetic would include, according to Monterastelli, a young couple ineligible for the population-controlling 'baby lottery' who break the law, create a child and then go on the run; and an android determined to live beyond its limited eight year life-span. His wife Olivia's addiction to the Sublimator would play a large part in the show's projected second year, with the pair becoming estranged due to her use of the machine and her retreat into a fantasy world: does Hume turn her in for treatment, or punishment — or can he help her himself?

***Above:** Michael Easton, as Hume, was a very different kind of hero than Arnold Schwarzenegger.*

For the first time in the series outline, Monterastelli makes a direct, explicit reference to the *Blade Runner* inspiration on the look of the show. "There are some similarities [in Hume's workspace] to the police structure used in the movie *Blade Runner*, where you had state-of-the-art equipment juxtaposed with furniture and an office space that was in a perpetual state of disrepair. Our series, however, will not be as relentlessly dark as *Blade Runner* and the interior of the Bureau headquarters will not be lit with the same heavy shadows and film noir style used in that film." Either minds were changed or the show's director of photography didn't read that part, as the eventual visual style of *Total Recall 2070* would heavily recall exactly the modern noir stark shadow lighting of *Blade Runner*.

In his character profile of Hume, Monterastelli points out that for most inhabitants of 'The City' life is good. "Although we are hinting at some dark secrets behind the sleek corporate veneer of this world, it must also not be forgotten that those same powerful corporations have done a lot of good over the previous fifty years. Hume and Olivia have an almost perfect life together…" There again is that tension between Monterastelli's desire to create a utopian world and the need for tension, conflict and crime to drive a twentieth century weekly television series.

Hume's android partner, Ian Farve, is described as being in his early 40s, a politically incorrect and deeply human character, almost more human than most humans. The clear intention here is that the revelation in the pilot that Farve is an android should come as a shock to both Hume and the audience. Farve was also positioned by Monterastelli as the comic relief figure in the series, partly through his politically incorrect viewpoints (perhaps reflecting the twentieth century viewer) and partly through the fact that he is an android struggling to be more human. This would be an example of the 'Pinocchio syndrome' made all too familiar by various *Star Trek* characters over the years, from the logical Vulcan Spock in the 1960s original, through the android Data from *Star Trek: The Next Generation* to shape-shifter Odo in *Star Trek: Deep Space Nine*, Borg drone Seven-of-Nine and the holographic Doctor in *Star Trek: Voyager*, back to logical Vulcan T'Pol in *Star Trek: Enterprise*.

Within the character profile of Farve, Monterastelli went on to outline the differences in the types of androids which would feature in the series. Whereas Farve was an Alpha-Class Android, the most sophisticated and human-like, the majority would be the service-oriented Beta-Class Androids. There is another class: Alpha-2 Androids, lacking in wit and imagination but used for highly complex and dangerous tasks, such as dismantling bombs or handling toxic waste, or deep space exploration.

Curiously, the series outline does not supply a separate specific character outline for Olivia, Hume's wife, although there are enough details of her character spread throughout the document to understand who she is and her function in the drama. The other characters specifically outlined were Lt. Martin Ehrenthal and Olan Chang. Ehrenthal is Hume and Farve's boss, the traditional precinct Captain. He's described as reporting to a "mysterious" superior, James Dedalus, but is essentially the traditional, gruff, no-nonsense police chief. He's the voice of reason and of the establishment against which, no doubt, Hume and Farve would find themselves tested. Chang is characterised as the 'Q' of the series, referring to the character in the James Bond movies who creates and supplies all the necessary gadgets. She is the series 'tech geek', who would no doubt explain in simple terms any high tech

Right: *Although it also dealt with the implications of science and technology, human drama was always at the centre of the series.*

equipment to Hume, so that the audience would also understand not so much what each McGuffin actually does or how it does it, but simply the reasons why it is important to the storyline of that week's episode. Although a technological boffin, Chang was described as not being a fan of the creation of artificial humans. She's also a friend of Olivia's, so crosses the professional and personal barriers around Hume, leading to other potential storylines.

Also key to generating storylines for the series and providing a sense of threat to the protagonists was the role of the Assessors, the internal affairs arm of the Interplanetary Council. It is an Assessor named Calley, according to the series outline, who assigns the android Farve to be Hume's partner. As the outline notes: "Over the series Calley will grow as a thorn in the side of and a nemesis for not only the investigators but also Ehrenthal." Additionally, because she works for the Transit Authority and was responsible for bringing the Johnny Cabs into the public transport system, the Assessors are also watching Hume's wife, Olivia. Thus Olivia's Sublimator addiction becomes important to Hume's professional standing as well as his private life.

Downplayed throughout the series outline so far has been the role of Mars, so central to both the originating Philip K. Dick short story, the Paul Verhoeven movie and the aborted *Total Recall*: The Series. Monterastelli does outline the basics of Mars in a similar way to the movie and the previous series document, but it seems clear that Mars would not be a central concern of the series. All the elements are present and correct: mining, mutants, a frontier-like Venusville, corporate politics and the seeds of rebellion. Mars introduces two additional proposed characters: Richard Collector, ruthless head of Minacom's private security arm, and Angeline, a cabaret singer in one of Venusville's exotic nightclubs (not The Last Resort!) who would eventually lead Hume and Farve to the truth about Mars' mutant population. Also mentioned in passing is a supposed spiritual leader for Mars named A-Showka (fulfilling the roles Kuato and Trask played in the abandoned series proposal). This would tie into an alliance between disgruntled miners and Martian mutants, as well as leading to the revelation of a pre-existing ancient culture on Mars, all concepts retained from earlier drafts of the *Total Recall* movie, but never fully explored.

Monterastelli's comprehensive bible ends with a summary of all the major characters, adding Vincent Nagle (who replaces Collector when he is sent to convalesce at a Rekall facility on the moon), SWAT team head Moralez, Felix Latham (inventor of the Rekall machine) and 'Johnny Zero', the most charismatic of the Johnny Cabs and the one who inadvertently spreads a virus through the system. There are also pages of definitions of the series' proposed institutions, technologies and terminologies.

It all adds up to a twenty-three-page document presenting a coherent, thought-through world which lays the groundwork for a whole variety of storylines drawing on Philip K. Dick's great themes of 'What is real?' and 'What is human?'. Even the complicated politics, which creates a variety of factions all struggling to control technology and humanity, echoes some of Dick's own set-ups for Earth's future in many short stories and novels. This was a pitch which did succeed, and led to Jeff King and Art Monterastelli embarking upon production of the first season of *Total Recall 2070*.

Distributor Alliance sold the first twenty-two-episode season to US cable broadcaster

Opposite: *Two promo sheets for* Total Recall 2070 *show slightly differing approaches to the series.*

Showtime (who had already enjoyed success with *Stargate SG-1*, the TV spin-off from the SF adventure B-movie *StarGate*), which allowed the producers to introduce a more adult sensibility to the show, meaning more swearing and nudity than network television might have allowed. Censored syndication versions of the episodes were also prepared…

Announcing the show to the press, producer Jeff King was keen to capitalise more on the connection to the original inspiration of Philip K. Dick than to the Paul Verhoeven film which gave the series its title. "We're relying on Philip K. Dick — who wrote the stories that *Blade Runner, Total Recall* and *Screamers* have all been based on — as our mentor into this world of the future and [we] pick up on his fascination with identity and levels of reality and unreality and the way that we communicate with each other."

King continued: "The kinds of things Philip Dick was writing about, his science fiction, isn't [of the] large planetary society scope that, say Asimov, or Pohl write; he writes small, intimate, personal stories, about heroes and anti-heroes and the human condition in a really great way. He embraces paranoia. So the brooding interior nature of his fiction is definitely an aspect of the series. That's all translated through Art Monterastelli's own unique vision of the future, which is really where our series departs strongly from Dick and *Total Recall*."

Art Monterastelli wrote the eighty-five-minute pilot episode, 'Machine Dreams'. "I wanted to move away from the world of the movie as much as I could without losing the audience that dug it in the first place," he claimed. Drawing on several elements from the series bible, the pilot movie introduced all the characters, sketching out their individual characteristics, and began several ongoing plot strands. Hume's partner is killed and replaced by android Farve, while Olivia begins her Sublimator addiction. The bulk of the action revolves around a group of rogue androids out to extend their lifespans. This involves a trip to Rekall and the kidnapping of a telepathic child (whose parents have their memories of their son wiped). There is a trip to Mars (largely via footage simply lifted from the *Total Recall* movie) and a rooftop confrontation between Hume and a dying android which is not a patch on the similar, but infinitely superior scene in *Blade Runner*.

Cast in the pilot movie (and subsequent series episodes) alongside Easton and Pruner were Cynthia Preston as Olivia, Michael Anthony Rawlins as Ehrenthal, Judith Krant as Olan Chang, Matthew Bennett as James Calley and rent-a-villain Nick Mancuso as Richard Collector. Easton and Pruner quickly came to terms with who their characters were. "Hume is like a regular guy who loves his wife, wants a family, defends his home," said Easton. "He's not comfortable with the way the world has become, is distrustful of all the machines and wants nothing more than to follow some good old fashioned pursuits…" After five auditions over two months, Pruner finally won the role of Farve. "The way Farve observes the world around him is similar to how a very intelligent hound views his surroundings," the actor noted. "He sees everything without judgement, without emotion or a psychological claiming of turf. His movements aren't exactly stilted, it's just that they don't flow into one another the way real human movements do."

Laying down a marker for the weekly series, the pilot movie opens with a special effects sequence which zooms in from a wide-angle view of 'The City', through a clock tower right down to the live-action main street. "I believe it's the longest continuous tracking sequence in a television show," claimed Emmy-award nominated visual effects director Jon

Campfens (whose previous work included *Mimic*, David Cronenberg's *Dead Ringers* and the first two *Darkman* movies). Working with a team of model builders and digital artists, Campfens and creature effects supervisor Gord Smith declared their intention for the series: "We don't just want to get the job done, we want it to be breathtaking."

Shooting on the pilot took place in Toronto, Canada in the summer of 1998. Jeff King set out to restrict all the live-action shooting to Toronto's Downsview Airforce Base, a former military supply depot, where elaborate wall-to-wall sets, designed by Taavo Soodor for the pilot and Peter Cosco for the series, were constructed. King hoped to avoid any additional location shooting, creating whatever was not shot on the soundstage via special effects and matte paintings, extending the real-world locations. "There are so many things you don't get to see until after it's shot," said King. "There are a lot of effects and green-screens or we are shooting plates and will put an effect in later. We've never really seen the whole city put together."

Shot between 29 June 1998 and March 1999, each episode of the series was set to cost around $1.5 million. The pilot, directed by pilot movie specialist Mario Azzopardi (*Stargate SG-1*, *Counterstrike* and *E.N.G.*), contained more than 125 different effects shots and sequences by Gazdecki Visual Effects of Toronto and Vancouver.

Costume designer Maxyne Baker deliberately set out to build on the *Blade Runner* vibe of the series by creating a wide range of outfits inspired by 1940s fashions, ranging from latex gowns to conservative dark-coloured ensembles for Minacon employees. Michael Easton and other members of the CPB were kitted out by Baker in suits with a 1940s inspiration.

The pilot was shot on what Azzopardi called "a maddeningly tight schedule" of only twenty days. Despite all the preparation and groundwork, the series leapt into production very quickly, so much so that star Michael Easton was a bit thrown at the beginning. "I was only cast a week before we started," he explained. "I came up immediately to Canada to do rehearsals. We literally got people cast the day before we started shooting. My original partner was cast two days before we started. So I come in and [start doing scenes] and talking about my partner, who gets killed, and I hadn't even met him yet. I was talking about my wife, and I hadn't even seen her picture yet."

***Above:** The key relationship in the show was between android Farve and the aptly-named human Hume.*

As the series progressed to shooting the individual episodes, Easton was impressed with the quality names attracted to feature in guest roles. "The cast here in Toronto is terrific, and we've been able to bring up some people from California and New York for recurring parts and guest roles. Anthony Zerbe plays my father. Peter Firth and David Warner have been up here." Firth, best known to SF fans as time traveller Dominick Hide in a pair of BBC-made TV movies of the 1980s, replaced Nick Mancuso's pilot movie role as Rekall's evil enforcer on the series.

The Toronto soundstages, housed in an old airport hangar, provided more than a million square feet of shooting space. One city set was spread across 300,000 square feet and featured a computerised system that allowed the filmmakers to create rain (much used on the series for that *Blade Runner* ambience), sunlight and fog as needed.

Following the pilot, *Total Recall 2070* moved on with the first stand alone episode, 'Self-Inflicted', which saw Hume and Farve investigate the origins of a lethal virus, leading them to uncover illegal germ warfare experiments at Minacom. 'Infiltration' introduced Peter Firth as the new head of Rekall security, as Hume and Farve investigated the death of a scientist involved in the manufacture of a new breed of androids. 'Nothing Like the Real Thing' saw black market 'recall' discs cause citizens to live out their twisted fantasies in real life. The investigation resulted in an emotional awakening for android Farve and guest-starred *24*'s Laura Harris.

Series star Michael Easton considered the seventh episode, 'Rough Whimper of Insanity', and episode nine, 'Baby Lottery', to be prime examples of the series at its best. "'Baby Lottery' was about manipulating children at — and also actually before — birth. If a child has a violent gene in him, that gene can be altered," he noted. "That helps make a pretty non-violent society even more non-violent, but it's also tampering with life. We do variations on that idea almost every week. They present this new technology to you and say, 'Look what we can do,' and then explore the ramifications. That's the overall philosophy.

"'Rough Whimper' is also interesting. We get into the notion of viruses. Somebody plants a virus in Farve, which causes him to act totally different from the way he normally does. He's usually very uptight and proper, and he ends up singing karaoke in a bar. It's a funny scene, but at the same time you know something's really wrong with [him]. It was a great episode for Karl [Pruner] to show his stuff."

The episodes of the second half of the season saw an arc story building towards the climax of the season finale. 'First Wave' highlights mankind's reliance on technology for everyday needs, while 'Brain Fever' deepens the audience's knowledge of Farve, as his investigation of the death of a union leader causes him to ask questions about his own creation. 'Begotten Not Made' continued the theme as Farve's 'creator' is implicated in a murder. 'Burning Desire', 'Brightness Falls', 'Astral Projections' and 'Paranoid' all feature paranoia, Sublimator abuse and hallucinations — all key Philip K. Dick themes — as well as some important choices for Hume in his relationship with Olivia.

The soap opera elements of the series developed alongside the SF future technology drama in a successful way rarely seen in episodic SF TV. 'Restitution' for example saw Olivia's ex kidnapped, and Hume faced with dealing with her loss of recall of their life together, while 'Bones Beneath My Skin' saw anti-android prejudice threaten Farve. 'Assessment' was the traditional 'clips show', and saw Hume undergo interrogation as he is forced to review his relationship with Farve (while viewers watched budget-saving excerpts from previous episodes). 'Eyewitness' had Olivia witness a murder, but her fragile state following her Sublimator addiction makes her recall untrustworthy. The final two episodes of the series — 'Virtual Justice' and 'Meet My Maker' — saw Hume uncover a conspiracy at the highest level in the justice system and investigate Farve's true origins. This results in Farve kidnapping Hume and the pair of them confronting Farve's true creator. (See the appendix for a full list of *Total Recall 2070* episodes.)

Although the series finished on a highly dramatic note, ratings were not deemed high enough to make a second series of adventures in the detailed future world of *Total Recall 2070* a reality. It's a shame the show didn't have further opportunity to develop, as it seems likely that in subsequent years the writers would have turned even more to the short stories and novels of Philip K. Dick to find inspiration for their episodes. (It's also a shame that, barring the pilot episode, the series has not to date been released on DVD.) As it is, the season that was made is far truer to Dick's themes than most of the movies directly based on his work. Spun off from a film that spiralled away from Dick's original work, the underappreciated *Total Recall 2070* TV series instead provided fans with twenty-two hours of solid Philip K. Dick-inspired drama. That's much more material than any of the movies... ■

WE CAN BUILD YOU

Impostor returns to Philip K. Dick's theme of 'What is human?' in a tale of android bombs and robot romance...

"I don't write about heroes. Heroes are really marvellous. Heroes give all the answers." — Philip K. Dick, *SF EYE*, #14, Spring 1996.

'Impostor' was the only story written by Philip K. Dick to be published in seminal pulp SF magazine *Astounding Science Fiction* (in June 1953). This core pulp fiction magazine had been founded in 1930 as an action-adventure title in which science was only ever featured where it could offer a sheen of realism to otherwise outlandish tales. It was *Astounding Science Fiction* that gave popular culture the clichéd magazine cover featuring a brawny spaceman rescuing a damsel-in-distress from some hideous space beast, an image which would go on to become a mainstay of science fiction movie posters of the 1950s. During the 1930s *Astounding* featured and helped to build the reputation of many of the classic pulp science fiction writers. Appearing in its pages were early stories by Jack Williamson, Eric Frank Russell, Murray Leinster, E. E. 'Doc' Smith, H. P. Lovecraft, C. L. Moore, Charles Fort (founder of all things Fortean) and John W. Campbell Jr.

By 1937 Campbell had become editor of *Astounding*, publishing the first works by writers such as Lester Del Rey and L. Ron Hubbard. The so-called Campbell 'golden age' began in 1939, with writers like Isaac Asimov, Theodore Sturgeon, Robert A. Heinlein and other key figures of SF literature in the 1940s and 1950s featuring regularly in the magazine.

By the 1950s, when Philip K. Dick was actively publishing his first short stories, *Astounding* was still a vital force, having driven off some strong competition through the years, but Campbell was taking the magazine in an odd direction, publishing Hubbard's first writings on Scientology and other pseudo-science features. Despite this, it was still the most important magazine for aspiring science fiction authors to be featured in, so Dick was very happy to have sold a story to the pre-eminent SF editor, even if his 'golden age' was somewhat tarnished by now. After all, *Astounding* continued to win Hugo Awards in 1953 (the year 'Impostor' was published), 1955, 1956 and 1957. Later, in the 1960s, *Astounding* published the novellas that formed Frank Herbert's *Dune*, and continued to win Hugos throughout the decade. Campbell remained at the helm until his death in 1971, when science fiction author Ben Bova took over.

Opposite: *Is he human, or an android bomb? Gary Sinise leads the cast of* Impostor.

Campbell's thirty-four year reign at *Astounding* is itself an astounding feat. In that period, he had developed a liking for his archetypal SF story: an action-adventure tale in which the science was taken for granted. The gadgets, devices and bizarre happenings

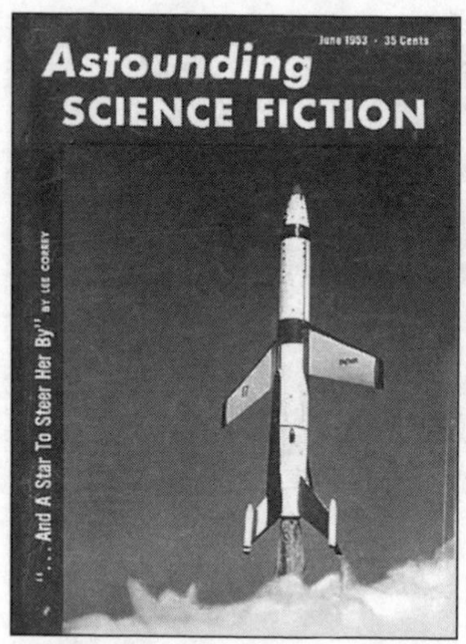

Above: *Dick's short story 'Impostor' was published in the June 1953* Astounding Science Fiction, *his only work to appear in the seminal pulp.*

would all be part of the protagonists' normal everyday life. It was a lesson Dick took to heart, creating across his fiction an often surprisingly convincing and consistent future world with its 'conapts', 'homeopapes' and 'autofacs', items which the characters in those stories and novels relate to in the way we do our contemporary real-life houses, newspapers and robot-operated factories.

While Campbell bought 'Impostor' from Dick, it was the only story of his to run in *Astounding*. *Divine Invasions*, Lawrence Sutin's biography of Dick, reports that the author felt that Campbell "considered my writing [to be] not only worthless but, as he put it, 'Nuts'." Dick was also aware that, as one of his many idiosyncrasies, Campbell considered psionics (mental processes such as telepathy, precognition and telekinesis) to be not optional but necessary elements of a good science fiction story. Perhaps in an attempt to sell another story to Campbell, Dick began writing a series of stories such as 'A World of Talent' (1954) and 'Psi Man' (1955) featuring such elements. However, it wasn't until his novels of the 1960s that Dick really engaged with ideas of precognition and mental powers in works such as *Martian Time Slip*, *The Three Stigmata of Palmer Eldritch* and *Ubik*.

In Dick's story 'Impostor', Earth is at war with the 'Outspacers', an enemy from Alpha Centauri. Spence Olham is a defence researcher developing new weapons to tip the balance of the ongoing battle in Earth's favour, but he is suspected of being an Outspacer agent, a 'humanoid robot' (a creation which Dick would later dub an 'android'). He's accused of killing and replacing the real Olham, but his programming is such that even he doesn't know that he's a robot replacement. Additionally, this 'impostor' robot unknowingly has a 'U-bomb' implanted within it, primed to be triggered when a certain crucial phrase is spoken...

Dick outlines how the robot "would become Olham in mind as well as body. He would look like him, have his memories, his thoughts and interests, perform his job." Olham can't convince the security forces that he is really human and so goes on the run, pursued by those who doubt his humanity. It's the realisation by Olham himself that he is, in fact, a robot replacement that triggers the U-bomb, destroying the world and concluding the story. Containing notions of implanted memories and false realities, 'Impostor' is one of the first short stories by Dick to fully explore those issues that would later become obsessions both in his fiction and in his life.

"'Impostor' was my first story on the topic of: Am I human? Or am I just programmed to believe I am human?" Dick pointed out in 1976, looking back on this story. "When you consider that I wrote this back in 1953, it was, if I may say so, a pretty damn good new idea in SF. Of course, by now I've done it to death. The theme still preoccupies me. It's an important theme because it forces us to ask: What is a human? And — what isn't?"

Reader identification is with Spencer Olham throughout the story, on the assumption that he is human, a terrible mistake has been made and his seemingly inhuman pursuers will ultimately get their comeuppance. Dick's trick ending (fresher in 1953 than it appears now, after countless stories and films with similar 'surprise' twists) takes the reader aback and plays out the 'What is human?' question to its logical conclusion: if the robot is more human than the real humans (at least as far as the author's manipulated sympathies of the reader are concerned) then who (or what) can truly be called 'human'? It was a question Dick would return to repeatedly and one that would frequently be at the centre of those stories of his adapted into films.

Above: *'Impostor' was Dick's earliest exploration of 'What is human?' What if a wife couldn't tell if her husband had been replaced by an android?*

In his academic study of Dick's work, Douglas A. Mackey noted of 'Impostor': "Dick implies it is important to be asking: 'What is it to be human? What can I know about myself and reality?' 'Impostor' is the classic statement of the ultimate paranoia that we ourselves may be the enemy. We may not be who we think we are, but rather a 'thing' with artificially implanted memories." Mackey concludes that in asking the question "Am I human?" we "must have the courage to take the consequences, even if it means the end of the world as we know it..." Patricia S. Warrick, who studies Dick's fiction in *Mind in Motion*, noted that in 'Impostor' Dick uses "the explosion as a metaphor for the event that shatters the illusions an individual believes to be truth and reality."

At its most basic, 'Impostor' is a clear initial statement of one of Dick's biggest themes, and provided the material for a movie version which, initially at least, intended to respect its origins as a short story. First planned as part of a trio of SF shorts, *Impostor*'s troubled journey to the screen resembled the plight of Spence Olham: the film didn't know what it was, wanted to be, or could be, and ended up self-destructing.

Impostor began life as one of three short science fiction films which would be released as one anthology movie, initially dubbed *The Light Years Trilogy*. Each tale would explore the theme of 'alien love', some more literally than others. The first segment of the movie, *Alien Love Triangle*, was shot by director Danny Boyle (*Trainspotting, 28 Days Later*) and starred Kenneth Branagh as a man who discovers his wife (played by *Friends* star Courteney Cox) is in fact a male alien from another world. Heather Graham also featured as Cox's alien wife.

The second segment of *The Light Years Trilogy* was intended to be *Impostor*, directed by Gary Fleder (at that time best known for his Tarantino-style gangster movie *Things to Do in Denver When You're Dead*). Three writers were hired — Scott Rosenberg, Mark Protosevich and Caroline Case — to write a forty-minute version of *Impostor*, which was filmed starring Gary Sinise as Spence Olham. When *The Light Years Trilogy/Alien Love*

Right: Impostor *envisages the future of 2079, with Earth's cities covered by protective domes.*

Triangle project fell apart, with two segments shot and an unnamed third story unmade (which some sources say later became Guillermo Del Toro's *Mimic*), the decision was taken to expand one of the two existing short films into a standalone movie. *Impostor* was chosen and new writers were hired to write around the existing material, expanding the forty minutes out to at least ninety, providing sensible story developments that would grow the tale organically. That, at least, was the initial plan.

The intention was for the third act of the full-length movie to be exactly as it was in the forty-minute short. Ehren Kruger, a screenwriter who'd worked with director Wes Craven at Miramax/Dimension (the studio for whom the feature film version of *Impostor* was being was being made) was tapped to work with director Fleder in developing the full-length film. It's unclear what Kruger contributed, but as 'insurance' Dimension executives also brought in writer-director David Twohy (*Pitch Black*, *Below*, *The Chronicles of Riddick*) to write alternate versions of key additional scenes. Twohy seems to have turned in around twenty-five pages before leaving the project and leaving many story problems unsolved. Next in line was screenwriter Richard Jeffries, apparently the last writer to tackle expanding *Impostor* from the short movie. He seems to have written or rewritten around sixty-five pages, reworking the second act mainly and developing bits of the first act. He cleaned up what then became the shooting script, ironing out some of the story problems Twohy had apparently left hanging at his departure.

Director Fleder offered a different spin on the development of *Impostor* when questioned about it during the film's many press junkets: "We shot the short as part of a trilogy we were doing for Miramax, kind of like *New York Stories*. Danny Boyle doing one, me doing one, Bryan Singer [*X-Men*] doing one. When the short was being shot, Bob Weinstein was so happy with the footage, he said, 'I'd love to make this as a feature.' And I said, 'You're nuts. We can't do that.' But, you know, Bob is not nuts. Bob is a really smart guy. So we began talking about how to do it. How to take the footage and create this bigger thing. David Twohy got involved, and we blew it up. We made it into a bigger story."

The film *Impostor* locked Dick's imprecise setting to 2079 (a year after *Screamers* is set, oddly enough, and sharing the decade of *Total Recall 2070*). The Earth has been at war with a (never seen) alien force for over a decade. As in the short story, Spencer Olham (Sinise) is a government scientist, working valiantly on new weapons in the battle to save the planet. He's accused of being an alien spy and becomes the subject of a nationwide manhunt. Olham's dilemma is two-tiered: can he prove his identity to his pursuers in time, and can he ultimately prove his identity to himself?

"It's the most terrifying conflict of all," noted Fleder, "to suddenly be accused of being someone else. How do you prove who you are? How do you prove you aren't who other people think you are? There have been many classic movies about fugitives or mistaken identity, but *Impostor* takes it one step further, adding in the technologically possible idea that Spencer Olham might not even be human. Even Spencer Olham has to entertain the fact that in the year 2079, the possibility for human-like replication exists."

Fleder's intention with the film was to create an unsettling mood, lifted from Dick's story, to have the audience doubt Olham's identity while being sympathetic to his fear and confusion as events unfold: "I wanted the audience to experience the same doubt that plagues the film's characters. They are made to believe, then not to believe. The film really plays with the variable nature of trust, belief and faith."

Having seen *Blade Runner* and *Total Recall*, Fleder was intent on going down the Harrison Ford path in terms of finding an actor suitable for the role of Spencer Olham, rather than the Arnold Schwarzenegger route. The director wanted a readily believable 'everyman', not a superhuman for whom the audience would feel no sympathy. "What struck me about Gary Sinise is that he's not the proto-typical macho hero," noted Fleder of his leading man. "He doesn't feel like a superhero, but more like the kind of guy who would endure and escape a terrible situation by the sheer force of his will. Gary really brings that quality and he also brings the essential elements of credibility and conviction to the part."

Sinise was attracted to the role for the very reasons that Fleder wanted him. "Spence is kind of an everyman character," said the actor, "who's vulnerable yet heroic, yet caught in a web of mistrust. He's got to prove something while up against the odds. The character also offered me a lot more in terms of being a leading man than some of the others I've done. He's more active." Sinise's other SF-related films had included the Brian De Palma dud *Mission to Mars*, real-life space thriller *Apollo 13* and the Stephen King dramas *The Stand* and *The Green Mile*.

When preparing for the original short film version of the movie, Sinise had read and enjoyed Dick's original short story. "What's interesting about the short story is that it was written in the 1950s. It's kind of remarkable when you think about it, how it relates to where we are today, current events and the threat of terrorism and paranoia, and what that makes the government do. Although it's a world far into the future, it's one person's vision, and it somehow relates to and reflects our own lives. That allows us, in our way, to identify with the story and understand it. A good SF piece can really make you think about that."

Above: *Madeleine Stowe, cast as Olham's wife Maya, was initially sceptical about expanding the short to full length.*

For his characterisation, Sinise drew on real-life scientists to develop his moral perspective on the story: "Like [Robert J.] Oppenheimer [creator of the atom bomb], my character has vast intelligence and knowledge, but he still feels very responsible for the creation of a weapon that can annihilate life."

Equally, the action element of the movie, expanded from the short story and stretched even further in the full-length version of the movie, was a major attraction for Sinise, an actor not usually associated with action hero roles. "I like that this is a very different sort of project for me, very intense and physical, a movie where all hell breaks loose for my character. I also like the way the story turns from being this sweet love story between Spencer Olham and his wife into a tense paranoid thriller. It's full of wild surprises."

Cast as Maya, Olham's wife, was Madeleine Stowe, whose only previous brush with SF was in Terry Gilliam's *12 Monkeys*. Stowe was reluctant to take part in the original short film, fearing that she would be able to bring little to the wife role. However, the prospect of working with Fleder and Sinise on a story she admitted intrigued her eventually won her over. Then the nature of the job changed. "It was very quick and brief," said Stowe of shooting the short, "and then the next thing you know, they wanted to turn it into a full-length feature. I was again [thinking], 'I don't know what I can really bring to it that is all that interesting.' They felt that if the character wasn't there, they didn't have a movie. I said, 'I think you're wrong.' And, you know, I think I even went on the record, when this was all coming around, saying, 'I don't know why they want to make [it full length],' because the short was perfect. I didn't know if I could trust the fact that they could expand it into something interesting."

Fleder saw the role of Maya, expanded in the feature film version of *Impostor*, as being pivotal to generating the audience sympathy for the main character that the film needed to attract if it was going to work successfully. "If you don't believe in the relationship, if you don't believe their love is at stake, the story doesn't work," admitted Fleder. "The core relationship of the film is Spencer and Maya, Gary and Madeleine. As husband and wife they are also best friends, and that's the closest we come to total belief and faith, usually. Can Maya look into Spencer's soul and believe that he is who he says he is? That's the question — and these two had to bring that to the fore."

Perhaps suspecting that the project to expand the movie was doomed, Stowe appeared reluctant to shoot the additional scenes required (including an opening bedroom scene) and doubted whether her character would be sufficiently developed in the full-length movie. "She didn't grow much. I mean, they just showed her at work. It was about opening up the film, more than anything else. And, you know, my inclination was to not [do it]. [But] because I was so fond of the people I was involved with, I just went ahead and did it. [In the short,] the hospital didn't exist. And there's a scene [added] with Vincent D'Onofrio and another where you see her being doctorly. All the other stuff was from the original."

Stowe had to dig deep into a role that was thinly written in order to develop any motivation for her character. "The interesting thing about Maya is that the audience has to always not know where she's standing. She's filled with ambiguities. She wakes in the morning and suddenly her husband is accused of being a cyborg bomb! Of course, it's unfathomable to her, but she knows the scientific possibilities, so she's truly conflicted. She has to question everything, even the reality that means the most to her, the reality of her love."

As his role was expanded for the full-length version of the movie, Vincent D'Onofrio found himself engaged in extra shooting on *Impostor* as Hathaway, the character in pursuit of Olham, convinced of his inhumanity. "Vincent has a very intense persona he brings to the role," said Fleder. "His Hathaway is a formidable opponent, who is at once complicated and charismatic."

"Although he is Spencer's greatest enemy," explained D'Onofrio, "he isn't a bad guy. He's just trying to catch the guy. He's just completely committed to the enormous responsibility he's been given to save humanity." Joining Olham on his newly extended odyssey through the world of 2079 is Cale, a disenfranchised member of this future society played by Mekhi Phifer. "My character is not one of Spencer Olham's friends, but he becomes a life-line," said Phifer. "Cale comes to respect Olham. He feels the need to help save his life."

In *Impostor* Gary Fleder wanted to create a realistically extrapolated vision of the future, something Steven Spielberg would achieve more convincingly with the later *Minority Report*. With a fraction of *Minority Report*'s resources, however, this director couldn't afford Spielberg's futurologist think tank approach (see Chapter 12), and had to work with his production designers to develop a vision of a practical and possible future on a tight budget. The switch from self-contained forty-minute short to ninety-eight-minute feature film made

Above: *Added to the expanded version of the film was Mekhi Phifer as Olham's guide through the future underworld.*

the job of coherently visualising this future that bit harder. "It was vital to me that everything in the film either be in the realm of possibility or already happening in one form or another," claimed Fleder. "We present the end results of research that is taking place now — everything from voice activation to automated houses [a mainstay of Dick's fiction] to next-generation medical technology, such as molecular-sized robots that can be injected into your body to fix things."

Drawing from Dick's fiction, and the lesson the author had learned from his editor at *Astounding*, John W. Campbell, Fleder was at pains to present in *Impostor* a world that was familiar and believable to a contemporary audience. Production designer Nelson Coates was tasked with realising this day-after-tomorrow future on screen. "We wanted to look at what's on the cutting edge now and project that seventy-five years into the future," explained Coates. "The challenge was to do this while keeping the look very different from other archetypes of SF that were out there, from *2001* to *Mad Max* to *Aliens*. Ours is a unique view of the future."

An example of this extrapolation would be the 'simcodes', embedded microchips which track and identify every human being in the world of *Impostor*. These micro-machine implants, which are scanned every time someone enters a building, makes a purchase or a phone call, grew out of the microchip identification tags already used to locate and track dogs and other animals, domestic and otherwise. This idea, and the all-pervasive Orwellian surveillance it allows, would also turn up in Spielberg's *Minority Report*, albeit further developed than in *Impostor*.

There was also a darker aspect to the world of the future which Coates wanted to bring to life, as it reflected the psychological state of the movie's central character. "Everything starts incredibly ordered, a very comforting and controlled environment," elaborated Coates. "As Spencer Olham's life falls apart, the sets start to highlight a greater sense of paranoia, of claustrophobia. You go from these lovely environments bathed in warm light and wood tones, to black, scary shapes. It's the same progression that's going on in Spencer Olham's brain, as he tries to face his humanity, or his uncertainty about his humanity. He's entering the realm of chaos."

Visual effects for the ambitious film were provided by Industrial Light & Magic (ILM) under supervisor Joe Grossberg. Producing the effects on a tight budget saw Grossberg using computer-generated 3D matte paintings to realise some of *Impostor*'s outlandish locations or difficult-to-achieve scenes. These included the landing of vehicles at stations and their progress through the portals in the dramatic domes which cover Earth's cities as protection from the constant attacks by alien forces. Also on Grossberg's schedule was the creation of working videophones, scanners and spy devices used in pursuit of the on-the-run Olham.

Adding to the paranoid atmosphere of the film, Fleder and production designer Coates took the decision not to show the story's threatening aliens from Alpha Centauri. "We decided to keep them entirely in the audience's imagination," said Coates, justifying in artistic terms a decision that was almost certainly driven by budgetary concerns. "We hear about them and see signs of them, but it's all very subtle, playing off our deepest fears."

In a strange coincidence that would almost certainly have amused and may even have spooked Dick, the building used to depict the HQ of the Earth Security Agency was that of eyewear manufacturer Oakley, whose founder Colin Baden was a huge Philip K. Dick fan. The building had actually been designed after the kind of buildings described in Dick's fiction. Although Baden had forbidden filming there previously, for a Dick-inspired project he was happy to relent.

Other locations used to depict the paranoid world of 2079 were the then newly-built California and Arizona Life Centres and the San Fernando Valley's Joseph Jensen Water Filtration Plant, which offered 36,000 square feet of blank, colourless, solid concrete against which Olham and Cale could flee the forces of the driven Hathaway.

There was a two-year gap between completion of the extended *Impostor* in Spring 2000 and its eventual release in January 2002. Delays in the work required to expand the film were partly to blame, as was concern about how some of the issues in the film would play with audiences in the wake of the 11 September 2001 terrorist attack on New York. However, according to Fleder, the main problem was with trying to get a certificate for the film from

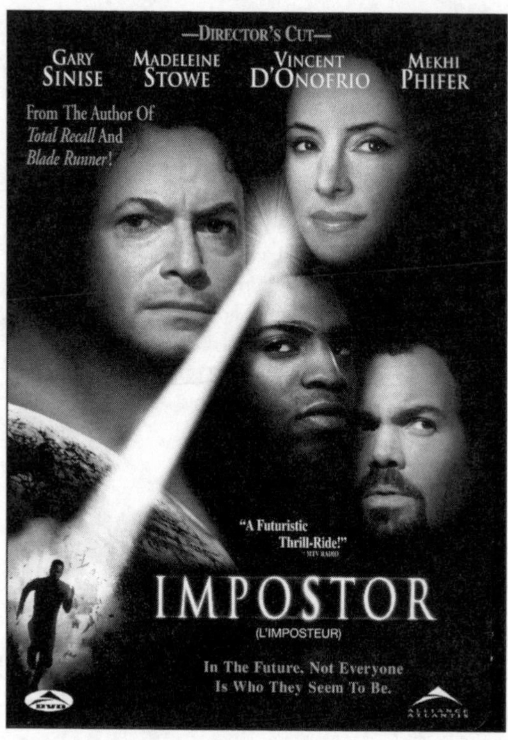

—Director's Cut—
Gary Sinise
Madeleine Stowe
Vincent D'Onofrio
Mekhi Phifer
From The Author Of Total Recall And Blade Runner!
"A Futuristic Thrill-Ride!"
IMPOSTOR
(L'IMPOSTEUR)
In The Future, Not Everyone Is Who They Seem To Be.

Above: *The DVD cover made sure to mention the key previous Philip K. Dick adaptations.*

the MPAA, the US movie censorship body.

"There were a lot of issues with the rating," the director admitted in discussions when the film was eventually released. "I delivered the film as an R rating about a year ago [January 2001]. That was before I began shooting *Don't Say a Word*. While I was gone, there was a conversation. You could see that things were happening, that films that were PG-13 were making more money. This film is designed to play, I think, pretty wide. But you also don't want to leave out younger kids, that *American Pie* audience. The big issue with time was just getting it cut right. We made some more trims. We re-previewed the film about two and a half months ago [October 2001], and the film previewed about twenty-five points higher than previously. I think making the film less horrific, less violent, made the film more accessible. The film's already pretty tough."

Fleder admitted to toning down the more visceral violence that featured in his initial cut. "The whole interrogation scene with Vincent D'Onofrio and Gary Sinise was much more brutal. The guy having this thing taken out of his chest was much more graphic. As a filmmaker, you can become inured to your own special effects. I realised, looking back, that the film was just too harsh. We toned it down. It took a lot of time to go back and forth and looking at different takes."

Another concern was the post-9/11 atmosphere in America. "The film is about a lot of these themes, the issues of the witch-hunt mentality and judging people not for who they are, but what they are. Everything from the bio-ethics of scanning people and DNA and that kind of obsession, I think those are issues raised."

Fleder felt that the movie effectively played up a kind of Cold War paranoia, something he'd detected in real life following the 2001 terrorist attacks on New York and the Pentagon. The unseen enemy hangs over the plot and action of *Impostor*. "In the film, you never see the Centauri. You never see the enemy. It's like that Philip Kaufman remake of *Invasion of the Body Snatchers*. It's this unseen, intangible evil. That goes back to 1950s sci-fi [from where the story originated]. If you had actually seen the aliens, it would have been a much more goofy movie. The fact is that not seeing it makes it relevant again in this context."

Dimension/Miramax even added an additional credit at the beginning of the movie, sourcing it to Philip K. Dick's short story, fearing that the filmmakers might have been accused of concocting their tale following the New York tragedy. "The only thing we added to the film, post-tragedy, was that little card that says the [story] was written in 1953," confirmed Fleder.

"It was the only thing we added. It was Bob's idea. Bob Weinstein said, 'You know, let's just remind people that this guy was prescient.' Dick wrote this thing fifty years ago."

Impostor cost around $40 million to produce and distribute, but it made only $6.11 million by the end of January 2002 at the US box office, a much more dramatic financial failure than that of even *Screamers* previously. Critic Peter Biskind, in *Down and Dirty Pictures*, his controversial exposé of Miramax and the independent movie scene of the 1990s, wrote of *Impostor*: "Gary Sinise couldn't open a can of tunafish, much less a movie", and described Bob Weinstein as being "too cheap to use stars [as well as being] unable to come up with pictures that packed the high concept punch of the *Scream* trilogy."

Released on 4 January 2002, *Impostor*, one of the first movies released in the new year, was treated harshly by the critics. According to Gary Dowell in the *Dallas Morning News*, *Impostor* had the look of a "low-budget, made-for-cable" feature. Most of the critics noted that it was originally intended as a forty-minute segment of a two-hour trilogy, then puffed up into a full-length feature. Eleanor Ringel Gillespie in the *Atlanta Journal-Constitution* observed that while the film "looks musty, dark, and cheap", it did have a few things going for it: "It gives its core audience — die-hard sci-fi freaks — a lot to like. There are the usual neato gadgets and a nifty twist that may not surprise everyone but is still satisfying." However, Michael Wilmington of the *Chicago Tribune* concluded: "*Impostor* starts as a tribute to Philip K. Dick and winds up selling its soul to Arnold Schwarzenegger." Geoff Pevere's review in the *Toronto Star* did give the newspaper's headline writer the opportunity to set down a phrase that otherwise would never have appeared in a family newspaper: "*Impostor* Doesn't Know Dick."

Like *Screamers* before it, *Impostor* is unfortunately something of a dull runaround in which cardboard characters, brought to life by actors giving often sub-par performances, fail to successfully flesh out the inventive ideas of Dick's fiction. The original short film (available on the US Region 1 DVD) is a snappier, faster-paced, less-padded version of the same tale of paranoia. At least it doesn't outstay its welcome, unlike the expanded version, which feels unnecessarily bloated with the addition of dull chase scenes and the comedy relief sidekick.

The one thing that *Impostor* does bring to the screen remarkably well is that key Dick theme of 'What is human?'. In an interview published in *Starlog* in 1990, Philip K. Dick outlined what was at the heart of his short story. "My original idea was that a guy could be an android and not know it. I wrote that in 'Impostor', very early, 1953, in *Astounding*. It was about a man who was getting ready to go to work at a big scientific research project and he's arrested by the FBI and told that he's not Spence Olham, he's an android who has been sent to Earth to replace Spence Olham, to carry a bomb into this great scientific research place to blow it up. He thinks he is Spence Olham. Well, it turns out he's wrong: he's an android, he has a bomb inside him, and the trigger that sets off the bomb is when he says, 'Good Lord, I am an android!' That's all it takes. As soon as he says that sentence, he blows up! That was one of the first stories I ever sold, so that idea is now public property. This is used all the time in science fiction, it's like time travel or ecology…"

If nothing else, the movie of *Impostor* brought that core Philip K. Dick idea to a wider audience than ever before. ■

DR FUTURITY

Steven Spielberg and Tom Cruise leap upon the Philip K. Dick movie bandwagon with the futuristic thriller *Minority Report*...

"My agent, Russell Galen, put it, 'Whenever a Hollywood film adaptation of a book works, it is always a miracle.' Because it just cannot really happen. It did happen with *The Man Who Fell to Earth* and it has happened with *Blade Runner*..." — Philip K. Dick, *Rod Serling's The Twilight Zone Magazine*, Vol. 2, No. 3, June 1982.

The Steven Spielberg-directed *Minority Report* began life as an idea for a sequel to *Total Recall*, which would have diverted even further from Philip K. Dick's original short story 'We Can Remember It For You Wholesale'. In the event, the film ended up being based on a different tale altogether.

Dick's short story 'The Minority Report', published in *Fantastic Universe* magazine in December 1954, depicts a future in which a percentage of human beings are born with a genetic mutation that results in the development of telepathic powers. Shunned by the population at large, these 'pre-cogs' (precognitives) find sanctuary with the government, who exploit their powers as the basis of a new crime fighting initiative dubbed the Pre-Crime Division. The pre-cogs are used to predict criminal acts that can then be averted before they occur, concentrating primarily on murder, thus saving lives and simultaneously solving the problem of overcrowded jails. Dick's plot followed the fate of Pre-Crime detective John Anderton, who becomes the subject of a manhunt after the pre-cogs finger him as the suspect in a murder yet to happen. Anderton, who doesn't know his supposed victim, is forced to go on the run. Dick's story explores notions of free will and fate, pitting Anderton against the system in which he has total faith, but which seems to have turned against him. In the end, Anderton feels compelled to fulfil the pre-cogs' prophecy because he believes the system is perfect and to do otherwise would contradict that belief. The movie's climax would take the totally opposite view, losing Dick's intended irony about the nature of Pre-Crime.

Dick's focus in the short story is not so much on the fear and ostracism suffered by the pre-cogs as a result of their differences from the rest of humanity, but instead is on the misuse by the government of the information that is derived from the pre-cogs' predictions. Precognition was a recurring Dickian theme, particularly in his early short fiction, featuring in stories such as 1954's 'A World of Talent'.

Opposite:
Spielberg's Minority Report *was built primarily around the star power of Tom Cruise, rather than the ideas of Philip K. Dick.*

The driving force behind 'The Minority Report' becoming a movie, distinct from the other proposed *Total Recall* sequels, was writer Gary Goldman. After *Total Recall*, Goldman had worked again with director Paul Verhoeven on the controversial *Basic Instinct*, and then he drafted an early version of superhero comic-book movie *X-Men* for *Titanic* director James

TOM CRUISE
PRECRIME
A STEVEN SPIELBERG FILM
MINORITY
REPORT

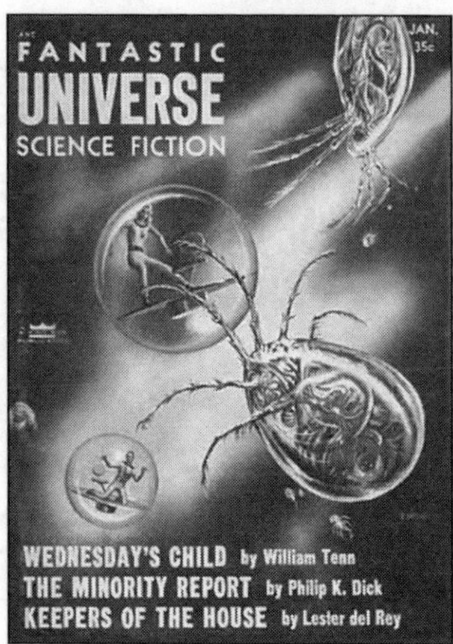

FANTASTIC
UNIVERSE
SCIENCE FICTION
JAN.
35c
WEDNESDAY'S CHILD by William Tenn
THE MINORITY REPORT by Philip K. Dick
KEEPERS OF THE HOUSE by Lester del Rey

Above: *Dick's original short story first appeared in the December 1954 issue of* Fantastic Universe.

Cameron. In 1992, a friend of Goldman's, himself an aspiring screenwriter, showed him Philip K. Dick's 1954 short story 'The Minority Report'. "I optioned it for myself to co-write and direct," Goldman said in an interview for this book. "I brought that project to Paul Verhoeven, to see if he would sponsor me by taking the role of executive producer. He suggested reshaping the project as a *Total Recall* sequel [see Chapter 7]. That seemed like an automatic movie, as we were reuniting the whole team from the original, including Ron Shusett, who came on board with me as co-writer and co-executive producer. [Writer Robert Goethals also became involved at this point]. Verhoeven lost interest in the project after reading our first draft. So after a year of dormancy at Carolco, Shusett and I got the project back, and we set it up at 20th Century Fox, with Jan de Bont attached to direct. Jan made the decision to change the project back to a straight adaptation, rather than a sequel to *Total Recall*.

"The [Philip K.] Dick situation is unique," said Goldman, discussing the attraction of the writer's work for film adaptation. "His stories have attracted the right kind of people. His best work has a combination of commercial ideas with profound insight." Goldman sees within the original Philip K. Dick stories ideas that are not only natural for film adaptation, but also have great commercial potential and would hence attract a broad, popular audience. That was certainly the case with Spielberg's *Minority Report*.

Goldman sees himself as being positioned in opposition to the traditional Hollywood filmmaking system, willing to take chances working on things that studio executives don't see as being hits… yet. "I liken myself to a 'pre-cog'. It has to do with a feeling of boredom I get with things the way they are. To a degree, I feel lucky to have had such a successful career being so contrary to the status quo."

With the script in development at 20th Century Fox, Goldman and Shusett worked on two further drafts before the project was taken away from them. Were those drafts closer to the Dick original, or in line with the resulting Spielberg movie? "All drafts were quite similar and quite faithful to the story," Goldman told the present author. "Our draft had lots of twists and turns and was about the hero's confusion in not knowing his motive." Later writers were to develop Goldman's foundations. "Jon Cohen's version was more straightforward. Scott Frank's draft blended our story structure with a lot of Cohen's futuristic visualisation, and then made it much darker, adding the element of the missing/dead child."

Having flirted with *Minority Report* as director, Jan de Bont ultimately left the project, but had interested Tom Cruise in starring. Through Cruise, the *Minority Report* screenplay found its way to director Steven Spielberg. "I read the script and sent it over to Spielberg because I saw great things in it. It's always difficult when you're looking for a film to do, but I love SF and I thought it was great, fascinating," noted Cruise.

Spielberg was struck by the central idea of the story, immediately seeing the screen potential. "I remember reading the script and liking the idea, especially for Tom [to star]," he said. Spielberg brought in Scott Frank to rewrite Jon Cohen's earlier reworking of Goldman and Shusett's original version. While Frank worked, harking back to Goldman and Shusett's draft, Spielberg went on to direct *A.I.: Artificial Intelligence*.

When he'd been hired to tackle a new version of 'The Minority Report,' screenwriter Jon Cohen had to admit that he'd "only vaguely ever heard of [Philip K. Dick]. I did not even truly understand that *Blade Runner* or *Total Recall* were based on his work, which shows you how attuned I am to sci-fi."

Cohen noted that he "kept the Dick story premise, the gimmick and a few lead characters, then completely changed everything. Dick wrote an impossible logic problem of a story. He was more interested in mental conceits than a propulsive visual story. I had to read it about a hundred times, and I still don't get it all."

For Cohen, though, the central conceit of the story eventually clicked the more he studied it, and his solution was to connect it directly to cinema, to ideas of seeing and sight and how viewers can be fooled about what they see. "The great thing about Philip K. Dick was his unconnectedness to the world," noted Cohen. "He never felt that he was part of the same world that you and I are part of. What drew me to his vision is that he is uncertain of the world, paranoid about the world, about what is real. *Minority Report* is about seeing, about looking into the future — that was how to shape the story. There's not a lot in the [short] story to work with in terms of gadgets or what the future world looks like. Dick doesn't elaborate on what his themes are. As soon as I began thinking about the pre-cogs, I found my theme for how I wanted to go at the story, which was 'sight': eyes, what do you see, what do the pre-cogs see, what does our hero see?"

Cohen admitted that his bottom line was that he "just made [the short story] into a cool 'innocent man on the run' movie. I loved the gimmick: Pre-Crime is an organisation that can predict a murder before it happens. You get arrested before you commit the crime. The head cop is accused of murdering someone, and must go on the run to figure it all out."

The next screenwriter on the project was Scott Frank, brought in to work on *Minority Report* at the behest of Spielberg. "The film is like nothing you've ever seen before," noted the writer. He saw in Dick's original tale the heart of a human story, rather than a soulless SF epic like *Total Recall* had turned out to be on screen. "I think ['The Minority Report'] is one of the few science fiction pieces that isn't cold, this is a very emotional story. We used to make genre movies for grown ups, not just action movies. We really tried to make a conscious effort to have the people in this be as real as we could." The challenges for Frank, coming in after the storyline had been drafted and redrafted to suit different studios and directors, mainly involved his immersion in an unfamiliar genre, as with Cohen. "It was also the hardest thing I've ever worked on because I don't normally like science fiction, I don't read it, and have never written it before. Also, the source material was virtually non-adaptable. Which is why I said I'd do it!"

Scott did read the original story as he approached drafting a new take on the script. He also worked his way through the pre-existing script drafts, although they were of variable use to him, given the story direction coming from Spielberg. "The concept of 'Pre-Crime' and people being arrested for crimes they're going to commit is from the short story," stated Frank. "The basic set up of the head of Pre-Crime being accused of a future murder is also from the short story. But that's it."

Frank had to untangle the various screenplays to pull out the elements Spielberg liked, dumping everything else. "Ron Shusett and Gary Goldman had worked with a guy

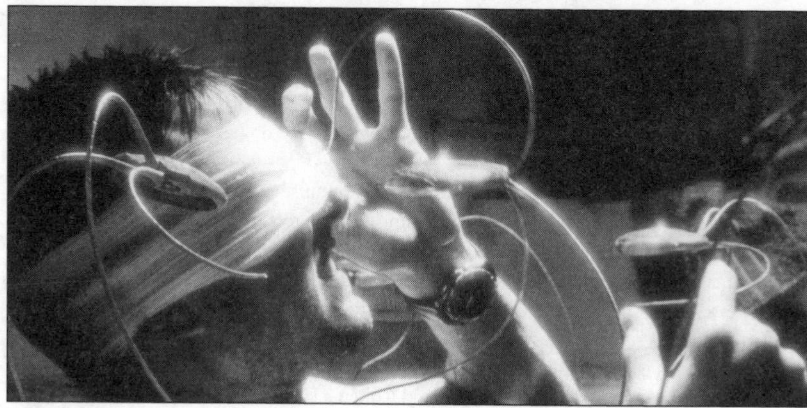

Right: *Screenwriter Jon Cohen expanded on the theme of sight and visions in* Minority Report.

named Bob Goethals, and the three of them wrote *Total Recall 2* based on the short story. Most of it takes place on Mars and ends with one of the moons of Mars crashing into another moon, so that it doesn't destroy Earth."

That was the final Carolco version of the script, but Frank also drew on Shusett and Goldman's solo redrafting of the story for 20th Century Fox. "[That one] adhered closely to the short story, but the film stalled for about two years. When Jan de Bont came on he hired Jon Cohen to write an entirely new script. At the end of 1998 Tom Cruise and Steven Spielberg committed to Cohen's rewrite of the earlier drafts of the *Minority Report* script."

In a scenario painfully familiar to Shusett, he and Goldman were sidelined by Spielberg. "[de Bont and Cohen] never read the earlier material, which pissed off Shusett and Goldman," claimed Frank. "Meanwhile, Steven hired me to rewrite Jon Cohen. This was the beginning of 1999 and shooting was to begin in April. Well, *Mission: Impossible II* went over schedule [tying up star Tom Cruise] and Steven suddenly realised he had more time. When we started looking at the material, we realised we wanted to make a different movie."

Even so, much of the previous work by all the preceding writers survived through to the final script. "A lot of what Jon Cohen did structurally, as well as in terms of sci-fi gadgets, and many other details, we kept. Shusett and Goldman meanwhile sent their script to Steven. He read it. I read it. The studio awarded credit to myself and Jon Cohen, which I think was fair..."

Shusett and Goldman didn't see it that way, and pursued arbitration regarding the on-screen credit through the Writer's Guild of America. When the film was finished, the studio had assigned preliminary writing credits to Cohen and Frank alone. Goldman claimed his case for credit was undermined by a myriad of Guild rules and technicalities. While final credit eventually went to Cohen and Frank, Goldman and Shusett retained their credits as executive producers for their development work on earlier script drafts.

However, Frank wasn't entirely happy with the final movie, as he told screenwriters-utopia.com: "Steven [Spielberg] often has a terrible ear for dialogue. When he lets actors ad lib or come up with lines on their own I often cringe. But he's the first to let you come up with something better, although there are a few [lines] in *Minority Report* that I could have done without."

The decision that the script was ready to be made was down to director Steven Spielberg: "Eventually I read a version that I liked enough to call time [on the development process] and say 'Yeah, I'll make this one…'" The attraction for Spielberg in this movie was the central ideas drawn from the Philip K. Dick short story. "The best SF is based on facts, or future facts, and the imagination gets a springboard from there." For star Tom Cruise, the attraction was the same: Dick's ideas: "There are some very strange things in this picture that I haven't seen before."

The central hook of Philip K. Dick's original short story — punishment before a crime has been committed and the potential fallibility of that system — was what intrigued Steven Spielberg. The director was no stranger to science fiction, having followed his breakthrough movie *Jaws* with his exploration of alien contact in *Close Encounters of the Third Kind*. This had been followed with *E.T.: The Extraterrestrial* and the revived dinosaurs of *Jurassic Park*. Spielberg's SF movies had taken a darker turn with his version of a film developed by the late Stanley Kubrick. *A.I.: Artificial Intelligence* tackled issues close to Dick's fiction: what is human, and if sophisticated robots can pass for the real thing, how can humanity make any claim to uniqueness?

Now, with the central conceit of *Minority Report* — what if it was possible to stop murder before it happened? — Spielberg was continuing to explore this darker, literary version of populist SF. "I think all of us would love to know what's just around the corner," Spielberg said. "We'd all love to know what's going to happen next — in the world, in our lives. This story flirts with the concept of what if we had the chance to know certain things about the future, especially things that come under the heading of 'life and death'."

In preparing for the film, Spielberg took a journey in two directions in time: back to the 1940s and the development of film noir (also an inspiration for the look of the world in *Blade Runner*) and into the real-world speculation about our own futures. "I wanted to tackle subjects I haven't really tackled before," the director explained. "I'm in a period in my life of experimentation and trying things that challenge me. *Minority Report* is really a mystery. It's a who-done-it or who-will-do-it, and you're along for the ride. It's also a very human story, about a man who has lived through a tragedy and is working through it."

Adopting the structure of the classic murder-mystery, with the twist that the murder is yet to happen, Spielberg had a story from which he could extrapolate a realistic vision of the future. As Dick's source story was light on description of the world in which it is set, beyond the notion of Pre-Crime, Spielberg had to find a way to invent the rest, as he would have to visually depict the world of fifty years into the future on screen for all to see.

Spielberg and Tom Cruise had long wanted to work together, but their first collaboration was delayed due to over-runs on Cruise's *Mission: Impossible II* and Spielberg's own commitment to *A.I.: Artificial Intelligence*. This allowed Spielberg's cohorts — screenwriter Scott Frank, production designer Alex McDowell and producers Bonnie Curtis and Walter Parkes — to concentrate on developing the story and the visual look of *Minority Report* in an extended period of pre-production.

Recalled Curtis, "Structuring this complicated story was a very daunting task. Steven wanted to weave a psychological thriller, so during the development process, he took great care to get all the layers of the story just right. In some ways, I think this is the most complicated film that Steven has ever made."

Above: *Driven by a vision of his own future, Pre-Crime operative John Anderton (Tom Cruise) goes on the run.*

The film initially entered pre-production for a six-month period in 1999, during which artists produced hundreds of concept drawings to illustrate the world of the future. The project was then put on hiatus, while *A.I.* was filmed, followed by a further six months of pre-production and three months of live action shooting from March 2001. "[The break] helped us," said Curtis. "We had prepped for six months, put it all in a warehouse for a year, entered a totally different fantasy world [that of *A.I.*] and then came back with a completely new perspective. I remember the first day Steven came in [after the hiatus]. We laid out all the drawings — months and months of drawings and concept illustrations. We literally threw out half of them."

Spielberg had decided early on in the development of the screenplay that he wanted the visual world of *Minority Report* to be an extrapolation of today's everyday life projected forward fifty years as accurately as possible. "I thought it would be a good idea to bring some of the best minds in technology, environment, crime fighting, medicine, health, social services, transportation, computer technology and other fields into one room to discuss what the future a half a century hence would be like," Spielberg noted.

"We tried to be as realistic as possible about our future," said Curtis. "Steven gave us an edict when we first started pre-production. He was like, 'Guys, I really don't want to create a science fiction world here. I want to create a future reality. We have this fantastic, odd idea that Philip K. Dick's brain has given us: let's really try to place it in the context of reality.' We had a 'think tank' where we brought together twenty or so futurists to gauge for us what our next fifty years are going to be like..."

From M.I.T. scientists such as John Underkoffler to urban planners, architects, inventors, writers (such as *Generation X* author Douglas Coupland), Spielberg assembled his think tank to develop concepts that would find their way into both the screenplay and the film's visuals. During a three-day conference, unique in the history of movie-making, the *Minority Report* think tank members came together at a hotel in Santa Monica, California, to hash out the social and technological details of the very near future of Washington D.C. Also attending were some of the filmmakers, including screenwriter Scott Frank and production designer Alex McDowell and his team. "We talked through the aspects of how society would be affected over a five, ten, twenty, thirty-year period," McDowell recalled. "What would change, what were the trends, and where would they logically end up? We knew that we would have to learn the answers to those issues, and to do that we would have to go into a consumer environment."

The conversations encompassed everything from advances in medicine, to how people would brush their teeth, to transportation, urban planning, architecture and art. "Steven wanted backgrounds that we were familiar with, that we could relate to, and — within the context of the familiar — have spectacular props," explained producer Bonnie Curtis.

One issue rapidly rose to prominence: the gradual loss of privacy. "The reason is not so people can spy on you," explained Scott Frank, "but so they can sell to you. In the not-too-distant future, it is plausible that by scanning your eyes, your whereabouts will be tracked. They will keep track of what you buy, so they can keep on selling to you." This is virtually happening today through mobile phones, so why not take things one step further, into the biological realm? Visitors to the United States are now regularly having their irises scanned, as well as their fingerprints taken…

"George Orwell's prophecy really comes true, not in the twentieth century but in the twenty-first," Spielberg believed. "Big Brother is watching us now and what little privacy we have will completely evaporate in twenty or thirty years, because technology will be able to see through walls, through rooftops, into the very privacy of our personal lives, into the sanctuary of our families."

Spielberg's vision for *Minority Report* was devoid of the natural disasters and wars that shaped many other futuristic films, such as the later *The Day After Tomorrow*. Noted McDowell, "The technology is benign and getting more and more efficient and serving the world better." The think tank vision of the future was one in which offices would be entirely portable and personal technology like computers and phones would become built-in human accessories, perhaps as an integral part of clothing.

Generation X author Douglas Coupland dreamed up a number of products for the Washington D.C. of 2054, such as the repellent sick-stick, a weapon that causes involuntarily vomiting — based on real crowd-control weapons being developed for use in urban environments, as well as 'spray meat' and boosted cats, which have been engineered to grow to the same size as dogs.

Though the think tank believed that corporations would drive these developments, such technologies would naturally prove valuable to law enforcement — to find and track suspects and, by extension, catch them. This brought their blue sky futurology right back to serving the needs of the movie and Philip K. Dick's original concerns in the 1954 short story version of 'The Minority Report'.

"Philip K. Dick was always interested in the consequences of technology and science," commented M.I.T. science advisor John Underkoffler, who for seventeen years worked at the institute's world-renowned Media Lab. "But Dick took it past where most other people stopped, because he was one of the few people who understood that good science fiction is actually social science fiction. Technology is a reflection or an echo of what's happening socially. Dick was interested in what the anthropological effect would be. I'm not sure if he ever passed a real judgment, but he was always asking [the questions]. That's what makes him so great."

Steven Spielberg shared Dick's aims in devising the film version of *Minority Report*: to get the audience thinking as well as entertaining them. "Steven wanted the audience to be split down the middle in their perception of this world," said McDowell, "whether it's a good world or a bad world, and not be black or white about it. He didn't want the audience to think everything about this future world was evil or dystopic, but an extension of a world that we absolutely recognise."

As Dick did throughout his fiction, Spielberg intended the technology of *Minority Report* to be a necessary background to his human story: "We want the audience to take the technology we show them for granted by having so much of it in the movie, so they can sit back and focus on the mystery."

For example, in the world of *Minority Report*, fossil fuels have clearly given way to the development of a Magnetic-Levitation (mag-lev) traffic system. While the existence of pre-cog telepaths and the potential to prevent murder as Dick portrayed it may be a truly science fiction idea, the rest of the world of *Minority Report* is as real as the scientists and futurologists hired by Spielberg could imagine it to be. That future may be an optimistic one, but it comes with a price. "To Steven's credit, the world we have in the film is edgier and more realistically gray than the kind of utopian world imagined by most futurists," admitted Underkoffler. "That's always a more exciting place and a more interesting place for a story to unfold."

The man handed the task of bringing this imagined future to the screen was production designer Alex McDowell (*Fight Club, The Crow*). "[Steven] wanted the audience to feel comfortable and familiar in the world of *Minority Report*," McDowell told *Cinescape* magazine. "I wanted an underlying logic to what we were going to build." McDowell and his design team produced a fifty-page 'bible' that described how the Pre-Crime process worked and itemised all the relevant technology associated with it. It also detailed the future world of 2054, from social structure to commerce, health, transportation and computers. "It was useful for the film — we got very detailed in the science." One of the dramatic changes from today is the transportation system, with those mag-lev cars parking 'inside' houses. "Your garage is actually an opening in the window of your living room. The car comes up the side of the building and connects like an airlock to that opening, the car door opens and you use the car essentially as a seating area..."

When fine-tuning the script Scott Frank, the final screenwriter on the project, faced the challenge of humanising the figure of John Anderton. As the Pre-Crime detective who is accused and goes on the run, Anderton has to serve as a point of identification for the audience, though he's one they must also feel could possibly be guilty of his 'future crime'. "What kind of person would embrace this kind of system?" Frank asked himself about the Pre-Crime concept. An addition to the film version of the story gave Frank a way of delving into Anderton's character, flaws and all. "Anderton has lost his son, who is presumed dead. He is still grieving some six years later, to a point that he obsesses about the very minute that he lost his son, the moment he turned away, and keeps replaying it over and over in his mind. His own guilt over what happened has led him to think he's a true believer in this system, because if it can prevent another set of parents from losing their child, then it must be a good thing."

Anderton is leader of the Pre-Crime Division of the Justice Department, and is responsible for analysing the visions of the trio of pre-cogs — psychics held in a womb-like chamber, suspended in fluid, who are able to see murders before they're committed. "The information goes from the Pre-Cogs to a computer, and John separates the pictures to analyze what it is he's looking at, where it is, and to glean information from what the pre-cogs are seeing," related Cruise, who saw playing the conflicted Anderton as something of an acting challenge.

Futurologist Underkoffler created a language of gestures that would allow Anderton to sort and almost 'conduct' the visual information he was getting from the pre-cogs. Commands were developed for stopping time, rolling backwards and forwards and making clips or changing his view. "Steven wanted to create a computer language but make it physical," noted

Cruise. "He wanted the specific hand movements to play like a dance — he even played music during the scene." The 'pre-vision' images (visual images of the crime before it happens) were created by effects house Imaginary Forces, which has designed opening titles for such films as *Se7en* and *The Mummy Returns*. "The pre-cogs see the future very prismatically," Spielberg explained. "They don't see things like film, with squares and cuts. The human eye sees in circles. Imaginary Forces made the pre-visions look actually organic."

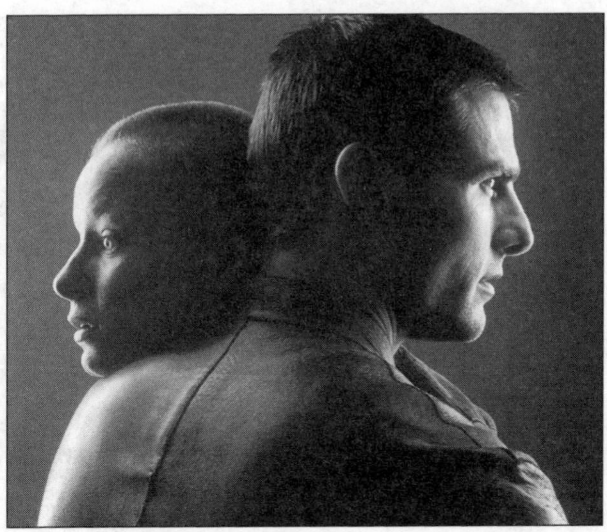

***Above:** Anderton makes a connection with pre-cog Agatha (Samantha Morton), who is the key to unravelling the truth.*

In *Minority Report*, the discovery of the psychic trio's precognitive visions was an accidental by-product of a completely different line of research, "an unintended result," explained Underkoffler. "But given that the researchers found that their subjects had these predictive abilities, then this whole Pre-Crime government institution was founded around them. This whole facility was built in response."

The three pre-cogs — Dashiell, Arthur and Agatha, named after crime authors Hammett, Conan-Doyle and Christie respectively — lie in an environmentally-controlled pool deep within Pre-Crime Headquarters, bathed in a fluid that is intended as both a biological nutrient and a medium that helps to channel their future visions. It also somehow filters the images, so the pre-cogs will only see murder. Though the outside world has no conception of who the pre-cogs are or how they were created or discovered, Anderton has lived with their visions and made a connection with the only female of the three: Agatha. Actress Samantha Morton joined Cruise on the film, describing Agatha as essentially "a child, but she has wisdom beyond her years. She sees people's feelings and emotions and feels their pain and suffering. It's a harsh reality for her."

"The three beings in the tank are not treated as humans," said Spielberg. "They're not even being treated as government workers. They're being treated like vegetables that spin a magic elixir that allows us to stop murders from happening. It takes Anderton a while to learn how to relate to the main pre-cog, Agatha."

"Anderton comes into this story with an air of professionalism, because he's the best at what he does," Spielberg explained. "But he's also under a very dark cloud, having lost his son and never found out who took his son six years ago, just before he came to work at Pre-Crime. Everybody he has trained to be good at stopping murders before they happen, all these trainees who are the best of the best, then come after him using all the techniques that he taught them."

"Anderton aggressively goes after people who are going to commit murder," said Scott Frank. "He is terrific at locating them, taking these little cues of information and piecing it

***Above:** To fulfil its summer blockbuster status, the film needed a full complement of action set pieces.*

all together to solve the murder. He is completely together and on top of it during the day, but at night you see a man who is completely fractured and falling apart."

Spielberg pointed out that Anderton is on two journeys. "One is a physical journey of discovering all the clues to either vindicate himself or determine that he, in fact, can and will murder. In addition, he is on an inner journey, an emotional struggle. So every scene is informed twice — once by the information he gathers and again as he lives his life. This makes this one of the more compelling roles Tom Cruise has ever had to play, and I think he pulls it off amazingly well."

Likewise, screenwriter Scott Frank had nothing but praise for the fearlessness with which Cruise approached the role. "From the very beginning of the project, Steven and I would periodically discuss with him what we were doing in terms of his character," Frank explained. "He's never been afraid of embracing dark characters and never once complained about any of those aspects. We tried hard to keep in mind that he's this great movie star and you want to have a great time and see him doing certain things. But at the same time he was all for going deep and making it as emotional as we needed it to be. He encouraged us to go as far as we possibly could, and I think he does his best work when we go really far with it."

It is only when Anderton finds himself outside the system that he once ran that he begins to see the faults in it. The first sign is when Justice Department official Danny Witwer, played by Colin Farrell, comes to Pre-Crime to audit the system and check for flaws, on the eve of the national referendum to implement it countrywide. Farrell described Witwer as "cocky and smug; he's there to do a job. Actually, he's there to infiltrate Anderton's department by pretending to be one of the lads. He'll step on anyone to get to the next step of the ladder, because he wants to get to the top." Spielberg gave Farrell a specific character through-line to consider in his portrayal: "You can tell when you first meet Witwer that he would love Anderton's job, that he likes Pre-Crime and thinks it's a great place for him."

Scott Frank noted that while Anderton is motivated by grief and guilt, Witwer is motivated by faith. "He's got a religious background and really believes in the pre-cogs as pseudo-deities," reckoned the screenwriter. "He thinks they have religious value beyond their value to solving murders. [That's why] he goes after Anderton rather zealously."

Swedish actor Max von Sydow portrayed Lamar Burgess, whom Frank described as "a father figure to Anderton. He has taken him under his wing and brought him in. He has also used tragedy not only motivate Anderton but also get people behind Pre-Crime. He's the perfect poster boy for Pre-Crime."

Burgess developed the institution of Pre-Crime based on the research of a scientist named Iris Hineman (Lois Smith). The pre-cogs are grown children whom the state has taken away from their unstable or drug-addicted parents, and turned into subservient predicting machines. "You harness them and stick them in this tank and force them to dream of violent crime and murder all the time," futurologist Underkoffler stated. "It has a very objectionable element. But the way Steven [Spielberg] has conceived and put this film together does a great job at just subtly suggesting that. All of our protagonists work for this agency, but at the same time the agency is engaged in something that many people might object to."

Frank knew his screenplay, as well as telling an exciting and entertaining story, had to engage with the ideas and issues raised in Dick's original tale, but in a twenty-first century context. "People can be against capital punishment until they lose a loved one," noted Frank. "We can be completely civilised until the murder rate goes way up and we need to figure out how to bring in the troops. That's how dictatorships get started; it's always for the 'greater good.' We use the Abraham Lincoln quote in the movie — sometimes it's better to sacrifice a limb to save the whole body. But how far do you go? By sacrificing the limb are you really controlling the whole body more than you are saving the whole body?"

Production on *Minority Report* commenced on 22 March 2001 in Los Angeles, with locations including the Ronald Reagan Federal Building and the Willard Hotel; other Southern California locations included Downtown LA, an abandoned mall in Hawthorne and a factory in Vernon. Filming also took place around the Federal Triangle Plaza in the Washington D.C. metro area. Back in Hollywood, Hennessy Street on the Warner Bros. lot and soundstages at Universal and Fox accommodated the sprawling production.

Post-production saw the addition of 447 special effects shots, the most that Spielberg had used in a film since *Close Encounters of the Third Kind*, twenty-five years before. According to producer Bonnie Curtis, most of the effects work was "to give us that [future] skyline and to give us the technology that we haven't attained yet." Spielberg agreed: "This movie is more story than effects, but there are a lot of gadgets in *Minority Report*. I was trying to get the futurists to inform me what cool toys will be out there for us to buy in fifty-two years…"

The reaction which greeted *Minority Report* was largely positive, with many critics seeing the film a something of a flawed masterpiece. Eric Harrison wrote in the *Houston Chronicle* that *Minority Report* "reaches towards greatness, but fails because it is too perfect a projection of its creator [Spielberg]. Nevertheless, we should celebrate it, because this makes it — flaws and all — more valuable than 1,000 soulless, committee-hatched flicks." In *Newsday*, critic John Anderson dubbed Spielberg's movie "fast-moving, entertaining, thought-provoking… [It] leaves you feeling vaguely empty because it might have been a classic."

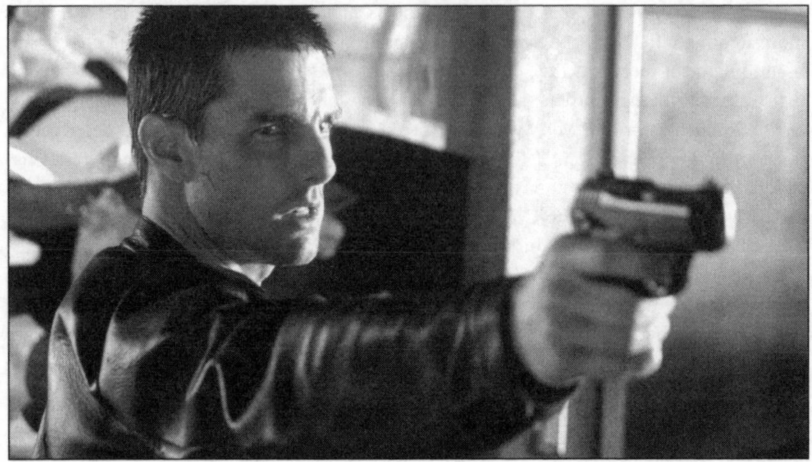

Right: *Self-determination versus destiny was the theme of the film, according to Spielberg. Anderton must ask himself whether he is capable of committing murder…*

Others were more directly positive about the film. Joel Siegel of ABC's *Good Morning America* felt "the story is so compelling, Spielberg's vision of the future is so smart, you don't think you're watching a great movie because you're having so much fun. But you are." *The New York Post* felt the film concluded with "an ending that seems a bit schmaltzy and pat," but added, "that's a small price to pay for one of Hollywood's most breathtaking glimpses of the near future — a heart-pounding experience that makes you think and contains a gallery of characters that will haunt your nightmares for years to come." Similarly, *The New York Times* thought the film offered too much didactic information at the end, with the effect of "explaining the fun away." The paper, though, called the movie "a kind of tour de force... magnificently creepy, a calculated bad dream."

Others weren't so taken with Spielberg's vision of a possible future. Critic Jami Bernard in *The New York Daily News* thought the film "by turns silly and amazing, a mishmash of Kubrickian devices accompanied by a steady Spielbergian drip of sentimentality." A fan of Philip K. Dick's work, and particularly the movies made from his stories, *The Chicago Sun-Times* critic Roger Ebert was upbeat, commenting: "This film is such a virtuoso high-wire act, daring so much, achieving it with such grace and skill. *Minority Report* reminds us why we go to the movies in the first place." Michael Wilmington of *The Chicago Tribune*, remarked that *Minority Report* was "a film that can get you high on the sheer magic and exhilaration of making movies." Taking the film's promotional slogan 'Everybody Runs', Mike Szymanski in *The Los Angeles Daily News* punned: "The report on *Minority Report* is that it's good, real good, and you should run... to go see it."

Minority Report was released in the US on 21 June 2002 and took $35.6 million, making it the biggest grossing movie of the week, beating Disney's *Lilo & Stitch* and the equally kid-friendly *Scooby-Doo* into second and third place in the box office charts. By the end of the film's US run in October 2002, total domestic takings totalled just over $132 million. *Minority Report* came sixth in the year's top ten highest grossing films on the international market for 2002 with a total take of $202.3 million. More popular that year (taking the top three slots) were the on-going franchise movies *Harry Potter and the Chamber of Secrets*, *Spider-Man* and *Star Wars*: Episode II *Attack of the Clones*. In fact, *Minority Report* was the highest grossing non-franchise film that year, falling just behind the fourth and fifth placed top international grossers *Men in Black II* and *The Lord of the Rings: The Two Towers*.

While Philip K. Dick's 'The Minority Report' may have been the inspiration for the central concept of Steven Spielberg's movie *Minority Report*, the film version has so expanded and distorted the source material that it can hardly be called a true adaptation. That's something Spielberg himself seems to agree with: "I don't think I tried to adapt [Dick] with *Minority Report* — I just took his brilliant premise and ran with it," admitted the director. "The Philip K. Dick story only gives you a springboard that really doesn't have a second or third act [echoes of *Total Recall*]. Most of the movie is not in the Philip K. Dick story — to the chagrin of the Philip K. Dick fans, I'm sure. The template became self-determination versus destiny. That's what interested me the most: If there is something in the stars, can you reconfigure them to either survive or write your own ending?"

Original screenwriter Gary Goldman saw the finished *Minority Report* as a brave take on the material, but agreed it failed to get to the roots of the Dick short story. Goldman had always intended the prophecy at the centre of the story to be fulfilled in the movie, that John Anderton would be able to exercise free will (in contradiction to the prediction) and spare his intended victim, Lee Crow. That fundamentally changed the ending of Dick's story. Goldman's explanation for this was that the pre-cogs had seen events from such an angle that their interpretation of the vision was simply wrong. The Spielberg movie did not follow through this intriguing 'point-of-view' notion. According to Goldman, the film "came very close to going all the way but doesn't go into [that] unexplored territory." The movie's climax wasn't close enough to Dick's thoughtful and challenging original for Goldman, who saw more material to be mined from the admittedly slight source story. "In his story, Dick is willing to contemplate that the system actually works, and if it does work, then we have to get used to new ideas about justice. Anderton's exercise of free will is accurately foreseen. He chooses to fulfil the prophecy — in part merely to prove that the system is infallible. But that's hard to wrap your mind around."

Goldman saw Spielberg, and before him Jan de Bont, as being unwilling to follow Philip K. Dick's ideas behind *Minority Report* through to their inevitable conclusion: "Jan and Steven took it as a given that there had to be free will, that the system was bad because it violated the constitution," Goldman noted, "[but] Dick was willing to question everything." However, Goldman, along with many critics, felt that *Minority Report* was a distinctive and serious SF movie from Spielberg, a director more usually associated with feel good wish-fulfilment in his SF cinema than engagement with challenging ideas.

As with *Blade Runner* and *Total Recall* before it, *Minority Report* simply took Dick's original story as a jumping off point, and the director was quite happy to totally alter it to suit his own cinematic needs. "Where I thought *Blade Runner* succeeded brilliantly was in its style and its look," said Spielberg. "I thought Ridley [Scott] did the most brilliant job of his career with its lighting... [but] there really wasn't much of a story to tell."

So it was with *Minority Report*: a slight story expanded into an imaginative, visually impressive film which despite the changes retained the essential questioning nature of the best of Philip K. Dick's work. ■

PRECIOUS ARTIFACTS

Got a pocketful of junk? Be careful: if you're the star of *Paycheck*, each item may be vital to your survival...

"That's the premise I start from in my work: that so-called "reality" is an mass delusion that we've all been required to believe for reasons totally obscure." — Philip K. Dick interviewed by Joe Vitale in *The Aquarian*, No. 11, October 11-18, 1978.

In his 1953 short story 'Paycheck', Philip K. Dick imbues a handful of very ordinary items with extraordinary significance. Only by decoding the nature of the items he had left for himself can the everyman engineer hero Michael Jennings save his own life. In an introduction to the story from 1976, Dick wrote: "How much is the key to a bus locker worth? One day it's worth twenty-five cents, the next day thousands of dollars. In this story, I got to thinking that there are times in our lives when having a dime to make a phone call spells the difference between life and death. Keys, small change, maybe a theatre ticket — how about a parking receipt for a Jaguar? All I had to do was link this idea up with time travel to see how the small and useless, under the wise eyes of a time traveller, might signify a great deal more. He would know when that dime might save your life. And back in the past again, he might prefer that dime to any amount of money, no matter how large..."

The 'Paycheck' short story opens right in the middle of the action: Jennings awakes on a small private rocket cruiser seated next to his employer Earl Rethrick. Two years have passed since the last thing Jennings can remember: autumn in New York. Things have changed since then: the Government has fallen, a pseudo-Fascist state has arisen and San Francisco Bay had been filled in. Jennings has been working as a 'mechanic' on a secret project. To preserve the secrecy he has agreed to have the last two years' events wiped from his memory in return for a fee of 50,000 credits. Now he's returning, with Rethrick, to the New York office to pick up his final paycheck.

Jennings is shocked, though, to discover that instead of the expected 50,000 credits he himself has instead substituted his big pay off with an envelope containing a seemingly random selection of junk: "Jennings stared down at what he held in his palm. From the cloth sack he had spilled a little assortment of items. A code key. A ticket stub. A parcel receipt. A length of fine wire. Half a poker chip, broken across. A green strip of cloth. A bus token. 'This, instead of 50,000 credits,' he murmured. 'Two years...'"

***Opposite:** The items in Jennings' envelope are a puzzle to be solved, suggests this poster for* Paycheck.

No sooner has the dazed Jennings left Rethrick Construction than he is picked up by the Security Police, who want to question him about his missing two years and his secret work for Rethrick. Due to the memory wipe procedure, he can't answer them, even if he wanted to. The trinkets, he reasons, must have a meaning far beyond their material value...

THE FUTURE
DEPENDS ON A PAST
HE WAS PAID TO FORGET.
FROM THE DIRECTOR OF
MISSION:
IMPOSSIBLE II
AND FACE/OFF
BEN AFFLECK
AARON ECKHART
UMA THURMAN
PAYCHECK

IMAGINATION
JUNE, 1953
35¢
STORIES OF SCIENCE AND FANTASY
THE STAR LORD By Boyd Ellanby

Above: 'Paycheck' *was one of the six stories by Dick that appeared in* Imagination *in 1953, this one in the June issue.*

otherwise, why would he have accepted them as payment? To survive, he must solve a puzzle of his own making. The answer comes to him as he instinctively uses the wire to short the lock on the police cruiser, then uses the bus token to escape the scene: each of the items he has bequeathed himself has a specific use and purpose — "Apparently the trinkets were going to see him through. A pocketful of miracles, from someone who knew the future!" — but how did he know what to leave himself?

Theorising he'd be safer from the Security Police back with the company, Jennings returns to Rethrick, also looking for answers to the mystery of his seeming knowledge of events yet to come. The ticket stub tells Jennings where he's been: Stuartsville, Iowa — the location of the Rethrick plant. Hooking up with Rethrick employee Kelly McVane, Jennings concludes that the company has developed an illegal 'time scoop', a previously theoretical device which allows people to not only see the future, but collect actual artefacts from it. The green cloth in Jenning's collection of odds and ends forms an armband that identifies him as a labourer and allows him access to the Rethrick plant. When the code key fails to gain Jennings access to the lab containing the time scoop, he suddenly begins to doubt the assumed omnipotence of his past self who saw his own future: "Surely he had known what he was doing? Like God, it had already happened for him. Predetermined. He could not err. Or could he? A chill went through him. Maybe the future was variable. Maybe this had been the right key, once. But not anymore!"

Evading security, Jennings gains access to the lab through that old pulp science fiction and B-movie stand-by, the ventilation shaft. Stealing documents that prove the existence of the time scoop, Jennings uses the doubtful code key to open the doors leading to the outside and escapes the Rethrick plant. Trusting the incriminating papers to Kelly, the pair separately make their way back to New York. Jennings' plan is to blackmail Rethrick into giving him a fifty per cent interest in the company, or else he'll turn Rethrick's secrets (he appears to be building an army to topple the State) over to the Security Police. For Jennings, big business provides a secure refuge from the forces that want the knowledge he deleted from his memory…

Jennings has two items left: the half poker chip and the parcel receipt. He realises that he's now caught up with the date on the receipt. Avoiding the curfew police, Jennings stumbles into a speakeasy casino where his half poker chip gains him entrance, and he hides out. Later, confronting Rethrick in his office, Jennings discovers that he'd personally disabled the 'mirror', a vital part of the time scoop, before leaving Rethrick's employ. Explaining that the company, which is fomenting a revolution, is a family concern, Rethrick refuses Jennings' claim for a share. He then reveals that Kelly, who has securely hidden the papers Jennings stole, is his daughter. Remembering the parcel receipt, dated the day before, Jennings realises the papers are stored in the Dunne National Bank. As Kelly gets the same slip of paper from her purse, a portal opens and the time scoop claw emerges — operated by Jennings in the past reaching into his own future — and snatches the parcel receipt from Kelly's hand. Referring to his all-seeing past self, Jennings comments: "I wondered when he would show up. I was beginning to worry." The story ends by implying that not only will Jennings run the company with Rethrick and lead it into the planned revolution, but he'll do that as Kelly's husband, thus maintaining the business as a family concern.

Published in *Imagination* in June 1953, 'Paycheck' was a superior example of Dick's ability to take the kernel of an idea and run with it, while still keeping the characters, their situations and the stakes relatively low key. *Imagination*, a US-digest sized pulp, ran for sixty-three issues, from October 1950 until October 1958. In each issue editor and publisher William L. Hambling would include a short novella, usually a standard space opera adventure, as well as an unusually high number of short stories with titles ending in dramatic exclamation marks! In 1953 alone, Dick had six short stories featured in *Imagination*: 'Mr Spaceship' (in January), 'Piper in the Woods' (February), 'Paycheck' (June), 'The Cosmic Poachers' (July), 'The Impossible Planet' (October) and 'Project: Earth' (December).

Unlike *Blade Runner, Total Recall* or *Screamers, Paycheck* did not undergo years of development and pass through many hands before reaching the screen. The process of adapting the story and getting the film made was a reasonably straightforward one, for a Philip K. Dick tale. It was also extremely lucrative.

According to Dick's agent, Russell Galen, Paramount Pictures had optioned the story 'Paycheck' under a deal that would bring Dick's estate about $2 million, one of the largest sums ever paid for a short story. Galen noted that's "about $200 a word" for the movie rights to a story that sold in the 1950s for $195. Paramount would not separately confirm the amount paid for the movie rights to 'Paycheck'.

Big changes were made to the story to make it suitable as a film. The positive outcome was to tie Jennings' reasons for going on the run and then confronting the company much more to the time viewer itself. In the original story, the time scoop is simply a tool that allows the story to happen, a mechanical solution to the narrative problem. However, in the movie it is the knowledge that use of the time viewer will remove free will from mankind and result in many more wars that causes Jennings to disable the device and then go on the run. The other major change is the introduction of the character of Rachel, a romantic figure for Jennings to protect and someone who can fill him in on his missing memories (essentially a developed version of the Kelly character in the story, but given much more to do). If the ending of the short story was somewhat weak, with Jennings seemingly forcing an arranged marriage with Kelly, the ending of the film, in which he has used the viewer to gain knowledge of future lottery numbers, thereby setting him and Rachel up for life after the destruction of the machine, is little more than audience wish-fulfilment, a feel-good buzz at the climax of the film for undiscerning moviegoers.

In a curious echo of the changes made to the climax of *Minority Report, Paycheck* manages to change the meaning of the storyline entirely. Whereas in both the short stories, Dick postulates that not only is knowledge of the future a good and useful thing to have, but that future is also set and unalterable, suggesting a lack of, or at least severe restrictions on, free will. In both films, knowledge of the future is looked upon as a negative thing from which no good can come, and free will is restored to the characters as they do something very different from the futures predicted for them. It's a curious change from the source material and equally odd that both films, made by different creative people, should change

Above: *Michael Jennings (Ben Affleck) tries to work out why he has left himself an envelope of junk instead of a fortune.*

their source stories in such similar ways.

Dean Georgaris was the screenwriter tapped by producers John Davis and Michael Hackett to turn Dick's brief story into a feature film script of at least ninety minutes in length for action director John Woo. As with many Philip K. Dick stories adapted for movies, it was the central concept that attracted the attention of the moviemakers. Unlike many adaptations, though, *Paycheck* was to remain fairly faithful to the plot dynamics of the source story, even if the details were changed significantly.

"I'm a big fan of Philip K. Dick, and I especially like the provocative moral issues he raises in 'Paycheck'," said Woo of the story he was to direct. "His heroes are very human, very grounded in reality, not superhuman like in a lot of science fiction. I find Dick to be a philosopher about faith and destiny, but his work is also very visual. It seems as if his books were written with movies in mind."

Dean Georgaris' screenplay builds upon this classic Dick conceit, the very human hero, updating it to a twenty-first century vision of the future rather than the 1950s version imagined by the author. In addition to building a more in-depth back-story for the character of Jennings, Georgaris virtually removes the classic Dick police-state elements, instead adding a more audience-friendly unremembered romance (thus allowing for a major female role in the movie) and squeezing in the high-speed-action vehicle chases required by almost all movie directors working in the commercial arena.

Like *Minority Report* before it, *Paycheck* attempts to merge Dick's dark concerns with a summer blockbuster thriller. "The short story had a terrific Hitchcockian engine for a movie: I have a pocket full of junk, and I don't know why..." said Georgaris, outlining his take on the movie to *The San Francisco Chronicle*. "It seems to be doing some magic stuff. What I thought was implied in the story, and would make a great foundation for a film, was: what kind of guy would willingly have his memory erased, for money, and why? He would probably be someone who felt that there are certain moments in life worth remembering and experiencing, but, frankly, there's a lot of stuff that you could sacrifice and still be who you are. I considered that to be a rather dark view of the world, but one that has a modern component. We live in a world in which we're forced to work harder and harder, with less time off, because that's what's deemed to be important."

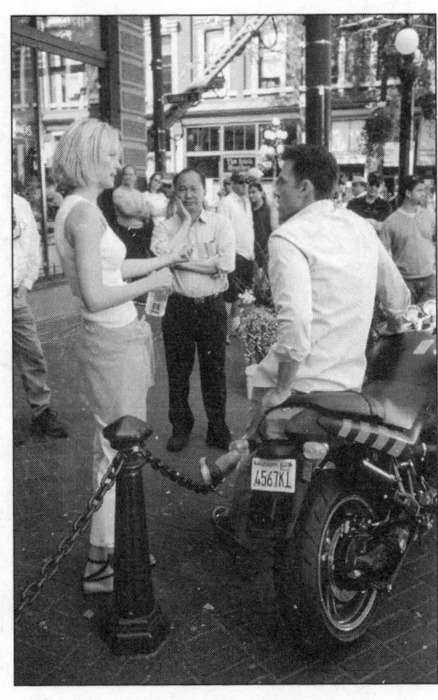

Above: *Director John Woo (centre) prepares a scene with Uma Thurman and Ben Affleck.*

Georgaris was also fascinated by how people would react if they were offered the ability to see into their own futures, as happens to Jennings. "In a strange way, seeing the future would be like seeing the highlights of your life... how it's all going to turn out... you've cut to the chase. Am I gonna win or lose, be President or not? By looking into this machine, you're essentially saying that everything leading up to it is not that important."

Although based on a short story that, when it was written, was set in the far future, Woo and Georgaris decided to set their movie only a few years from the present. That way, the world could look pretty much like ours (making it dramatically easier and cheaper to film), yet the outlandish technology required to set the story in motion could still exist. "The more it looks like our world, the closer we can identify with the story," claimed Georgaris. "There's nothing in the story that requires flying saucers. The junk in the envelope is all stuff that's from our world, and it makes Jennings' dilemma more fun to watch."

The nature of the story, though, is that it revolves around a piece of fantasy technology. The how and why of the workings of 'the machine' don't really matter: it's what results that's important — information. For the characters in *Paycheck*, what is important is how they react to the information they get from the future and from their suppressed memories. "In every case, Dick uses technology to dramatise something incredibly human, whether it be a search for God or a search for information," Georgaris said. "You can go back to the Oracle at Delphi; people have always talked about knowing their destiny. Someday, machines may allow us to do that, but it won't be the machines that hurt us, it will be what we do with that knowledge."

John Woo, one of the legends of the Hong Kong school of action cinema, admitted to not being a great fan of the science fiction genre. Ironically, his introduction to Philip K. Dick came through watching *Blade Runner*. "I really loved *Blade Runner*," said Woo. "Visually, it was fantastic, and it was the only science fiction movie that made me cry. I don't

Above: *Uma Thurman's Rachel was developed significantly from the character of Kelly in the original short story.*

usually expect much from science fiction films... maybe some amazing special effects shots, but this one [*Paycheck*] had suspense and wonderful characters."

It was Dean Georgaris' script that brought actor Ben Affleck to the leading role of Michael Jennings in *Paycheck*. "The script was extremely smart, interestingly complicated and well-written," claimed Affleck. "When you combine high concept science fiction source material from Philip K. Dick, whose work has already been proven to work well on the screen, with a master of the visual medium like John Woo directing, you have the makings of something extraordinary."

Attractive to Affleck was the emotional side of the character. Jennings was to be portrayed in the film as more than just the clichéd cold science fiction scientist, obsessed with his work: in this case reverse-engineering equipment to benefit commercial competitors in the cutthroat world of high tech innovation. "As dedicated as Jennings is to his work, we can see in the way he flirts with Rachel (Uma Thurman) a side of the man that is very vulnerable," noted Affleck. "While it's true that when we first meet him, Jennings may appear to be just some genius making one gigantic paycheck after the next, he definitely starts to rethink his work as the stakes get higher, it suddenly isn't about the money anymore. It's about discovering who he really is and unravelling what he's done."

The human side of the character of Jennings, and the 'everyman' nature of the character — as with so many of Dick's 'ordinary' heroes — was core to the appeal of the role to Affleck. "He's not a super agent, super spy or superhuman," said the actor of Jennings in both Dick's story and the movie screenplay. "He's an engineer, a man who uses his brains to work backwards out of problems, and now he's got to work backwards to figure out his life." While director John Woo had worked with larger than life super-characters before, in *Face/Off* for example, in *Paycheck* he determined to remain true to the characters in the source material in a way films like *Total Recall* (in casting Arnold Schwarzenegger) had not.

The role of Rachel Porter was expanded from the short story character by Woo and Georgaris to give the film a strong female co-starring role. It was Woo who felt that the female character had to be a catalyst behind Jenning's change of ethics and he suggested Uma Thurman, fresh from Quentin Tarantino's two-part epic *Kill Bill*, for the part. "Uma has intelligence and a strong physical presence, both of which are perfect character traits for Rachel," explained Woo.

In meeting the director, Thurman was hoping to fulfil a long-standing desire to work with him. However, first Woo had to explain the importance of her role to the overall concept of the film: "He said it was the most important part of the movie to him — the idea that love can change your life," the actress recalled. "I love the way this magnificent action director was so incredibly dedicated to the beautiful love story within this film. He really makes it a true romantic action thriller."

The role of Rachel becomes central to Jenning's attempt to discover the secrets of his own past. "He has to find me in order to find out what happened to him and who he really is," noted Thurman of her character. "In one scene, he actually doesn't remember me, and as a woman he supposedly loves, it kind of boggles her mind." Jennings' memories have been erased so he doesn't recall his own past or the role Rachel has played in his life. "Your ego would have you believe that you left some kind of stamp on him, and it's devastating to her that he could lose that," elaborated Thurman. "Still, even though his mind gets wiped, the brain holds some deep memory, and memories of Rachel come back to him in flashes. It's a fascinating film."

Another character dramatically expanded from that in the short story was the villain of the piece, billionaire entrepreneur Jimmy Rethrick. Aaron Eckhart won the role and was struck by the personal nature of the relationship between the hero and the villain. "Rethrick and Jennings were buddies who wanted to save the world through technology," he noted. "Along the way Rethrick alters his idealist vision in favour of personal power and ambition. Now he wants to use technology to change the world, not save it. He's a Machiavellian character. He sees the machine his company has developed as his legacy which will change the course of the Earth."

Producer Terence Chang saw Eckhart's Rethrick as following in a long line of John Woo movie villains, ordinary guys who were not overtly evil so much as misguided or corrupted by other forces. "That's why we tapped Aaron for the role," explained Chang. "He's got just the right charisma and unique ability to play a tortured good soul that has been turned to evil."

The four-month long shoot for *Paycheck* took place entirely in Vancouver, Canada, which doubled for the film's setting of Seattle. Over the past two decades Vancouver has become known as 'Hollywood North', with many movies and even more TV series shooting in studios and on location in the city, to take advantage of exchange rate savings and the city's ability to double for almost any US location.

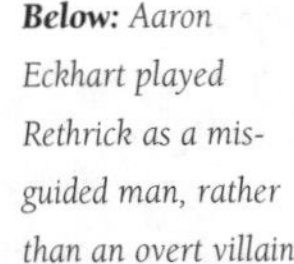

***Below:** Aaron Eckhart played Rethrick as a misguided man, rather than an overt villain.*

The pre-production period saw production designer William Sandell and his team of illustrators and model-builders flesh out the vision of the film contained in the script and outlined in production meetings by director John Woo. "John has a way of making the smallest things magical," claimed Sandell, who liked the fact that the film mixed in a solid mystery and a love story into the high concept science fiction elements. "We decided to design the production as a stylish mystery, not your average

Above: *While the film stayed broadly true to Dick's concepts, Woo also found time for some spectacular action sequences.*

high concept futuristic design that can have a tendency to look artificial. Instead, we went with a slick, clean look, which we felt better served the sophisticated nature of the story."

Sandell had been warned that Woo was a director who liked to have a lot of physical freedom to explore his movie sets with his camera, allowing for maximum flexibility when it came time to shoot each scene. Taking this into account, Sandell designed many of the sets for *Paycheck* so they could be divided up or segmented in any number of ways to allow Woo and his camera maximum access. "I got a little wild," the production designer admitted, "making it possible for each set to break apart like a puzzle box. John wanted to be able to move in and out at will, so the sets turned out to be huge." The sound stages in Vancouver played host to the sets for Rachel's apartment, the FBI offices, the interrogation rooms and Rethrick's office. The biggest set of the movie, the biolab, was also built there, but it was Rachel's domestic setting that was Sandell's favourite. "It's a beautiful little jewel, surrounded by a translight reflecting a local location that has a very sophisticated design feel. We extrapolated from the exterior design and built the inside of Rachel's apartment to reflect the sophistication of all that surrounded it."

Sandell also faced the challenge of constructing a semi-operational subway system in under three weeks. Built under a huge circus tent, the production designer and his team constructed 250 feet of tunnels and tracks which allowed Woo to direct a more realistic and exciting chase sequence in the subway tunnel than could have been achieved through working on location or even on a smaller, more contained studio set.

Costume designs, realised by Erica Edell Philips, similarly avoided any overtly futuristic looks or styles in an attempt to avoid the film becoming rapidly dated. 'Stylised and sleek' was the instruction from John Woo, while Philips wanted the looks for the main characters to be rooted in contemporary aesthetics. "John didn't want to make a statement with the wardrobe," explained Philips. "Rather, he wanted the characters' subtle attire to evoke a clean modernism."

There was a definitive cinematic throwback, though, in the look suggested by the director for the lead character of Michael Jennings. Woo wanted Ben Affleck's look to be modelled very closely after that of Cary Grant in Alfred Hitchcock's *North by Northwest*, one of the director's favourite films. Philips was required to manufacture forty-seven different but identical custom-tailored grey suits, suitable for a serious-minded engineer. The clothes designed for the film had to be tough enough to withstand the inevitable stunt work involved in a John Woo production, so many of the outfits worn by the leads featured concealed harnesses, padding and protective gear built in. Many multiples of all the key outfits had to be created as stand-bys, as the clothes were rapidly worn out due to the rigours of filming, especially with two distinct units operating at the same time.

While not opting for an overtly futuristic look, Philips did take the opportunity to put the saying that 'clothes maketh the man' into operation. The natures of many of the characters in the story were reflected in the outfits she designed, from Jennings' serious, business-like suits to the khaki green and tan colours of the Allcom biologists, which blend with their greenhouse working environment, to the darker, sombre business suits worn by the villains of the piece, Rethrick and Wolfe, played by Aaron Eckhart and Colm Feore.

The most demanding action sequence for the director and stunt teams on *Paycheck* was the motorcycle chase. Ben Affleck's Jennings finds himself careening through traffic —

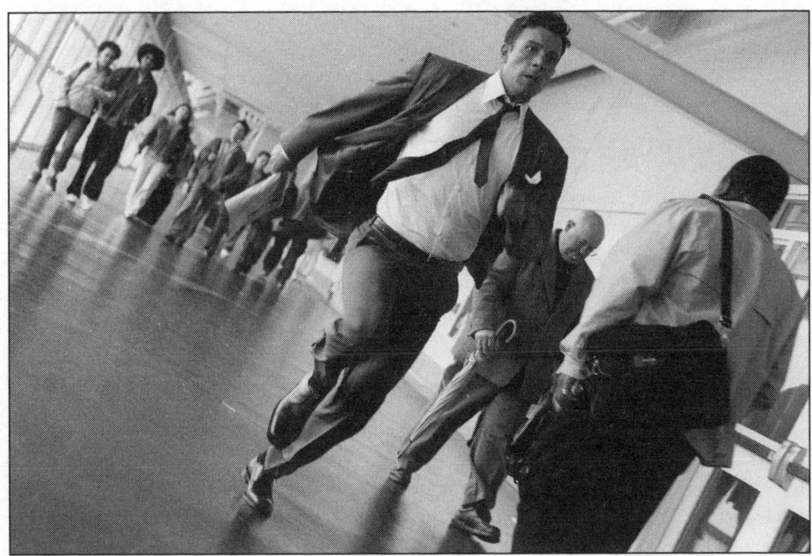

Left: *Director Woo wanted Affleck's look to be modelled closely after that of Cary Grant in* North by Northwest.

Above: *Colm Feore (centre) played Wolfe, Rethrick's right hand man.*

often against oncoming traffic — on a motorcycle with Uma Thurman's Rachel on the back. Second unit director Brian Smrz and his brother, the film's stunt co-ordinator Gregg Smrz, prepared the sequence by producing a series of incredibly detailed storyboards, so everyone involved in realising the sequence would know exactly what was required of them, from the actors through to the vehicle wranglers and the background action co-ordinators.

Remote mechanical camera rigs were used to put the viewer in the midst of the action, where no human cameraman could go. To intensify the action even further, a 'descender' was used: a device which allows an unmanned camera to drop on a cable from a great height at a rapid pace. Travelling rigs additionally allowed another unmanned camera to travel along a cable for the length of an entire city block, in tandem with the motorcycle and other vehicles featured in the sequence. Other cameras were elevated above the rooftops to offer Woo a bird's eye view of the action. The director then had multiple action-driven takes of the sequence to cut together, allowing him to both excite audiences in a visceral manner while still clearly capturing the characters' momentum and moving the story forward.

Visual effects supervisor Gregory L. McMurty knew that John Woo was a director who notoriously liked to rely on 'in-camera' effects — actual footage and physical stunt work — to achieve his ends, rather than techniques such as computer-generated imagery. "John presented me with quite a challenge: I had to avoid doing visual effects and look for 'natural' solutions…" Even so, on a science fiction film derived from a short story by Philip K. Dick, special effects would be very hard to avoid entirely. McMurty was up to Woo's challenge, though. "When he was unable to do something [required by the story] with the camera or an actor, it was up to me to find a way to accomplish what he wanted, while retaining his signature visual style."

McMurty's solution to many of these challenges was a process he dubbed 'enhanced photography'. A series of extreme close-up images, which a traditional camera lens cannot capture, were generated by computer. These images, some vivid and hyper-real, others less defined, appear among the visions of the future and memories of the past seen in Jennings' mind or through the future-revealing machine he has created.

Woo wanted the machine at the centre of the story to have a very traditional 'palm-reading' quality. The images seen were to distinctly reflect the future from the uniquely personal perspective of each individual being scanned. "To do this we had the computer project the person's future in fleeting hologram imagery by scanning his or her palms with light," explained McMurty. "To make it more believable, we tried to keep the futuristic technology to a minimum, and grounded the sequence in today's technology as much as possible."

For additional images to form Jennings' memories, McMurty turned to dream imagery as a source, surveying his co-workers and other members of the film's production team to find out how different people dreamt. "Strangely enough, some said they have dreams in which they see themselves actually watching themselves" — a very phildickian result. McMurty drew on this revelation and included elements from it in the scanning sequence: "That meant that there was actually two of them in their dreams…

"Memories don't always have to be shown from an individual's point of view, and often dream memories are impressions and not necessarily literal images," McMurty observed. "That's why in this film we felt at liberty to use both."

Below: *Using the 'time scoop', Jennings uncovers a sinister future awaiting mankind.*

An avid fan of Philip K. Dick, McMurty felt that the author touched people in a very personal way: "A lot of science fiction stories deal with grand ideas like going from planet to planet, but Dick's stories are often about who we are and what drives us. I see *Paycheck* as a story not just about knowing how the future can affect us, but how *we*, as individuals, can affect the future."

Handing a film project such as *Paycheck* to director John Woo guarantees a certain focus on action. Often imitated by other directors throughout the 1990s, Woo's signature action sequences manage to not only thrill and excite audiences, but often include within them a degree of character development, a trick which imitators often forget to duplicate as they concentrate on spectacle over content.

Weapons specialist Robert Galotti had worked on many of Woo's previous movies, maintaining all the firearms involved and ensuring that they are used under the safest circumstances. He also ensured that the guns reflected the characters.

Training actors in the proper way to use movie weapons fell under Galotti's remit.

"People think the guns used in films are not real weapons, that they're replica firearms used only for movies, but that's not true. They are real, albeit modified by professionals to fire blank ammunition, but they function as true weapons," explained Galotti. "A load is a blank cartridge — basically a round without a projectile — [but] blanks are almost as dangerous as a live round because people think they are safe."

Ramping up the action quotient of Philip K. Dick's story to suit a director of Woo's style had fallen to scripter Dean Georgaris in the first instance, but during production it was the job of the director, storyboard artists and weapons and stunt specialists to get that action on screen safely.

The classic Mexican standoff, where protagonist and antagonist face off against each other, guns drawn, is an iconic John Woo movie moment and naturally features in *Paycheck*. "I really like doing close gunfire like that," admitted Galotti. "I like doing things that people say can't be done, but there are ways to do shots that are amazing and look insanely dangerous, if you know what you are doing, have confidence in your equipment and do the proper testing."

Getting the actors used to handling the weapons properly was one of the early priorities for Galotti. "I'm a stickler for making sure the weapons are properly held so they look believable to audiences. Holding a weapon sideways, which you see all the time in music videos, is just wrong. People who fire weapons do not carry their guns that way."

Matching specific weapons to characters, so that the weapon reflects something about the character, is something of a John Woo speciality that Galotti continued on *Paycheck*. "The weapons are all different, and I essentially audition a firearm and 'cast' it accordingly," he explained. "One weapon we always have in a John Woo film is the Beretta handgun. John's used them since [working in] Hong Kong and he likes their look." Other weapons featured in the *Paycheck* armoury were modified sniper rifles, MP5 machine guns, Walther P5s and a variety of other 9mm handguns.

Special effects co-ordinator Alfred DiSarro was responsible for adding the 'fire' to the firearms, making them more effective on film through the addition of fireballs, sparks and shattering glass props. The destruction of the biolab was the most concentrated sequence for DiSarro and his team. "That was one of the most dramatic scenes in the film. We had to make sure that the film-makers had gotten every last bit of footage they needed on the biolab set, because there was no turning back once we set off the explosives."

Released on 25 December 2003, *Paycheck* was up against some tough competition at the Christmas box office. With the final instalment in Peter Jackson's film trilogy of *The Lord of the Rings*, *The Return of the King*, topping the chart with a first week take of $50 million, other releases suffered. Behind the Tolkien movie in the top ten were comedy *Cheaper by the Dozen* ($27.5 million), drama *Cold Mountain* ($14.5 million) and Jack Nicholson vehicle *Something's Gotta Give* ($13.8 million). *Paycheck* came in at number five, drawing $13.4 million, and may have topped the chart at another less hectic time of year. By March 2004, *Paycheck* had grossed a total of $53.7 million in the US against an estimated total budget of $60 million. Additional worldwide grosses helped push the film towards profitability.

At the time of *Paycheck*'s release, star Ben Affleck was suffering much media attention over his troubled relationship with Jennifer Lopez and the abject failure of their movie *Gigli*, and this inevitably affected reviewers approaching his new film. "Ben Affleck must have signed on to this bloated action film to collect a fat check. That would make more sense than if he claimed to be mesmerised by this ridiculous story," wrote Claudia Puig in *USA Today*. Jack Mathews in *The New York Daily News* observed: "You can't really blame [Affleck] for picking up his own fortunes for his film work. He's a good-looking guy with zero screen presence, and if the studios want to keep throwing money at him to play heroic figures, that's their problem." Manohla Dargis, writing in *The Los Angeles Times*, wondered if the film's budget just wasn't enough to do the central idea justice. "The film feels cheap, frayed around the edges…" Michael Wilmington in *The Chicago Tribune* observed that one of the film's gimmicks was a device that erases memories. "Unfortunately, after watching *Paycheck*, you may wish you had the picture's gimmickry at your disposal, so you could erase your own memory of it," he wrote.

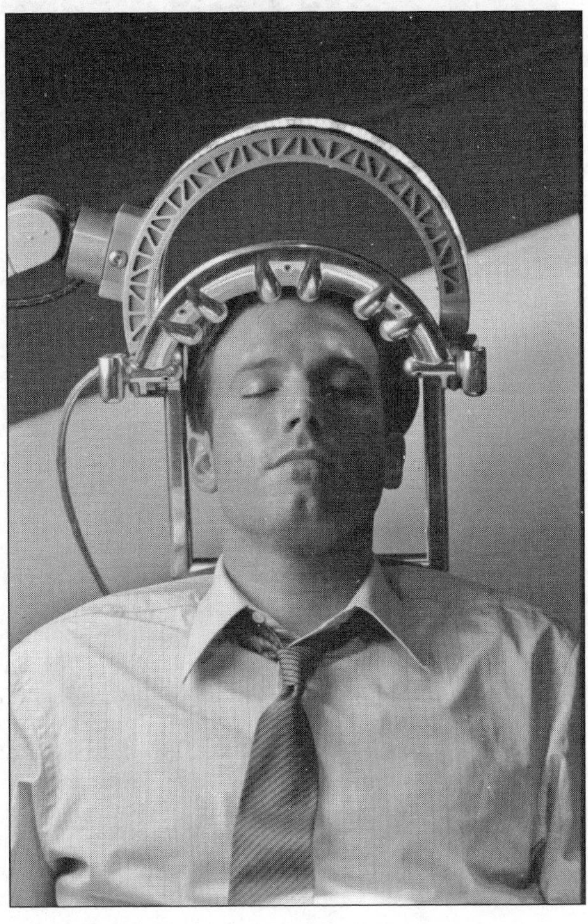

Above: *An iconic Dickian image, as man and machine interface and memory suffers!*

In the August 1953 edition of *Imagination*, letter writer Darryl Sharp commented on 'Paycheck': "In writing 'Paycheck', Philip K. Dick came through with another terrific story. Obviously, he's a regular so I know there will be more of him in the future…"

There were to be many more Philip K. Dick short stories of course, and 'Paycheck' was indeed a fine example of his work from the 1950s. That it was not a success as a movie may have been down to expectations being higher than the film could deliver, especially following the likes of *Blade Runner* and *Total Recall*. John Woo fell short of his own trademark poetic ultraviolence, while both Ben Affleck and Uma Thurman seemed uncomfortable in their roles. While better than *Screamers, Paycheck* nonetheless did not achieve the intellectual satisfaction of *Blade Runner* or the sheer entertainment value of *Total Recall*. Its major problem, though, may have been that the central time travel idea is an old science fiction gimmick, and not one central to Dick's work and themes. There's no 'What is human?' or 'What is real?' theme in *Paycheck*, just a time travel-driven romp which failed to find an appreciative audience. ■

GAME PLAYERS

Philip K. Dick's fractured reality is explored in Richard Linklater's *A Scanner Darkly*, a tale of drug abuse and surveillance inspired by the author's real life...

"I am not a character in the novel; I am the novel." — Philip K. Dick, Author's Note, *A Scanner Darkly.*

A Scanner Darkly grew out of one of the most troubled periods in Philip K. Dick's personal life. His marriage to Nancy Hackett had collapsed, and Dick had thrown his home open to all-comers, partly to overcome the isolation he felt being separated from his wife and daughters. The result, though, was that his house in San Raphael became a kind of counter-culture hangout where drug taking (including Dick's own habit, which was spiralling out of control) was not only tolerated, but actively encouraged.

Living through the early 1970s, the last thing on Dick's mind was the possibility that he might write about his experiences. In a 1973 letter to critic and author John Sladek, Dick wrote of *A Scanner Darkly*: "I spent all of 1971 doing first-hand research for it… although I did not know this at the time. I just thought I was 'turning on' with all my friends. Toward the start of 1972, I woke up one day and noticed that all my friends either were dead, had burned-out brains, were psychotic, or all of the above."

In talking with interviewer Gregg Rickman in *Philip K. Dick: In His Own Words*, Dick recognised that the world of drug users throws up multiple identities for those involved: one of the author's favourite themes. Using the example of Donna Hawthorne, main protagonist Bob Arctor's girlfriend in the novel, he talked of the writing process as an act of remembering real-life events. "I got it down on paper, before the memory left. How else can you be if you're a drug dealer who's also working with a police inspector? [The real-life inspiration for Donna] had three identities: she had a regular job, and she still lived with her parents. She had to conceal from everybody that she dealt dope. Also, she was an addict… She led a very complicated life. Under those circumstances, how could she be up front with anybody at any time?"

However, by 1973 Dick was off the drugs, married to his fifth and final wife Tessa Busby and enjoying the kind of critical acclaim for his work that had previously eluded him. It was in this more stable environment that he was able to look back at the beginning of the new decade and write *A Scanner Darkly*, taking the paranoid fears of the time and turning them into a contemporary fiction masterpiece, with little in the way of science fiction involved.

***Left:** As this teaser poster shows, computer-based rotoscoped animation gives* A Scanner Darkly *a unique look.*

présence du futur
philip k. dick
substance mort
denoël

Above: *The French title plays on the nature of the drug in the book, Substance-D, nicknamed 'Death'.*

In his 'Author's Note' which closes the novel, Dick writes of his friends and acquaintances whose lives were blighted by the drugs they took as "... children playing in the street; they could see one after another of them being killed — run over, maimed, destroyed — but they continued to play anyhow. If there was any 'sin', it was that these people wanted to keep on having a good time forever, and were punished for that... the punishment was far too great."

A Scanner Darkly fused Dick's yearnings to write 'realist' fiction (as he'd attempted in the 1950s) with his paranoid science fiction fantasies perfectly. It's a novel that realistically captures the feeling of the end of the 1960s: that the party was truly over and now there was a price to be paid, a reckoning which no one involved could escape. At the same time, it's a tale of split identities that relies on SF ideas to drive the plot and characters forward. It's one of Dick's finest works.

Although Dick, as was still his style, wrote the novel quickly, between February and April 1973, he spent the next two years revising and rewriting it — not a working method he'd ever employed in his fast-and-loose pulp days of the 1950s and 1960s. Editor Judy-Lynn del Rey, of Del Rey Books, was invaluable in convincing Dick that it was worth his while to really work on a novel for a period of time, revising and improving his writing. This was new to Dick, and became a working method he'd adopt for the remainder of his life, hence the dramatic slowdown in productivity in his final decade.

A Scanner Darkly chronicles the exploits of Fred, an undercover cop who adopts a fake identity known as Bob Arctor, a small time dealer, allowing him to track down the suppliers of a potent new drug called Substance-D, also known as 'Death'. An SF gadget allows Fred to become Arctor: the book features a 'scramble suit', which changes Fred's physical identity completely. "The wearer of the 'scramble suit' was Everyman and in every combination," writes Dick in the novel. "Hence any description of him — or her — was meaningless..."

Lifting his title from St Paul's I Corinthians 13:12 ("For now we see through a glass, darkly") Dick incorporates the ultimate surveillance device, the scanner, into his novel. This puts Arctor and his housemates under direct observation twenty-four hours a day, causing Fred to muse whether the scanner sees "into the head? Down into the heart? Into me clearly or darkly?"

Apart from the technological gimmicks of the scanner and the scramble suit, *A Scanner Darkly* offers a realistic account of the effects excessive drug use had on many practitioners at the end of the 1960s. Fred/Bob watches as one by one his friends succumb to the consequences of their lifestyle choices. Based on real people from his life at the turn of the decade, Dick writes horribly believable vignettes which strip drug-taking of any glamour it might still have possessed. Jerry Fabin spends hours in the shower, washing away imaginary bugs; Charles Freck experiences the world as a film running in his head; while Jim Barris concocts 'real' Coke from Solarcaine and psychedelics extracted from mushrooms. In his 'Author's Note' Dick names many of those who provided inspiration and lists the consequences they suffered, including himself with "permanent pancreatic damage."

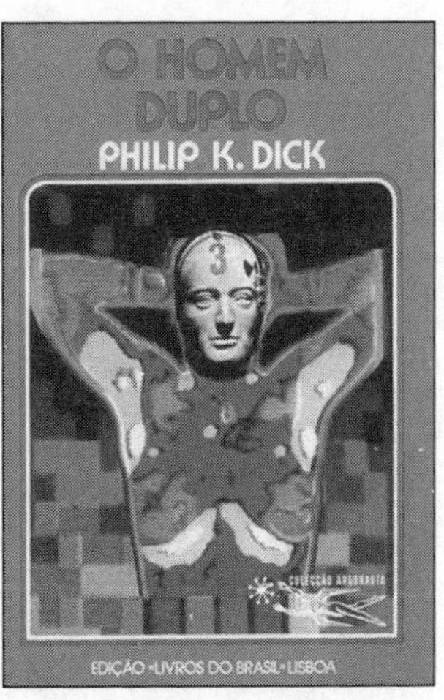

Many of his then-friends were dead by the middle of the decade when he came to work on the novel.

Beyond the street drug scene where Arctor thrives, the novel also covers Fred's 'straight' world of the police station where he is tasked with watching himself in action as an undercover narc, so deep undercover that he forgets who he is. As Fred's behaviour becomes more erratic, he is sent by his police bosses for tests of his mental condition. These determine that the hemispheres of his brain are separating as a result of the drugs he's using to maintain his cover. Fred and Bob are no longer co-operating. Instead, they're competing. Is he a narc undercover in the drug world, or is he now an addict pretending to be a cop? Beyond this there are further layers of deception, as Fred ends up an inmate at New-Path, a drug recovery centre modelled on X-Kalay in Vancouver, where Dick spent time in the early 1970s. Fred's breakdown has been engineered so he can function undercover in New-Path, which is suspected of being merely a cover for a drug dealing operation. Additionally, Fred/Bob's girlfriend Donna is also an undercover agent, investigating a much larger conspiracy than even Fred is aware of… Dick writes of Donna thinking: "Warm eyes, warm face, warm fucking fake smile, but inside I'm cold all the time, and full of lies." She's just the latest of Dick's characters to be described as inhuman, android-like. As always with Dick, reality is not what it appears, identity is fluid and changeable, and there are layers within layers…

Above: *The Portuguese title of the novel translates as 'The Double Man'.*

The end of the novel, which sees Fred working on a farm, zombie-like, secretly and unknowingly cultivating the very flower from which the deadly Substance-D is made, is a metaphor for the death of the human spirit right up there with *Nineteen Eighty-four*'s boot stamping on a human face forever. As critic Douglas A. Mackey wrote of *A Scanner Darkly* in his critical study of Dick's work: "Never did Dick write with such fierce conviction, emotional power, and sense of grief as in this shattering novel." First published in 1977, it has remained in print ever since. In fact, according to the publishers, *A Scanner Darkly* is one of their three top-selling Philip K. Dick novels.

The film of *A Scanner Darkly* went through various transformations before reaching the screen in 2006 in the form of Richard Linklater's beautifully animated movie, starring Keanu Reeves as Fred and Bob Arctor.

Accent Films, a French company, had been first in line to make a film from Philip K. Dick's darkest novel in 1984, in the wake of *Blade Runner*. Accent had been behind the production of several movies featuring Jean-Paul Belmondo and in the mid-1980s had produced a historical mini-series, called *A.D.*, for American broadcaster NBC, as well as a movie version of *La Traviata*. This French interest in making the movie no doubt came on the back of the critical acclaim and academic attention which Dick's work had garnered in France in the late 1970s and early 1980s, and which would eventually lead to the French film of *Confessions of a Crap Artist*.

Things were quiet around the film option on *A Scanner Darkly* for a long time, as the movie of *Total Recall* came and went in 1990. There was a report in the Philip K. Dick

Above: *Another French cover emphasises the shattered nature of Fred/Bob Arctor's personality.*

Society Newsletter of May 1990 that a 'major Hollywood production company' had once again expressed interest in the novel, but as with so many possible film options, nothing came of it.

At one stage director Terry Gilliam was seriously interested in adapting some of Philip K. Dick's work to film. "After *The Fisher King*, Richard LaGravenese, who wrote the film, and I went to the studio with his script for Philip K. Dick's *A Scanner Darkly*," the director is reported as saying by the online Gilliam fanzine, *Dreams*. "Nobody's done a Dick novel right yet; *Blade Runner* was stunningly good, but Dick's idea was missing — that people were killing replicants to buy real animals. I saw how to make *Scanner* cheaply, and for it to be disturbing. But did the studio say, 'These two guys just made us our second most profitable film of the year, let's give them the money to develop the idea?' No. I simply wasn't understanding the rules of this place called Hollywood."

It was 1999 before another planned film of the book was in development. Australian film director Emma-Kate Croghan graduated from the Victorian College of the Arts and made a splash with her début movie, 1996's *Love & Other Catastrophes*. The low-budget Australian film was hailed as the equivalent to the personally financed early films of Gregg Araki, Kevin Smith or Robert Rodriguez. The legend had it that the film was shot on Super-16 film stock for only A$25,000. This ignored the later-revealed fact that the budget had ballooned to A$45,000 by the end of the three-week shoot and the Australian Film Commission had 'rescued' the production with a A$500,000 'completion budget', which allowed for the film to be blown up to 35mm, covered incurred costs remaining to be paid off and included another A$45,000 to be spent on marketing the film. Not quite the kitchen sink success story that the hype had suggested, but that's the business of movie publicity…

Nevertheless, Croghan's film was a huge international success, and was followed by 1998's *Strange Planet*, which chronicled the ups and downs of some young GenX-ers in Sydney. Croghan had been attached to a film of *A Scanner Darkly* since 1997 (it was first reported in *Variety* on 4 June 1997), during the buzz around her début. The project was to be produced by Danny DeVito's Jersey Films, who had been behind such acclaimed movies as *Pulp Fiction* and *Get Shorty*.

Croghan cited *A Scanner Darkly* as one of her favourite novels, one in which she saw much filmic potential. *The Australian* national newspaper carried an interview with the director on 9 October 1999. "I don't want to end up making romantic comedies for the rest of my life," she offered, by way of explanation for her change of direction into the weird worlds of Philip K. Dick. "It is a kind of departure and it isn't. It deals with the kind of caustic, loser sense of humour that you see in Dick's writing but hasn't made it on to the screen. If anything it reminds me of [comic strip artist] Robert Crumb." Croghan also cited George Miller's *Babe: Pig in the City* and Alex Proyas' *Dark City* as inspirations for her planned approach to the film, which certainly conjures up an intriguing prospect.

The script for Croghan's aborted take on *A Scanner Darkly* was written by Charlie

Kaufman, the maverick screenwriter with a reputation for writing offbeat scripts that disrupt the very form of movies themselves. His first success came in 1999, in conjunction with director Spike Jonze. In *Being John Malkovich*, John Cusack's meek puppeteer finds a mysterious portal that allows him to possess real-life actor John Malkovich. Kaufman followed this up with a trio of films in 2002. First came the critically mauled flop *Human Nature*, directed by Michel Gondry, in which scientist Tim Robbins attempts to help a hirsute feminist and a man who thinks he's a monkey. This was followed by his film version of the book *The Orchid Thief*, entitled *Adaptation*. Directed by Spike Jonze, the film is about the process of adaptation itself, and stars Nicolas Cage as both 'Charlie Kaufman' and a fictional twin brother, Donald. Donald is a hack writer, but more successful than the tortured Charlie. As the film progresses, it actually turns into the film Donald is writing, adopting all the Hollywood thriller clichés, from double-crosses to car chases and beyond... Kaufman next brought his talents to the supposed true story of *Gong Show* host Chuck Barris, in the George Clooney-directed *Confessions of a Dangerous Mind*. Elements of his script for *A Scanner Darkly* are echoed in the fantastical imaginings of Barris, who claimed to be a government hit man as well as a top TV producer and star. Kaufman and Gondry redeemed themselves after *Human Nature* with the fantastic *Eternal Sunshine of the Spotless Mind*, an incredibly 'phildickian' romance, which featured Jim Carrey and Kate Winslet as lovers who have erased each other from their memories, only to repeat the same love story once more...

Kaufman's unproduced script for *A Scanner Darkly* pre-dated all of these projects. This first and apparently only draft is dated 20 December 1997 and is very faithful to the novel, while also working very well as a blueprint for a movie. Kaufman presents a group of funny, yet sad characters whose stoned ramblings are amusing but also a symptom of the damage they are doing to themselves. While the multiple identity material (Arctor and Fred being one and the same, Donna being both junkie and Fed) may not throw a twenty-first century audience, it is nonetheless faithful to Dick's plotting. Like the book, Kaufman's screenplay opens with Jerry Fabin and his invisible bugs, and introduces Charles Freck. Although Freck goes on to be part of the Arctor/Luckman/Barris/Donna circle, it's really the subsequently introduced Arctor/Fred who is the central character, who the potential audience follows through to the New Path farm at the end, where he ends up cultivating the flowers that become Substance-D.

In *Adaptation*, Kaufman had the character named after him address one of the conceits of *A Scanner Darkly*: "The only idea more overused than serial killers is multiple personality. On top of that you explore the notion that cop and criminal are really two aspects of the same person." Thankfully, Dick's novel and Kaufman's unmade screenplay are both smarter than the average tired example of that genre. Kaufman avoids the temptation to import the kind of clichéd action that features (albeit ironically) at the end of *Adaptation* into *A Scanner Darkly*. Dick's novel is a character piece, a psychological exploration of the effect of drugs on a community, and the Kaufman screenplay follows that faithfully. There are comedic situations and funny dialogue, but almost everything is drawn from Dick, and Kaufman resists the opportunity to thrust some of his own trademark weirdness into proceedings — after all, Dick's work is weird enough. There are hallucinations, day-dream fantasies and such unreal elements as visible thought bubbles above characters' heads which

sf NARRATIVA D'ANTICIPAZIONE
CAPOLAVORI DI FANTASCIENZA MODERNA
PHILIP K. DICK
SCRUTARE NEL BUIO
«Credo che questo romanzo sia un capolavoro, forse l'unico capolavoro che scriverò mai...
(P.K.Dick)
EDITRICE NORD

***Above:** The scramble suit is brought to life on this Italian cover.*

can be seen by select others, but these all reflect elements in the novel. The whole script suggests a vibe similar to that of another phildickian movie, *Fight Club*, made by David Fincher from Chuck Palahniuk's novel, which features a plot driven forward by the main character's nonexistent alter-ego. One scene has Fred watching himself as Arctor on screen (the 'scanner' of the title), pausing the action and then entering into the scene himself through the monitor. The Kaufman script is essentially a streamlined, higher-impact version of the novel.

There are nevertheless some distinctly weird elements in the screenplay. Coca-Cola is given a prominent position, from scenes of its nationwide distribution in the film's opening moments (not in Dick's novel, but possibly mirroring the distribution of Substance-D?), to a Coke bottle appearing in tests carried out on Fred, and the Coca-Cola corporation being cited by Donna as an example of a monopoly corporation which should be outlawed (the latter two examples are in the original novel). Although a caption card at the beginning gives the setting of the movie as 1994, Charles Freck has a 1970s-style eight-track cassette player in his car and the characters' speech is peppered with 1960s verbal ticks, as in Dick's novel. Donna at one point refers to an all-night screening of all eleven *Planet of the Apes* movies at the Torrance Drive-In (that's also directly from Dick's novel, but there were only five *Apes* movies, so Dick obviously anticipated the series continuing longer…)

"Yeah, *A Scanner Darkly*… it didn't get made," said Kaufman in a rare interview with *Bizarre* magazine. "It pretty much fell apart when the director left. It was kind of an unpleasant experience working on it, for me. I don't want to say too much [about it]. I love Philip K. Dick and I really like that book, I'd love to see a movie of it. I heard Richard Linklater is going to make an animated version of it, but I'm pretty certain they're not using my script…" With an untitled horror movie going into production for Columbia Pictures in 2005, once again teaming him with Spike Jonze, Charlie Kaufman seems likely to continue his phildickian approach to cinema — even if the chance to directly adapt a Dick novel slipped through his fingers with *A Scanner Darkly*.

In the early twenty-first century *A Scanner Darkly* passed through Universal, with *Titanic* and *The Aviator* actor Leonardo DiCaprio being talked of as the star. British pop promo director Chris Cunningham, who was once an artist for the UK's sci-fi comic *2000AD* (as Chris Halls), was involved around the same time, without success. "I spent most of last year [2002] trying to adapt *A Scanner Darkly* into a workable screenplay," Cunningham told *Resolution* magazine in 2003. "As far as science fiction goes, it's got just the right level of implausibility. It's just trippy and paranoid enough. But in order to get it into a filmable shape, I would have to change it so much and I didn't want to. The thing that put me off in the end was that I didn't want it to be a film about drugs. I couldn't figure out how to approach it without ruining the essentials. It was a lesson for me, that I should have more faith in a world of my own, rather than attempt any kind of cannibalism," he said of the failed project.

Known for his controversial music videos for Aphex Twin and Bjork, Cunningham had also attempted to adapt William Gibson's Dick-influenced *Neuromancer* as a movie in 2000. Earlier he'd worked in a design capacity on David Fincher's *Alien*³ and with Stanley Kubrick on the original development of *A.I.: Artificial Intelligence*. "It's just embarrassing," Cunningham admitted to *Time Out*. "All I ever do is talk about films and then not make them. As a result I thought: just shut up about it — make a film then talk about it when it's done. After three or four years tinkering with other people's material I came to the conclusion that I just had to develop my own material from scratch."

It's a shame, as Cunningham was a huge fan of *Blade Runner*, so was keen to embark on his own Philip K. Dick movie adaptation. "I'd seen stills from it in magazines," he told *The Daily Telegraph* of his favourite movie, "but there was something about them that hadn't appealed to me — probably because I had been gorging on *Star Wars* since I was seven, and *Blade Runner* didn't appear to have much hardware in it."

For Cunningham, it was Dick's ideas and the atmosphere of the film, rather than Ridley Scott's lush visuals, which captured his attention. "I can't think of another film that has such a strong atmosphere, melancholy, and the strangest feeling of nostalgia for a place and time that never was. When I was a teenager, I would put the film on in the same way you might put a moody record on, just to soak up the feeling. The love scene in Deckard's apartment is so beautiful and strange. If Deckard is supposed to be a replicant, then this is basically an uncomfortable dialogue between two non-humans, one of whom is about to have their first sexual encounter. I love the way the music, sound design and different lighting environments change as they move around the apartment. It was an idiosyncratic film for the mainstream — almost European."

According to the would-be director, the wrong people are making films from the work of authors like Dick, and are focussing on the wrong elements of the source material. "Science fiction always attracts the wrong people [to make movies]," Cunningham told celebrity rock photographer Anton Corbijin in an interview. "[They say] something like: 'Gee, there is technology in this movie so let's use a flying car.' The exciting thing about people in the future doesn't lie in their environment. It is not the futuristic technology that makes [these] books so interesting. I am crazy about the idea of filming a science fiction movie using only a 200mm lens, so that you never get to see the backgrounds."

When the Chris Cunningham version of *A Scanner Darkly* failed to materialise, the rights came into the hands of independent filmmaker Richard Linklater. Warner Brothers initially optioned *A Scanner Darkly* for Stephen Soderbergh to direct, but turned the project over to Linklater when he expressed his interest. A new deal was struck with Warner Independent Films ensuring that all involved worked for basic 'scale' payments to ensure that Linklater could realise his unique vision for the film. He was the one to finally get the film made, bringing it to the screen starring Keanu Reeves and with the enthusiastic backing of the Philip K. Dick Trust, represented by the author's daughters Laura Leslie and Isa Dick-Hackett. "I'm a fan. I think anybody who reads more than a few of the books becomes a fan [of Philip K. Dick]. I think you either like his characters and his thinking or you don't," Linklater confirmed in an interview for this book.

By the time of *Waking Life* in 2001, writer and director Richard Linklater had eight movies under his belt. Acclaimed for his second and third movies *Slacker* and *Dazed and Confused*, Linklater also directed the romance *Before Sunrise* (and its later sequel *Before Sunset*), before the animated *Waking Life* brought him to Philip K. Dick.

Linklater's dissatisfaction with previous film adaptations of Dick's work led him to approach *A Scanner Darkly* in a particular way. "While I like a lot of the movies made from Dick's books, particularly *Blade Runner* and *Total Recall*, I was always a little disappointed when I saw some of them... It's like they took the central ideas, but they didn't really do the whole thing... There's always a mild disappointment on things like *Minority Report*. These films are always going to reflect the director, so if you have John Woo [*Paycheck*], it's going to be an action thriller with a lot of shoot-outs... With Spielberg, it's going to have his touches. I always thought 'Wouldn't it be great if someone would just make the whole book or short story?'"

Linklater had started out with an aborted attempt to make a film of *Ubik*, the novel Dick himself had adapted as an unproduced screenplay in the mid-1970s. "I thought *Ubik* would be an interesting adaptation with things to say about the present: the notion of half-life, being kept alive to communicate with loved ones... That book was having rights problems — the non-exclusive rights were owned by somebody else. The [Dick] estate didn't control it, so I segued onto thinking *A Scanner Darkly* would make a good movie. That one always hit me as Dick's most personal book. I knew it wouldn't be an action-packed film, it could be more my kind of movie, actually... just people talking!"

Like *Before Sunrise*, Linklater's *Waking Life* had been a 'talking' movie, in which

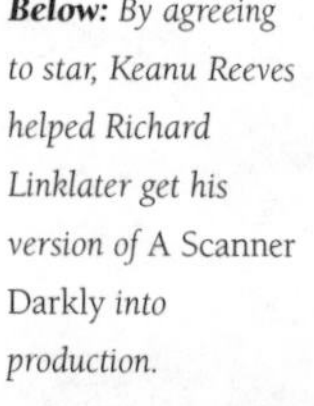

Below: *By agreeing to star, Keanu Reeves helped Richard Linklater get his version of* A Scanner Darkly *into production.*

Above: *Winona Ryder was cast as Donna, drug addict and undercover Fed.*

characters discuss the meaning of life and explore abstract ideas and emotional states. Taking this concept a step further than in *Before Sunrise*, Linklater wanted *Waking Life* to have the feeling of a dream. He shot the entire film as live-action footage with actors and props, as he would any other movie, but then animated over the top in the style of the ancient movie art of rotoscoping. The effect was an uncannily life-like animation, with the characters clearly resembling the actors playing the parts.

In the course of the film, there's an analysis of Dick's novel *Flow My Tears, The Policeman Said* (delivered by the director himself), which came from Linklater's own interest in Dick's work. "I'd actually talked about Philip K. Dick books as possible future film projects, and of doing them as animated films… I like it now that reference is in there because it points to the future in a good way, I think…"

When it came to reviving the long-gestating project to film *A Scanner Darkly*, Linklater seemed like the ideal candidate, and he was keen to make the new film using the realistic but weirdly off-kilter animated technique of *Waking Life*. "*Scanner* was good for animation, not only because of the scramble suit but because the animation would put the viewer into a similar headspace as Robert Arctor. There's a certain brain split, because that's the way your brain sees it: something's real, something's not real as you see this animation… There were some practical considerations too. Time-consuming though animation is, it still kept us in the low budget realm. Hollywood wasn't exactly clamouring to do *A Scanner Darkly* as a movie. It's not a subject matter they go for."

In adapting the novel into a screenplay, being faithful to the original "was certainly my goal," noted Linklater. "It wasn't like I was on a huge crusade to do a faithful adaptation, I just thought that would make the story work. Maybe I just didn't have the additional ideas

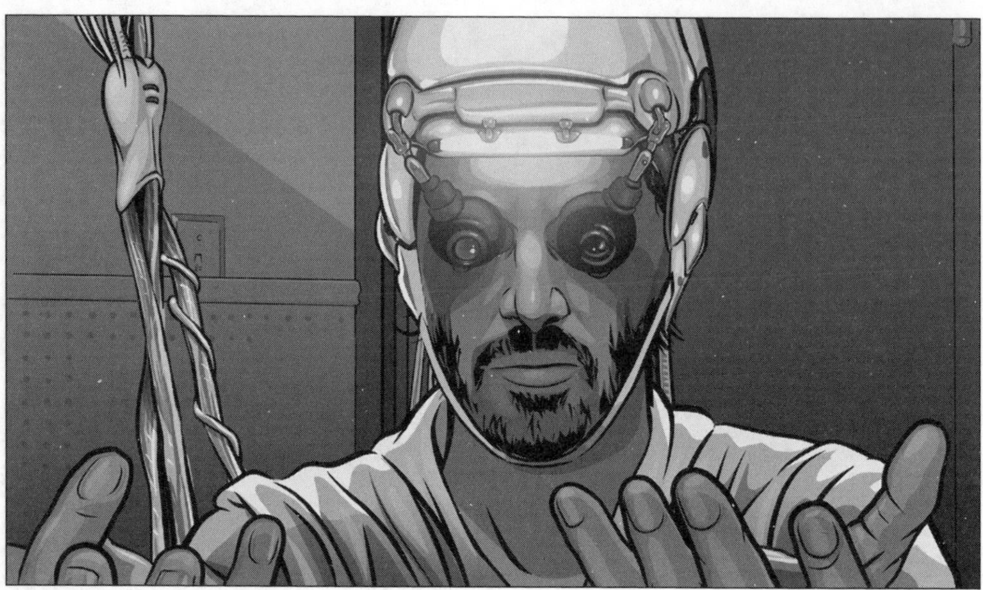

Above: *That iconic Dickian image again, as man and machine meld in the mental realm.*

to turn it into an action thriller? I don't think that way. I felt I was probably the right person to film all these long conversations that don't go anywhere, whereas a lot of people would cut those on the basis that 'It doesn't move the story forward.' I see it and go 'Oh, that's great,' because, actually, they *do* go somewhere and there's something going on there… My take was to be as faithful as I could. It still needed an adaptation: it was written in the 1970s and set in the early 1990s… I set it in the near future, but it seemed particularly apt for these times that we're living in, with 9/11 and the crackdown in the US and the world, this new cloud we're all living under. It seemed like a logical extension that the war on terror would join with the war on drugs. There would be bigger government and private corporate interests taking over those wars, with endless profiteering from unwinnable wars… Philip K. Dick saw the future very clearly."

Getting from the concept to actually filming the project was to be no easier for Richard Linklater than it had been for any of the other directors attached through the years. In Peter Biskind's exposé of Miramax, *Down and Dirty Pictures*, Linklater's *Before Sunrise* star Ethan Hawke was quoted regarding the difficulties he and Linklater were having raising the finance for the film, despite their joint pedigree. "You can't get a film made for $10 million," claimed Hawke, pointing out that without big star names attached, low-to-mid budget movies were impossible to get made. "[Richard] Linklater has this incredible screenplay of a Philip K. Dick story, *A Scanner Darkly*, and I want to be in it. After *Training Day* [which won Hawke's co-star Denzel Washington an Oscar], I can get you $30 million if you want to do a cop movie, but we can't get anyone to give us $10 million for that."

It wasn't until his mainstream success as director of the hit Jack Black comedy *School of Rock* that Linklater earned enough clout to make not only a follow-up to *Before*

Sunrise, with the original cast of Hawke and Julie Delpy, but also *A Scanner Darkly*, though with the star of *The Matrix* attached instead of Hawke.

One of the key factors in getting a studio greenlight for *A Scanner Darkly* was the involvement of Keanu Reeves. Like Linklater, Reeves was a self-confessed Philip K. Dick fan who was pleased to play any role in bringing one of the writer's odder books to the screen. Casting Reeves as Bob Arctor brought a lot of other idiosyncratic actors to the film, giving it even greater 'underground' cachet. Richard Linklater felt that the man who was the stoner Ted in *Bill & Ted's Excellent Adventure* was ideal for the divided Arctor. "I approached Keanu in 2001, as I'd always thought he'd be a good Robert Arctor. I always did. He was still in *The Matrix* world at that moment, and couldn't really wrap his head around it," said Linklater of his attempts to secure Reeves. "In early 2004, I took another run at Keanu and he wanted to talk about it. I was really happy when he came aboard. Keanu's pretty fearless that way. He cares about the ideas. He really loves Philip K. Dick. Dick's his kind of writer."

Although Linklater saw Reeves as the best actor for the split part of Arctor and Fred, having the star of *The Matrix* aboard was an extra bonus. "It certainly helps. I wasn't even thinking about people seeing the movie, I was just thinking about getting the movie made. Even though we were low budget, there is a certain kind of thinking in the movie business that it is hard to go up against. They would almost rather it be a live action movie at $20-$25 million than an animated movie at $6 million… The animated thing is much more of a wild card, as they don't know whether adults want to go see animation. It's not yet proven in their minds. As Keanu came aboard, and then Robert Downey Jr, Winona Ryder, Woody Harrelson, it made it so that they had to do it… It's how you get anything made these days that is out of the commercial mainstream: you get everybody working for very little, for scale, basically, the minimum payments, and they share in the back-end. The budget is low enough, and suddenly the script I wrote which everybody thought was kind of weird has improved a little… improved enough that, in fact, it could get done."

Left: *Woody Harrelson joined the ensemble cast as Luckman.*

For many, the casting of Keanu Reeves, who'd been miscast previously in the film of William Gibson's *Johnny Mnemonic*, in Francis Ford Coppola's *Dracula* and the comic book movie *Constantine*, looked like the first mis-step on the project. Although he'd been acclaimed for his performance in the initial film of the *The Matrix* trilogy — which, like *A Scanner Darkly*, dealt with a kind of alternative reality — many Dick fans were doubtful of Reeves' suitability for the nuanced and potentially complicated dual roles of Bob Arctor and Fred. Anguished online comments ran the gamut from "Keanu Reeves as (arguably) Dick's single most complex and difficult character? I don't think I've ever seen a performance by him that wasn't in at least some way jarring," to "I've read this novel eight times and each of those times I did *not* consider Keanu Reeves even playing the phantom dogshit on Arctor's car engine!"

However, Dick's daughters Laura and Isa (who were running their father's literary estate, and heavily supported this version of the movie) applauded Linklater's choice and welcomed the involvement of the other actors who came together to give life to their father's vision. "After agreeing that this project was the right way to go, we were delighted to hear that this group of gifted actors would be playing the characters: Keanu Reeves as Arctor, Winona Ryder as Donna, Robert Downey Jr as Barris, Woody Harrelson as Luckman, and Rory Cochrane as Freck. We think each person brings a unique quality and passion to the project."

Throwing himself wholeheartedly into the movie, Reeves gave his all to the live-action shooting element of the project, even though he was aware that he and the other actors were to be animated over. Linklater shot all his live-action material in Austin, Texas, wrapping on 30 June 2004. Although the actors were effectively finished, a long road still lay ahead for the director to complete his version of *A Scanner Darkly*. He could have released the film as was, but the animation idea had taken deep root, especially as it allowed Linklater to retain control over the project. "If we'd gone live action and the budget had jumped to $25 million I would be getting directives to cut the scene where they talk about the bicycle pump because it doesn't advance character or move the story forward. They'd be asking 'Can we make it more cops and robbers?' We'd have to introduce other elements to justify the story at $25 million… All things considered, animating was the best way to do it and be off the charts, below the radar of the industry… Just give us our $6 million and let us do our thing…!"

Following *Waking Life*, Linklater knew the weird-looking animation over recognisable movie stars would give a unique look, suitable for this Dick adaptation. "The animation has this quality of elevating the mundane, and this movie is guys sitting around talking about cars and things, so there's a certain banal dialogue element to it…"

Once shooting was complete and the live-action footage was edited, Linklater's company Detour Film Productions brought over thirty animators together to turn it into the finished film, via *Waking Life*'s Bob Sabiston and his rotoscope-inspired animation technique.

Despite their previous experience on *Waking Life*, all sorts of problems were faced by the animation team working on *A Scanner Darkly*. "We're trying to have this movie have more of a unified look than *Waking Life*," commented Sabiston. "It's more of a finely detailed comic book with fine lines and real accuracy, a very polished look."

Using software developed by Sabiston, *A Scanner Darkly*'s animators, including Mike

Layne and his team from Flat Black Films, traced over the initial footage, turning it into a combination comic book and watercolour look. "We've been divided into teams," explained Layne to *The Austin Chronicle*. "Each team starts off with a scene, people try to nail that particular aesthetic, and then it all becomes a question of speed. Bob's software has evolved tremendously since what we used during *Waking Life*. It's really unlike anything else that's out there."

Making sure that the animated versions of the characters looked just like the star actors in the film was central to the technique. "With *A Scanner Darkly*, we're trying to be much more cohesive, because we've got A-list actors and those guys need to be recognizable," confirmed Layne. "If you've got somebody like Robert Downey Jr, who is made of elastic — there is nothing on him that is stationary at any time — capturing all of his expressions and doing justice to someone who is that great an actor is a real challenge. It's interesting to see him in particular, because you never really notice how much goes into acting until you see a guy who is going into the scene that way, and you see every little nuance that goes into each little piece of his performance. It's incredibly complex and detailed, and we've really got to capture that in the animation."

***Above:** The animation team went to great lengths to ensure that stars like Ryder remained recognisable.*

For Richard Linklater, animation was the only way to go with *A Scanner Darkly* even though it raised a whole new set of daunting challenges. "You're sort of re-imagining the film, certainly. It was much more difficult than what we did with *Waking Life*. The artistic style of this movie demanded more. We wanted it to look like a graphic novel and to have a certain level of detail. There were a few scenes of *Waking Life* that had that level of detail, but for the most part they didn't. Once we committed to that, it upped the hours. We animated 24fps (frames per second) instead of the 12fps we did on *Waking Life*. Everything about *A Scanner Darkly* was more difficult: it was a huge managerial thing, the consistency of the look had to be maintained, we had to imagine things like the scramble suit. It was difficult. I think at the end of the day it was 500+ hours per minute of animation… It was such a huge, gargantuan undertaking that I don't think I'll be doing another animated film for some time…"

Another attraction for the director in Dick's work was the humour evident in his stories and novels. "That was my biggest single note on the other Dick films I'd seen. I wanted to bring out the comedy. I always thought Philip K. Dick was hilarious. I read his books and I laugh out loud. I go with the ideas. They get very dark — and in the case of *Scanner*, tragic — and yet the humour always struck me, the wicked humour of Dick's work. Having gone through it, I can see why people do lose it. It's a battle of tones, which works fine in novels and short stories, but doesn't work as well in movies. A movie is much more like a finely crafted short story, and you have one tone. You don't have a lot of room for deviation. To combine a tragedy with a comedy, not just in the way of comic relief, but to have a full-blown comedy… I knew we were making a comedy on one hand, but on the other hand we were making a tragedy. That was a huge challenge. I wish other films didn't drop the comedy."

Only too aware of the previous movie adaptations of Dick's work and the pitfalls some of them had fallen into, Linklater was determined to take a very different, individualistic approach to *A Scanner Darkly*. "I always felt a personal connection to *A Scanner Darkly* because it was personal to Dick. You read it and he'd clearly lived in that house, he clearly was that guy…: to some degree, he knew these people. The book is a loving tribute to those people. The human connection rang out, as I think it does to all readers. It struck me as his most personal work. Doing some research, and later talking with his daughter, confirmed that. Isa was like, 'Yeah I lived in that house…' Both her parents are in the dedication at the back of the book, which is also at the end of the movie. That confirmed what I felt."

In fact, Linklater was the only filmmaker to date who has built a strong relationship with the Dick estate, in the form of his daughters Laura Leslie and Isa Dick-Hackett. "It seemed natural to me," he said of involving Dick's daughters on the project. "On a holistic level, knowing what a personal book it was, you want the blessing of the people who were closest to him. On another level, they wanted to meet me too before I did it: they had to sign off on me. I went up to the Bay Area and hung out with them. It was very sweet: they gave me their father's own copy of his book, his own paperback of *A Scanner Darkly*, with his name in it… It was like a talisman. I think they were very concerned with how I was

Below: *Although it features outlandish technology, Linklater regarded* A Scanner Darkly *as more of a dark comedy than a science fiction film.*

Above: *Winona Ryder as Donna.*

going to treat the book. I think the drug element, the story in general and the sensibility was important to them. They were curious about my take on it. They said they'd like to work more like this in future. They're completely supportive and understanding. It meant everything to me that they liked my script, that they liked where it was going and they liked that it had a tribute at the end. It meant a lot to the cast to be able to talk to them. It confirmed a lot of my ideas, 'Oh yeah, my dad was hilarious…' They said how creative, funny and what a good guy he was."

Laura and Isa even went so far as to issue a statement during production, backing Linklater and the film in a way they had not backed any other film or moviemaker. "This project is very exciting for us — not only because of the calibre of talent behind it, but because we believe that it will be the very first faithful adaptation of a Philip K. Dick story," ran the statement, posted at the official philipkdick.com web site, run on behalf of the estate. The sisters were fully aware of the legacy left behind by their prolific father and were clearly intent on both exploiting and protecting that legacy in a way not previously attempted. "Philip K. Dick is now 'the most adapted SF author in the history of film.' Wonderful opportunities have been realised in bringing his stories to the screen. In fact, some of the greatest filmmakers, writers and actors have been involved in film adaptations of his work. And the most important benefit of these adaptations has been that they have brought new readers to his work. (Each time we have been told of a 'green light', we have marvelled at the odds of it!) But there has always been the nagging question of whether or not any of the films have adequately captured this depth of spirit of his work. We have long awaited the opportunity for a faithful adaptation of our father's work."

As far as the sisters were concerned, they were convinced that Linklater was the man to make a faithful version of *A Scanner Darkly*. "This amazing group of filmmakers (true Philip K. Dick fans) and the Philip K. Dick Trust came together to get this project made. We were originally approached by producer Tommy Pallotta with the enticement of a faithful adaptation. When we read Richard Linklater's fantastic screenplay, and then had the opportunity to meet with him and discuss his and our visions of *Scanner*, we knew this was the right way to go."

The movie was co-financed by Warner Independent Pictures, founded in August 2003 as a new division of Warner Bros., devoted to serious films with modest budgets. The plan was to release up to ten feature films each year, each budgeted under $20 million (a move that would in part answer Ethan Hawke's criticisms of the movie industry). *A Scanner Darkly* was to be one of their first projects, although the film was actually produced by Section 8 partners George Clooney and Steven Soderbergh (once a possible director for this film), along with Jonah Smith and Palmer West, whose company Thousand Words was co-financing the film with Warner Independent Pictures.

"Five years ago, Philip K. Dick's vision of the future seemed at the very least a bit fanciful or paranoid, but now it seems like a highly plausible possibility," said Mark Gill, president of co-financier Warner Independent. "That topicality, combined with a stellar group of actors and a director at the top of his career — introducing us to a new look at the art form of film — make *A Scanner Darkly* irresistible."

More than the likes of *Blade Runner* or *Total Recall*, the film of *A Scanner Darkly* was a deeply personal experience for Laura and Isa. After all, the autobiographical nature of the novel meant that a slice of their father's own life (albeit heavily fictionalised) was to be put on screen. It was important that they trust the director and that the screenplay be as faithful as possible, in spirit as well as in detail, to the realism of the original novel. "*A Scanner Darkly* is one of our father's most personal stories," noted the sisters' joint statement, "because much of it is based on his own experiences. For this reason, it was especially important to us that it be done with all of the right intentions. His struggle with drug abuse is well documented, and he (and we) have witnessed many casualties. The novel is filled with his humour and his own tragedies. We believe that Richard's screenplay manages to capture these key elements — he has even included our father's poignant afterword in his adaptation."

The sisters' involvement extended to several trips to see the filming and meet all those involved. They even supplied some of their father's personal items — such as his coffee cup and a bottle of Dean Swift Snuff — to be placed in the backgrounds of scenes for fans to spot as a series of in-film 'Easter eggs'. "Laura and I visited the set during filming and had a chance to speak with the actors about some of the more personal aspects of this story. Without exception, every person we spoke to — actors, producers and crew was entirely gracious and enthusiastic about the work of Philip K. Dick. They have welcomed our input, and made us feel a part of this project."

Release of the movie was delayed from autumn 2005 to summer 2006, as the animation process took its toll on the dedicated team of animators. Throughout it all, the involvement of Dick's daughters helped Linklater stay on track. "It made it easier for me to do this whole process having their support, because there is pressure," the director

told this author. "I tried not to think about it too much, but it's the pressure you feel when you adapt a beloved work, whether it's *Fear and Loathing*, *The Da Vinci Code* or anything else… Millions of people have read this book and have their own ideas about it. Dick has a fan following which is very unlike most authors. His fans take this stuff very personally — he's not just a writer. He's not just some guy that wrote books. It goes beyond that, and for good reason. I knew there would be scrutiny, more so on this than anything I've ever done. Laura and Isa's support made that all manageable, and confirmed what I was feeling and hoping anyway, that I was the right guy to do this."

Above: *Keanu Reeves was a Philip K. Dick fan keen to appear in any film based on his work.*

Two months before release, *A Scanner Darkly* was selected to be showcased as part of the out-of-competition 'Un Certain Regard' section of the 2006 Cannes Film Festival. The graphic novel of the film from Pantheon appeared on 4 July, described as "one of the most exciting collaborative graphic novels ever published." *American Splendor* writer Harvey Pekar contributed to the faithful adaptation, utilizing a landscape (or 'widescreen') book format, with the art drawn directly from the animated film source.

Calling the distinctive look of Richard Linklater's film "a graphic novel come to life", Philip K. Dick's daughters Laura and Isa were pleased that their father's novel had been captured on screen as "a haunting, highly stylized vision of the future. We all hope that when fans watch this film, they will feel that the interpretation reflects the true spirit of the original story, and also know that the genesis of the project is the love and respect for Philip K. Dick." ■

TIME PAWN

Philip K. Dick fans Gary Goldman, Jason Koornick and Nicolas Cage team-up to bring 'The Golden Man' to the screen...

"We are bombarded with pseudo realities manufactured by very sophisticated people. I distrust their power. It is an astonishing power: that of creating whole universes, universes of the mind. I ought to know. I do the same thing." — Philip K. Dick, 'How to Build a Universe That Doesn't Fall Apart Two Days Later' (written 1978), published in *I Hope I Shall Arrive Soon* (1985).

Following *A Scanner Darkly*, the next film adapted from the work of Philip K. Dick to enter production was in fact called *Next*, drawn from the short story 'The Golden Man'. *Next* was written by Gary Goldman, who had previously scripted *Total Recall* (not to mention developing its aborted sequels, and the film that eventually resulted: *Minority Report*). Under the direction of Lee Tamahori, who previously helmed the James Bond movie *Die Another Day*, Nicolas Cage plays Cris Johnson, a man who can see a short way into the future and so change events to his advantage before they even happen. Going beyond using this precognition for personal gain, Cage's hero has to use his unusual gift to outsmart a secret government plan to capture him and use him for their own ends. Additionally, he's faced with preventing a terrorist attack and winning the hand of Liz (Jessica Biel), the woman he loves. Eventually, he is forced to choose between saving the world or saving himself. Potentially typical blockbuster Hollywood movie fare, in other words.

Below: *'The Golden Man' provided the title for a UK collection of Dick's short stories.*

'The Golden Man' was published in science fiction pulp magazine *If* in April 1954. Dick had written the story the previous year, and it was his attempt to break into what was then a popular style of science fiction story — the psi-powers tale. "In the early 1950s much American science fiction dealt with human mutants and their glorious super-powers and super-faculties," noted Dick in his 1978 comments on 'The Golden Man'. "They would presently lead mankind to a higher state of existence, a sort of 'promised land'."

The concentration on psi-powers and 'mind over matter' in science fiction short stories had been promoted by John W. Campbell Jr, the editor of *Analog*. He demanded of his writers that their stories must deal with mentally super-powered mutants who were always benevolent and often rose to a position of power. 'The Golden Man' was Dick's response to these plot diktats. "I intended to show that the mutants might not be good, at least for the rest of mankind, for us 'ordinaries' and [they may] not be in charge, but sniping at us as a bandit would, a feral mutant who potentially would do us more harm than good." That approach did not endear Dick to Campbell: "This was specifically the view of psionic mutants that Campbell loathed, and the theme in fiction that he refused to publish… so my story appeared in *If*!"

Dick believed the idea that mutants would be a benevolent, misunderstood and persecuted minority who would one day rise to power was a fantasy which reflected a kind of wish-fulfilment for deluded science fiction fans. Dick commented, "As far as I was concerned, for psionic mutants to rule us would be to put the fox in charge of the hen house…"

The movie of 'The Golden Man' began life with writer Gary Goldman. "After failing to get the rights to 'Paycheck', which I had pursued, I adopted an indirect approach in allying with Jason Koornick, the creator of philipkdick.com, whose site was being acquired by the Dick estate as their official web site," explained Goldman, in an interview for this book. "In return, the estate offered Jason an option on a short story of his choice. We formed a partnership. I advised him to choose 'The Golden Man' and agreed to adapt it. To me, the key to a successful adaptation is to retain Phil Dick's subversive questioning of all assumptions. You have to embrace his ideas, not run from them."

For Goldman, adapting this story was different to tackling 'We Can Remember It For You Wholesale' or 'The Minority Report'. "'The Golden Man' was different from my earlier adaptations in that it's main interest to me was technical and cinematic: the opportunity to present on screen a new way of seeing and storytelling, based on the precognitive ability of the hero."

Another fan of Philip K. Dick's writing was enlisted to star in the movie, a development which at first led to problems. "Nicolas Cage had apparently been looking for a Phil Dick project. I worked with his company, Saturn Films, in the early stages of the development. We had some friendly creative differences, but since I controlled the material, I was the one who left. When I finished the screenplay on spec, I sent it back to them, and they liked what I had done. And we teamed up again." At the time of writing, the screenplay was credited to Gary Goldman and Jason Koornick, and both were also executive producers on the film.

Director Lee Tamahori told web site Sci Fi Wire that he and Cage, who was also producing along with his Saturn Films partner Norm Golightly, were still defining their approach to the film. "I know that sounds elusive, but this is a very tricky project," he said. "This movie is about time shifting, and time shifting in movies has always been tricky. Nic Cage and I are both looking for a new approach. We're looking for something that is visually arresting as well as physically fascinating and believable. The technique can wear itself out and become boring very fast. We don't want to turn this into a science fiction movie without the science fiction." With Julianne Moore also joining the cast, *Next* entered production in March 2006, aiming for a 2007 release. ■

Top: *The original story first appeared in* If *in April 1954.*

Above: *'The Golden Man' collection was also published in this US edition.*

SALES PITCH

The ones that got away: many options have been taken out on Philip K. Dick properties over the years and some intriguing projects almost made it to the screen...

"The basic tool for the manipulation of reality is the manipulation of words. If you can control the meaning of words, you can control the people who must use the words." — Philip K. Dick, 'How to Build a Universe That Doesn't Fall Apart Two Days Later' (written 1978), published in *I Hope I Shall Arrive Soon* (1985)

For every film adapted from a novel or short story by Philip K. Dick, there have been many others that did not reach the screen, a secret alternate history of the Philip K. Dick adaptations that might have been. Although *Blade Runner* was less than successful at the box office, the year after it was released saw several movie options taken out on Dick's work. It seemed that the floodgates had finally been opened for others to option Dick's tales of mind-bending alternate realities and attempt to bring them to the screen.

The 1970 novel *A Maze of Death*, in which a group of colonists experience weird happenings on the uninhabited planet Delmark-O, was optioned by a young Hollywood director/producer named C. Jerry Kutner in 1983. *A Maze of Death* is closely related to *Ubik* and *Eye in the Sky*, in that the protagonists discover their perceived reality is not what's really going on at all.

Dick himself noted, "*A Maze of Death* is a really desperate attempt to come up with something new. In no way is it new! It repeats familiar things, with reality versus irreality. That's the last gasp of those things that had become my stock-in-trade. At that point I couldn't go on. I had exhausted all the possibilities in that type of thing..." In the case of *A Maze of Death*, the colonists are in fact trapped upon a damaged rocket ship, collectively dreaming up the 'reality' they are experiencing as a device to keep them sane while awaiting rescue, a rescue which may never come. Kutner had produced one previous film in 1977 (*In MacArthur Park*, written and directed by Bruce Schwartz), and later became a writer and web curator for the surrealist art of Richard M. Powers, and a producer on the Traci Lords-starring movie *Object of Desire*. *A Maze of Death*, however, never found its way out of development hell.

There was also an active option on *The Man in the High Castle* in 1983, taken out by hopeful LA-based producer Charles Swartz, who wanted to make the movie, but lacked the finance to even develop the project. Dick had found *High Castle* to be one of his easiest novels to write and it had found much acclaim. "It required no outline, no plot structure in advance," he admitted to Gregg Rickman in an interview. "It just happened. The book had just built up in me."

The year 1983 also saw *Flow My Tears, The Policeman Said* attract the interest of influential blues musician and DJ Alexis Korner and his one-time producer Del Taylor, through their company Monsoon Management. The pair was hoping to mount a UK-based production of the novel, adapting it to turn Jason Taverner from a TV personality into a rock star, a milieu Korner was more familiar with. It appears no agreement was reached on actually taking an option, and Korner died the following year in 1984. In early 1991, a further option would be sought for *Flow My Tears* by a pair of producers, Dale Rosenbloom and John Alan Simon, who had a shopping list of Dick projects they wished to option. (Simon's name will crop up again in this history of unmade Philip K. Dick projects.) The book was one Dick was very close to: "*Flow My Tears* was written in 1970, the worst period of my life. Nancy had left me while I was working on the book, and I finished the book, even though she had taken our daughter and left. The theme of the book became autobiographical because I was suffering so much from that loss..." *The Cosmic Puppets*, Dick's first published novel, was also in negotiation for an option in 1983 by a wannabe film-maker called John Reynolds, but nothing seems to have come of that one...

It seems that 1983 was something of a banner year for Dick, with the believed lost self-penned screenplay for *Ubik* being rediscovered among his papers, and *Blade Runner* winning the Hugo Award for Best Science Fiction Movie of 1982.

***Above:** A Hungarian cover for* A Maze of Death, *one of the Philip K. Dick films that got away.*

The dawning of 1984 may have been feared by readers of the work of George Orwell, but for fans of Philip K. Dick it not only marked the beginning of the posthumous boom in the release of his unpublished works (both *Puttering About in a Small Land* and *The Man Whose Teeth Were All Exactly Alike* made their début), but also saw a continued growing interest in optioning Dick's work for film.

The estate, at the time administered by Paul Williams, who'd written the influential 1974 *Rolling Stone* profile of Dick, was in serious negotiations with the US Public Broadcasting Service (PBS) for a television movie based on Dick's 1953 short story 'The Defenders', previously adapted for *X Minus One* on NBC radio. Producer Geoffrey Haines-Stiles had previously adapted Ursula K. LeGuin's reality-twisting novel *The Lathe of Heaven* for TV in an acclaimed production. By 1984, Haines-Stiles had been trying to persuade PBS to adapt Dick's story for around five years, and had explained to Dick's literary agent Russ Galen that he was deeply committed to bringing the story to the screen. By the end of the year, PBS had closed a deal with the estate and a first draft screenplay was written. Discussion had progressed as far as changing the title, so the new show would not be confused with the 1960s US TV courtroom drama *The Defenders*. By the beginning of 1988, though, all development on the project had halted, so the option was cancelled by the Dick estate.

Dick's 1955 short story 'The Mold of Yancy' featured a concept which an anonymous film producer was interested in optioning towards the end of 1984: what if a electronic human image was so convincing (as portrayed in the Al Pacino-starring movie *S1m0ne*) that it could be manipulated into successfully functioning as the political leader of an unsuspecting nation? This is an example where the details of the actual Dick story were not required, but an idea featured in the story proved attractive as the basis for a film. The notion that a population could be led by a perfect, but non-existent, political leader was

Above: The Finnish cover for The Man in the High Castle. *The novel was considered for film treatment in 1983.*

certainly echoed in much of Dick's fiction. Dick himself claimed that the character of Yancy was based on Eisenhower. "During his reign we were all worrying about the man-in-the-grey-flannel-suit problem; we feared that the entire country was turning into one person and a whole lot of clones," said Dick in 1978. "I liked this story enough to use it as the basis for my novel *The Penultimate Truth*, in particular the part where everything the government tells you is a lie. Watergate, of course, bore the basic idea of that story out..."

Dick himself was aware of an attempt to get a film of *The Penultimate Truth* under way in the early 1980s, just before his death. "The guy involved is [Vernon] Zimmerman," said Dick. Zimmerman was a writer, director and producer active in the 1970s and 1980s. "He did *Fade to Black*," noted Dick, citing Zimmerman's 1980 film about an obsessive film fan embarking on a killing spree. "I haven't heard from them in a long time, [so] I don't think they're going to pursue it. They have no money. I think it would make a great film."

While those initial approaches seemingly did not progress, in 1989 *M*A*S*H* writer Gary Markowitz (who also later contributed to sci-fi TV shows *ALF* and *Eerie, Indiana* and went on to create several TV series) attempted to option not only 'The Mold of Yancy' but also Dick's 1964 novel *The Penultimate Truth* (which as Dick admitted, featured the same central idea). It's possible Markowitz was also behind one of the earlier approaches, but none of them resulted in a film reaching cinemas. By late 1992, the Markowitz options had expired, though apparently negotiations continued, so this film may yet eventually emerge.

Clans of the Alphane Moon is a true Dickian potboiler, published in 1964. Surprisingly, this tale of the inmates of a lunar mental hospital who revolt and form a functioning society in which Dick parodies the mental heath caste system (naming his groupings after paranoids, schizophrenics, depressives and obsessive-compulsives among others), was the subject of a concerted attempt to make a film. According to Dick, *Clans of the Alphane Moon* was "a labour of love. The story of the survival value of various forms of psychosis... Did they have any utility? It seemed to me they did, if not in our culture, in other cultures perhaps..."

During 1986, Gary Walkow, a director on the spoof detective TV series *Sledge Hammer*, obtained an option on *Clans of the Alphane Moon*. By the middle of 1987, Walkow had developed a screenplay and was trying to raise finance through his company Frolix Productions (named after Dick's *Our Friends from Frolix 8*). By then, Walkow had co-written and directed *The Trouble With Dick* (see Chapter 17), an indirect homage to Philip K. Dick, showing he was serious about getting a Dickian project underway. Walkow appealed through the Philip K. Dick Society Newsletter for investors in his project, but finance proved to be a continual problem, as it had for so many attempting to mount films based on little-known Philip K. Dick works. By mid-1990, Walkow was a director on short-lived SF comedy TV series *They Came From Outer Space* and the equally short-lived *She-Wolf of London*. At the same time, World Film Services, a New York-based film financier, and Island Pictures expressed an interest in obtaining an option on *Clans of the Alphane Moon*. There's no indication if Walkow (or his screenplay) was still involved in this version. In 1991 the option was confirmed but the film did not materialise, and the novel is not listed by the Dick estate as currently being under option.

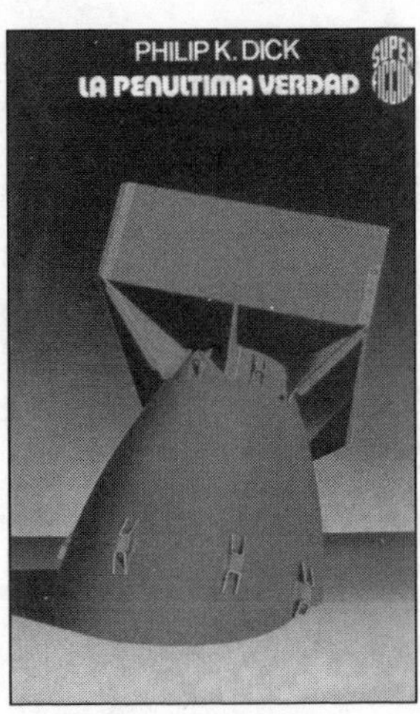

Above: *Dick was aware of plans to film* The Penultimate Truth *(a Spanish cover is shown here).*

Time Out of Joint, Dick's 1959 novel of a dissolving reality behind which is another truth altogether, may seem an odd choice to adapt to film in the twenty-first century. It's certainly very filmic, but so much of this tale of a man living in what he believes to be a perfect 1950s world, only to discover that he's being watched and manipulated by a higher power, already shares much thematically with two key 'phildickian' films of the 1990s: *The Truman Show* and *The Matrix*. However, Warner Bros. has long held an option on the book, which has now been exercised.

Despite being an early novel, one of Dick's obsessions appeared fully formed in *Time Out of Joint*. "I had become obsessed with the idea of fake reality," Dick admitted to Gregg Rickman. "That's a pivotal book, the first novel in which I wrote that the entire world is fake. This was to be essentially the premise of my entire corpus of writing, my underlying premise. The world that we experience is not the real world. It's as simple as that..."

Ragle Gumm is the hero of *Time Out of Joint* who witnesses the breakdown of his reality of 1958 California. A key cinematic moment from the novel could include the disintegration of a soft drink stand before Gumm's eyes, to be replaced by a piece of paper simply stating 'soft drink stand'. Like *The Matrix* or *The Truman Show*, the truth is that Gumm is trapped within a simulation. It is forty years later, and Gumm's actions are being used to influence the outcome of a major war. This observed and monitored 'fake reality' may seem like an old idea now, but was groundbreaking when the novel was published and only became acceptable in cinema during the 1990s, by which time Dick's cinematic star was riding high.

Warner Bros. had originally optioned *Time Out of Joint* in 1987. A screenplay was commissioned — there's no indication of who the writer was, just that a screenplay was completed fairly soon after the initial option. The project was simply listed as "in development" through 1988.

During 1989 *Daily Variety* reported that screenwriter Sam Hamm, who wrote the Tim Burton 1989 *Batman* movie and was then lined up for the sequel *Batman Returns*, had placed a screenplay for *Time Out of Joint* with Guber-Peters, producers of *Batman*. They had a deal at Warner Bros., but were then hired by Sony to run Columbia Pictures, which caused a legal battle between the studios. All of this seems to have killed off the Sam Hamm version of *Time Out of Joint*.

The project was not entirely dead as the 1990s dawned. Warner Bros. maintained their interest and, more importantly, continued to pay out to renew their option. Screenwriter Mike Duncan (who appears to have had no significant credits since) was brought in to rework the Hamm script, but there was still no sign of a director or cast as the decade wore on. By 1992 Duncan was history, but future-*Matrix* producer Joel Silver was attached to the film. To date the movie remains in "active development", but no serious news has emerged from within Warner Bros. for some considerable time. It's possible the success of the similarly themed *The Matrix* and *The Truman Show* has caused the studio to rethink the project, although their success may alternatively have spurred the studio into a

Philip K. Dick
TIME
OUT OF
JOINT
A man's genius
turns the world
into a futuristic
nightmare!

Above: Time Out of Joint *was in development at Warner Bros. for many years.*

new period of development on *Time Out of Joint*, precisely because of its similarities. Such is Hollywood.

As the 1980s gave way to the 1990s and *Total Recall* renewed studios' interest in all things Philip K. Dick, there was another attempt to get some of Dick's work on television. *Logan's Run* author William F. Nolan hoped to include a Philip K. Dick story as part of a horror anthology he was scripting for ABC TV for transmission late in 1990. If Nolan had succeeded that year's *Trilogy of Terror II* TV movie would have included an adaptation of Dick's 1954 short story 'The Father-Thing'. Dick said of this story, "I always had the impression when I was very small that my father was two people, one good, one bad. The good father goes away and the bad father replaces him. I guess many kids have this feeling [but] what if it were so?"

Nolan commented, "In my opinion, the best segment of all would have been my adaptation of Philip K. Dick's 'The Father-Thing', but it got dropped at the last moment and replaced with Richard Matheson's 'Bobbie'. My Dick teleplay was very frightening, but no one ever got a chance to see it."

John Lennon, killed two years before Dick's own untimely death, had long been interested in making a film of the author's *The Three Stigmata of Palmer Eldritch*. (Lennon himself would feature in Dick's *The Transmigration of Timothy Archer*, which opens on the day the musician was shot.) It seems unlikely that Lennon's early interest progressed much beyond talk in interviews (members of the Beatles were also keen on making a film of J. R. R. Tolkien's *The Lord of the Rings* long before Peter Jackson finally did so). Like the Beatles, much of Dick's life and work involved a search for spiritual enlightenment, and *The Three Stigmata of Palmer Eldritch* was one of several books that charted his path. "That was written in connection with my becoming involved in Christianity," said Dick. "Evil was as real a force as good, there was a God and an Anti-God. It's essentially a diabolical novel, in which the 'good' side was Humans and the 'evil' side was [the] deity, like Man being confronted with a murderous God."

There was more serious interest in filming *The Three Stigmata of Palmer Eldritch* in 1990, when the novel was optioned by Vanguard Films. Vanguard was a New York-based independent project packager which enjoyed relationships with Columbia, Act III Productions and Touchstone. The script was to be drafted by TV writer Howard Rodman, but the project soon lost momentum.

A couple of other minor options were taken out early in the 1990s. Following *Confessions D'un Barjo*, another French director expressed an interested in a Philip K. Dick project. Didier Haudepin sought out the rights to film Dick's mainstream novel *Puttering About in a Small Land*. "That wasn't half bad," said Dick of his then-unpublished non-SF novel. "It's about a man who is not as educated as his wife, the story of a guy who is essentially an artisan, a craftsman, a guy who repairs TV sets. His wife is a college graduate. It's the story of how eventually her economic ambitions and her social ambitions and her education undermine his own respect. His self-confidence is so undermined, he's destroyed as a person." Haudepin's paperwork pitching for the rights outlined the film, in fractured

English, as follows: "Coming of age of a man despite his incredulity, through lucid women, at an age when precisely he would think he'd already become an adult." Although the project did not progress, it was further evidence that only the French seem to be interested in making Dick's realist mainstream novels of 1950s life into movies.

At the same time that Gary Goldman optioned 'The Minority Report' in 1992, Universal also optioned the short story 'The Short Happy Life of the Brown Oxford'. While *Minority Report* eventually became a blockbusting Steven Spielberg movie, we're still waiting for 'The Short Happy Life of the Brown Oxford', Universal's option having now lapsed.

Above: Fantasy and Science Fiction *for January 1954 ran 'The Short Happy Life of Brown Oxford'.*

One of the most intriguing unmade Philip K. Dick projects was a Brian Aldiss adaptation of Dick's 1964 novel *Martian Time-Slip*, for a proposed BBC TV mini-series in the 1980s. The novel itself seemed cursed, at least in Dick's eyes. "That was my attempt to escalate to the next level of quality, complexity and value. It was badly received in the marketplace. No hardcover publisher would touch it. I felt it was a very good book, a very serious [and] important book. There was no response, the book just disappeared. It didn't sell many copies..."

The BBC had apparently adapted the novel once before for radio in the 1960s, but sadly little is known about this version. During the mid-1980s a concerted effort was made at the BBC to mount a five-part, 275-minute television mini-series faithfully adapted from Dick's *Martian Time-Slip*. Dick admirer and fellow SF writer Aldiss was involved in adapting the book to TV script form, and the mini-series was set to be produced through his company Avernus.

Aldiss had started by trying to get a movie of Dick's *Martian Time-Slip* underway, and he decided to start at the top of the film-making tree. "I pressed Stanley [Kubrick] to film a novel of Philip K. Dick's I admired, *Martian Time-Slip*," wrote Aldiss in his online movie-making memoirs. "This novel, written in the 1960s, possessed my imagination, not least because I saw how it could be brought up to date without altering the plot structure. Stanley simply swept my suggestion out of the way. No discussion. No time to be wasted."

Below: *Brian Aldiss adapted* Martian Time-Slip *in the mid-1980s.*

That rejection did not put Aldiss off this project, however. "I did not give up on Phil Dick," he wrote. "Dick was a friend and a wonderfully creative man. I wasted much time and effort trying to get *Time-Slip* screened. In that endeavour, I was assisted by Frank Hatherley, an Australian buddy. Frank and I put in a proposal to BBC TV for a televised version of Phil Dick's novel. We met with Michael Wearing, who was then, if memory serves, in charge of Serial Drama. He wanted to be convinced that the idea of humans living on Mars was not fantasy. That serious approach was much to my taste."

To his delight, Aldiss was asked to begin development work. "I wrote Wearing a paper on how we could soon journey to Mars, and what might then happen in the way of terraforming. And of how sectors of Mars might come under the jurisdiction of various United Nations states. Wearing was convinced."

That resulted in a screenplay for this major project being financed by

Above: *The French cover for* Valis, *a novel which may yet find its way to the big screen.*

the BBC. "Frank and I were commissioned to write a screenplay in five parts, fifty-five minutes a part," Aldiss continued. "Two hundred and seventy-five minutes air time! Wow! What luxury! A real spread at last for serious SF, based on psychology rather than gimmickry... We had a good script editor, Susan Hogg, who worked with Wearing. Sue was entirely supportive and never made anything but sensible suggestions."

Although it was not his natural working environment, novelist Aldiss thoroughly enjoyed the challenge of adapting one of Dick's finest novels for the small screen, along with Frank Hatherley. "We delivered an outline of the five parts. Eventually, after long afternoons spent in dusty classrooms, working with a whiteboard, and evenings with a computer, we drew up an outline of the entire thing and put the first episode together. We sent it to Wearing without a qualm."

To the shock of Aldiss and Hatherley, their screenplay was rejected. "Wearing's position in the BBC had altered. We never heard from him directly. We learnt, however, that he was now looking for something with 'contemporary relevance'. As if exploitation were an irrelevance. So yet another cop show went on in our spot."

Although back to square one, Aldiss refused to let his work on *Martian Time-Slip* go to waste. He now had a screenplay that could be used to attract other producers to the project. "We knew we had a terrific drama to offer," claimed Aldiss. He arranged to meet the new head of Paramount in the UK, Ileen Maisel. Discussions went so well that on a subsequent visit to see Maisel, Aldiss and Hatherley were expecting to sign a contract on the project. Picking up a copy of *Variety* en route to the Wardour Street meeting in London, the pair were dismayed to discover that Maisel had been sacked. Her pet project, a film of *Jane Eyre* shot in the UK, had failed at the box office and she'd been replaced. Maisel herself had discovered she'd been fired through reading the same *Variety* story. *Martian Time-Slip* was once again a project in limbo. It was now 1989. Hatherley returned to Australia and Aldiss moved on to write a screen adaptation of his novel *Frankenstein Unbound* for Roger Corman, which resulted in the movie starring Michael Hutchence, John Hurt and Bridget Fonda. Aldiss would go on to work with Kubrick and then Steven Spielberg on an adaptation of his short story 'Super-Toys Last All Summer Long' which eventually became *A.I.: Artificial Intelligence*. Although a film or TV series of *Martian Time-Slip* did not emerge, Aldiss returned to Dick for his 1991 play *Kindred Blood in Kensington Gore: Philip K. Dick in the Afterlife — An Imaginary Conversation*.

Beyond *A Scanner Darkly* and the film version of 'The Golden Man' called *Next* (see Chapter 15) there are several other 'live' Philip K. Dick movie options which could come to fruition over the next few years. One is *Time Out of Joint*, still held by Warner Bros. In addition, there are the novels whose movie rights are currently held by elusive independent producer John Alan Simon.

Simon's sole Hollywood credit is as a producer on the 1994 remake of the Steve McQueen movie *The Getaway*, which starred Kim Basinger and Alec Baldwin. Simon is an industry executive, rather than a creative movie-making producer. He's been involved in the financing and distribution of various movies, including *The Wicker Man*, starring Edward Woodward, *The Haunting of Julia*, with Mia Farrow and Tom Conti, *Basket Case* and *Out of the Blue*, starring and directed by Dennis Hopper. Simon is also president of Discovery Productions (not connected to the Discovery Channel) and was previously a journalist and film critic. He is partnered with Dale Rosenbloom of Rosenbloom Entertainment. Simon's Discovery company has acquired the rights to *Flow My Tears, The Policeman Said*, *Valis* and *Radio Free Albemuth*. Simon himself has written the script for *Flow My Tears* and claims he has done a deal to produce the movie with Paramount Pictures in conjunction with Tom Cruise/Paula Wagner Productions and Oliver Stone's Illusion Entertainment. Simon also claimed to have a 'provisonal purchase agreement' on Dick's self-penned *Ubik* screenplay at one point, but this has been denied by the Philip K. Dick Trust.

***Above:** A French cover for* Radio Free Albemuth, *one of the Dick novels currently under option.*

In an online interview, Simon addressed some of the questions surrounding his options on these three Dick novels. "I'm a huge fan. I started reading PKD back in the 1970s when I was an undergraduate at Harvard. When I read *The Three Stigmata of Palmer Eldritch*, I realised that he was a major, major writer. I've read everything published (and some unpublished stuff)… The definitive PKD movie has yet to be made. The closest in spirit (though not based on PKD) to me is Terry Gilliam's *12 Monkeys*, written by David Peoples."

Simon has developed a script combining *Valis* and *Radio Free Albemuth* into one movie, which makes sense, as one is really an earlier draft of the other. "The script is based at this point almost entirely on *Radio Free Albemuth*. The financiers like the title *Valis* better, so that's the tentative title. Since *Radio Free Albemuth* is essentially the first draft of *Valis*, we ended up with rights to both from the estate of PKD. If *Radio Free Albemuth* is successful, *Valis* the book would form the basis for the sequel to *Valis* the movie. In other words, the story of *Valis* would form the basis for [the movie] *Valis* 2. The script for *Radio Free Albemuth* is very close to the book. There are bound to be changes, but it's my job to make sure the spirit of the book remains intact."

Simon has consistently maintained that this project is in pre-production, with casting agent Mike Fenton (*E.T., Total Recall, The Getaway*) attached. The film is apparently being financed by Charles Fries' Fries Entertainment Group, who partially financed *Screamers*. Simon raises finance for his movies through pre-sales, meaning he sells an unmade film territory-by-territory across the world to raise the budget to then actually make the film.

As for *Flow My Tears*, Simon maintains: "My adaptation was optioned by Paramount for Tom Cruise's production company and I did a re-write under Oliver Stone's supervision." Future announcements on these projects were promised, but to date none of these films have actually commenced production.

Various short stories have been optioned and lapsed in recent years, among them 'Adjustment Team' (still active) and 'King of the Elves'. One thing at least is certain: there will surely be more movies from the work of Philip K. Dick in the future. After all, there are countless imaginative short stories and many brilliant novels yet to be adapted… ■

THE GOLDEN MAN

Philip K. Dick's legacy and influence spreads far beyond the movies adapted from his stories...

"I feel mortality closing in on me. Age is the name of the tune they are playing, age and fatigue. Wow, do I sense it. ... I blame *Blade Runner*; negotiating with them had worn me down. ... I am burned out." — Philip K. Dick, letter to Gregg Rickman, 26 June 1981, reprinted in *Philip K. Dick: In His Own Words.*

The Philip K. Dick business is clearly a good one for movie producers to be in. The irony is, of course, the fact that Dick himself failed to benefit from the fruits of his own imagination. While he struggled through a hand-to-mouth existence, those now selling his stories to the movies and protecting his legacy are able at last to generate a decent income from the work of one of the twentieth century's most imaginative writers.

"The whole phenomenon of Philip K. Dick short stories selling for a lot of money started with *Total Recall*," Dick's long-serving literary agent Russell Galen told *Wired* magazine. It wasn't *Blade Runner* that created the opportunities for Dick's fiction to flourish on the cinema screen, although Ridley Scott's film laid much of the groundwork. It was the millions grossed by *Total Recall* in 1990 that made Hollywood executives sit up and take notice of Philip K. Dick. What they found were thirty-six novels and over 150 short stories packed with brain-warping ideas, any one of which could form the basis of a high-octane action thriller given a respectable edge by actually featuring complex philosophical ideas at its core. Over the next fifteen years, Hollywood gingerly stuck its toes into the Philip K. Dick business, beginning with action movies like *Screamers*, but eventually creating more thoughtful films truer to Dick's ideas, such as *A Scanner Darkly*. Over the decade-and-a-half between *Total Recall* and *A Scanner Darkly*, Philip K. Dick became the most adapted SF author in cinema history.

The new Hollywood respect for Philip K. Dick's work was sealed when Tom Cruise and Steven Spielberg took on *Minority Report*. From Gary Goldman's initial version of the story as a potential sequel to *Total Recall*, to its very changed appearance on screen, the fact that Hollywood titans like Cruise and Spielberg were attracted to Dick's ideas was enough to guarantee that his remaining fiction would be heavily mined by idea-starved studios, writers and directors out to create entertainment that is smarter than the average summer blockbuster.

"I think what appeals to Hollywood is the idea of a high concept in Phil Dick's works," noted Mark Steensland, director of the documentary *The Gospel According to Philip K. Dick*, in a feature in the *Seattle-Post Intelligencer*. "These things can be summed up in a one-line pitch." The fact that most of Dick's complex ideas and stories can be reduced to an intriguing one-liner — cop sees crimes before they're committed (*Minority Report*), cop falls

Left: *The adaptation that started it all. The reissued book that Dick insisted upon, complete with movie logo.*

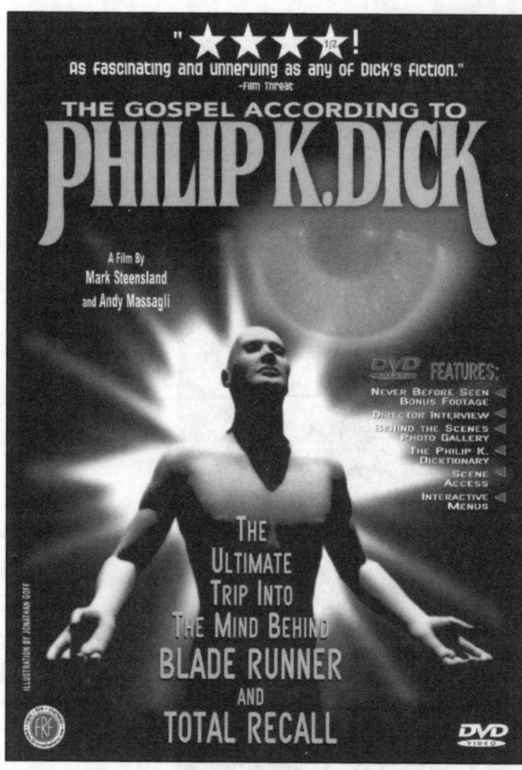

"★★★★1/2!
As fascinating and unnerving as any of Dick's fiction."
-Film Threat
THE GOSPEL ACCORDING TO
PHILIP K. DICK
A Film By
Mark Steensland
and Andy Massagli
DVD FEATURES:
Never Before Seen Bonus Footage
Director Interview
Behind the Scenes Photo Gallery
The Philip K. Dicktionary
Scene Access
Interactive Menus
The Ultimate Trip Into The Mind Behind
BLADE RUNNER
AND
TOTAL RECALL
DVD VIDEO

***Above:** Mark Steensland and Andy Massagli's documentary feature explores the life and work of Philip K. Dick.*

in love with android he's hunting (*Blade Runner*), murderous robots evolve to look and act just like the humans they're battling (*Screamers*), memory implants of a fake adventure reveal the existence of a real one… or do they? (*Total Recall*) — has made them utterly accessible to those in Hollywood with the ability to greenlight a project. Ironically, that has often meant the core idea being taken and a Hollywood action movie being built around it, while the true depth of Dick's analysis of these ideas is neglected.

"It's very difficult to be true to Phil Dick and make a Hollywood movie," noted Gary Goldman. For Goldman, Dick's imagined worlds and the real world have converged to such an extent that Hollywood filmmakers can see in his fiction a relevancy to today that may have escaped his original readers in the 1950s and 1960s. "Phil understood the world better than most sci-fi writers," Goldman said in an interview for this book. "So his vision of the future is still relevant. Science has actually gone in the direction he imagined: virtual reality, altered states, simulations, artificial intelligence. Phil questioned everything that Hollywood is trying to affirm. If you fight Phil's ideas, the movie based on his story is unlikely to hold together. So you need a subversive director who isn't afraid of ideas and who is strong enough to defy the studio, which will try to take all interesting ideas (or all ideas altogether) out of the movie."

Despite this tendency to take Dick's smart ideas and build dumb movies around them, *Paycheck* star Ben Affleck believes that movies based on Dick's work have something extra to offer. "I've always been a fan of Philip K. Dick, both his writings and the movie adaptations. They're big-budget movies for smart people," he told *Wired*.

At the heart of most of Dick's tales is the 'human factor'. They may feature strange technology, even stranger worlds and events, but at their core is the reaction of a simple everyman to these events. The mechanics, repairmen and salesmen of his short stories and novels engage with the counterfeit worlds they face. In the movies, these meek figures who rise to a challenge become Arnold Schwarzenegger and Tom Cruise: buffed up Hollywood heroes who cinema audiences don't doubt will succeed…

This is a Hollywood-style change to the core of his work that Dick would not have appreciated. "You would have to kill me and prop me up in the seat of my car with a smile painted on my face to get me to go near Hollywood," said Dick in a 1980 interview, before his *Blade Runner* experiences changed his view of the movie-making machine for the better. A life-long movie fan, he would secretly have been overjoyed at any movie adaptations of his work (whatever their various failings) and he would certainly have enjoyed the income that such movies could have generated for him.

The 'cult' of Philip K. Dick that flourished post-*Blade Runner* reached far and wide beyond movies, although it was in cinemas that Dick's ideas were most regularly to be exploited. The author himself featured in many magazine cover stories over the years, from *The New York Times Book Review* to *The New Republic* as his work was reassessed; his later novel *Valis* became an opera performed at the Pompidou Centre in Paris; stage productions of his work multiplied, prime among them being the Brian Aldiss' low key show *Kensington Blood in Kindred Gore*, Geoff Ryman's various productions of *The Transmigration of Timothy Archer* and the Mabou Mines professional mounting of *Flow My Tears, The Policeman Said*; while many previously unpublished works joined the re-issues of the SF classics on bookshelves worldwide.

The *Valis* opera would have amused Dick — a huge classical music and opera aficionado himself — and the fact that his influence has also resulted in several bands naming themselves or their songs after people, places and concepts from his work would also surely have brought a wry smile to his face. From Phil Oakey of the Human League basing the track 'Circus of Death' on "the devolving world portrayed in *Ubik*", to a band named Chew-Z, after the drug in *The Three Stigmata of Palmer Eldritch*, and Philadelphia-based The Bunnydrums releasing an album called 'PKD' in 1983, Dick's presence popped up in the most unusual places.

The author had written himself as a fictional character in his own work, notably in *Valis* and *Radio Free Albemuth*, so it wouldn't have surprised him that he became a character in other writers' fictions. From Michael Bishop's uncannily PKD-like *The Secret Ascension* (later retitled *Philip K. Dick is Dead, Alas*) through David Bischoff's *Philip K. Dick High* to the short stories 'The Transmigration of Philip K.' by Michael Swanwick, Richard Lupoff's 'The Digital Wristwatch of Philip K. Dick' and Thomas M. Disch's 'The Girl with the Vita-Gel Hair', Dick became the SF author's favourite SF author! Dick's life — or at least the 1974 'vision of God' events — were even the subject of a Robert Crumb comic strip entitled *The Religious Experience of Philip K. Dick*. Dick is seen as the godfather of the 'cyberpunk' literary movement begun in the early-1980s by William Gibson's novel *Neuromancer*. Even the architect Philippe Starck claims that his work displays a conscious Philip K. Dick influence…

As well as the films directly adapted from Dick's work, there are other curiosities out there, from the appearance of frustrated science fiction author Dick Kendred (Tom Villard) in Gary Walkow's 1986 film *The Trouble With Dick* to the fan-produced documentary *The Gospel According to Philip K. Dick*, in which Dick appears as an animated character.

The Trouble With Dick sees unsuccessful SF writer Dick Kendred try to follow his publisher's (Mr Samsa, a Kafka reference) advice to write something "new and unusual, like everyone else is selling." Sub-letting a room, the would-be author finds his time and energy sapped by the unwanted advances of the mother and daughter from whom he's renting, while the boundaries between his mundane reality and the world of the fictions he is writing begin to break down. Billed as a 'Frolix Production', the film sees Kendred reading Dick's *The Zap Gun* at one point.

It's actually not a bad film, and it improves as it develops, but it really has very little to do with Philip K. Dick directly. SF fans will spot interesting in-jokes, like a phone call from "Arthur in Sri Lanka" being a reference to *2001* author Arthur C. Clarke, and the

phrase "See you next Wednesday" being a reference to a line featured in many John Landis movies, including *An American Werewolf in London*. The SF B-movie pastiche featured throughout looks little worse than most of *Screamers*, and features the interesting concept of a sentient, talking gun. The other main characters are a pretentious artist type who litters her speech with French phrases, a reckless schoolgirl and a repressed scientist. Later moments certainly show some flair from director Gary Walkow, such as the 'word room' fever dream, the flour montage and the sequences when, as his reality crumbles, Kendred watches himself on TV, or sees himself referred to in TV ads. His psychotic break sees him hallucinate the three women in his life as threatening alien life forms. By the end, both Kendred and the character he's created, Lars (named after a character in *The Zap Gun*), escape their captivity. The film won the Grand Prize at the US Film Festival in 1987 and was nominated for the Critic's Award at the Deauville Film Festival. As mentioned in the previous chapter, Walkow had serious ambitions to follow this project with a movie of Dick's *Clans of the Alphane Moon*, but nothing ever came of it.

Other productions have directly referenced their use of Dick's ideas by closely naming characters after the author. The *RoboCop* TV mini-series *Prime Directives* saw actor Geraint Wyn Davies play David Kaydick, the villain of the piece. An episode of *The 4400*, the hit TV series about returnee abductees resuming their lives, featured an Ira Steven Behr-scripted episode called *Life Interrupted* in its second season. As the main character finds himself trapped in an alternate reality where the abduction of 4400 random people did not happen, he encounters a character called Kendrick, an amalgamation of Dick's middle and last names. It's a nice tip-of-the-hat from Behr to those who recognise his inspiration.

Beyond the films made directly from his novels and short stories, the speculative fiction of Philip K. Dick has clearly influenced many movies made post-*Blade Runner*. From the mid-1980s, just as Dick's fiction was being widely re-issued, fake realities proliferated in the cinema. David Cronenberg's *Videodrome*, a tale of technology invading the body and the mind, might have been more visceral than any of Dick's writings, but the disjointed reality that Max Renn (James Woods) experiences is very like those written about by Dick. Similarly, as 'Rowdy' Roddy Piper and Keith David face an alien invasion in John Carpenter's *They Live*, they have to break through the veil that has been drawn over the perceptions of mankind (by wearing groovy sunglasses!).

Into the 1990s, there were other Dick-like movies released, including Terry Gilliam's time-travelling conundrum *12 Monkeys*, which sees the characters played by Bruce Willis and Brad Pitt cause the very incident they had set out to avert (drawing heavily from Chris Marker's 1962 short *La Jetee*, which in turn owes a direct debt to Dick). Adrian Lyne's *Jacob's Ladder* saw Tim Robbins' Vietnam vet hovering between two worlds, unsure which — if any — is real. A 1995 TV movie drawn from Kurt Vonnegut's short story, *Harrison Bergeron* posits a future often seen in Dick's fiction, one of surveillance and mind-control where everyone is moulded to be mediocre. David Fincher's *The Game* saw the creation of a counterfeit world in the real world, as Michael Douglas finds himself caught up in a series of reality-manipulations which push him over the edge — literally. *Gattaca* tackled genetic manipulation and societal control, again favourite themes of Dick's.

Opposite: *The world of his cheesy SF stories comes to life for frustrated author Dick Kendred in* The Trouble With Dick.

The Dickian theme most often exploited by mainstream cinema has been that of the fake reality, as in *The Game*. *Dark City, The Truman Show, eXistenZ, The Thirteenth Floor*, and *The Matrix* all explore this theme to varying degrees, from *The Matrix*'s all encompassing computer-created false world in which humanity is trapped, through to *The Truman Show*'s creation of an ideal world for one individual, watched by millions more as entertainment. Cronenberg's *eXistenZ* is a replay of *Videodrome* to a large extent, exploring the attractions and repulsions of an accessible fake world to which characters can retreat or escape… *The Thirteenth Floor* is like *The Matrix* in that its inhabitants are not aware that their world is false to begin with, but the film does play with layers of reality in a way that Dick would have recognised as his own.

Before *Minority Report*, Tom Cruise was the driving force behind *Vanilla Sky*, the Hollywood remake of Spanish movie *Abre los ojos* (*Open Your Eyes*), which sees a traumatised magazine publisher alternating between two possible realities. *Equilibrium* and *Cypher* are action movies set in worlds familiar to readers of Dick's fiction, so much so that they may as well have been adaptations of Dick's work.

The memory manipulations of *Eternal Sunshine of the Spotless Mind*, in which Jim Carrey and Kate Winslet face the consequences of using a service that can selectively delete memories, and the identity dilemmas of *Being John Malkovich* mine the weirder edges of Dick's oeuvre (both scripted by Charlie Kaufman, who'd made an attempt at scripting *A Scanner Darkly*), as do oddball movies like *Donnie Darko, Code 46*, and *Man Facing Southeast*. Even *Memento*, with its backwards storytelling and questioning of memory recalls Dick's novel *Counter-Clock World*. Even this lengthy list only begins to scratch the surface of Philip K. Dick's influence on the high concept movies filling multiplexes today.

As well as influencing future movies, Dick actually managed to make a few accurate future predictions in his work. Dick rarely put dates to his fiction, suffering from the science fiction writer's perennial fear of redundancy when the idea comes to pass sooner, or the year stated flies by with no sign of the prediction coming true. Those stories and novels which are precisely dated are now anachronistic. So, when Dick was asked specifically to look ahead for *The Book of Predictions* in 1981, it is amazing to see what he got right (among much else that was wrong). Dick said that by 1985 there would be a "titanic nuclear accident in the USSR or United States, resulting in the shutting down of all nuclear power plants." The Chernobyl disaster came in 1986, though nuclear power stations are still firmly with us. The world of the Internet, well entrenched by 1995, was a glimmer in Dick's fertile imagination.

Above: *Replicants of a different kind... Dick's work has even inspired these Japanese action figures: 'Android Hunter' and 'Android 001'.*

However, by 1989 Dick saw the creation of "one vast metacomputer as a central source of information available to the entire world", which is a pretty good description of the World Wide Web. Dick's fiction often featured computers and computer-driven devices as commonplace items, so his view of the world of 1995 featuring "computer use by ordinary citizens" which would transform the public "from passive viewers of TV into mentally alert, highly trained information-processing experts" was not so unusual. Dick also claimed that by 1993 "an artificial life form will be produced in a lab." Some would claim that computer viruses or other artificial intelligences would constitute just such a life form, but what about the infamous clone Dolly the Sheep, created/born in 1997? Dick saw the end of the USSR by 2010 (it happened in 1989 with the removal of the Berlin wall), and while some might espouse a science fiction explanation for AIDS, Dick feared that "an alien virus, brought back by an interplanetary ship, will decimate the population of Earth." Of course, there's much Dick got plain wrong. He predicted particle-beam weapons by 1983, the elimination of the need for oil by 1984, colonies on the moon and Mars by 1997 and time travel by 2010. Which just goes to prove that making specific predictions can be a frustratingly hit-and-miss business, no matter how much of a 'pre-cog' Dick might appear in his writings.

Hollywood has long used ideas from literature as the basis for movies, often not giving due credit to the source material. Is Ian Holm's Ash in *Alien*, the company man later revealed to the rest of the *Nostromo* crew to be an android, anything more than a misplaced Philip K. Dick character? What is the fake consensual reality of *The Matrix* but a Philip K. Dick counterfeit world, thrown up onto the big screen wholesale? The idea, revealed in the sequels, that mankind would willingly submit to this subjugation by machine is also very 'dickian'. Would *Eternal Sunshine of the Spotless Mind* have even been possible without the groundwork laid in popular culture by Dick and the ideas spun off from his fiction?

After all, aren't movies themselves a form of alternate reality? J.P. Telotte, Professor of Literature, Communication and Culture at Georgia Tech, regards cinema as "fundamentally a kind of time machine, a device that effectively freed both its audience and its early users from a conventional sense of place and time." Going to the movies, audiences are essentially transported into the alternate reality conjured up by a director. Where some of the movies based on Philip K. Dick's work have failed is in capturing the author's ideas beyond the high concept of the one-line pitch. "As a writer I'd like to see some of my ideas, not just the special effects of my ideas, used," said Dick in reaction to the early footage he saw of *Blade Runner*.

While we will certainly see further adaptations of Dick's work in the cinema, it is to be hoped they include more films like *Confessions d'un Barjo* and *A Scanner Darkly*, alongside the action epics such as *Total Recall* and *Next* (there is also surely scope for a biopic chronicling Dick's own turbulent, wild life in the style of one of his novels). "The fundamental elements of his stories are ageless, and his works translate into film in ways those of other best-selling authors don't," noted one of Dick's protégés, James Blaylock, in *The San Francisco Chronicle*.

Below: *Different countries had varying takes on the Blade Runner tie-in edition. This one is Yugoslavian.*

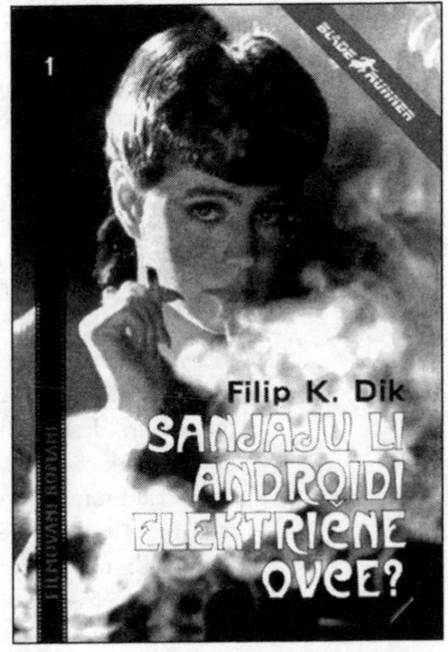

Philip K. Dick often feared that his reality was not all there was: he'd have been even more amazed by a future reality in which he was such a central character, in literature, in the movies and as a fictional hero in disparate fictions created by others. Would he laugh or be embarrassed by the fact that college courses teach both his writings as fiction to be studied, and as key philosophical texts to be investigated alongside Descartes and Sartre? "He would never have been that Hollywood thing, ever," claimed Dick's daughter Laura, one of the custodians of his estate. "The thought of the general public knowing who he was… he would have been out of his mind." He would, though, have had no choice but to accept it. As Dick himself wrote: "Reality is that which, when you stop believing in it, doesn't go away."

In 2005, Philip K. Dick returned to life. That June's NextFest exposition in Chicago saw Dick return to his birthplace — as an android. In a delicious, perfect irony, artificial intelligence scientists from Hanson Robotics recreated a lifelike replicant of Philip K. Dick that was able to answer questions and engage in conversations with fascinated visitors. It was as if the robot Dick had walked out of his novel *We Can Build You*. The head, modelled after photos of the author, relied on thirty-six servo-motors to mimic facial expressions, and was coated in a skin-like polymer cheekily dubbed 'Frubber'. Motion trackers allowed the fake PKD to make eye contact with visitors, while artificial intelligence and speech software enabled the android to participate in seemingly sophisticated conversations. "It invents new ideas using a mathematical model of Philip K. Dick's mind extracted from his vast body of writing," claimed David Hanson of Hanson Robotics. Calling the creation a "robotic portrait" of their father, Dick's daughters Isa and Laura supported the offbeat project. They admitted that this "memorial" to their father "may sound like something from a long lost Philip K. Dick manuscript, but it is reality." The project's instigator had consulted with the Dick estate, winning their backing. "We anticipate that the robot may stir some controversy because it breaks ground using the human form. We consider the project to be artistically ground-breaking and innovative, as well as a powerful tribute to him and his work." The arrival of 'robo-Phil' is one of the weirdest happenings in the counterfeit worlds of Philip K. Dick, and it is one that the author, never entirely sure what was real and what wasn't in his daily life, may have been thrown by. Returning to the world he'd left (but had increasingly influenced in the years after his death) in android form would perhaps have seemed to Philip K. Dick to be a kind of inevitable apotheosis.

Dick's legacy is now under the control of the three people who run the literary estate. They are his two daughters Isa Dick-Hackett and Laura Leslie, and their half-brother Christopher. Between them, they consider all requests for movie rights and control how Dick's material is used, with expert guidance from longtime literary agent Russell Galen and recently retained Hollywood agent Michael Siegel. Following Dick's own example, they are happy to see the original novels re-issued in movie tie-in editions, but are unwilling to allow short stories, which have been expanded in order to be turned into movie, or scripts which have departed significantly from their source novel, to be re-novelised. In *Valis*, the character of 'Phil Dick' is told that the government has plans to write and publish novels in his name after his death, expressing one of the author's own fears. In this respect, Isa, Laura and Chris are only continuing to honour their father's wishes over *Do Androids Dream of Electric Sheep?*, the movie adaptation that started it all…

In talking about the nature of death, which came all too soon for him, Philip K. Dick even used movies as an analogy. "If you go see a movie, eventually they flash a sign up on the screen saying 'The End'. Did you expect the movie to go on forever? The movie has a time-span in which it unfolds… Death is not the tragedy. Untimely death is the tragedy. There's no such thing as timely death, not really." Isa and Laura were profoundly affected by the success of *Minority Report*, and belatedly woke up to the worth in their father's work. "We didn't realise what a phenomenon our Dad was," Laura told *Wired* magazine. "He's going to live forever. He transcended death." The sisters had little idea of the effect their father's philosophically questioning work could have in the world of mainstream blockbuster movies. "That was just my dad," said Laura. "The concept of alternate realities — I thought that was the way everybody talked…" Thanks to the steady stream of adaptations over the years since *Blade Runner*, and the ever-increasing number of Hollywood movies which owe a big debt to Dick's work, his ideas of false humans, fake realities and counterfeit worlds have become commonplace.

We all talk like Philip K. Dick now. ■

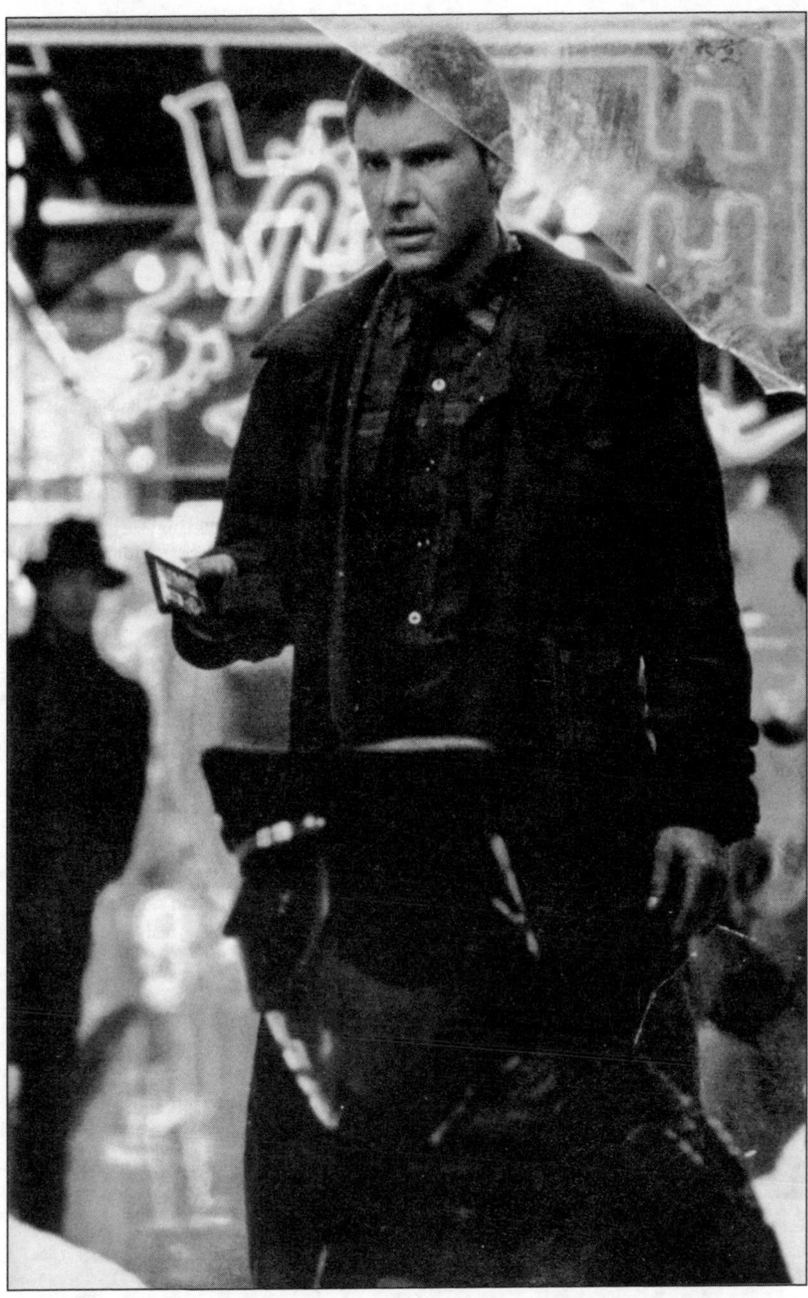

Left: Blade Runner: *The first and, for many, still the best movie adaptation of Philip K. Dick's work.*

APPENDIX

1. FILMS ADAPTED FROM THE WORKS OF PHILIP K. DICK

***Blade Runner* (1982)**
US Release Date: 25 June 1982
Directed by Ridley Scott
Writing credits Philip K. Dick (novel, *Do Androids Dream of Electric Sheep?*); Hampton Fancher; David Peoples
Cast: Harrison Ford (Rick Deckard), Rutger Hauer (Roy Batty), Sean Young (Rachael), Edward James Olmos (Gaff), M. Emmet Walsh (Bryant), Daryl Hannah (Pris), William Sanderson (J. F. Sebastian), Brion James (Leon), Joe Turkel (Tyrell), Joanna Cassidy (Zhora), James Hong (Chew), Morgan Paull (Holden)
Producers: Michael Deeley (producer), Hampton Fancher (executive producer), Brian Kelly (executive producer), Jerry Perenchio (co-executive producer), Ivor Powell (associate producer), Run Run Shaw (associate producer), Bud Yorkin (co-executive producer), Ridley Scott (co-producer)
Original Music: Vangelis
Cinematography: Jordan Cronenweth
Production Design: Lawrence G. Paull
Art Direction: David Snyder
Costume Design: Michael Kaplan, Charles Knode

***Total Recall* (1990)**
US Release Date: 1 June 1990
Directed by Paul Verhoeven
Writing credits: Philip K. Dick (short story, 'We Can Remember It For You Wholesale', wrongly credited onscreen as Phillip K. Dick), Ronald Shusett (screen story) & Dan O'Bannon (screen story) and Jon Povill (screen story), Ronald Shusett (screenplay) & Dan O'Bannon (screenplay) and Gary Goldman (screenplay)
Cast: Arnold Schwarzenegger (Douglas Quaid/Hauser), Rachel Ticotin (Melina), Sharon Stone (Lori), Ronny Cox (Vilos Cohaagen), Michael Ironside (Richter), Marshall Bell (George/Kuato), Roy Brocksmith (Dr. Edgemar), Robert Picardo (Voice of Johnnycab)
Producers: Buzz Feitshans (producer), Robert Fentress (associate producer), Mario Kassar (executive producer), Elliot Schick (associate producer), Ronald Shusett (producer), Andrew G. Vajna (executive producer)
Original Music: Jerry Goldsmith, Bruno Louchouarn (songs)
Cinematography: Jost Vacano
Production Design: William Sandell
Art Direction: José Rodríguez Granada, James Tocci
Costume Design: Erica Edell Phillips

***Confessions d'un Barjo* (1992)**
France Release Date: 13 May 1992
Directed by Jérôme Boivin
Writing credits Jacques Audiard, Jérôme Boivin, Philip K. Dick (novel, *Confessions of a Crap Artist*)
Cast Richard Bohringer (Charles), Anne Brochet (Fanfan), Hippolyte Girardot (Barjo), Consuelo De Haviland (Madame Hermelin), Renaud Danner (Michel), Nathalie Boutefeu (Gwen), Jac Berrocal (Mage Gerardini), El Kebir (Le gardien de l'usine)
Producers: Françoise Galfré (executive producer), Patrick Godeau (producer)
Original Music: Hugues Le Bars
Cinematography: Jean-Claude Larrieu
Production Design: Dominique Maleret
Costume Design: Caroline de Vivaise

***Screamers* (1995)**
US Release Date: 26 January 1996
Directed by Christian Duguay
Writing credits: Philip K. Dick (short story, 'Second Variety'), Dan O'Bannon (screenplay) and Miguel Tejada-Flores (screenplay)
Cast: Peter Weller (Hendricksson), Roy Dupuis (Becker), Jennifer Rubin (Jessica), Andy Lauer (Ace Jefferson), Charles Powell (Ross), Ron White (Elbarak), Michael Caloz (David), Liliana Komorowska (Landowska), Jason Cavalier (Leone), Leni Parker (Cpl. McDonald), Bruce Boa (Secretary Green)
Producers: Franco Battista (producer), Josée Bernard (co-executive producer), Tom Berry (producer), Charles W. Fries (executive producer), Antony I. Ginnane (supervising producer), Masao Takiyama (co-executive producer), Stefan Wodoslawsky (associate producer)

Original Music: Normand Corbeil
Cinematography: Rodney Gibbons
Production Design: Perri Gorrara
Art Direction: Michael Devine
Costume Design: Trixi Rittenhouse

***Impostor* (2002)**
US Release Date: 4 January 2002
Directed by Gary Fleder
Writing credits: Philip K. Dick (short story, 'Impostor'), Scott Rosenberg (adaptation), Caroline Case (screenplay) and Ehren Kruger (screenplay) and David Twohy (screenplay)
Cast: Gary Sinise (Spencer Olham), Madeleine Stowe (Maya Olham), Vincent D'Onofrio (Maj. D.H. Hathaway), Tony Shalhoub (Nelson Gittes), Tim Guinee (Dr. Carone), Mekhi Phifer (Cale), Gary Dourdan (Capt. Burke), Lindsay Crouse (Chancellor), Elizabeth Peña (Midwife), Rachel Luttrell (Scan Room nurse), Mac Sinise (Young Spence), Tracey Walter (Mr. Siegel)
Producers: Gary Fleder (producer), Cary Granat (co-producer), Marty Katz (producer), Daniel Lupi (producer), Michael Phillips (executive producer), Andrew Rona (co-producer), Gary Sinise (producer), Amber Stevens (associate producer), Bob Weinstein (co-executive producer), Harvey Weinstein (co-executive producer), David Witz (line producer), Michael Zoumas (co-producer)
Original Music: Mark Isham
Cinematography: Robert Elswit
Production Design: Nelson Coates
Art Direction: Kevin Cozen
Costume Design: Abigail Murray

***Minority Report* (2002)**
US Release Date: 21 June 2002
Directed by Steven Spielberg
Writing credits Philip K. Dick (short story, 'The Minority Report'), Scott Frank (screenplay) and Jon Cohen (screenplay)
Cast: Tom Cruise (Chief John Anderton), Max von Sydow (Pre-Crime Director Lamar Burgess), Steve Harris (Jad), Neal McDonough (Officer Gordon 'Fletch' Fletcher), Patrick Kilpatrick (Officer Jeff Knott), Jessica Capshaw (Evanna), Klea Scott (Pre-Crime cop), Colin Farrell (Danny Witwer), Stephen Ramsey (FBI Agent Jucket), Tom Choi (FBI Agent Payment), Tom Whitenight (FBI Agent Price), Billy Morts (FBI Agent Foley), Samantha Morton (Agatha), Daniel London (Wally the caretaker), Michael Dickman (Arthur), Matthew Dickman (Dashiell), Lois Smith (Dr. Iris Hineman), Tim Blake Nelson (Gideon), Arye Gross (Howard Marks), Ashley Crow (Sarah Marks), Joel Gretsch (Donald Dubin), Peter Stormare (Dr. Solomon Eddie), Cameron Crowe (Bus passenger, uncredited), Cameron Diaz (Woman on metro, uncredited)
Producers: Jan de Bont (producer), Bonnie Curtis (producer), Michael Doven (associate producer), Gary Goldman (executive producer), Sergio Mimica-Gezzan (associate producer), Gerald R. Molen (producer), Walter F. Parkes (producer), Ronald Shusett (executive producer)
Original Music: John Williams
Cinematography: Janusz Kaminski
Production Design: Alex McDowell
Art Direction: Ramsey Avery, Leslie McDonald, Seth Reed
Costume Design: Deborah L. Scott

***Paycheck* (2003)**
US Release Date: 25 December 2003
Directed by John Woo
Writing credits: Philip K. Dick (short story, 'Paycheck'), Dean Georgaris (screenplay)
Cast: Ben Affleck (Michael Jennings), Aaron Eckhart (James Rethrick), Uma Thurman (Dr. Rachel Porter), Paul Giamatti (Shorty), Colm Feore (John Wolfe), Joe Morton (Agent Dodge), Michael C. Hall (Agent Klein). Peter Friedman (Atty. Gen. Brown), Kathryn Morris (Rita Dunne)
Producers: Arthur Anderson (co-producer), Terence Chang (producer), John Davis (producer), Michael Hackett (producer), Keiko Koyama (co-producer), Stratton Leopold (executive producer), Caroline Macaulay (co-producer), David Solomon (executive producer), John Woo (producer)
Original Music: James McKee Smith, John Powell, John Ashton Thomas
Cinematography: Jeffrey L. Kimball, Gregory Lundsgaard
Production Design: William Sandell
Art Direction: Sandy Cochrane
Costume Design: Erica Edell Phillips

A Scanner Darkly (2006)
US Release Date: March 2006
Directed by Richard Linklater
Writing credits: Philip K. Dick (novel, *A Scanner Darkly*), Richard Linklater (screenplay)
Cast: Keanu Reeves (Fred/Bob Arctor), Robert Downey Jr. (Barris), Woody Harrelson (Luckman), Winona Ryder (Donna), Dameon Clarke (Mike), Rory Cochrane (Freck), Christopher Ryan (New Path Resident)
Producers: George Clooney (executive producer), Sara Greene (associate producer), Tommy Pallotta (producer), John Sloss (executive producer), Jonah Smith (producer), Steven Soderbergh (executive producer), Erwin Stoff (producer), Anne Walker-McBay (producer), Palmer West (producer)
Original Music: Graham Reynolds
Cinematography: Shane F. Kelly
Production Design: Bruce Curtis
Costume Design: Kari Perkins

Next (2006)
US Release Date: 2006
Directed by Lee Tamahori
Writing credits: Philip K. Dick (short story, 'The Golden Man'), Gary Goldman (screenplay)
Cast Nicolas Cage (Cris Johnson), Julianne Moore (Callie Ferris)
Producers: Nicolas Cage (producer), Gary Goldman (executive producer), Norman Golightly (producer), Jason Koornick (executive producer)

2. WORKS BY PHILIP K. DICK UNDER OPTION FOR FILM ADAPTATION

Novel, *Time Out of Joint* (Purchased by Warner Bros.)
Novels, *Valis, Radio Free Albemuth, Flow My Tears the Policeman Said* (Purchased by independent producer John Alan Simon)
Short story, 'Adjustment Team', under option

3. RELATED PHILIP K. DICK FILMS/DOCUMENTARIES

***The Trouble With Dick* (1987)**
Comedy about a sci-fi author with writer's block, loosely inspired by Philip K. Dick
US Release Date: January 1987 (US Film Festival)
Directed by Gary Walkow
Writing credits Paul Freedman (story) and Gary Walkow (story), Gary Walkow (screenplay)
Cast: Tom Villard (Dick Kendred), Susan Dey (Diane), Elaine Giftos (Sheila), Elizabeth Gorcey (Haley), David Clennon (Lars), Marianne Muellerleile (Betty Ball), Johnna Johnson (Lottie), Jack Carter (Samsa)
Producers: Robert V. Augur (executive producer), Albert Barosso (line producer), Charlie Mullin (associate producer), Leslie Robins (co-producer), Gary Walkow (producer)
Original Music: Roger Bourland
Cinematography: Daryl Studebaker
Production Design: Eric Jones, Pui-Pui Li
Costume Design: Ted Sewell

***Arena: Philip K. Dick – A Day in the Afterlife* (1994)**
Fascinating BBC TV documentary on the cult of Philip K. Dick
UK Transmission Date: April 1994
Directed by Nicola Roberts
Writing credits:
Featuring: Terry Gilliam, Thomas A. Disch, Philip K. Dick, Elvis Costello, Kim Stanley Robinson, Kleo Mini, Brian Aldiss, Lawrence Sutin, Barry Spatz, Paul Williams (programme advisor), Anne Dick, Tim Powers, Tessa A. Dick, Fay Weldon, Jim Blaylock, Russell Galen, Gregg Proops (readings)
Producer: Nicola Roberts
Series Editors: Nigel Finch, Anthony Wall

***The Nervous Breakdown of Philip K. Dick* (1996)**
Short comedy – 22 mins – this is a darkly comic journey through Berkeley in 1968, as seen through the paranoid eyes of Philip K. Dick
US Release Date: Film Festival screenings only
Directed by Judy Bee
Writing credits: Juliet Bashore

Cast: Brian Brophy (Philip K. Dick), Lisa Zane (Tessa)
Producer: Alan Stern
Web: Available on DVD from *www.bigfilmshorts.com*

***On the Edge of Blade Runner* (2000)**
TV documentary on the phenomenon of *Blade Runner*
UK Transmission Date: 15 July 2000, Channel 4, UK
Directed by Andrew Abbott
Writing credits: Mark Kermode
Featuring: Mark Kermode (presenter), Brian Aldiss, Michael Arick, Joanna Cassidy, Michael Deeley, Philip K. Dick, David Dryer, Hampton Fancher, Katherine Haber, Daryl Hannah, Rutger Hauer, James Hong, Syd Mead, Lawrence G. Paull, David Webb Peoples, Terry Rawlings, William Sanderson, Ridley Scott, David L. Snyder, Douglas Trumbull, Joe Turkel, M. Emmet Walsh, Bud Yorkin, Richard Yuricich
Producer: Russell Leven
Original Music: Duncan Moore
Cinematography: Andrew Begg, Danny Dimitroff

***The Gospel According to Philip K. Dick* (2001)**
Film documentary portrait of Dick's life-changing vision in 1974
US Release Date: 29 May 2001 (San Francisco, limited)
Directed by Mark Steensland
Featuring: Paul Williams, Robert Anton Wilson, Scott Apel, Jay Kinney, Ray Nelson, Miriam Lloyd, Jason Koornick, Duncan Watson, Sharon Perry
Producer: Andy Massagli
Animation: Da'gum Animation
Original Music: Kevin Keller
Web: available on DVD from Amazon.com or direct from First Run Features at *www.firstrunfeatures.com*

***Drug-Taking and the Arts* (1994)**
Drama-documentary film about the role of drugs in creativity, featuring Philip K. Dick's *A Scanner Darkly*
US Release Date: no theatrical release
Directed by Storm Thorgerson
Featuring Works by: Charles Baudelaire, Paul Bowles, Elizabeth Barrett Browning, William S. Burroughs, Jean Cocteau, Samuel Taylor Coleridge, Thomas De Quincey, Philip K. Dick, Allen Ginsberg, Robert Graves, Aldous Huxley, Jack Kerouac, Ken Kesey, Jay McInerney, Anaïs Nin, Edgar Allan Poe, Arthur Rimbaud
Cast: Bernard Hill (Presenter), Phil Daniels (Thomas De Quincey), Jon Finch (Gérard de Nerval), Daniel Webb (Jean Cocteau), Diana Quick (Anaïs Nin), John Sessions (William Burroughs/Ken Kesey, voice)
Featuring: Brian Aldiss, J.G. Ballard, Virginia Berridge, Paul Bowles, Andy Warhol, Allen Ginsberg, Francis Huxley, Laura Huxley, Timothy Leary, George Melly, Hubert Selby Jr, Ian Walker
Producer: Jon Blair
Original Music: David Gilmour

4. AUDIO ADAPTATIONS OF WORKS BY PHILIP K. DICK

***The Defenders* (1956)**
US Transmission: 22 May 1956, *X Minus One*, NBC Radio
Writing credits: George Lefferts (script), Philip K. Dick ('The Defenders', short story)
Cast: Lydia Bruce, Warren Parker, Grant Richards, Mike Ingram, Stan Early, Fred Collins (announcer)
Producer: Van Woodward

***Colony* (1956)**
US Transmission: 10 October 1956, *X Minus One*, NBC Radio
Writing credits: Ernest Kinoy (script), Philip K. Dick ('Colony', short story)
Cast: Bill Quinn, Fredericka Chandler, John Larkin, James Stevens, Larry Robinson, Alan Bergman, Fred Collins (announcer)
Producer: Van Woodward

Additional Radio Scripts (mid-1950s)
Philip K. Dick apparently wrote three additional radio scripts which were aired in the mid-1950s on a show narrated by John W. Campbell Jr. on the Mutual Broadcasting System. The precise date that these aired is unknown.

***Valis* Opera (1987)**
An opera for six voices, hyperkeyboard, hyperpercussion and live computer electronics

Premiere Performance: 2-10 December 1987, Paris, France
Libretto by Tod Machover, based on the book by Philip K. Dick. **Commissioned by** Centre Georges Pompidou, Paris to celebrate its 10th anniversary.
Musicians: Ensemble InterContemporain/IRCAM.
Conductor: Tod Machover (Available on CD from Bridge)

***Omnibus: Philip K. Dick* (1990)**
Radio portrait of the 'science fiction writers' science fiction writer
UK Transmission Date: 4 November 1990
Written by Mark Burnam
Featuring: Gregg Rickman, Ray Nelson, Paul Williams, Tim Powers, Jim Blaylock, Ann Dick
Producer: Richard Dunn

5. TELEVISION ADAPTATIONS OF WORKS BY PHILIP K. DICK

***Out of This World: Imposter* (1962)**
UK Transmission: 21 July 1962, ABC TV, UK
Directed by Peter Hammond
Writing credits: Terry Nation (teleplay), Philip K. Dick ('Impostor', short story)
Cast: Patrick Allen (Major Peters), John Carson (Roger Carter), Glyn Owen (Frank Nelson), Angela Browne (Jean Baron)
Producer: Irene Shubik
Designer: Robert Fuest

(?) *Martian Time-Slip*
Apparently aired on the BBC sometime in the 1960s, though this may be a confused report of the unmade Aldiss version.

(?) 'The Cookie Lady' (mid-1970s)
Half-hour show by Metromedia that aired sometime in the 1970s. No further details are known.

***Total Recall 2070* (1999)**
22 one-hour TV episodes, based on Philip K. Dick's 'We Can Remember It For You Wholesale', but drawing widely on many Dickian themes and ideas…
Series Created by Art Monterastelli
Writing credits: Philip K. Dick ('We Can Remember It For You Wholesale', short story)
Regular Cast: Michael Easton (David Hume), Karl Pruner (Ian Farve), Cynthia Preston (Olivia Hume), Michael Rawlins (Martin Ehrenthal), Judith Krant (Olan Chang), Matthew Bennett (James Calley)
Producers: Dennis Chapman (line producer), Jeff King (supervising producer), Robert Lantos (executive producer), Drew S. Levin (executive producer), Ted Mann (consulting producer), Art Monterastelli (executive producer), Elliot Stern (producer)
Original Music: Zoran Boris
Cinematography: Derick V. Underschultz, Peter Wunstorf ('Machine Dreams', pilot episode)
Production Design: Peter Cosco

'Machine Dreams' (pilot, 90 minutes)
US Transmission: 5/12 January 1999
Writer: Art Monterastelli
Director: Mario Azzopardi
Guest stars: Nick Mancuso (Richard Collector), Angelo Pedari (Mario Soodor), Kathryn Winslow (Maria Soodor), Thomas Kretschmann (Nick Blanchard)
David Hume and new partner investigate a gang of 'smart' androids created through the use of experimental memory implant technology from Rekall. Hume's new partner, Farve, is also an android…

'Nothing Like the Real Thing'
US Transmission: 19 January 1999
Writer: Elliot Stern
Director: Terry Ingram
Guest stars: Peter Firth (Vincent Nagle), Laura Harris (Elana), Mark Humphrey (The Messenger), Nicole Oliver (Joy Pauley)
Black market Rekall fantasy discs lead Hume and Farve to Elana, an 'actress' who awakens Farve's emotional and sexual capabilities.

'Self-Inflicted'
US Transmission: 2 February 1999
Writer: Ted Mann
Director: Jorge Montesi
Guest stars: Vanessa L. Williams (Violet Whims), Sara

Botsford (Maria Schviller), Bruce Clayton (Flat), Kerry Dorey (Ian Whims)
A lethal virus leads Hume and Farve to Minacon, where experiments in germ warfare are being covered-up. Olivia buys a sublimator.

'Allure'
US Transmission: 9 February 1999
Writer: Jeff F. King
Director: Fred Gerber
Guest stars: Monika Schnarre (Rachel Vespers/Marissa Lett), Tig Fong (Mister Ho), Robert Haley (Martin Brett)
Identical genetically enhanced courtesans have a weird effect on Hume.

'Infiltration'
US Transmission: 16 February 1999
Writer: W. K. Scott Meyer
Director: Mario Azzopardi
Guest stars: Peter Firth (Vincent Nagle), Lori Hallier (Barbara Raymond), Andrew Airlie (Michael Leland), Tim Lee (Joseph Granger)
A doctor who works for android manufacturer Uber Braun is assassinated, drawing Hume and Farve into a conspiracy.

'Rough Whimper of Insanity'
US Transmission: 23 February 1999
Writer: Ted Mann
Director: Ken Girotti
Guest stars: Andreas Apergis (The Technician), Paulino Nunes (Janitor Jack), David Eisner (Vereen), Heather Hodgson (Tolman)
Investigation of a rogue android leads to questions about Farve's creation.

'First Wave'
US Transmission: 2 March 1999
Writer: Elliot Stern
Director: Jorge Montesi
Guest stars: Chad Allen (Eddie Miller), Tara Rosling (Newt), Karen Glave (Helena Ehrenthal), Alan C. Peterson (Deputy Chief Atkins)
An anti-android cult member holds hostages to force the police department to shut down.

'Baby Lottery'
US Transmission: 9 March 1999
Writer: Michael Thoma
Director: David Warry-Smith
Guest stars: Clint Howard (Pontifex), Joseph Griffin (Howard Manning), Noam Jenkins (Shelley), Adrian Hough (Bill)
A baby with a rare gene is kidnapped, the trail leads to consortium company Variable Dynamics.

'Brain Fever' (Part One)
US Transmission: 16 March 1999
Writer: Elliot Stern
Director: George Mandeluk
Guest stars: David Warner (Dr. Felix Latham), Beau Starr (Lorne Atwater), Richard Eden (Unknown), Dina Barrington (McCall)
Questions about Farve's creator become central when he is connected to the would-be assassin of a union leader.

'Begotten Not Made' (Part Two)
US Transmission: 23 March 1999
Writer: W. K. Scott Meyer
Director: David Warry-Smith
Guest stars: David Warner (Dr. Felix Latham), J.C. MacKenzie (Brendan McGuire), Carolyn Mackenzie (Detective Vecchio)
Leading neurosurgeon Dr. Felix Latham is implicated when an advanced brain implant containing technology used in building Farve's memory system, is found to have motivated a murder.

'Brightness Falls'
US Transmission: 30 March 1999
Writer: Rod Pridy
Director: Kris Dobkin
Guest stars: Anthony Zerbe (Tyler Hume), Kristin Booth (Ashley Ambrose), Jason Cadieux (Mark Preston)
Hume and Farve investigate the Level Four cult after their leader is murdered. Hume has to deal with his father's paranoia.

'Burning Desire'
US Transmission: 6 April 1999
Writer: Jeff F. King
Director: Mario Azzopardi
Guest stars: Kevin Jubinville (Kroczek), Carolyn Dunn (Jenna Hannah), Katherine Ashby (Yvonne), Jed Dixon (Gerold Hannah)
Sublimator addiction is uppermost in Hume's mind as users are found dead and the Nexus Dating Service leads them to a top secret Rekall project gone wrong.

'Astral Projections'
US Transmission: 13 April 1999
Writer: Michael Thoma
Director: David Warry-Smith
Guest stars: Ron White (Machado), Larissa Laskin (Jill Evans), Andrew Tarbet (Ingles), David Keeley (Kaplan)
Hume and Farve travel to a crashed interplanetary cargo transport – which carried an ancient artifact known as the Brancusi Stone – that went down in the freezing 'New Territories.' Were the crew murdered?

'Paranoid'
US Transmission: 20 April 1999
Writer: Michael Thoma
Director: Rod Pridy
Guest stars: Anthony Zerbe (Tyler Hume), Kamar de los Reyes (Jack Brant), Richard Waugh (Simon), Victoria Snow (Surgeon)
Investigating the murder of the head of the Nexus dating service, Farve finds a list of people implanted by a Rekall mind-control project: Hume's wife Olivia is on it. Adding to Hume's trouble is his father, who once again has problems with his retirement home.

'Restitution'
US Transmission: 27 April 1999
Writer: Elliot Stern
Director: Jorge Montesi
Guest stars: Peter Firth (Vincent Nagle), Kamar de los Reyes (Jack Brant), Roman Podhora (Jonathan Crane)
Brant is kidnapped on his way to a Mars safe house, and the assessor's office is prepared to pay the 40 million credits ransom in fear of losing him to Rekall. Hume's personal problems continue as Olivia's memory fails.

'Bones Beneath My Skin'
US Transmission: 4 May 1999
Writer: Ted Mann
Director: Mark Sobel
Guest stars: Henry Gibson (Belasarius), Hugh Thompson (Meadows), Victoria Snow (Surgeon), Paulino Nunes (Delta Supervisor Mike)
Farve and Hume investigate the destruction of an android at a chemical company, and anti-android worker Belasarius. Meanwhile David and Olivia split up, while they deal with the fact that she was under Rekall's control during their entire relationship.

'Assessment'
US Transmission: 11 May 1999
Writer: Jeff F. King
Director: Terry Ingram
Guest stars: Steven Williams (Brack), Xenia Seeberg (Sela), Deborah Odell (Bayliss), Claudia Difolco (Anchor), Chris Crumb (Angry Man)
Investigating a report about berserk androids, Farve and Hume are ambushed and captured by a rogue section of the assessor's office. They seek Hume's help in discovering Farve's part in what they see as a plot by machines to eradicate humans.

'Eye Witness'
US Transmission: 18 May 1999
Writer: Elliot Stern
Director: Jorge Montesi
Guest stars: Art Hindle (Frank Trower), Jayne Heitmeyer (Robin Trower), Nigel Bennett (Esterhaus), Dan Lett (Fedderman)
When visiting a friend's apartment Olivia hears screaming, and finds her friend's rich husband standing over a bloody corpse. She is willing to testify, but given her recent memory problem, did she just imagine the whole thing?

'Personal Effects'
US Transmission: 25 May 1999
Writer: Kris Dobkin
Director: Jorge Montesi

Guest stars: Titus Welliver (Henry Sumners), Mimi Kuzyk (Jackson Rami), Kevin Hare (Android), John Bekavac (Robbie the Android)
Olan decides to keep a vial found on corpse in a crashed shuttle out of her report. Its owners, Vari Dyne Inc., want it back.

'Virtual Justice'
US Transmission: 1 June 1999
Writer: Jeff F. King
Director: Mark Sobel
Guest stars: Heino Ferch (Franco Kasten), Johanna Black (Amber Nelson), Martin Sheen (Praxis), Deborah Odell (Bayliss)
After seeing a fellow cop killing a prison escapee, Hume finds that the cop may have been taking the law into his own hands.

'Meet My Maker' (Series Finale)
US Transmission: 8 June 1999
Writer: Ted Mann
Director: Mario Azzopardi
Guest star: Karl Pruner (The Maker)
After Hume nearly dies trying to interface with Farve's back-up memory banks, Farve finally takes Hume to meet the alpha-android's creator.

6. THEATRICAL PERFORMANCES ADAPTED FROM WORKS BY PHILIP K. DICK (SELECTED)

***Ubik/The Three Stigmata of Palmer Eldritch* (1984)**
Adapted and performed by The Voluntary Tinware Troupe
Debut Performance: 25 February 1984
Venue: Suzunari Theatre, Shimokitazawa, Tokyo, Japan

***The Transmigration of Timothy Archer* (1984)**
Adapted and directed by Geoff Ryman, Three-act play
Cast: Angel Archer (Kim Campbell), uncredited others
Debut Performance: 27 May 1984
Venue: Literary SF convention TyneCon II: The Mexicon, Newcastle-Upon-Tyne, UK

***Ubik* (1984)**
Adapted by Joel Gersmann
Debut Performance: August 1984
Venue: Broome Street Theatre, Madison, Wisconsin, USA

***Solar Lottery* (under the title *El Primer Magistrado*) (1985)**
A 'technotheatre' piece freely adapted and directed by Stephanie Olry
Performed by the Extincteur theatre group
Debut Performance: 1985
Venue: Paris, France

***Flow My Tears the Policeman Said* (1985)**
Adapted by Linda Hartinian
Directed by Bill Raymond
Performed by Mabou Mines
Cast: Jason Taverner (Greg Mehrten), Felix Buckman (Christopher Martin), Alys Buckman (Ellen McElduff), Taverner (Greg Mehrten), Heather Hart (Rosemary Quinn) Mary (Linda Hartinian), Ruth Rae (Ruth Maleczech), Letter Reader (Anne Dominick)
Debut Performance: 18-30 June 1985
Venue: Boston Shakespeare Theatre, Boston, USA

***Martian Time-Slip* (1987)**
Adapted by Joel Gersmann
Debut Performance: 1987
Venue: Broome Street Theatre, Madison, Wisconsin, USA

***Philip K. Dick: The Play* (1988)**
A one-man play, written John Dowie
Performed by John Joyce
Debut Performance: 18 October 1988
Venue: Finborough Theatre Club, London, UK

***Radio Free Albemuth* (1991)**
Directed by Lisa Morton, Two-act play
Produced by Mookie Martorana
Performed by Theatre of N.O.T.E (New One-Act Theatre Ensemble)
Cast: Phil (David LaPorte), Nick (Paul Clemens), Sadassa Silvia (Esther Ives Williams), Ferris Fremont (James Higdon), FBI Agent (Hy Pike), Rachel Brady (Christina Artelis)

Debut Performance: 22 January-27 February 1991
Venue: Hollywood Boulevard, Los Angeles, USA

Take Them to the Garden (1991)
Written and performed by John Dowie
Debut Performance: 19 October 1991
Venue: Epping Forest College, Loughton, Essex, UK [Part of the Philip K. Dick: A Celebration event]

What is Human? (1991)
Written and performed by John Joyce
Debut Performance: 19 October 1991
Venue: Epping Forest College, Loughton, Essex, UK [Part of the Philip K. Dick: A Celebration event]

Kindred Blood in Kensington Gore (1991)
Tells the story of the various conversations of Philip K. Dick in the Afterlife with someone who might be his dead sister, VALIS, or both.
Written by Brian Aldiss
Directed by Frank Hatherley
Albert Memorial backdrop by Sylvia Starshine
Cast: Philip K. Dick (Brian Aldiss), Jane/VALIS (Petronilla Whitfield)
Debut Performance: 20 October 1991
Venue: Epping Forest College, Loughton, Essex, UK [Part of the Philip K. Dick: A Celebration event]

2-3-74 The Exegesis of Philip K. Dick (2003)
Written by Jonathan A. Goldberg
Debut Performance: April 2003
Venue: The Producer's Club, West 44th Street, New York, USA

800 Words: The Transmigration of Philip K. Dick (2003)
Written by Victoria Stewart
Directed by Erica Gould
Performed by The New York City Theatre Company
Debut Performance: 11-13 December 2003
Venue: Hinton Battle Theatre Lab, West 42nd Street, New York, USA

7. VIDEO GAMES ADAPTED FROM WORKS BY PHILIP K. DICK (SELECTED)

Ubik Video Game (1998)
Published by Cryo Interactive Entertainment
A third-person science fiction mystery, based on the Philip K. Dick novel. The player takes the role of the main character from the book, Joe Chip, working for a company called Runciter Associates in Los Angeles (in the year 2019). Chip's job is to protect companies against industrial espionage through ESP. With genetic engineering and the development of Replicants both sides have Psi-powers. The player leads, trains and equips a squad of selected individuals (with various abilities, kinds of weapon skills or Psi-skills) through 3D-realtime rendered maps, where they can interact with the enviroment or even talk to some individuals. Connecting those missions are many rendered cinematic cut-scenes.
Available for Playstation, Windows PC

Blade Runner Video Game (1999)
Published by Westwood/Electronic Arts
RPG/Adventure game based on the movie *Blade Runner*, which was based on the Philip K. Dick novel *Do Androids Dream of Electric Sheep?*
Game Directed by Joseph D. Kucan
Writing credits: Philip K. Dick (*Do Androids Dream of Electric Sheep?*, novel), Hampton Fancher (1982 screenplay), Joseph D. Kucan, David Leary, David Peoples (1982 screenplay), David Yorkin
Cast (voices): Martin Azarow (Dino Klein), Mark Benninghoffen (Ray McCoy), Warren Burton (Runciter), Brion James (Leon), James Hong (Dr. Chew), Joseph D. Kucan (Crazylegs Larry), Michael McShane (Marcus Eisenduller), Stephen Root (Early Q), William Sanderson (J.F. Sebastian), Vincent Schiavelli (Bullet Bob), Joe Turkel (Eldon Tyrell), Sean Young (Rachael)
Available for Windows PC and Macintosh

Minority Report Video Game (2002)
Published by Activision
Bland chase-and-fight movie tie-in, which had no input from Tom Cruise or Steven Spielberg
Available for Xbox, GameCube, PS2 and Gameboy Advance

8. COMICS/MAGAZINES ADAPTED FROM WORKS BY PHILIP K. DICK

The Official Comics Adaptation of *Blade Runner* (1982)
Stan Lee Presents A Marvel Super Special, Vol 1, #22
Adapted by Archie Goodwin
Pencilled by Al Williamson and Carlos Garzon
Inked by Al Williamson, Dan Green and Ralph Reese
Coloured by Marie Severin
Lettered by Ed King
Edited by Jim Salicrup
Covers by Jim Steranko
Editor-in-Chief Jim Shooter
Published: September 1982

***Blade Runner* Souvenir Magazine: Official Collector's Edition (1982)**
Interviews by Vic Bulluck
Design: Robert Altemus
Publisher: Ira Friedman, Inc., New York

***The Religious Experience of Philip K. Dick* (1986)**
An eight-page illustrated feature about Philip K. Dick
Written and Drawn by Robert Crumb
Published: *Weirdo* #17 (Summer 1986)

***A Scanner Darkly* (2006)**
Hardcover graphic novel adaptation, based on the Richard Linklater 'animated' film.
Publisher: Pantheon

BIBLIOGRAPHY

1. NOVELS BY PHILIP K. DICK

Solar Lottery (1955)
The World Jones Made (1956)
The Man Who Japed (1956)
Eye in the Sky (1957)
The Cosmic Puppets (1957)
Time Out of Joint (1959)
Dr. Futurity (1960)
Vulcan's Hammer (1960)
The Man in the High Castle (1962) (1963 Hugo Award Winner for Best Science Fiction Novel)
The Game-Players of Titan (1963)
The Penultimate Truth (1964)
Martian Time-Slip (1964)
The Simulacra (1964)
Clans of the Alphane Moon (1964)
The Three Stigmata of Palmer Eldritch (1965)
Dr. Bloodmoney, or How We Got Along after the Bomb (1965)
Now Wait for Last Year (1966)
The Crack in Space (1966)
The Unteleported Man (1966)
The Zap Gun (1967)
Counter-Clock World (1967)
The Ganymede Takeover (with Ray Nelson) (1967)
Do Androids Dream of Electric Sheep? (1968)
Galactic Pot-Healer (1969)
Ubik (1969)
A Maze of Death (1970)
Our Friends from Frolix 8 (1970)
We Can Build You (1972)
Flow My Tears, the Policeman Said (1974) (1974 John W Campbell Memorial Award Winner)
Confessions of a Crap Artist (1975)
Deus Irae (with Roger Zelazny) (1976)
A Scanner Darkly (1977)
VALIS (1981)
The Divine Invasion (1981)
The Transmigration of Timothy Archer (1982)
The Man Whose Teeth Were All Exactly Alike (1984)
Radio Free Albemuth (1985)
Puttering About in a Small Land (1985)
In Milton Lumky Territory (1985)
Humpty Dumpty in Oakland (1986)
Mary and the Giant (1987)
The Broken Bubble (1988)
Nick and the Glimmung (1988)
Gather Yourselves Together (1994)
Lies, Inc. (2004)

2. UNPUBLISHED PHILIP K. DICK NOVELS

Voices from the Street (written circa 1952-53)
Lost Manuscripts - *Pilgrim on the Hill*; *Nicholas and the Higs*

3. COMPLETE PHILIP K. DICK SHORT STORY COLLECTIONS

Beyond Lies the Wub: Volume 1 of the Collected Short Stories of Philip K. Dick (Grafton Books, 1990)

Second Variety: Volume 2 of the Collected Short Stories of Philip K. Dick (Grafton Books, 1990)

The Father-Thing: Volume 3 of the Collected Short Stories of Philip K. Dick (Grafton Books, 1990)

The Days of Perky Pat: Volume 4 of the Collected Short Stories of Philip K. Dick (Grafton Books, 1991)

We Can Remember it for You Wholesale: Volume 5 of the Collected Short Stories of Philip K. Dick (Grafton Books, 1991)

4. PHILIP K DICK'S COLLECTED LETTERS

Dick, Philip K., Kausch, Allan (co-ord), Williams, Paul (series ed): *The Selected Letters of Philip K. Dick 1938-1971* (Underwood Books, 1996)

Dick, Philip K., Kausch, Allan (co-ord), Williams, Paul (series ed): *The Selected Letters of Philip K. Dick 1972-1973* (Underwood-Miller, 1993)

Dick, Philip K., Kausch, Allan (co-ord), Williams, Paul (series ed): *The Selected Letters of Philip K. Dick 1974* (Underwood-Miller, 1991)

Dick, Philip K., Kausch, Allan (co-ord), Williams, Paul (series ed): Don Herron (ed), *The Selected Letters of Philip K. Dick 1975-76* (Underwood-Miller, 1992)

Dick, Philip K., Kausch, Allan (co-ord), Williams, Paul (series ed): Herron, Don (ed), *The Selected Letters of Philip K. Dick 1977-79* (Underwood-Miller, 1993)

Dick, Philip K., Kausch, Allan (co-ord), Williams, Paul (series ed): *The Selected Letters of Philip K. Dick 1980-82* (unpublished)

5. OTHER SIGNIFICANT WORKS BY PHILIP K. DICK

The Dark-Haired Girl (Mark V. Ziesing, 1988)

Ubik: The Screenplay (Corroboree Press, 1985)

6. BOOKS ABOUT PHILIP K. DICK AND HIS WORKS

Apel, D. Scott (ed): *Philip K. Dick - The Dream Connection* (The Impermanent Press, 1999)

Bukatman, Scott: *BFI Modern Classic - Blade Runner* (British Film Institute, 1997)

Butler, Andrew M.: *Pocket Essentials - Philip K. Dick* (Pocket Essentials, 2000)

Carrere, Emmanuel: *I Am Alive and You Are Dead - A Journey into the Mind of Philip K. Dick* (Metropolitan Books, 2004)

Gillespie, Bruce: *Philip K. Dick - Electric Shepherd* (Norstrilia Press, 1975)

Kerman, Judith: *Retrofitting Blade Runner - Issues in Ridley Scott's Blade Runner and Philip K. Dick's Do Androids Dream of Electric Sheep?* (Popular Press, 1991)

Lacey, Nick: *York Film Notes - Blade Runner* (York Press/Pearson Education, 2000)

Mullen, R.D., Csicsery-Ronay, Jr, Istvan, Evans, Arthur B. and Hollinger, Veronica (eds): *On Philip K. Dick - 40 Articles from Science Fiction Studies* (Terre Haute & Greencastle/SF-TH Inc, 1992)

Olander, Joseph D. & Greenberg, Martin Harry (eds): *Writers of the 21st Century Series - Philip K. Dick* (Taplinger, 1983)

Palmer, Christopher: *Philip K. Dick - Exhilaration and Terror of the Postmodern* (Liverpool University Press, 2003)

Pierce, Hazel: *Philip K. Dick* (Starmont House, 1982)

Mackey, Douglas A.: *Philip K. Dick* (Twayne/G.K. Hall & Co, 1988)

Merrifield, Jeff & Joyce, John: *Philip K. Dick - A Celebration* (Connections/Community Education Epping Forest College, 1991)

Robinson, Kim: *The Novels of Philip K. Dick* (UMI Research Press, 1984)

Rickman, Gregg: *Philip K. Dick - The Last Testament* (Fragments West/The Valentine Press, 1985)

Rickman, Gregg: *Philip K. Dick - In His Own Words* (Fragments West/The Valentine Press, 1988)

Rickman, Gregg: *To The High Castle - Philip K. Dick: A Life 1928-1962* (Fragments West/The Valentine Press, 1989)

Sammon, Paul F.: *Future Noir - The Making of Blade Runner* (Harper Prism, 1996)

Sauter, Elaine and Lee, Gwen (ed): *What If Our World Is*

Their Heaven - The Final Conversations With Phillip K. Dick (The Overlook Press, 2000)
Stephensen-Payne, Phil: *Philip Kindred Dick - Metaphysical Conjuror* (Borgo Press, 1990)
Sutin, Lawrence: *Divine Invasions - A Life of Philip K. Dick* (Paladin, 1991)
Sutin, Lawrence (ed), Dick, Philip K.: *In Pursuit of Valis - Selections from the Exegesis* (Underwood Miller, 1991)
Sutin, Lawrence (ed): *The Shifting Realities of Philip K. Dick - Selected Literary and Philosophical Writings* (Pantheon Books, 1995)
Taylor, Angus: *Philip K. Dick and the Umbrella of Light* (T-K Graphics, 1975)
Umland, Samuel J.: *Philip K. Dick - Contemporary Critical Interpretations* (Greenwood Press, 1995)
Warrick, Patricia S.: *Mind in Motion - The Fiction of Philip K. Dick* (Southern Illinois University Press, 1987)
Williams, Paul: *Only Apparently Real - The World of Philip K. Dick* (Arbor House, 1986)

7. OTHER RELEVANT BOOKS

Biskind, Peter: *Down and Dirty Pictures: Miramax, Sundance and the Rise of Independent Film* (Simon & Schuster, 2004)
Clarke, James: *Ridley Scott* (Virgin, 2002)
Fass, Ekbert: *Young Robert Duncan: Portrait of the Poet as Homosexual in Society*, (Black Sparrow Press, 1983)
Rodley, Chris (ed): *Cronenberg on Cronenberg* (Faber & Faber, 1992)
van Scheers, Rob: *Paul Verhoeven* (Faber & Faber, 1996)
Thompson, David: *A Biographical Dictionary of Film* (Andre Deutsch, 1994)

8. BOOKS FEATURING PHILIP K. DICK AS A FICTIONAL CHARACTER

Bishop, Michael: *Philip K. Dick Is Dead, Alas* (ORB/Tom Doherty Associates, 1987)
Anton, Uwe (ed): *Welcome to Reality - The Nightmares of Philip K. Dick* (Broken Mirrors Press, 1991)
Bischoff, David F.: *Philip K. Dick High* (Wildside Press, 2000)

9. RADIO/AUDIO MATERIAL FEATURING PHILIP K. DICK

Cartoon Pleroma: KUCI, 88.9FM, Irvine, California 'Interview with Linda Hartinian & Fred McCollister', 3 May 1999 (transcribed by Frank C. Bertrand, at *www.philipkdickfans.com*)
Hour 25: KPFK-FM, North Hollywood, California 'A Talk With Philip K. Dick, Hosted by Mike Hodel', 26 June 1976 (transcribed by Frank C. Bertrand, audio hosted at *www.philipkdickfans.com*)

10. FILM PRESS NOTES

Blade Runner, Total Recall,
Screamers, Impostor,
Minority Report, Paycheck
Alliance Atlantis, *Total Recall: The Series* 'Press to Date' (unpublished)

11. MAGAZINE/NEWSPAPER ARTICLES

Aguirre-Sacasa, Roberto: 'Primal Screamers', *Fangoria* #146, September 1995
Anton, Uwe & Fuchs, Werner: 'So I Don't Write About Heroes', *SF Eye* #14, Spring 1996
Atherton, Tony: 'New Sci-Fi Series A Pleasant Surprise', *The Ottawa Citizen*, 2 January 1999
Axmaker, Sean: 'Philip K. Dick's Dark Dreams Still Fodder For Films', *Seattle Post-Intelligencer*, 26 June 2002
Bernstein, Richard: 'The Electric Dreams of Philip K. Dick', *New York Times*, 3 November 1991
Boutillier, James G.: 'Philip K. Dick Scores Another Media Hit With the New TV Series Total Recall 2070', *Science Fiction Age*, March 1999
Brandon, Carl: 'Total Recall: Dan O'Bannon On Why It Doesn't Work', *Cinefantastique*, Vol. 21, #5, April 1991
Bzdeck, Vincent P.: 'Philip K. Dick's Future Is Now', *Washington Post*, 28 July 2002
Cohen, David S.: 'Revolution Turns to Sci-fi', *Variety*, 11 November 2004
Corliss, Richard: 'That Old Feeling - You Know Dick', *Time*

Magazine, 12 January 2004
Doherty, Thomas: 'Blade Runner', *Cinefantastique*, Vol. 23, #5, February 1993
Doherty, Thomas: 'Total Recall - The Vision of Philip K. Dick, Saddled With Body Slam Schtick', *Cinefantastique*, Vol. 21, #3, December 1990
Dretzka, Gary: 'Late Writer's Clever Ideas Have Launched Many A Hollywood Science Fiction Vehicle', *San Francisco Chronicle*, 27 December 2003
Epstein, Daniel Robert: 'Michael Almereyda, Director of This So-Called Disaster', *suicidegirls.com*
Florence, Bill: 'Schwarzenegger - Total Recall', *Cinefantastique*, Vol. 21, #1, July 1990
Florence, Bill: 'Pumping Irony - Total Recall', *Cinefantastique*, Vol. 21, #3, December 1990
Florence, Bill: 'Behind-the-Scenes - Total Recall', *Cinefantastique*, Vol. 21, #5, April 1991
Frank, Scott: 'Scott Frank Minority Report Chat', *screnwritersutopia.com*, 6 December 2001
Gibson, Thomasina: 'Sublimator Dreaming', *SFX* #56, October 1999
Godfrey, Alex: 'Eternal Sunshine of the Spotless Mind', *Bizarre*, April 2004
Grove, Christopher: 'Switching Channels', *Cinescape*, May/June 1999
Hackett, Isa: 'A Note from The Philip K. Dick Trust Regarding the Film Adaptation of A Scanner Darkly'
Hettrick, Scott: 'Showtime Future for Total Recall', *The Hollywood Reporter*, November 10-16 1998
Hobson, Louis B.: 'Scream(er) Therapy - Roy Dupuis', *Edmonton Sun*, 29 January 1996
Kipen, David: 'Visionary's Total Precall - Minority Report's Future World the Work of Sci-fi Writer Philip K. Dick', *San Francisco Chronicle*, 25 June 2002
Kipp, Jeremy: 'Michael Almereyda Profile', *sensesofcinema.com*, February 2003
Koornick, Jason: 'The Minority Report on Minority Report: A Conversation with Gary Goldman', *philipkdick.com*, July 2002
Lee, Gwen & Sauter, Doris E.: 'Thinker of Antiquity', *Starlog* #150, January 1990
Lee, Gwen & Sauter, Doris E.: 'Worlds of Sound & Color', *Starlog* #165, April 1991
Lethem, Jonathan: 'The Many Voices of Philip K. Dick', *The Editor*, *The Guardian*, 7 September 2002
L'Officier, Randy & Jean-Marc: 'Blade Runner Special Section', pp36-51, *Starlog* #184, November 1992
Lucas, Tim: 'Cronenberg Under the Knife (Part Two)', *Fangoria* #80, February 1989
Manoharan, Raj: 'Total Recall 2070 - Head Games', *Sci-Fi TV*, June 1999
McKay, John: 'Futuristic Set Dominates Total Recall TV Series', *Syndicated to Canadian Press*, 24 December 1998
McKie, Robin: 'What A Clever Dick', *The Observer*, 23 June 2002
Monterastelli, Art: 'Total Recall - Series Outline', *Alliance Atlantis*, unpublished
Oliver, Greg: 'Total Recall 2070 Set to Debut in January', *Jam! Showbiz*, 12 December 1998
Oliver, Greg: 'Total Recall 2070 Will Live With X-Files Comparisons', *Jam! Showbiz*, 5 January 1999
Oliver, Greg: 'Geek Beauty Loves Work on Total Recall', *Jam! Showbiz*, 12 January 1999
Orrison-Labby, Katherine: 'The Dangerous Days of Blade Runner', *Cult Movies* #27, 1998
Parker, James: 'Substance', *The Boston Globe*, 25 July 2002
Perenson, Melissa J.: 'Mining Minority', *Sci-Fi Magazine*, Vol. 8, #4, August 2002
Petrikin, Chris: 'Croghan on Scanner', *Variety*, 4 June 1997
Powers, John: 'Majority Report', *On*, 21-27 June 2002
Rees, Chuck: 'Sites Keep the Magic of Science Fiction Radio Alive', www.therevu.com/other/scifi-radio.html
Rose, Frank: 'The Second Coming of Philip K. Dick', *Wired*, December 2003
Rothkerch, Ian: 'Will the Future Really Look Like Minority Report', *Salon*, 10 July 2002
Sammon, Paul M.: 'The Making of Blade Runner', *Cinefantastique*, Vol 12 No 5/Vol 12 No 6, July-August 1982
Savlov, Marc: 'Dream Job - Inside the Production of Richard Linklater's A Scanner Darkly', *Austin Chronicle*, 21 January 2005
Shusett, Ron: 'Total Recall - The Series Bible', *Alliance*

Atlantis, April 1997, *unpublished*
Sigesmund, B.J.: 'A Writer's Wars', *Newsweek*, 20 June 2002
Simpson, Mark: 'Men at Arms', *The Independent*, 24 April 2005
Spelling, Ian: 'Total Recall 2070 Set to Debut as Showtime Series', *Inside Sci-Fi & Trek*, *New York Times*, March 1999
Spelling, Ian & Lee, Patrick: 'The Creators of Impostor Wrestle Philip K. Dick to the Big Screen', *Science Fiction Weekly*, January 2002
Star, Alexander: 'The God in the Trash - The Fantastic Life and Oracular Work of Philip K. Dick', *The New Republic*, Vol. 209, #23, 6 December 1996
Star, Alexander: 'The Filming of Philip K. Dick', *Culture Box*, *Slate* (*slate.msn.com*), 25 April 2002
Swedko, Pamela: 'On Set - Total Recall 2070', *Playback*, 10 August 1998
Toth, Robert J.: 'A Life of Fantasy; A Literature of Fantasy', *The Wall Street Journal*, 27 April 1999
Tunison, Michael: 'Brave New World View – Minority Report: Alex McDowell', *Cinescape* #62, July 2002
Unknown: 'Un héros très discret', *www.filmfestivals.com/cannes96/cfile3.htm*, May 1996
Unknown: 'Thought Policeman', *Starlog* #261, April 1999
Unknown: Scott Frank/Jon Cohen interviewed, *Scr(i)pt Magazine*, May/June 2002
Unknown: 'Cage Toplines New PKD Film', *Sci-Fi Wire*, 15 April 2005
Widner, James F.: 'To Boldly Go…', www.otr.com/sf.html, 1995-2002
Williams, Paul (ed): *The Philip K. Dick Society Newsletter* #1-23, The Estate of Philip K. Dick, 1983-89

12. FILM SCRIPTS

Shusett, Ron & Goldman, Gary: 'Total Recall II' (Undated draft)
Fancher, Hampton: 'Blade Runner', 24 July 1980
Cohen, Jon: 'Minority Report', 15 August 1997 (Rewrite)
Kaufman, Charlie: 'A Scanner Darkly', 20 December 1997 (First draft)

13. SELECTED WEB SITES

www.philipkdick.com
Primary official web site, run by the Philip K. Dick estate and featuring occasional contributions from Dick's daughter's Isa and Laura as well as internet-exclusive documents and photos. Also home to the excellent cover gallery
www.philipkdickfans.com
Jason Koornick's once near-official site is now the primary fan site, packed with in-depth material accumulated over a number of years
www.wired.com/wired/archive/11.12/philip.html
Wired magazine's in-depth piece on Philip K. Dick.
www.philipkdickaward.org
Official home of the annual award for the best paper-back debut SF novel
www.philipkdickfans.com/weirdo.htm
The Robert Crumb comic-strip based on Philip K. Dick's 1974 visions.
www.boingboing.net/2005/06/23/philip_k_dick_robot.html
Philip K. Dick's bizarre resurrection as an android. How fitting!
www.otrsite.com/logs/logsx1001.htm
Jerry Haendige's Vintage Radio Logs
www.bladezone.com
In depth *Blade Runner* fan site
www.brmovie.com
Another good *Blade Runner* fan site, with links to many more
www.apbnews.com
Blade Runner Author Suspected Syphilis Plot: Dick's FBI Files & more on the author's paranoia
www.geocities.com/SoHo/3661/dick/interv.htm
An interview with would-be Dick film producer John Alan Simon
www.geocities.com/pkdbooks2/pulpsframe.html
A wonderful collection of science fiction pulp magazine covers featuring Dick's work
www.brianwaldiss.com/html/life_outside_movies_1.htm
A fascinating four-part feature by Aldiss about his movie work, including his experiences trying to mount an adaptation of Dick's *Martian Time-Slip*

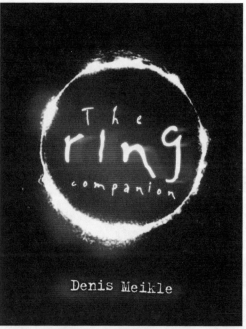